PLACE IN RETURN BOX to remove this checkout from your record.
TO AVOID FINES return on or before date due.

DATE DUE	DATE DUE	DATE DUE

6/15 K:/Proj/Acc&Pres/CIRC/DateDueForms_2015.indd - pg.1

CHRONICLES
OF THE
American Revolution

General Washington on White Charger

CHRONICLES
OF THE
American Revolution

Edited by ALDEN T. VAUGHAN

Originally compiled by HEZEKIAH NILES *as*
"Principles and Acts of the Revolution in America"

With an introduction by
HENRY STEELE COMMAGER

GROSSET & DUNLAP
NEW YORK

INTRODUCTION

by Henry Steele Commager

THE MEN WHO FOUGHT THE REVOLUTION and set up the new nation were deeply concerned with history, but mostly they were too busy making it to write it. All of them were, in a sense, historians, and we turn now to what they wrote for authentic, though not impartial, history: *The Farmer's Letters, Common Sense, Notes on Virginia, Letters of an American Farmer, The Defense of the Constitutions, The Federalist Papers.* But these did not count as formal histories like those stately Old World productions—Voltaire's *Age of Louis XIV* or Gibbon's *Decline and Fall of the Roman Empire* or David Hume's multi-volume *History of England.* No, that kind of history would have to wait. Meantime history was to be read in the documents, and the public papers, of the participants. To be sure, a few bold, or impatient, authors tried their hands at history even as the new nation was finding itself. There was the Reverend William Gordon, who made himself a national nuisance by his appeals for materials, and then went off to England and constructed his history out of the *Annual Register* after all; what a disappointment that was. There was Dr. Ramsay down in Charleston, a better historian, a better craftsman, and a better man, too, than Gordon, who wrote both state and national history. There was the sprightly Mercy Warren, who was on the inside of everything and whose *History* of the Revolution brought down on her the wrath of John Adams, who thought he was unjustly disparaged. There were local historians, like the lively Jeremy Belknap of New Hampshire, who was a theologian, and a novelist to boot, or the forgotten Hugh Williamson of North Carolina, whose mother had been captured by the pirate Blackbeard (imagine that) and who was even more versatile than

[v]

his New Hampshire colleague: he was a medical doctor, an astronomer, a mathematician, a merchant, a politician, and, almost by accident, an historian. There was General James Sullivan, who took time out from being Governor of Massachusetts to write a history of Maine, and Robert Proud, who was a Tory but whose *History of Pennsylvania* was none the worse for that. There were those two indefatigable purveyors to the public taste, Noah Webster and Jedediah Morse, who, to be sure, came a bit late on the scene and wrote mostly for schoolchildren. Jefferson's favorite poet, Joel Barlow, planned a history of the Revolution—or Jefferson planned it for him—but he was much too busy making a fortune over in Paris, and too easily distracted by politics and society, to settle down to the drudgery of history. Benjamin Trumbull projected a comprehensive history in three volumes, but managed to produce only the first; the Reverend Abiel Holmes did get through the Revolution, but his *American Annals* was merely a chronology. Surprisingly enough, it was John Marshall who came closest to writing the long-awaited history of the Revolution. But his five-volume biography of Washington—less a biography than a history—was, as might have been expected, highly partisan, and the Jeffersonians would have none of it; only later was it discovered that it had not even the merit of originality.

Clearly things were in a bad way. Scholarly Americans had a choice between the Englishman George Chalmers's *History of the Revolution of the American Colonies,* which was readable but unfriendly, and—a bit later —the Italian Charles Botta's *History of the War of Independence,* which was friendly enough but, in translation at least, not very readable. The less scholarly contented themselves with the myths and the fairy tales of the good Parson Weems.

Many of the Founding Fathers who thought about the matter concluded that the history of the Revolution simply could not be written until the documents had all been collected, nor were they persuaded that it was possible ever to collect them or that, if collected, they would tell the truth. As early as 1782 John Adams—who took this whole problem more seriously than any of his contemporaries—wrote to the eager and presumptuous Abbé Mably that "it is premature to undertake a general history of the American Revolution. . . . The whole of a long life, to begin at the age of twenty years, will be necessary to assemble from all nations and from all parts of the world in which they are deposited the documents proper to form a complete history. . . ." A generation later Adams was still discouraged. "Who shall write the history of the American Revolution?" he asked. "Who can write it? Who will ever be able to write it? The most essential documents . . . were all in secret, and are now lost forever."

Elbridge Gerry of Massachusetts had moved in the Continental Congress that each state appoint an official to collect historical materials, but nothing came of this. John Jay, too, proposed the preparation of a documentary history, but was too busy to undertake it himself. Noah Webster and Gordon and Ramsay had all collected such documentary materials as they could lay their hands on, but to little purpose. The persistent Ebenezer Hazard, for a time postmaster of the United States, had resolutely set himself to compile a documentary history and had actually published two volumes, but these, alas, carried the story only to the New England Confederation of 1643!

To old John Adams, sitting in his library in Braintree and living over again the great days of the Revolution, it was all very discouraging. Who would do justice to the daring and the courage and the wisdom of the Argonauts? Who would appreciate the trials and perils through which they had gone to win the Golden Fleece of Liberty?

But be of good cheer. The age of the Bollandists and of the Acta Sanctorum had already dawned, the age of the collectors and the editors, and John Adams could be sure that he would be numbered among the Saints. And after them came, almost inevitably, the storytellers and the philosophers!

Down in Baltimore, Hezekiah Niles, who had failed at many things, was publishing his *Register,* which was a tremendous success. It had all the news, all the information, all the reports from the best journals, and it had all the documents, too; in addition it was one of the most patriotic of American journals. With Hezekiah Niles patriotism was inborn, for when he was still in the womb a British grenadier had "charged bayonet on my mother, to kill, as he gallantly said, two rebels at once," and Niles had that on his mind, just as Jackson had that saber cut! He had grown up in Philadelphia with the Argonauts as it were, where Washington and Jefferson and Hamilton and John Adams were famous figures; as a boy he had listened to debates in Independence Hall, and he became not only an ardent patriot but an ardent republican as well. When, in 1805, he took on his first paper—it was the Baltimore *Evening Post*—he wrote that Jefferson had "exalted the country to a pinnacle of happiness and glory which the sages of ancient or modern times but dreamed of." Six years later Niles launched his *Weekly Register,* containing "political, historical, geographical, scientific, astronomical, statistical, biographical documents, essays, and facts, together with notices of the arts and manufactures, and a record of the events of the times." It did indeed contain all of those things, and more. It was national, it was authoritative, it was indispensable.

In mid-February of 1818 John Adams sent off one of a series of letters to editor Niles: he was trying to explain to a new generation what the Revolution had really been like, and how logical to turn to that editor who every week proclaimed an ardent nationalism and a lively appreciation of the importance of documents. The real Revolution, wrote the aged Adams—he was eighty-two at the time—was the change in principles, opinions, sentiments, and affections, and it was this the historian must understand and explain.

> To this end it is greatly to be desired that young men of letters in all the states, especially in the thirteen original states, would undertake the laborious but certainly interesting and amusing task, of searching and collecting all the records, pamphlets, newspapers, and even handbills, which in any way contributed to change the temper and views of the people, and compose them into an independent nation.

And he added a word of caution:

> In this research, the gloriole of individual gentlemen, and of separate states, is of little consequence. The *means and the measures* are the proper objects of investigation. These may be of use to posterity, not only in this nation, but in South America and all other countries. . . .

Niles needed little urging: indeed he had already begun to collect documents in a modest way. By the summer of 1819 he had concluded that "the task seemed to be imposed on us as a duty," and he promised to execute it to the best of his ability. Meantime, through the pages of his *Weekly,* he invited "every patriot" to give his aid. The response was gratifying, the documents came pouring in—eventually a "cart load" of them, too much really for the busy editor—and in 1822 the long-awaited volume appeared.

Principles and Acts of the Revolution was, as Niles himself admits, more principles than acts. The Revolution, as it emerges from these pages, was an intellectual, a philosophical, even a sedate affair. It did not consist of men fighting and killing each other, Indian massacres, patriots and tories applying coats of tar and feathers to their enemies, starvation at Valley Forge or Morristown, and retreats and defeats and occasional victories— all that was relegated to the historians. Rather the Revolution consisted of Addresses, Sermons, Proceedings, Speeches, Proposals, Instructions, Resolutions, Proclamations, and Letters. Now and then the editor permitted an anecdote or a biographical sketch to remind us that there were real fights and that flesh-and-blood men and women were involved. But he was, as he confessed, concerned with "feelings and sentiments": the feelings were almost invariably patriotic and the sentiments elevated.

It was a very one-sided compilation in other ways as well. The British got short shrift, and so did the Loyalists. Where they are allowed to speak it is only in what might be called accommodating tones. Burke and Chatham and Fox are here, and John Wilkes, but George III and his ministers are not permitted to present their side of the case, and as for Lord Howe and General Clinton and Gentleman Johnny Burgoyne, they appear only in defeat and disgrace.

Niles's volume opened the floodgates, as it were, and the next two decades saw something like a torrent of documents flow over the land. Jedediah Morse, who doubled as an historian, brought out his *Annals of the American Revolution* in 1824, a feeble enough production. The first volume of Jared Sparks's *Diplomatic Correspondence of the American Revolution* made its bow in 1829, and thereafter the indefatigable Sparks published one great collection after another, the *Writings* of Washington and the *Works* of Benjamin Franklin among them. Gales and Seaton's *Register of the Debates in Congress* began to appear in 1825, and their invaluable collection of *American State Papers*—eventually to fill thirty-eight massive volumes— was launched in 1832. Jonathan Elliot's collection of *Debates of the Federal Constitution*—a compilation still not supplanted—appeared between 1827 and 1830. Peter Force, eventually the greatest of documentary editors, began to compile historical materials as early as 1822, but it was 1837 before the first of the great folio volumes of *The American Archives* was ready.

All these were substantial and impressive compilations. By comparison with them Hezekiah Niles's *Principles and Acts* looks modest enough, modest and amateurish. It was indeed both a modest and an amateurish affair. But it has three distinctions, which have assured it a lasting place in our literature. It was, in the first place, a pioneering work and commands something of the interest that always attaches to such an enterprise. It was, second, if not well edited, then well selected, filled with valuable documents not easily available elsewhere. And, finally, a very practical consideration: it covered the whole of the Revolution from its philosophical inception in the sixties to the Peace of Paris and beyond, in a single, manageable volume. The appearance of this third edition of *Principles and Acts,* almost a century and a half after the first, is a testimony to that continued usefulness.

PREFACE

Almost one hundred and fifty years have passed since Hezekiah Niles began collecting materials relating to the American Revolution. It was 1816, America was basking in the after-glow of the "Second War for Independence," and the time seemed propitious for reviving the words of those who had guided us through the first struggle with Great Britain. The task proved an embarrassment of riches. By 1822 Niles had gathered enough documents to justify their publication as a separate volume; that summer the American public was treated to the first edition of *Principles and Acts of the Revolution in America: or, an Attempt to Collect and Preserve some of the Speeches, Orations, and Proceedings with Sketches and Remarks on Men and Things*. . . .

Niles's collection was an important contribution to the field of American history, but it had serious shortcomings. Much of the material in the volume was of limited value—at least so it now seems. Furthermore, Hezekiah Niles was a busy man, and he did not find time to arrange his documents into any logical order, leaving the reader to wade through a random assortment of some five hundred double-column pages with only an index as guide. Nonetheless, such drawbacks seem to have dissuaded very few potential readers: enough of them paid the three dollar price to make its editor a handsome profit and eventually to create a demand for a reissue of the collection.

The second edition of *Principles and Acts of the Revolution* was the work of Samuel V. Niles, Hezekiah's grandson. This later edition appeared in 1876 as the nation gaily celebrated its first century of independence and was appropriately entitled "Centennial Offering." Popular interest in a new edition was perhaps to be expected on such a significant anniversary, but Samuel Niles did not undertake the task until he had cautiously solicited opinions as to its feasibility from several dozen leading statesmen and jurists—among them Vice-President Henry Wilson, Secretary of State Hamilton Fish, General Benjamin Butler, Charles Francis Adams, and members of the Supreme Court. The editor not only took the advice of these correspondents to reissue *Principles and Acts,* but added luster to the new edition by including as a preface extracts from the replies of thirty-eight dignitaries.

Unfortunately, in the selection and arrangement of the contents, the second edition of *Principles and Acts* was only a slight improvement on its predecessor. Samuel Niles included all of the material—good, bad, and indifferent—that his grandfather had compiled. And while the younger Niles did attempt to improve the organization, his solution left much to be desired. In place of the purely random presentation of the first edition, Samuel Niles devised nineteen categories, with the items in each arranged in chronological order. This certainly added convenience for the reader, but the categories did little to bring meaning to the material: the first thirteen were the names of the original thirteen states, the other categories were "Continental Congress," "British Parliament," "George Washington," "Benjamin Franklin," "Continental Navy," and "Miscellaneous." Still, the second edition, like the first, found a warm reception, and it too has long been out of print.

In preparing a third edition of Hezekiah Niles's *Principles and Acts of the Revolution in America,* I have tried to avoid the pitfalls that marred the previous editions. The contents are organized so that the reader may have a sense of the way events unfolded and ideas evolved in the era of the American Revolution. Thus both the broad categories and the documents within them are arranged in chronological order for the most part, but exceptions have been made whenever a topical presentation seemed more meaningful. And in order that the documents of this collection may be read, if desired, as a continuous narrative, I have added introductions to each part and chapter and have inserted brief identifying notes at the beginning of each document. Occasionally I have injected explanatory comments within the text of a document; in such cases my remarks are enclosed in square brackets. I have also, in some instances, modernized the typography as a convenience for the modern reader.

The present edition also sharply curtails the quantity of documents of the original collection; this is an abridgment that attempts to preserve the spirit and value of the original without burdening the reader with material that is either trivial or repetitious. Many items have been entirely omitted; others have been condensed—in which case the places of deletion have been indicated by the customary ellipses. But those items of the original edition that have stood the test of time are offered here for the reader's enjoyment and edification. These selections, it is hoped, will adequately fulfill Hezekiah Niles's desire "to represent the feelings that prevailed in the 'times that tried men's souls.' "

A.T.V.
Columbia University
1965

CONTENTS

ILLUSTRATIONS

HEZEKIAH NILES

PRINCIPLES AND ACTS

OF THE

REVOLUTION IN AMERICA:

OR, AN ATTEMPT

TO COLLECT AND PRESERVE SOME OF THE

SPEECHES, ORATIONS, & PROCEEDINGS,

WITH SKETCHES AND REMARKS

ON

MEN AND THINGS,

AND OTHER FUGITIVE OR NEGLECTED PIECES,

BELONGING TO THE

REVOLUTIONARY PERIOD IN THE UNITED STATES;

WHICH, HAPPILY, TERMINATED IN THE

ESTABLISHMENT OF THEIR LIBERTIES:

WITH A VIEW

TO REPRESENT THE FEELINGS THAT PREVAILED IN THE "TIMES THAT TRIED MEN'S SOULS," TO EXCITE A LOVE OF FREEDOM, AND LEAD THE PEOPLE TO VIGILANCE, AS THE CONDITION ON WHICH IT IS GRANTED.

DEDICATED TO THE

YOUNG MEN OF THE UNITED STATES.

BY H. NILES.

——————*" Collecta revirescunt."*

BALTIMORE:

PRINTED AND PUBLISHED FOR THE EDITOR, BY WILLIAM OGDEN NILES.

1822.

Facsimile of the title page of the 1822 edition

TO

THE YOUNG MEN

OF THE

UNITED STATES,

THIS VOLUME OF

REVOLUTIONARY PAPERS, SPEECHES, &c.,

IS, RESPECTFULLY, DEDICATED;

IN THE HOPE

That they may be encouraged to adhere to the simplicity of Truth,

AS SET FORTH BY THE

PRINCIPLES AND ACTS OF THEIR FATHERS,

AND EMULATE THE NOBLEST DEEDS WHEN THE

LIBERTIES OF THEIR COUNTRY ARE ENDANGERED,

BY FOREIGN ENEMIES OR DOMESTIC ENCROACHMENTS,

SO THAT

THE BLESSINGS WHICH THESE PATRIOTS WON

MAY DESCEND TO POSTERITY,

And our Republic forever continue to be the pride of Humanity, and an Asylum for the

OPPRESSED OF ALL NATIONS:

BY THEIR SINCERE FRIEND,

H. NILES.

Baltimore, April, 1822.

Facsimile of the dedication page of the 1822 edition

PART ONE

Defining the
Rights of Englishmen
1765-1775

Defining the Rights of Englishmen

1765-1775

THE AMERICAN COLONIST of the 1760's was proud to be a British subject. After more than a century of intermittent warfare with France and Spain, Great Britain had gained undisputed control of the North American continent. By 1763 the British flag flew over most of the settled areas of the North American mainland; it also flew over most of the profitable Caribbean islands, over the choicest parts of India, over scattered outposts in Africa and Asia, as well as over the united kingdom of England, Ireland, Scotland, and Wales. It was a glorious time to be an Englishman.

Yet the British Empire contained the seeds of its own downfall. Its very success had earned it a legion of enemies who waited for a chance to reverse its fortune, its colonies no longer needed protection from Spanish and French encroachment, and its victories had left a legacy of debt that could not be met without major innovations. In short, despite its newly won glory, the British Empire had immense new problems, which demanded prudent leadership, wise planning, and efficient administration. But none of these qualities was possessed by the imperial government in the critical period from 1763 to 1776. Rather, Britain's statesmen bluffed, blundered, and eventually prodded thirteen of their mainland colonies into open revolt.

The first steps toward the American Revolution were deceptively peaceful. Several measures proposed by the British government during the French and Indian War (1754-1763) raised constitutional issues in which American colonists and British statesmen took opposite stands. In Virginia a dispute over clerical salaries dramatized the question of the Crown's right to

veto acts of colonial legislatures, and thus thrust a fundamental issue before the people. It also brought to prominence an articulate spokesman for
the colonial position in young Patrick Henry. In Massachusetts a similar
commotion was caused by a dispute over the use of writs of assistance—the
blank search warrants which seemed so threatening to the civil liberties of
the colonists. Again the imperial government won its case, but once more
it raised an issue that would not down, and another colonial spokesman
emerged, James Otis of the Bay Colony. Still other points of controversy
irritated the populace from New Hampshire to Georgia, especially after
1763 when the British government decided to revamp its colonial system.

In rapid order the ministry of Lord George Grenville established a
limit on westward expansion (1763), imposed a revenue tax on sugar and
related items (1764), prohibited the use of paper money in the colonies
(1764), and required colonial governments to furnish barracks and supplies
for the 10,000 British troops that were to be stationed in the American
colonies (1765). Loud protests came from every colony, but they were un-
organized and, compared to what came later, rather tepid. This was a period
of debate—often passionate, sometimes unruly, but seldom violent. The colonies and the mother country were having a family quarrel: Britain was imposing new regulations on her distant progeny which the colonists claimed
were depriving them of the rights their brethren back home in England
possessed.

Unfortunately the rights of an Englishman, especially one transplanted
to a British colony, were not so easy to define. Beginning in the late 1750's,
Englishmen in all walks of life, on both sides of the Atlantic, began to
argue, proclaim, and debate what they thought were the rights of Englishmen, an issue that assumed paramount importance with the enactment in
1765 of the Stamp Act. The chronicles that follow illustrate the course of
that debate in the decade from the Stamp Act of 1765 to the outbreak of
hostilities at Lexington, Massachusetts, in the spring of 1775.

I

FROM STAMP ACT TO MASSACRE,

1765-1770

Parliament's passage of the Stamp Act aroused the first concentrated colonial opposition to the new imperial policies and at the same time brought forth the first comprehensive body of American constitutional principles. Designed to raise some £60,000 per year through duties on such printed matter as newspapers, almanacs, pamphlets, and on most legal transactions, the Stamp Act was Parliament's first direct tax on the American colonies. The colonial response was vehement. Stamp agents were forced to resign before they had even received their official appointments, stamped paper was confiscated before it could be put into circulation, and courts and lawyers closed their doors rather than abide by the new requirements. So universal was the reaction in North America that the colonies drew together and began to cooperate with one another in their resistance to the Crown.

In the fall of 1765, representatives of nine colonies met in New York City to draft a joint protest against the Stamp Act in particular and against British encroachment on colonial rights in general. After several weeks of discussion the Stamp Act Congress issued moderate but forthright petitions to the King and to each house of Parliament. As the journal of its proceedings (p. 7) and a letter from a delegate (p. 20) reveal, the members of the Congress were fully aware of the importance and seriousness of their undertaking. At the same time, the leaders of the government in Great Britain were apprehensive of the colonial resistance movements, as Benjamin Franklin discovered in his talks with English officials (p. 21). In the end, the colonies went far beyond verbal protest and effectively thwarted the use of stamped paper. As the instance of South Carolina illustrates (p. 23), the Stamp Act was a nullity throughout the colonies.

[5]

Under pressure from British merchants who were suffering heavy losses through an American boycott of British goods, Parliament in 1766 repealed the Stamp Act. But its Declaratory Act, passed at the time of the repeal, reasserted Parliament's right to tax the colonies, a prerogative the government put to use the next year. The Townshend duties of 1767 levied small charges on imports such as glass, lead, paints, paper, and tea. In conjunction with a companion measure, the act also instituted a major revision in the administration of the American colonies: it provided for the payment of salaries to civil officials from imperial rather than colonial sources (a threat to colonial control of appointed officeholders), authorized the use of writs of assistance in the execution of the act, established vice-admiralty courts to adjudge without jury trial infractions of the act, and set up a new board of customs commissioners at Boston. The colonists vehemently protested against all features of this newest imperial scheme. To many British Americans, it appeared to be a deliberate system of oppression designed to undermine the fundamental rights of Englishmen. Resistance now took many forms, the most effective of which was a well enforced program of non-importation (pp. 25, 26, and 30). Parliament finally succumbed, and early in 1770 repealed all of the duties except that on tea—left as a symbol of Parliamentary prerogative. But even after its repeal, the Townshend Act indirectly touched off a major episode in the growing rift between America and Great Britain.

In its attempt to enforce the Townshend duties, the British government had stationed imperial troops in several potential trouble spots. Violence soon followed. Soldiers and civilians clashed in New York City on a number of occasions, with some injuries on both sides. But it was in Boston that the friction between British troops and rebellious citizens resulted in the first fatalities of the Revolution. On the evening of March 5, 1770, a detachment of soldiers fired into a heckling mob. Three civilians were killed outright, two more died of wounds (p. 31). Although the soldiers received a fair trial and no further violence occurred, the memory of the Boston Massacre served in the coming years as a catalyst for resentment of British policy and as a focal point for patriotic rhetoric (pp. 33 and 39).

1. THE COLONIES UNITE AGAINST THE STAMP ACT

JOURNAL OF THE STAMP ACT CONGRESS
[*Extracts from the official journal of the Stamp Act Congress,
New York, 1765*]

Delegates to the Congress of 1765.

MASSACHUSETTS
  James Otis,
  Oliver Partridge,
  Timothy Ruggles.
RHODE ISLAND
  Metcalf Bowler,
  Henry Ward.
CONNECTICUT
  Eliphalet Dyer,
  David Rowland,
  William S. Johnson.
NEW YORK
  Robert R. Livingston,
  John Cruger,
  Philip Livingston,
  William Bayard,
  Leonard Lispenard.

NEW JERSEY
  Robert Ogden,
  Hendrick Fisher,
  Joseph Borden.
PENNSYLVANIA
  John Dickinson,
  John Morton,
  George Bryan.
DELAWARE
  Thomas McKean,
  Caesar Rodney.
MARYLAND
  William Murdock,
  Edward Tilghman,
  Thomas Ringgold.
SOUTH CAROLINA
  Thomas Lynch,
  Christopher Gadsden,
  John Rutledge.

NEW HAMPSHIRE,
VIRGINIA,
NORTH CAROLINA,
AND
GEORGIA

} Were not represented in this congress. But their assemblies wrote that they would agree to whatever was done by the congress.

THE JOURNAL

BOSTON, June, 1765

SIR—The house of representatives of this province, in the present session of general court, have unanimously agreed to propose a meeting, as soon as may be, of committees from the houses of representatives or burgesses, of the several British colonies on this continent, to consult together on the present circumstances of the colonies, and the difficulties to which they are and must be reduced by the operation of the acts of parliament, for levying duties and taxes on the colonies; and to consider of a general and united, dutiful, loyal and humble representation of their condition to his majesty and to the parliament, and to implore relief.

The house of representatives of this province have also voted, to propose that such meeting be at the city of New York, in the province of New York on the first Tuesday in October next, and have appointed the committee of three of their members to attend this service, with such as the other houses of representatives or burgesses, in the several colonies, may think fit to appoint to meet them: and the committee of the house of representatives of this province, are directed to repair to the said New York, on the first Tuesday in October next, accordingly: if, therefore your honorable house should agree to this proposal, it would be acceptable, that as early notice of it as possible might be transmitted to the speaker of the house of representatives of this province.

SAMUEL WHITE, Speaker.

In consequence of the foregoing circular letter, the following gentlemen met at New York, in the province of New York, on Monday, the 7th of October, 1765, viz:

From the province of Massachusetts Bay, } JAMES OTIS, OLIVER PARTRIDGE, TIMOTHY RUGGLES.

Who produced their appointment as follows, viz:

TO JAMES OTIS, OLIVER PARTRIDGE, AND TIMOTHY RUGGLES, ESQUIRES.

Gentlemen,—The house of representatives of this province, have appointed you a committee to meet at New York on the first Tuesday in October next, such committees as the other houses of representatives or burgesses in the several colonies on this continent, may think fit to appoint, to consult together on the present circumstances of the colonies, on the difficulties to which they are, and must be reduced by the operation of the late acts of parliament. By this choice, the house has reposed in you a trust of singular importance, and have just reason to expect you will give your utmost attention to it. In case you should receive advice that the house of representatives or burgesses of the other colonies, or any of them, agree to such committees, to join you in this interesting affair, you are directed to repair to New York at the time appointed, and endeavor to unite with them in sentiment, and agree upon such representations, as may tend to preserve our rights and privileges. And it is the opinion of this house, that no address or representation shall be esteemed the act of this house, unless it is agreed to and signed by the major part of their committee.

If it should be said, that we are in any manner represented in parliament, you must by no means concede to it; it is an opinion which this house cannot see the least reason to adopt.

Further, the house think that such a representation of the colonies as British subjects are to enjoy, would be attended with the greatest difficulty, if it is not absolutely impracticable, and therefore, you are not to urge or consent to any proposal for any representation, if such be made in the congress.

It is the expectation of the house, that a most loyal and dutiful address to his majesty and the parliament, will be prepared by the congress, praying as well for the removal of the grievances the colonies labor under at present, as for preventing others for the future; which petitions, if drawn up, as far as you shall be able to judge, agreeable to the mind of the house, you are empowered to sign and forward; and you are to lay a copy of the same before this house, and make report of your proceedings upon your return.

It is the hearty prayer of this house, that the congress may be endued with that wisdom which is from above, and that their councils and determinations may be attended with the divine blessing.

SAMUEL WHITE, Speaker

[The instructions of the other colonies to their delegates followed, all expressed in terms similar to those of Massachusetts.]

Then the said committees proceeded to choose a chairman by ballot; and TIMOTHY RUGGLES, Esq. on sorting and counting the votes, appeared to have a majority—and thereupon was placed in the chair.

Resolved, nem. con. That Mr. John Cotton, be clerk to this congress during the continuance thereof.

Then the congress took into consideration the several appointments of the committees from New York, New Jersey, and the government of the lower counties on Delaware—and

Resolved, nem. con. That the same are sufficient to qualify the gentlemen therein named, to sit in the congress.

Resolved also, That the committee of each colony, shall have one voice only, in determining any questions that shall rise in the Congress.

Then the congress adjourned until tomorrow morning, 9 o'clock.

Tuesday, Oct. 8th, 1765, A.M.— The congress met according to adjournment. . . . Voted, that Mr. justice Livingston, Mr. McKean and Mr. Rutledge be a committee to inspect the proceedings and minutes, and correct the same.

Then the congress took into consideration the rights and privileges of the British American colonists, with the several inconveniences and hardships to which they are and must be subjected by the operation of several late acts of parliament, particularly the act called the stamp act; and after some time spent therein, the same was postponed for further consideration.

Then the congress adjourned until to-morrow morning, 9 o'clock.

Wednesday, Oct. 9th, 1765, A.M.—Then the congress met according to adjournment. The congress resumed the consideration of the rights and privileges of the British American colonists, etc., the same was referred after sundry debates, for further consideration.

Then the congress adjourned until tomorrow morning, 11 o'clock.

Thursday, Oct. 10th, 1765, A.M.—Then the congress met according to adjournment, and resumed, etc., as yesterday—and then adjourned to 10 o'clock, to-morrow morning. . . .

[*For the period October 11-18 the Journal entries follow the pattern of October 10.*]

Saturday, Oct. 19th, 1765, A.M.—Then congress met according to adjournment, and resumed, etc., as yesterday; and upon mature deliberation, agreed to the following declarations of the rights and grievances of the colonists in America, which were ordered to be inserted.

The members of this congress, sincerely devoted, with the warmest sentiments of affection and duty to his majesty's person and government; inviolably attached to the present happy establishment of the protestant succession, and with minds deeply impressed by a sense of the present and impending misfortunes of the British colonies on this continent; having considered as maturely as time would permit, the circumstances of the said colonies, esteem it our indispensable duty to make the following declarations, of our humble opinion, respecting the most essential rights and liberties of the colonists, and of the grievances under which they labor, by reason of several late acts of parliament.

1st. That his majesty's subjects in these colonies, owe the same allegiance to the crown of Great Britain, that is owing from his subjects born within the realm, and all due subordination to that august body, the parliament of Great Britain.

2d. That his majesty's liege subjects in these colonies are entitled to all the inherent rights and privileges of his natural born subjects within the kingdom of Great Britain.

3d. That it is inseparably essential to the freedom of a people, and the undoubted rights of Englishmen, that no taxes should be imposed on them, but with their own consent, given personally, or by their representatives.

4th. That the people of these colonies are not, and from their local circumstances, cannot be represented in the house of commons in Great Britain.

5th. That the only representatives of the people of these colonies, are persons chosen therein, by themselves; and that no taxes ever have been, or can be constitutionally imposed on them, but by their respective legislatures.

6th. That all supplies to the crown, being free gifts of the people, it is unreasonable and inconsistent with the principles and spirit of the British constitution, for the people of Great Britain to grant to his majesty the property of the colonists.

7th. That trial by jury is the inherent and invaluable right of every British subject in these colonies.

8th. That the late act of parliament, entitled, an act for granting and applying certain stamp duties, and other duties in the British colonies and plantations in America, etc., by imposing taxes on the inhabitants of these colonies, and the said act, and several other acts, by extending the jurisdiction of the courts of admiralty beyond its ancient limits, have a manifest tendency to subvert the rights and liberties of the colonists.

9th. That the duties imposed by several late acts of parliament, from [the] peculiar circumstances of these colonies, will be extremely burthensome and grievous, and from the scarcity of specie, the payment of them absolutely impracticable.

10th. That as the profits of the trade of these colonies ultimately centre in Great Britain, to pay for the manufactures which they are obliged to take from thence, they eventually contribute very largely to all supplies granted there to the crown.

11th. That the restrictions imposed by several late acts of parliament, on the trade of these colonies, will render them unable to purchase the manufactures of Great Britain.

12th. That the increase, prosperity and happiness of these colonies, depend on the full and free enjoyment of their rights and liberties, and an intercourse, with Great Britain, mutually affectionate and advantageous.

13th. That it is the right of the British subjects in these colonies, to petition the king or either house of parliament.

Lastly, that it is the indispensable duty of these colonies to the best of sovereigns, to the mother country, and to themselves, to endeavor by a loyal and dutiful address to his majesty, and humble application to both houses of parliament, to procure the repeal of the act for granting and applying certain stamp duties, of all clauses of any other acts of parliament, whereby the jurisdiction of the admiralty is extended as aforesaid, and of the other late acts for the restriction of the American commerce.

Upon motion, voted, that Robert R. Livingston, William Samuel Johnson and William Murdock, Esqrs. be a committee to prepare an address to his majesty, and lay the same before the congress on Monday next.

Voted also, that John Rutledge, Edward Tilghman and Philip Livingston, Esqrs. be a committee to prepare a memorial and petition to the lords in parliament, and lay the same before the congress on Monday next.

Voted also, that Thomas Lynch, James Otis and Thomas McKean, Esqrs. be a committee to prepare a petition to the house of commons of Great Britain, and lay the same before the congress on Monday next.

Then the congress adjourned to Monday next, at twelve o'clock.

Monday, Oct. 21st, 1765, A.M.—The committee appointed to prepare and bring in an address to his majesty, did report, that they have essayed a draught for that purpose, which they laid on the table, and humbly submitted to the correction of the congress.

The said address was read, and, after sundry amendments, the same was approved of by the congress, and ordered to be engrossed.

The committee, appointed to prepare and bring in a memorial and petition to the lords in parliament did report that they had essayed a draught for that purpose, which they laid on the table, and humbly submitted to the correction of the congress.

The said address was read, and after sundry amendments, the same was approved of by the congress, and ordered to be engrossed.

The committee appointed to prepare and bring in a petition to the house of commons of Great Britain, did report that they had essayed a draught for that purpose, which they laid on the table, and humbly submitted to the correction of the congress.

The said address was read, and after sundry amendments, the same was approved of by the congress, and ordered to be engrossed.

Then the congress adjourned to to-morrow morning at 9 o'clock.

Tuesday, Oct. 22d, 1765, A.M.—The congress met according to adjournment. The address to his majesty being engrossed, was read and compared, and is as follows, viz:

To THE KING'S MOST EXCELLENT MAJESTY,

The petition of the freeholders and other inhabitants of the Massachusetts Bay, Rhode Island and Providence Plantations, New Jersey, Pennsylvania, the government of the counties of New Castle, Kent and Sussex upon Delaware, and province of Maryland,

Most humbly sheweth,

That the inhabitants of these colonies, unanimously devoted with the warmest sentiments of duty and affection to your sacred person and government, and inviolably attached to the present happy establishment of the protestant succession in your illustrious house, and deeply sensible of your royal attention to their prosperity and happiness, humbly beg leave to approach the throne, by representing to your majesty, that these colonies were originally planted by subject of the British crown: who, animated with the spirit of liberty, encouraged by your majesty's royal predecessors, and confiding in the public faith for the enjoyment of all the rights and liberties essential to freedom, emigrated from their native country to this continent, and, by their successful perseverance in the midst of innumerable dangers and difficulties, together with a profusion of their blood and treasure, have happily added these vast and extensive dominions to the empire of Great Britain.

That, for the enjoyment of these rights and liberties, several governments were early formed in the said colonies, with full power of legislation agreeable to the principles of the English constitution;—that under those governments, these liberties, thus vested in their ancestors, and transmitted to their posterity, have been exercised and enjoyed, and by the inestimable blessings thereof, under the favor of Almighty God, the inhospitable deserts of America have been converted into flourishing countries; science, humanity and the knowledge of divine truths diffused through remote regions of ignorance, infidelity, barbarism; the number of British subjects wonderfully increased, and the wealth and power of Great Britain proportionably augmented.

That, by means of these settlements and the unparalleled success of your majesty's arms, a foundation is now laid for rendering the British empire the most extensive and powerful of any recorded in history; our connection with this empire we esteem our greatest happiness and security, and humbly conceive it may now be so established by your royal wisdom, as to endure to the latest period of time; this with the most humble submission to your majesty, we apprehend will be most effectually accomplished by fixing the pillars thereof on liberty and justice, and securing the inherent rights and liberties of your subjects here, upon the principles of the English constitution. To this constitution these two principles are essential; the right of your faithful subjects freely to grant your majesty such aids as are required for the support of your government over them, and other public exigencies, and trials by their peers. By the one they are secured from unreasonable impositions, and by the other from the arbitrary decisions of the executive power. The continuation of these liberties, to the inhabitants of America, we ardently implore, as absolutely necessary to unite the several parts of your wide extended dominions, in that harmony so essential to the preservation and happiness of the whole. Protected in these liberties, the emoluments Great Britain receives from us, however great at present, are inconsiderable, compared with those she has the fairest prospect of acquiring. By this protection, she will forever secure to herself the advantages of conveying to all Europe, the merchandise which America furnishes, and for supplying through the same channel, whatsoever is wanted from thence. Here opens a boundless source of wealth and naval strength. Yet these immense advantages, by the abridgement of those invaluable rights and liberties, by which our growth has been nourished, are in danger of being forever lost, and our subordinate legislatures in effect rendered useless by the late acts of parliament imposing duties and taxes on these colonies, and extending the jurisdiction of the courts of admiralty here, beyond its ancient limits; statutes, by which your majesty's commons in Britain undertake absolutely to dispose of the property of their fellow subjects in America without their consent, and for the enforcing whereof, they are subjected to the determination of a single judge, in court unrestrained by the wise rules of the common law, the birthright of Englishmen, and the safeguard of their persons and their properties.

The invaluable rights of taxing ourselves and trial by our peers, of which we implore your majesty's protection, are not, we most humbly conceive, unconstitutional, but confirmed by the Great Charter of English liberties. On the first of these rights the honorable house of commons found their practice of originating money; a right enjoyed by the kingdom of Ireland, by the clergy of England, until relinquished by themselves; a right, in fine, which all other your majesty's English subjects, both within and without the realm, have hitherto enjoyed.

With hearts, therefore, impressed with the most indelible characters of gratitude to your majesty, and to the memory of the kings of your illustrious house, whose reigns have been signally distinguished by their auspicious influence on the prosperity of the British dominions, and convinced by the most affecting proofs of your majesty's paternal love to all your people, however distant, and your unceasing and benevolent desires to promote their happiness, we most humbly beseech your majesty that you will be graciously pleased to take into your royal consideration the distresses of your faithful subjects on this continent, and to lay the same before your majesty's parliament, and to afford them such relief, as in your royal wisdom their unhappy circumstances shall be judged to require.

And your petitioners will pray, etc.

The memorial to the lords in parliament being engrossed, was read and compared, and is as follows, viz:

TO THE RIGHT HONORABLE THE LORDS SPIRITUAL AND TEMPORAL OF GREAT BRITAIN, IN PARLIAMENT ASSEMBLED.

The memorial of the freeholders and other inhabitants of Massachusetts Bay, Rhode Island and Providence Plantations, New Jersey, Pennsylvania, the government of the counties of New Castle, Kent and Sussex upon Delaware, and province of Maryland, in America.

Most humbly sheweth,
That his majesty's liege subjects in his American colonies, though they acknowledge a due subordination to that august body, the British Parliament, are entitled, in the opinion, of your memorialists, to all the inherent rights and liberties of the natives of Great Britain, and have, ever since the settlement of the said colonies, exercised those rights and liberties, as far as their local circumstances would permit.

That your memorialists humbly conceive that one of the most essential rights of these colonists, which they have ever till lately uninterruptedly enjoyed, to be trial by jury.

That your memorialists also humbly conceive another of these essential rights, to be the exemption from all taxes, but such as are imposed on the people by the several legislatures in these colonies, which rights they have also, till of late enjoyed. But your memorialists humbly beg leave to represent to your lordships, that the act for granting certain stamp duties in the British colonies in America, etc., fills his majesty's American subjects with the deepest concern, as it tends to deprive them of the two fundamental and invaluable rights and liberties above mentioned; and that several other late acts of parliament, which extend the jurisdiction and power of courts of admiralty in the plantations beyond their limits in Great Britain, thereby make an unnecessary, unhappy distinction, as to the modes of trial between us and our fellow subjects there, by whom we never have been excelled in duty and loyalty to our sovereign.

That, from the natural connection between Great Britain and America, the perpetual continuance of which your memorialists most ardently desire, they conceive that nothing can conduce more to the interest of both, than the colonists' free enjoyment of their rights and liberties, and an affectionate intercourse between Great Britain and them. But your memorialists (not waiving their claim to these rights, of which, with the most becoming veneration and deference to the wisdom and justice of your lordships, they apprehend they cannot reasonably be deprived) humbly represent, that from the peculiar circumstances of these colonies, the duties imposed by the aforesaid act, and several other late acts of parliament, are extremely grievous and burthensome; and the payment of the several duties will very soon, for want of specie, become absolutely impracticable: and that the restrictions on trade by the said acts, will not only distress the colonies, but must be extremely detrimental to the trade and true interest of Great Britain.

Your memorialists, therefore, impressed with a just sense of the unfortunate circumstances of the colonies, the impending destructive consequences which must necessarily ensue from the execution of these acts, and animated with the warmest sentiments of filial affection for their mother country, most earnestly and humbly entreat your lordships will be pleased to hear their council in support of this memorial, and take the premises into your most serious consideration, and that your lordships will also be thereupon pleased to pursue such measures for restoring the just rights and liberties of the colonies, and preserving them forever inviolate, for redressing their present, and preventing future grievances, thereby promoting the united interest of Great Britain and America, as to your lordships, in your great wisdom, shall seem most conducive, and effectual to that important end.

And your memorialists will pray, etc.

Then the congress adjourned to to-morrow morning, 9 o'clock.

Wednesday, Oct. 23d, 1765, A.M.—The congress met according to adjournment.

The petition to the house of commons being engrossed, was read and compared, and is as follows, viz:

To the Honorable the Knights, Citizens and Burgesses of Great Britain, in Parliament Assembled.

The petition of his majesty's dutiful, loyal subjects, the freeholders and other inhabitants of the colonies of the Massachusetts Bay, Rhode Island and Providence Plantations, New Jersey, Pennsylvania, the government of the counties of New Castle, Kent, and Sussex upon Delaware, and province of Maryland, in America.

Most humbly sheweth,

That the several late acts of parliament, imposing divers duties and taxes on the colonies, and laying the trade and commerce under very burthensome restrictions, but above all, the act for granting and applying certain stamp duties in America, have filled them with the deepest concern and surprise, and they humbly conceive the execution of them will be attended with consequences very injurious to the commercial interest of Great Britain and her colonies, and must terminate in the eventual ruin of the latter. Your petitioners, therefore, most ardently implore the attention of the honorable house to the united and dutiful representation of their circumstances, and to their earnest supplications for relief from their regulations that have already involved this continent in anxiety, confusion, and distress. We most sincerely recognize our allegiance to the crown, and acknowledge all due subordination to the parliament of Great Britain, and shall always retain the most grateful sense of their assistance and approbation; it is from and under the English constitution we derive all our civil and religious rights and liberties; we glory in being subjects of the best of kings, having been born under the most perfect form of government. But it is with the most ineffable and humiliating sorrow that we find ourselves of late, deprived of the right of granting our own property for his majesty's service, to which our lives and fortunes are entirely devoted, and to which on his royal requisitions, we have been ready to contribute to the utmost of our abilities.

We have also the misfortune to find, that all the penalties and forfeitures mentioned in the stamp act, and divers late acts of trade extending to the plantations, are, at the election of the informers, recoverable in any court of admiralty in America. This . . . renders his majesty's subjects in these colonies, liable to be carried at an immense expense from one end of the continent to the other. It always gives us great pain to see a manifest distinction made therein between the subjects of our mother country and the colonies, in that the like penalties and forfeitures recoverable there only in his majesty's courts of record, are made cognizable here by a court of admiralty. By this means we seem to be in effect, unhappily deprived of two privileges essential to freedom, and which all Englishmen have ever considered as their best birth-rights; that of being free from all taxes but such as they have consented to in person, or by their representatives, and of trial by their peers.

Your petitioners further shew, that the remote situation and other circumstances of the colonies, render it impracticable that they should be represented but in their respective subordinate legislatures, and they humbly conceive that the parliament adhering strictly to the principle of the constitution, have never hitherto taxed any but those who were therein actually represented: for this reason, we humbly apprehend, they never have taxed Ireland, nor any other of the subjects without the realm.

—But were it ever so clear, that the colonies might in law be reasonably represented in the honorable house of commons, yet we conceive that very good reasons from inconvenience, from the principles of true policy, and from the spirit of the British constitution, may be adduced to shew, that it would be for the real interest of Great Britain, as well as her colonies, that the late regulations should be rescinded, and the several acts of parliament imposing duties and taxes on the colonies and extending the jurisdiction of the courts of admiralty here beyond their ancient limits, should be repealed.

We shall not attempt a minute detail of all the reasons which the wisdom of the honorable house may suggest, on this occasion, but would humbly submit the following particulars to their consideration:

That money is already very scarce in these colonies, and is still decreasing by the necessary exportation of specie from the continent for the discharging of our debts to British merchants, that an immensely heavy debt is yet due from the colonies for British manufacture, and that they are still heavily burthened with taxes to discharge the arrearages due for aids granted by them in the late war; that the balance of trade will ever be much against the colonies, and in favor of Great Britain, whilst we consume her manufactures; the demand of which must ever increase in proportion to the number of inhabitants settled here, with the means of purchasing them. We therefore humbly conceive it to be the interest of Great Britain to increase rather than diminish those means, as the profit of all the trade of the colonies ultimately centre there to pay for her manufactures as we are not allowed to purchase elsewhere, and by the consumption of which, at the advanced prices the British taxes oblige the makers and venders to set on them, we eventually contribute very largely to the revenues of the crown.

That, from the nature of American business, the multiplicity of suits and papers used in matters of small value, in a country where freeholds are so minutely divided, and property so frequently transferred, a stamp duty must be ever very burthensome and unequal.

That it is extremely improbable that the honorable house of commons should at all times be thoroughly acquainted with our condition, and all facts requisite to a just and equal taxation of the colonies.

It is also humbly submitted whether there be not a material distinction, in reason and sound policy at least, between the necessary exercise of parliamentary jurisdiction in general acts, and the common law, and the regulations of trade and commerce, through the whole empire, and the exercise of that jurisdiction by imposing taxes on the colonies.

That the several subordinate provincial legislatures have been moulded into forms as nearly resembling that of the mother country, as by his majesty's royal predecessors was thought convenient; and these legislatures seem to have been wisely and graciously established, that the subjects in the colonies might, under the due administration thereof, enjoy the happy fruits of the British government, which in their present circumstances they cannot be so fully and clearly availed of any other way.

Under these forms of government we and our ancestors have been born or settled, and have had our lives, liberties and properties protected; the people here as every where else, retain a great fondness of their old customs and usages, and we trust that his majesty's service, and the interest of the nation, so far from being obstructed, have been vastly promoted by the provincial legislatures.

That we esteem our connection with and dependence on Great Britain, as one of our greatest blessings; and apprehend the latter will be sufficiently secure, when it is considered that the inhabitants in the colonies have the most unbounded affection for his majesty's person, family and government, as well as for the mother country, and that their subordination to the parliament is universally acknowledged.

We, therefore, most humbly entreat that the honorable house would be pleased to hear our council in support of this petition, and take our distressed and deplorable case into their serious consideration, and that the acts and clauses of acts so grievously restraining our trade and commerce, imposing duties and taxes on our property, and extending the jurisdiction of the court of admiralty beyond its ancient limits, may be repealed; or that the honorable house would otherwise relieve your petitioners as in your great wisdom and goodness shall seem meet.

And your petitioners shall ever pray, etc.

Then the congress adjourned until to-morrow morning, 10 o'clock.

Thursday, Oct. 24th, 1765, A.M.—The congress met according to adjournment.

The congress took into consideration the manner in which their several petitions should be preferred and solicited in Great Britain, and thereupon came to the following determination, viz:

It is recommended by the congress to the several colonies to appoint special agents for soliciting relief from their present grievances, and to unite their utmost interest and endeavors for that purpose.

Voted unanimously, that the clerk of this congress sign the minutes of their proceedings, and deliver a copy for the use of each colony and province.

By order of the congress,
JOHN COTTON, Clerk

CAESAR RODNEY WRITES FROM NEW YORK

[Extract of a letter from Delaware statesman Caesar Rodney to his brother Thomas, New York, Oct. 20, 1765]

When I wrote to you last, I expected that congress would have ended in eight or ten days from that time; but, contrary to expectation, we have not yet finished. You and many others are surprised, perhaps, to think we should sit so long, when the business of our meeting seemed only to be the petitioning the king, and remonstrating to both houses of parliament; but when you consider that we are petitioning and addressing that august body, the great legislature of the empire, for redress of grievances,—that, in order to point out those grievances, it was likewise necessary to set forth the liberty we have and ought to enjoy (as free-born Englishmen) according to the British constitution. This we are about to do by way of declaration, in the nature of resolve, as a foundation to the petition and address; and was one of the most difficult tasks I ever yet saw undertaken, as we had carefully to avoid any infringement of the prerogative of the crown and the power of parliament—and yet in duty bound fully to assert the rights and privileges of the colonies. However, after arguing and debating two weeks, on liberty, privileges, prerogatives, etc. in an assembly of great abilities, we happily finished them, and now have the petitions and addresses before us, and expect to finish in three or four days.

BENJAMIN FRANKLIN REPORTS FROM LONDON

[Extract of a letter from Benjamin Franklin to his son William]

London, Nov. 9, 1765

I had a long audience on Wednesday with lord Dartmouth. He was highly recommended to me by lords Grantham and Besborough, as a young man of excellent understanding, and the most amiable dispositions. They seemed extremely intent on bringing us together. I had been to pay my respects to his lordship on his appointment to preside at the board of trade; but during the summer he has been much out of town, so that I had not, till now, the opportunity of conversing with him. I found him all they said of him. He even exceeded the expectations they had raised in me. If he continues in that department, I foresee much happiness from it to the American affairs. He inquired kindly after you, and spoke of you handsomely. I gave it him as my opinion, that the general execution of the stamp-act would be impracticable, without occasioning more mischief than it was worth, by totally alienating the affections of the Americans, and thereby lessening their commerce. I therefore wished that advantage might be taken of the address expected over, (if expressed, as I hoped it would be in humble and dutiful terms) to suspend the execution of the act for a term of years, till the colonies should be more clear of debt, and better able to bear it, and then drop it on some decent pretence, without ever bringing the question of right to decision.

And I strongly recommend either a thorough union with America, or that government here would proceed in the old method of requisition, by which I was confident more would be obtained in the way of voluntary grant, than could probably be got by compulsory taxes laid by parliament. I stated that particular colonies might at times be backward, but at other times, when in better temper, they would make up for that backwardness, so that on the whole it would be nearly equal. That to send armies and fleets to enforce the act, would not, in my opinion, answer any good end: That the inhabitants would probably take every method to encourage the soldiers to desert, to which the high price of labor would contribute, and the chance of being never apprehended in so extensive a country, where the want of hands, as well as the desire of wasting the strength of an army come to oppress, would incline every one to conceal deserters, so that the officers would probably soon be left alone: That fleets, indeed, might easily obstruct their trade, but withal must ruin great part of the trade of Britain; as the properties of American and British or London merchants were mixed in the same vessels, and no remittance could be received here; besides the danger, by mutual violences, excesses and severities, of creating a deep rooted aversion between the two countries, and laying the foundation of a future total separation.

I added, that, notwithstanding the present discontents, there still remained so much respect in America for this country, that wisdom would do more towards reducing things to order, than all our forces, and that, if the address expected from the congress of the colonies should be unhappily such as could not be made the foundation, three or four wise and good men, personages of some rank and dignity, should be sent over to America, with a royal commission to enquire into grievances, hear complaints, learn the true state of affairs, giving expectations of redress where they found the people really aggrieved, and endeavoring to convince and reclaim them by reason, where they found them in the wrong: That such an instance of the considerateness, moderation and justice of this country towards its remote subjects would contribute more towards securing and perpetuating the dominion, than all its forces, and be much cheaper.

A great deal more I said on our American affairs; too much to write. His lordship heard all with great attention and patience. As to the address expected from the congress, he [thought] some difficulty would arise about receiving it, as it was an irregular meeting, unauthorized by any

American constitution; I said I hoped government here would not be too nice on that head; that an address of the whole there seemed necessary, their separate petitions last year being rejected. And to refuse hearing complaints and redressing grievances, from punctillios about form, had always an ill effect, and gave great handle to those turbulent, factious spirits who are ever ready to blow the coals of dissension. He thanked me politely for the visit and desired to see me often.

It is true that inconveniences may arise to government here by a repeal of the act, as it will be deemed a tacit giving up the sovereignty of parliament, and yet I think the inconveniences of persisting much greater, as I have said above. The present ministry are truly perplexed how to act on the occasion: as, if they relax, their predecessors will reproach them with giving up the honor, dignity, and power of their nation. And yet even they, I am told, think they have carried things too far; so that if it were indeed true that I had planned the act (as you say it is reported with you) I believe we should soon hear some of them exculpating themselves by saying I had misled them. I need not tell you, that I had not the least concern in it. It was all cut and dried, and every resolve framed at the treasury ready for the house, before I arrived in England, or knew any thing of the matter; so that if they had given me a pension on that account, (as is said by some,) it would have been very dishonest in me to accept it. I wish an enquiry was made of the Dutch parsons how they came by the letter you mention, which is undoubtedly a forgery, as not only there were no such facts, but there is no such person as the queen's chaplain. I think there is no doubt, but that though the stamp act should be repealed, some mulct or punishment will be inflicted on the colonies that have suffered the houses of officers, etc., to be pulled down; especially if their respective assemblies do not immediately make reparation.

South Carolina Defies the Stamp Act

[*From the Memoirs of William Drayton, a prominent South Carolina citizen and Chief Justice of his state*]

Having received the stamp-act, the lieut. governor, (in the absence in England of Thomas Boone, the governor), manifested a desire of complying with its requisitions, in causing it to be executed, (the governor of the province being, by the terms of the act, sworn with its due execution); but his powers at that time were insufficient to effectuate the same.

Encouraged by this weakness, and by the public opinion which was hostile to the act, the members of assembly deliberated in what manner they might most embarrass and elude its operations. And, as the best mode they could devise, they addressed the lieutenant governor on the occasion, requesting to be informed whether the stamp-act, said to have been passed in parliament, had been transmitted to him, and if it had through what channel; and whether he had received it from a secretary of state, the lords of trade, or from any other authentic source? These were questions of a singular nature—however, his honor, from a desire to soften as much as possible the fermentations which existed, answered, he had received it from Thomas Boone, the governor of the province. The assembly replied, that, while Mr. Boone was out of the bounds of his government they could not consider him in any other light than as a private gentleman; and the act being received through such a channel, was not sufficiently authentic, to place the lieutenant governor under the obligation of enforcing it.

The stamps soon reached Charleston, and were deposited at Fort Johnson. The people finding the lieutenant governor and crown officers determined to circulate them, resolved to counteract all their movements, and obtain possession of the stamped paper.

About one hundred and fifty volunteers were soon organized and armed for the purpose; and two nights after, boats being provided at Lamboll's bridge, on the west end of South Bay, they formed and marched towards that place for embarkation. From thence, they proceeded in boats across Ashley river, and landed after twelve o'clock at night, on James Island, between Style's plantation and the fort. They then proceeded towards the fort, and halting at a small distance from it, a reconnoitering party was sent forward. This party proceeded to the draw-bridge unnoticed, or challenged by sentries; and finding it down, through the omission of the garrison, they immediately returned and reported the same.

The whole body of volunteers then advanced upon the fort; and arriving at the bridge, they crossed it without opposition—pressed through the inner gate, which was not secured, and immediately possessed themselves of the fort. Only one soldier was found awake; and before he could give the alarm, the remainder of the garrison was secured except Lloyd, its commander, who had not slept there that night. The garrison was then placed under a guard—the bridge was drawn up—and a search commenced for the obnoxious stamped paper. This, to the great joy of the volunteers, was at length found in one of the rooms of the barracks, and a guard was placed over it. Preparations were then made for maintaining the fort against any attack which might be made upon it by the sloop-of-war, when day light should arrive; and for this purpose, the cannon on the platform were loaded with ball and grape shot, matches were provided, and a number of men were stationed at each gun; and a flag, showing a blue field, with three white crescents, which the volunteers had brought with them for the purpose, was hoisted on the flag staff of the fort.

2. THE TOWNSHEND DUTIES MEET STUBBORN RESISTANCE

CONNECTICUT ENCOURAGES DOMESTIC PRODUCTION

[Report of a town meeting in New Haven, Connecticut, February 22, 1768]

. . . The committee appointed in consequence of a letter from the selectmen of the town of Boston to the selectmen of this town, to consider of some measures to be agreed upon for promoting economy, manufactures, etc. report, That it is their opinion, that it is expedient for the town to take all prudent and legal measures to encourage the produce and manufactures of this colony, and to lessen the use of superfluities, and more especially the following articles imported from abroad, viz:

Carriages of all sorts, house furniture, men's and women's hats, men's and women's apparel, ready made household furniture, men's and women's shoes, sole leather, gold, silver, and thread lace, gold and silver buttons, wrought plate, diamond, stone, and paste ware, clocks, silver-smith's and jeweller's ware, broad cloths, that cost above ten shillings sterling per yard, muffs, furs, and tippets, starch, women's and children's toys, silk and cotton velvets, gauze, linseed oil, malt liquors, and cheese.

And that a subscription be recommended to the several inhabitants and house holders of the town, whereby they may mutually agree and engage, that they will encourage the use and consumption of articles manufactured in the British American colonies, and more especially in this colony, and that they will not, after the 31st day of March next, purchase any of the above enumerated articles, imported from abroad, after the said 31st of March, and that they will be careful to promote the saving of linen rags, and other materials, proper for making paper in this colony.

The foregoing report being considered by the town, was by a full vote approved of and accepted.

MARYLAND IMPOSES NON-IMPORTATION

[Resolutions of a meeting of county representatives at Annapolis,
Maryland, June 29, 1769]

Several of the counties having entered into resolutions of non-importation of British superfluities, and the province, in general, being invited by the gentlemen of Anne Arundel county, to request some people from each county, to meet at this place, on the 20th instant, in order that a general resolution of non-importation might be formed—There was accordingly a very full meeting, at which the following resolutions were entered into; and it was agreed, that twelve copies should be printed and transmitted to each county, to be signed by the people, which, it is expected, will be done with great readiness throughout the province.

We, the subscribers, his majesty's loyal and dutiful subjects, the merchants, traders, free-holders, mechanics, and other inhabitants of the province of Maryland, seriously considering the present state and condition of the province, and being sensible that there is a necessity to agree upon such measures, as may tend to discourage, and as much as may be, prevent the use of foreign luxuries and superfluities, in the consumption of which we have heretofore too much indulged ourselves, to the great detriment of our private fortunes, and, in some instances, to the ruin of our families; and, to this end, to practice ourselves, and as much as possible, to promote, countenance, and encourage in others, a habit of temperance, frugality, economy, and industry, and considering also, that measures of this nature are more particularly necessary at this time, as the parliament of Great Britain, by imposing taxes upon many articles imported hither from thence, and from other parts beyond sea, has left it less in our power, than in time past, to purchase and pay for the manufactures of the mother-country; which taxes, especially those imposed by a late act of parliament, laying duties on tea, paper, glass, etc., we are clearly convinced have been imposed contrary to the spirit of our constitution, and have a direct and manifest tendency to deprive us, in the end, of all political freedom, and reduce us to a state of dependence, inconsistent with that liberty we have rightfully enjoyed under the government of his present most sacred majesty, (to whom we owe, acknowledge, and will always joyfully pay all due obedience and allegiance) and of his royal predecessors, ever since the first settlement of the province, until of very late time—have thought it necessary to unite, as nearly as our circumstances will admit, with our sister colonies, in resolutions for the purpose aforesaid; and, therefore, do hereby agree and bind ourselves, to and with each other, by all the ties and obligations of honor and reputation, that we will strictly and faithfully observe, and conform to the following resolutions:

First, That we will not, at any time hereafter, directly or indirectly, import, or cause to be imported, any manner of goods, merchandise, or manufactures, which are, or shall hereafter be, taxed by act of parliament, for the purpose of raising a revenue in America (except paper not exceeding six shillings per ream, and except such articles only as orders have been already sent for) but, that we will always consider such taxation, in every respect, as an absolute prohibition to the articles that are, or may be taxed.

Secondly, That we will not hereafter, directly or indirectly, during the continuance of the aforesaid act of parliament, import, or cause to be imported, from Great Britain, or any other part of Europe, (except such articles of the produce or manufacture of Ireland, as may be immediately and legally brought from thence, and also, except all such goods as orders have been already sent for) any of the goods herein after enumerated, to wit, horses, spirits, wine, cider, perry, beer, ale, malt, barley, peas, beef, pork, fish, butter, cheese, tallow, candles, oil, except Salad-oil, fruit, pickles, confectionary, British refined sugar, mustard, coffee, pewter, tin-ware of all kinds, whether plain or painted, waiters, and all kinds of japan-ware, wrought copper, wrought and cast brass, and bell-metal, watches, clocks, plate and all other gold and silversmiths' work trinkets, and jewelry of all kinds, gold and silver lace, joiners' and cabinet work of all sorts, looking-glasses, upholstery of all kinds, carriages of all kinds, ribbons and millinery of all kinds, except wig-ribbon, lace, cambric, lawn, muslin, kenting, gauze of all kinds, except Boulting-cloths, silks of all kinds, except raw and sewing silk, and wig cauls, velvets, chintzes, and calicoes of all sorts, of more than twenty-pence per yard, East-India goods of every kind, except salt-petre, black pepper, and spices, printed linens, and printed cottons, striped linens, and cottons, check linens, and cotton checks of all kinds, handkerchiefs of all kinds, at more than ten shillings per dozen; cotton velvets, and all kinds of cotton, or cotton and linen stuffs, bedbunts, and bed-ticking of all sorts, cotton counterpanes and coverlids, British manufactured linens of all kinds, except sailcloth, Irish and all foreign linens, above one shilling and six pence per yard; woolen cloth, above five quarters wide, of more than five shillings per yard; narrow cloths of all sorts, of more than three shillings per yard: worsted stuffs of all sorts, above thirteen pence per yard, silk and worsted, silk and cotton, silk and hair, and hair and worsted stuffs of all kinds, worsted and hair shags, mourning of all and every kind, stockings, caps, waistcoat and breeches patterns of all kinds, rugs of all sorts, above eight shillings; blankets, above five shillings, per blanket; men's and women's ready made clothes and wearing apparel of all kinds, hats of all kinds, of more than two shillings per hat; wigs, gloves, and mits of all kinds, stays and bodices of all sorts, boots, saddles, and all manufactures of leather, and skins of all kinds, except men's and women's shoes, of not more than four shillings per pair, whips, brushes, and brooms of all sorts, gilt, and hair trunks, paintings, carpets of all sorts, snuff-boxes, snuff, and other manufactured tobacco, soap, starch, playing cards, dice, English china, English ware, in imitation of China, delph and stone ware, of all sorts, except milk-pans, stone bottles, jugs, pitchers, and chamber pots, marble and wrought stone of any kind, except scythe-stones, mill-stones, and grind-stones, iron castings, iron-mongery of all sorts, except nails; hoes, steel, handicraft and manufacturers' tools, locks, frying-pans, scythes and sickles, cutlery of all sorts, except knives and forks, not exceeding three shillings per dozen; knives, scissors, sheep shears, needles, pins and thimbles, razors, chirurgical instruments and spectacles, cordage, or tarred rope of all sorts, seines, ships' colors ready made, ivory, horn and bone ware of all sorts, except combs.

Thirdly, That we will not, during the time aforesaid, import any wines, of any kind whatever, or purchase the same from any person whatever, except such wines as are already imported, or for which orders are already sent.

Fourthly, That we will not kill or suffer to be killed, or sell, or dispose to any person, whom we have reason to believe intends to kill, any ewe-lamb that shall be yeaned before the first day of May in any year, during the time aforesaid.

Fifthly, That we will not, directly or indirectly, during the time afore-said, purchase, take up, or receive, on any terms, or conditions whatever, any of the goods enumerated in the second resolution, that shall, or may be imported into this province, contrary to the intent and design of these resolutions, by any person whatever, or consigned to any factor, agent, manager, or storekeeper here, by any person residing in Great Britain, or else-where; and if any such goods shall be imported, we will not upon any consideration whatever, rent or sell to, or permit any way to be made use of by any such importer, his agent, factor, manager, or store-keeper, or any person, on his, or their behalf, any store-house, or other house, or any kind of place whatever, belonging to us, respectively, for exposing to sale, or even se-curing any such goods, nor will we suffer any such to be put on shore on our respective properties.

Sixthly, That if any person shall import, or endeavor to import, from Great Britain or any part of Europe, any goods whatever, contrary to the spirit and design of the foregoing resolutions, or shall sell any goods which he has now, or may hereafter have on hand, or may import, on any other terms than are herein expressed, we will not, at any time hereafter, deal with any such person, his agent, manager, factor, or store-keeper, for any commodity whatever; and that such of us as are, or may be sellers of goods, will not take any advantage of the scarcity of goods, that this agreement may occasion, but will sell such as we have now on hand, or may hereafter import, or have for sale, at the respective usual and accustomed rates for three years last past.

Seventhly, That we will not, during the time aforesaid, import into this province, any of the goods above enumerated for non-importation in the sec-ond resolution, which have been, or shall be imported from Great Britain, or some part of Europe, from any colony, or province, which hath not entered, or shall not, within two months from the date hereof, enter into resolutions of non-importation, nor will we purchase, take up, or receive, on any terms, or conditions whatever, any such goods, from any person or persons, that may import the same; nor will we purchase, take up, or receive, on any terms, or conditions, any of the said goods, which may be imported from any province, or colony, which has entered, or may enter into such resolutions, unless a certificate shall accompany such goods, under the hands of a com-mittee of merchants (if any) of the place from whence such goods shall come or if no such committee, then under the hands of at least three of the prin-cipal merchants there, who have entered into resolutions of non-importa-tion, that such goods were imported before such resolution was entered into in such place. And that we will not purchase, take up, or receive, on any terms, or conditions whatever, after the expiration of six months, from the date thereof, from any colony, or province aforesaid, any of the said enumer-ated articles, which have been, or shall be imported from Great Britain.

Eighthly, We, the tradesmen and manufacturers, do likewise promise, and agree, that we will not avail ourselves of the scarcity of European goods, proceeding from the resolutions for non-importation, to raise or enhance the prices of the different articles, or commodities, by us wrought up, or manu-factured; but that we will sell and dispose of the same, at the usual and ac-customed rates we have done for these three years past.

Lastly, That, if any person, or persons, whatever, shall oppose, or contravene the above resolutions, or act in opposition to the true spirit and design thereof, we will consider him, or them, as enemies to the liberties of America, and treat them on all occasions, with the contempt they deserve; provided that these resolutions shall be binding on us, for and during the continuance of the before mentioned act of parliament, unless a general meeting of such persons at Annapolis, as may, at any time hereafter, be requested by the people of the several counties in this province to meet, for the purpose of considering the expediency of dispensing with the said resolutions, or any of them, not exceeding four from each county, or a majority of such of them as shall attend, shall determine otherwise.

BALTIMORE MERCHANTS ENFORCE NON-IMPORTATION

[Report of a meeting of Baltimore merchants for the non-importation of European goods, November 14, 1769]

JOHN SMITH, Chairman—
The committee of enquiry having reported, that William Moore, jun. had imported a cargo of goods in the Lord Cambden, captain John Johnston, from London, of the value of £900 sterling, which they were in doubt were not within the terms of the association. The following question was put, whether William Moore, jun. has imported the said cargo within the terms mentioned in the agreement of the 30th of March last, to which he was a signer? Upon which question, the gentlemen present were unanimously of opinion, that the said cargo was imported contrary to that agreement. Of which determination William Moore being informed, he alleged, as a justification of his conduct, that at the time he signed the agreement, he objected to Mr. John Merryman, who then had the carriage thereof, (and who is now absent in London) that he would not sign, unless he had liberty to send off his orders for fall goods, and to import the same: That some few days afterwards Mr. Merryman informed him that the merchants of the town would give leave to send off the orders, and receive the fall goods; and that, in consequence of this information, he signed the agreement, without any such condition, written or expressed, in the same opposite to his name. After which the question was put, whether Mr. Moore should have liberty to land and vend his whole cargo? Which was determined in the affirmative. . . .

The committee of enquiry having also reported that Benjamin Howard had imported a cargo of goods, of the value of £1700 sterling, in the Lord Cambden, captain John Johnston, London, which they were in doubt were not within the terms of the association of 30th March. Upon which the following question was put, whether Benjamin Howard be permitted land and vend the said cargo, he having alleged that he never signed the association of the 30th March, being then an inhabitant of Anne-Arundel county, and that he apprehended he was entitled to import within the terms of the general association of the 22d June, to which he was subscriber, his orders for the said cargo having been transmitted the 1st of May. Resolved in the affirmative. . . .

3. THE BOSTON MASSACRE DEEPENS THE RIFT

REMINISCENCES OF THE MASSACRE

*[A recollection probably written by Hezekiah Niles as related
to him by an eyewitness]*

At that time there was only one house on the east side of what is called Pearl Street, in which then resided Charles Paxton, esq. On the west side of the street, stood four or five rope-walks, extending from the upper to the lower end of the street, which were all burnt in 1794. On Saturday afternoon, on the 3d March, 1770, a British soldier of the 29th regiment, accosted a negro who was employed in one of the rope walks, by inquiring "whether his master wanted to hire a man." (The soldiers who were mechanics were sometimes hired as journeymen.) The negro answered that his "master wished to have the vault emptied, and that was a proper work for a Lobster ["Redcoat" or British soldier]." This produced a conflict between the soldier and the negro, and, before relief came to his assistance, the negro was very severely beaten. Some ropewalk men, (among whom was Mr. Gray, the foreman of the walk), came up and parted them. Mr. Gray, (who was a very respectable man), told the soldier that "as he had obtained satisfaction for the insult, he had better go to his barracks." The soldier "damned him" and said that "for six-pence he would drub him as he had done the negro."—A contest then took place between them in which the soldier received a much worse beating than the negro, and went off to his barracks over Fort-hill, on Wheelwright's (now Foster's) wharf swearing revenge. In about half an hour the soldier returned with about seventy of his comrades, who came over the hill huzzaing, armed with pipe staves split into bludgeons, which they obtained at a cooper's shop, and made the attack with great fury. Each party was brave and intrepid, but the science in this kind of warfare, which the ropewalk men had obtained in their "Pope Day" battles gave them a decided superiority, and in their pursuit of the soldiers, halted on Forthill, and gave three cheers in token of victory.

The noise of the shouting and huzzaing resounded far around, and excited the curiosity of those at a distance. At that time Mr. Hallowell, (grandfather of the present Admiral Hallowell, in the British navy), owned and resided in the house in Battery March-street, now occupied by Mr. Goodrich, near which he also owned a ship yard, about where now stands the Commercial Coffee House, in which he usually employed about fifty or sixty men. There was a mast yard a little south and several wood wharfs, on all which were also employed hardy laborers, who, together with the blacksmiths, blockmakers, and other athletic mechanics in the neighborhood, (whose brawny arms could wield a club with as much dexterity as an Highlander could manage his broadsword), all ran towards the scene of combat. The bravery of the soldiers was not doubted, and accordingly, preparations were made to repel another attack which was expected, and in which they were not disappointed. —The shouting of the soldiers, issuing from the barrack-yard, to the number of more than three hundred, headed by the sergeant-major, moving over the hill towards Pearl street, soon gave the alarm. The soldiers pulled down the fence in High street, then called Cow lane, which inclosed the field, where now stands Quincy place. The rope-walk men pulled down the fence on the opposite side in Pearl street, when both parties rushed on each other with equal intrepidity. —But the Herculean strength of virtuous labor, united with the activity and science of the Yankees, soon obtained a triumph over an idle, inactive, enervated, and intemperate, though brave soldiery.

The effect of this rencontre was seen in the countenances and conduct of the soldiers the next and following day, who looked vengeance on the inhabitants, especially those whom they suspected to be concerned in the affray on Saturday; and those of them, who were friendly to the citizens, advised them to remain at home on Monday evening, as revenge would then be taken.

The soldiers asserted on Sunday morning, that one of their men had died of his wounds, but as the body was never shewn, it was supposed to be only a pretence to justify the horrid scene which ensued on the Monday evening following. . . .

The threats of the soldiers, as mentioned in my last communication, were put in execution on Monday evening the 5th of March, 1770, by insulting and abusing many inhabitants in various parts of the town, which resulted in what was called the "horrid massacre," by which four persons were instantly killed, one died of his wounds a few days succeeding, and about seventeen in the total killed and wounded.

Language cannot describe the horror and indignation which was excited through the town by this dreadful event. The bells rang a terrific peal, which roused the whole population. More than five thousand citizens were collected in State street and its vicinity. The 29th regt. was marched into the same street. The 14th regt. was under arms at their barracks. What a scene for contemplation! Lieut. governor Hutchinson, and the king's council, were assembled in the council chamber, even at the solemn hour of midnight! Many of the venerable citizens repaired to them and demanded the surrender of the criminals to justice. The high-sheriff appeared in the balcony of the state house, and ordered silence!!! An awful stillness ensued—when, with a loud voice, he declared, that he was authorized by his honor the lieutenant governor and his majesty's council with the consent of col. Dalrymple, to say that Capt. Preston, and the men who had committed the outrage, should be immediately delivered to the civil power, and requested the citizens to retire peaceably to their dwellings; which, after the soldiers had marched off, was complied with. . . .

The funeral of the unfortunate victims was attended with great pomp and parade. Thousands came from the country; and the whole number that followed them to the grave, was supposed to exceed ten thousand! . . .

Joseph Warren Commemorates the Massacre, 1772

[Excerpts from a speech by Dr. Joseph Warren in Boston on the occasion of the second anniversary of the Massacre, March 5, 1772]

It was . . . attachment to a constitution [that is, the British Constitution—unwritten but very real nevertheless], founded on free and benevolent principles, which inspired the first settlers of this country—they saw with grief the daring outrages committed on the free constitution of their native land—they knew nothing but a civil war could at that time restore its pristine purity. So hard was it to resolve to embrue their hands in the blood of their brethren that they chose rather to quit their fair possessions and seek another habitation in a distant clime. When they came to this new world, which they fairly purchased of the Indian natives, the only rightful proprietors, they cultivated the then barren soil, by their incessant labor, and defended their dear-bought possessions with the fortitude of the christian, and the bravery of the hero.

After various struggles, which, during the tyrannic reigns of the house of Stuart, were constantly kept up between right and wrong, between liberty and slavery, the connection between Great Britain and this colony was settled in the reign of king William and queen Mary, by a compact, the conditions of which were expressed in a charter, by which all the liberties and immunities of British subjects, were confided to this province [Massachusetts], as fully and as absolutely as they possibly could be by any human instrument which can be devised. And it is undeniably true, that the greatest and most important right of a British subject, is, that he shall be governed by no laws but those to which he, either in person or by his representatives hath given his consent: and this I will venture to assert, is the great basis of British freedom: it is interwoven with the constitution; whenever this is lost, the constitution must be destroyed.

The British constitution (of which ours is a copy) is a happy compound of the three forms (under some of which all governments may be ranged) viz., monarchy, aristocracy, and democracy; of these three the British legislature is composed, and without the consent of each branch, nothing can carry with it the force of a law; but when a law is to be passed for raising a tax, that law can originate only in the democratic branch, which is the house of commons in Britain, and the house of representatives here.—The reason is obvious; they and their constituents are to pay much the largest part of it; but as the aristocratic branch, which, in Britain, is the house of lords, and in this province, the council, are also to pay some part, their consent is necessary; and as the monarchic branch, which in Britain is the king, and with us, either the king in person, or the governor whom he shall be pleased to appoint to act in his stead, is supposed to have a just sense of his own interest, which is that of all the subjects in general, his consent is also necessary, and when the consent of these three branches is obtained, the taxation is most certainly legal.

Let us now allow ourselves a few moments to examine the late acts of the British parliament for taxing America—Let us with candor judge whether they are constitutionally binding upon us;—if they are, in the name of justice let us submit to them, without one murmuring word.

First, I would ask whether the members of the British house of commons are the democracy of this province? if they are, they are either the people of this province, or are elected by the people of this province, to represent them, and have therefore a constitutional right to originate a bill for taxing them; it is most certain they are neither; and therefore nothing done by them can be said to be done by the democratic branch of our constitution. I would next ask, whether the lords, who compose the aristo-cratic branch of the legislature, are peers of America? I never heard it was (even in those extraordinary times) so much as pretended, and if they are not, certainly no act of theirs can be said to be the act of the aristocratic branch of our constitution. The power of the monarchic branch we, with pleasure, acknowledge resides in the king, who may act either in person or by his representative; and I freely confess that I can see no reason why a proclamation for raising in America issued by the king's sole authority would not be equally consistent with our own constitution, and therefore equally binding upon us with the late acts of the British parliament for taxing us; for it is plain, that if there is any validity in those acts, it must arise altogether from the monarchical branch of the legislature; and I fur-ther think that it would be at least as equitable; for I do not conceive it to be of the least importance to us by whom our property is taken away, so long as it is taken without our consent; and I am very much at a loss to know by what figure of rhetoric, the inhabitants of this province can be called free subjects, when they are obliged to obey implicitly, such laws as are made for them by men three thousand miles off, whom they know not, and whom they never empowered to act for them, or how they can be said to have property when a body of men, over whom they have not the least control, and who are not in any way accountable to them, shall oblige them to deliver up any part, or the whole of their substance without even asking their consent: and yet whoever pretends that the late acts of the British parliament for taxing America ought to be deemed binding upon us, must admit at once that we are absolute slaves, and have no property of our own; or else that we may be freemen, and at the same time under a neces-sity of obeying the arbitrary commands of those over whom we have no control or influence, and that we may have property of our own, which is entirely at the disposal of another. Such gross absurdities, I believe will not be relished in this enlightened age: and it can be no matter of wonder that the people quickly perceived, and seriously complained of the inroads which these acts must unavoidably make upon their liberty, and of the hazard to which their whole property is by them exposed; for, if they may be taxed without their consent, even in the smallest trifle, they may also, without their consent, be deprived of every thing they possess, although never so valuable, never so dear. Certainly it never entered the hearts of our ancestors, that after so many dangers in this then desolate wilderness, their hard-earned property should be at the disposal of the British parliament; and as it was soon found that this taxation could not be supported by reason and argument, it seemed necessary that one act of oppression should be enforced by another, and therefore, contrary to our just rights as possessing, or at least having a just title to possess, all the liberties and immunities of British subjects, a standing army was established among us in time of peace; and evidently for the purpose of effecting that, which it was one principal design of the founders of the constitution to prevent, (when they declared a standing army in a time of peace to be against law) namely, for the enforcement of obedience to acts which, upon fair examination, appeared to be unjust and unconstitutional.

The ruinous consequences of standing armies to free communities may be seen in the histories of Syracuse, Rome, and many other once flourishing states: some of which have now scarce a name! their baneful influence is most suddenly felt, when they are placed in populous cities; for, by a corruption of morals, the public happiness is immediately affected! and that this is one of the effects of quartering troops in a populous city, is a truth, to which many a mourning parent, many a lost, despairing child in this metropolis must bear a very melancholy testimony. Soldiers are also taught to consider arms as the only arbiters by which every dispute is to be decided between contending states;—they are instructed implicitly to obey their commanders without enquiring into the justice of the cause they are engaged to support; hence it is, that they are ever to be dreaded as the ready engines of tyranny and oppression. And it is too observable that they are prone to introduce the same mode of decision in the disputes of individuals, and from thence have often arisen animosities between them and the inhabitants, who, whilst in a naked, defenceless state, are frequently insulted and abused by an armed soldiery. And this will be more especially the case, when the troops are informed that the intention of their being stationed in any city is to overawe the inhabitants. That this was the avowed design of stationing an armed force in this town is sufficiently known; and we, my fellow citizens, have seen, we have felt the tragical effects!—The fatal fifth of March, 1770, can never be forgotten—The horrors of that dreadful night are but too deeply impressed on our hearts—Language is too feeble to paint the emotion of our souls, when our streets were stained with the blood of our brethren—when our ears were wounded by the groans of the dying, and our eyes were tormented with the sight of the mangled bodies of the dead.—When our alarmed imagination presented to our view our houses wrapt in flames, our children subjected to the barbarous caprice of the raging soldiery,—our beauteous virgins exposed to all the insolence of unbridled passion,—our virtuous wives, endeared to us by every tender tie, falling a sacrifice to worse than brutal violence, and perhaps like the famed Lucretia, distracted with anguish and despair, ending their wretched lives by their own fair hands. When we beheld the authors of our distress parading in our streets, or drawn up in a regular battalia, as though in a hostile city, our hearts beat to arms; we snatched our weapons, almost resolved, by one decisive stroke, to avenge the death of our slaughtered brethren, and to secure from future danger, all that we held most dear: but, propitious heaven forbade the bloody carnage, and saved the threatened victims of our too keen resentment, not by their discipline, not by their regular array,—no, it was royal George's livery that proved their shield—it was that which turned the pointed engines of destruction from their breasts. The thoughts of vengeance were soon buried in our inbred affection to Great Britain, and calm reason dictated a method of removing the troops more mild than an immediate resource to the sword. With united efforts you urged the immediate departure of the troops from the town—you urged it, with a resolution which ensured success—you obtained your wishes, and the removal of the troops was effected, without one drop of their blood being shed by the inhabitants.

The immediate actors in the tragedy of that night, were surrendered to justice.—It is not mine to say how far they were guilty? they have been tried by the country and acquitted of murder! and they are not to be again arraigned at an earthly bar; but, surely the men who have promiscuously scattered death amidst the innocent inhabitants of a populous city, ought to see well to it, that they be prepared to stand at the bar of an omniscient judge! and all who contrived or encouraged the stationing troops in this place have reasons of eternal importance, to reflect with deep contrition, on their base designs, and humbly to repent of their impious machinations.

The infatuation which hath seemed, for a number of years, to prevail in the British councils, with regard to us, is truly astonishing! what can be proposed by the repeated attacks made upon our freedom, I really cannot surmise; even leaving justice and humanity out of question. I do not know one single advantage which can arise to the British nation, from our being enslaved:—I know not of any gains, which can be wrung from us by oppression, which they may not obtain from us by our own consent, in the smooth channel of commerce: we wish the wealth and prosperity of Britain; we contribute largely to both. Doth what we contribute lose all its value, because it is done voluntarily? the amazing increase of riches to Britain, the great rise of the value of her lands, the flourishing state of her navy, are striking proofs of the advantages derived to her from her commerce with the colonies; and it is our earnest desire that she may still continue to enjoy the same emoluments, until her streets are paved with American gold; only let us have the pleasure of calling it our own, whilst it is in our own hands; but this it seems is too great a favor—we are to be governed by the absolute command of others; our property is to be taken away without our consent —if we complain, our complaints are treated with contempt; if we assert our rights, that assertion is deemed insolence; if we humbly offer to submit the matter to the impartial decision of reason, the sword is judged the most proper argument to silence our murmurs! but this cannot long be the case —surely the British nation will not suffer the reputation of their justice and their honor, to be thus sported away by a capricious ministry; no, they will in a short time open their eyes to their true interest: they nourish in their own breasts, a noble love of liberty; they hold her dear, and they know that all who have once possessed her charms, had rather die than suffer her to be torn from their embraces—they are also sensible that Britain is so deeply interested in the prosperity of the colonies that she must eventually feel every wound given to their freedom; they cannot be ignorant that more dependence may be placed on the affections of a brother, than on the forced service of a slave; they must approve your efforts for the preservation of your rights; from a sympathy of soul they must pray for your success: and I doubt not but they will, ere long, exert themselves effectually, to redress your grievances. Even in the dissolute reign of king Charles II when the house of commons impeached the earl of Clarendon of high treason, the first article on which they founded their accusation was, that "he had designed a standing army to be raised, and to govern the kingdom thereby." And the eighth article was, that "he had introduced an arbitrary government into his majesty's plantation." A terrifying example to those who are now forging chains for this country.

You have, my friends and countrymen, frustrated the designs of your enemies, by your unanimity and fortitude: it was your union and determined spirit which expelled those troops, who polluted your streets with innocent blood. You have appointed this anniversary as a standard memorial of the bloody consequences of placing an armed force in a populous city, and of your deliverance from the dangers which then seemed to hang over your heads; and I am confident that you never will betray the least want of spirit when called upon to guard your freedom.

BENJAMIN CHURCH COMMEMORATES THE MASSACRE, 1773

[*Excerpts from a speech by Dr. Benjamin Church in Boston on the occasion of the third anniversary of the Massacre, March 5, 1773*]

When rulers become tyrants, they cease to be kings: they can no longer be respected as God's vicegerents, who violate the laws they were sworn to protect. The preacher may tell us of passive obedience, that tyrants are scourges in the hands of a righteous God to chastise a sinful nation, and are to be submitted to like plagues, famine and such like judgments: such doctrine may serve to mislead ill-judging princes into a false security: but men are not to be harangued out of their senses; human nature and self-preservation will eternally arm the brave and vigilant, against slavery and oppression.

As a despotic government is evidently productive of the most shocking calamities, whatever tends to restrain such inordinate power, though in itself a severe evil, is extremely beneficial to society; for where a degrading servitude is the detestable alternative, who can shudder at the reluctant poignard of a Brutus, the crimsoned axe of a Cromwell, or the reeking dagger of a Ravillac.

To enjoy life as becomes rational creatures, to possess our souls with pleasure and satisfaction, we must be careful to maintain that inestimable blessing, liberty. By liberty, I would be understood, the happiness of living under laws of our own making, by our personal consent, or that of our representatives. . . .

Numberless have been the attacks made upon our free constitution; numberless the grievances we now resent: but the Hydra mischief, is the violation of my right, as a British American freeholder, in not being consulted in framing those statutes I am required to obey.

The authority of the British monarch over this colony was established, and his power derived from the province charter; by that we are entitled to a distinct legislation. As in every government there must exist a power superior to the laws, viz. the power that makes those laws, and from which they derive their authority: therefore the liberty of the people is exactly proportioned to the share the body of the people have in the legislature; and the check placed in the constitution, on the executive power. The state only is free, where the people are governed by laws which they have a share in making; and that country is totally enslaved, where one single law can be made or repealed, without the interposition or consent of the people.

That the members of the British parliament are the representatives of the whole British empire, expressly militates with their avowed principles: property and residence within the island, alone constituting the right of election; and surely he is not my delegate in whose nomination or appointment I have no choice; but however the futile and absurd claim of a virtual representation, may comport with the idea of a political visionary, he must (if possible) heighten the indignation, or excite the ridicule of a freeborn American, who by such a fallacious pretext would despoil him of his property.

An American freeholder, according to the just and judicious conduct of the present ministry, has no possible right to be consulted, in the disposal of his property: when a lordly, though unlettered British elector, possessed of a turnip garden, with great propriety may appoint a legislature, to assess the ample domains of the most sensible, opulent American planter. . . .

But let us not forget the distressing occasion of this anniversary: the sullen ghosts of murdered fellow-citizens haunt my imagination "and harrow up my soul;" methinks the tainted air is hung with the dews of death, while Ate, hot from hell, cries havoc, and lets slip the dogs of war. Hark! the wan tenants of the grave still shriek for vengeance on their remorseless butchers. . . .

II

A NEW PERIOD OF CRISIS,

1773-1774

THE TWO AND a half years between the Boston Massacre of March 1770 and the Boston Tea Party of December 1773 were the quiet before the storm. Occasional episodes such as the burning of the revenue cutter *Gaspee* marred the general tranquillity of the period, but these disturbances had only local repercussions. To many observers it seemed that the crisis in imperial relations had passed; only the duty on tea remained to impress the colonial mind with Parliament's ability to tax, with or without representation.

But new troubles were just over the horizon. In May 1773 Parliament attempted to salvage the financial wreckage of the British East India Company by permitting it to sell its surplus tea directly to agents in the colonies without paying the usual duties. British tea would now undersell any other tea and might thereby monopolize the American market, a matter of concern not only to American tea merchants but to all who feared British undermining of the colonial commercial structure. If permitted to stand, a monopoly on one commodity could be followed by a monopoly on any other. To the colonists, what Parliament intended as a specific emergency measure had become another broad encroachment on the rights of Englishmen.

Boston's violent reaction to the Tea Act is best understood in the context of Massachusetts politics. Since his accession to the governorship in 1770, Thomas Hutchinson had been at odds with his legislature (pp. 42, and 54). The running battle between the chief executive of the colony and the representatives of the people had helped to make the Bay Colony a leader in the growing resistance to royal authority (pp. 62 and 64). It also helped to incite the Boston mobs against the local consignees of the tea, among whom were three relatives of the Governor. Of course, they never got their hands on the tea. On the night of December 16, 1773, a mob of Massachusetts patriots disguised as Indians boarded the tea ships and dumped 342 chests of tea leaves into Boston Harbor (p. 67).

Although many Americans condemned the destruction of private property and agreed with Parliament that the Boston "Mohawks" had gone too far, most colonists supported the principle, if not the practice, of Boston's stand (pp. 65, 68, and 72). Armed in part by the backing of its neighbors and in part by its own determination to brook no opposition from the Governor, the legislature of Massachusetts increased its efforts to stimulate intercolonial cooperation through committees of correspondence. This led to a new clash with Governor Hutchinson (pp. 73, and 74). By the spring of 1774 relations between the colonies and the mother country had reached a new crisis. John Hancock used the fourth anniversary of the Boston Massacre to review the deterioration of imperial ties (p. 76).

1. MASSACHUSETTS WRANGLES WITH ITS GOVERNOR

GOVERNOR HUTCHINSON LECTURES THE LEGISLATURE

[*A portion of Governor Thomas Hutchinson's speech of February 16, 1773, in which the Governor criticized the House of Representatives*]

GENTLEMEN OF THE COUNCIL, AND GENTLEMEN OF THE HOUSE OF REPRESENTATIVES.

The proceedings of such of the inhabitants of the town of Boston . . . at a legal town meeting, denying, in the most express terms, the supremacy of parliament, and inviting every other town and district in the province, to adopt the same principle, and to establish committees of correspondence . . . appeared to me to be so unwarrantable, and of such a dangerous nature and tendency, that I thought myself bound to call upon you in my speech at opening the session, to join with me in discountenancing and bearing a proper testimony against such irregularities and innovations.

I stated to you fairly and truly, as I conceived, the constitution of the kingdom and of the province, so far as relates to the dependence of the former upon the latter; and I desired you, if you differed from me in sentiments, to show me, with candor, my own errors, and to give your reasons in support of your opinions, so far as you might differ from me. I hoped that you would have considered my speech by your joint committees, and have given me a joint answer: but as the house of representatives have declined that mode of proceeding, and as your principles in government are very different, I am obliged to make separate and distinct replies. . . .

GENTLEMEN OF THE HOUSE OF REPRESENTATIVES:

I shall take no notice of that part of your answer, which attributes the disorders of the province, to an undue exercise of the power of parliament; because you take for granted, what can by no means be admitted, that parliament had exercised its power without just authority. The sum of your answer, so far as it is pertinent to my speech, is this.

You allege that the colonies were an acquisition of foreign territory, not annexed to the realm of England; and therefore, at the absolute disposal of the crown; the king, having, as you take it, a constitutional right to dispose of, and alienate any part of his territories, not annexed to the realm: that Queen Elizabeth accordingly conveyed the property, dominion, and sovereignty of Virginia, to Sir Walter Raleigh, to be held of the crown by homage and a certain render, without reserving any share in the legislative and executive authority: that the subsequent grants of America were similar in this respect; that they were without any reservation for securing the subjection of the colonists to the parliament, and future laws of England; that this was the sense of the English crown, the nation, and our predecessors, when they first took possession of this country; that, if the colonies were not then annexed to the realm, they cannot have been annexed since that time; that, if they are not now annexed to the realm, they are not part of the kingdom; and, consequently, not subject to the legislative authority of the kingdom; for no country, by the common law, was subject to the laws or to the parliament, but the realm of England.

Now, if this foundation shall fail you in every part of it, as I think it will, the fabric which you have raised upon it must certainly fall.

Let me then observe to you, that as English subjects, and agreeable to the doctrine of feudal tenure, all our lands and tenements are held mediately, or immediately, of the crown, and although the possession and use, or profits, be in the subject, there still remains a dominion in the crown. When any new countries are discovered by English subjects, according to the general law and usage of nations, they become part of the state, and, according to the feudal system, the lordship or dominion, is in the crown; and a right accrues of disposing of such territories, under such tenure, or for such services to be performed, as the crown shall judge proper; and whensoever any part of such territories, by grant from the crown, becomes the possession or property of private persons, such persons, thus holding, under the crown of England, remain, or become subjects of England, to all intents and purposes, as fully as if any of the royal manors, forests, or other territory, within the realm, had been granted to them upon the like tenure. But that it is now, or was, when the plantations were first granted, the prerogative of the kings of England to alienate such territories from the crown, or to constitute a number of new governments, altogether independent of the sovereign legislative authority of the English empire, I can by no means concede to you. I have never seen any better authority to support such an opinion, than an anonymous pamphlet, by which, I fear, you have too easily been misled; for I shall presently show you, that the declarations of king James the I, and of King Charles the I, admitting they are truly related by the author of this pamphlet, ought to have no weight with you; nor does the cession or restoration, upon a treaty of peace, of countries which have been lost or acquired in war, militate with these principles; nor may any particular act of power of a prince, in selling, or delivering up any part of his dominions to a foreign prince or state, against the general sense of the nation, be urged to invalidate them; and, upon examination, it will appear, that all the grants which have been made of America, are founded upon them, and are made to conform to them, even those which you have adduced in support of very different principles.

You do not recollect that, prior to what you call the first grant by queen Elizabeth to Sir Walter Raleigh, a grant had been made by the same princess, to Sir Humphrey Gilbert, of all such countries as he should discover, which were to be of the allegiance of her, her heirs and successors; but he dying in the prosecution of his voyage, a second grant was made to Sir Walter Raleigh, which, you say, conveyed the dominion and sovereignty, without any reserve of legislative or executive authority, being held by homage and a render. To hold by homage, which implies fealty and a render, is descriptive of soccage tenure, as fully as if it had been said to hold, as of our manor of East Greenwich, the words in your charter. Now, this alone was a reserve of dominion and sovereignty in the queen, her heirs and successors; and, besides this, the grant is made upon this express condition, which you pass over, that the people remain subject to the crown of England, the head of that legislative authority, which, by the English constitution, is equally extensive with the authority of the crown, throughout every part of the dominions. Now, if we could suppose the queen to have acquired, separate from her relation to her subjects, or in her natural capacity, which she could not do, a title to a country discovered by her subjects, and then to grant the same country to English subjects, in her public capacity as queen of England, still, by this grant, she annexed it to the crown. Thus, by not distinguishing between the crown of England and the kings and queens of England, in their personal or natural capacities, you have been led into a fundamental error, which must prove fatal to your system. It is not material, whether Virginia reverted to the crown by Sir Walter's attainder, or whether he never took any benefit from his grant, though the latter is most probable, seeing he ceased from all attempts to take possession of the country after a few years trial. There were, undoubtedly, divers grants made by King James the I of the continent of America, in the beginning of the seventeenth century, and similar to the grant of queen Elizabeth, in this respect, that they were dependent on the crown. The charter to the council at Plymouth, in Devon, dated November 3, 1620, more immediately respects us, and of that we have the most authentic remains.

By this charter, upon the petition of Sir Ferdinando Gorges, a corporation was constituted, to be, and continue by succession, forever in the town of Plymouth aforesaid, to which corporation, that part of the American continent, which lies between 40 and 48 degrees of latitude, was granted, to be held of the king, his heirs and successors, as of the manor of East Greenwich, with powers to constitute subordinate governments in America, and to make laws for such governments, not repugnant to the laws and statutes of England. From this corporation, your predecessors obtained a grant of the soil of the colony of Massachusetts-Bay, in 1627, and in 1628, they obtained a charter from king Charles the I making them a distinct corporation, also within the realm, and giving them full powers within limits of their patent, very like to those of the council of Plymouth, throughout their more extensive territory.

We will now consider what must have been the sense of the king, of the nation, and of the patentees, at the time of granting these patents. From the year 1602, the banks and sea coasts of New England had been frequented by English subjects, for catching and drying cod-fish. When an exclusive right to the fishery was claimed, by virtue of the patent of 1620, the house of commons was alarmed, and a bill was brought in for allowing a free fishery; and it was upon this occasion, that one of the secretaries of state declared perhaps as his own opinion, that the plantations were not annexed to the crown, and so were not within the jurisdiction of parliament. Sir Edwin

Sandys, who was one of the Virginia company, and an eminent lawyer, declared, that he knew Virginia had been annexed, and was held of the crown, as of the manor of East Greenwich, and he believed New England was so also; and so it most certainly was. This declaration, made by one of the king's servants, you say, shewed the sense of the crown, and, being not secretly, but openly declared in parliament, you would make it the sense of the nation also, notwithstanding your own assertion, that the lords and commons passed a bill, that shewed their sense to be directly the contrary. But if there had been full evidence of express declarations made by king James the I and king Charles the I they were declarations contrary to their own grants, which declare this country to be held of the crown, and consequently it must have been annexed to it. And may not such declarations be accounted for by other actions of those princes, who, when they were soliciting the parliament to grant the duties of tonnage and poundage, with other ads, and were, in this way, acknowledging the rights of parliament, at the same time requiring the payment of those duties, with ship money, etc., by virtue of their prerogative?

But to remove all doubts of the sense of the nation, and of the patentees of this patent, or character, in 1620, I need only refer you to the account published by Sir Ferdinando Gorges himself, of the proceedings in parliament upon this occasion. As he was the most active member of the council of Plymouth, and, as he relates what came within his own knowledge and observation, his narrative, which has all the appearance of truth and sincerity, must carry conviction with it. He says, that soon after the patent was passed, and whilst it lay in the crown office, he was summoned to appear in parliament, to answer what was to be objected against it; and the house being in a committee, and Sir Edward Coke, that great oracle of the law, in the chair, he was called to the bar, and was told by Sir Edward, that the house understood that a patent had been granted to the said Ferdinando, and divers other noble persons, for establishing a colony in New England, that this was deemed a grievance of the commonwealth, contrary to the laws, and to the privileges of the subject, that it was a monopoly, etc., and he required the delivery of the patent into the house. Sir Ferdinando Gorges made no doubt of the authority of the house, but submitted to their disposal of the patent, as, in their wisdom, they thought good: "not knowing, under favor, how any action of that kind could be a grievance to the public, seeing it was undertaken for the advancement of religion, the enlargement of the bounds of our nation, etc. He was willing, however, to submit the whole to the honorable censures." After divers attendances, he imagined he had satisfied the house, that the planting a colony was of much more consequence, than a simple disorderly course of fishing. He was, notwithstanding disappointed; and, when the public grievances of the kingdom were presented by the two houses, that of the patent for New England was the first. I do not know how the parliament could have shewn more fully the sense they then had of their authority over this new acquired territory; nor can we expect better evidence of the sense which the patentees had of it, for I know of no historical fact, of which we have less reason to doubt.

And now, gentlemen, I will shew you how it appears from our charter itself, which you say I have not yet been pleased to point out to you, except from that clause, which restrains us from making laws repugnant to the laws of England; that it was the sense of our predecessors, at the time when the charter was granted, that they were to remain subject to the supreme authority of parliament.

Besides this clause, which I shall have occasion further to remark upon before I finish, you will find that, by the charter, a grant was made of exemption from all taxes and impositions upon any goods imported into New England, or exported from thence into England, for the space of twenty-one years, except the custom of five per cent, upon such goods as, after the expiration of seven years, should be brought into England. Nothing can be more plain than that the charter, as well as the patent to the council of Plymouth, constitutes a corporation in England, with powers to create a subordinate government or governments within the plantation, so that there would always be subjects of taxes and impositions both in the kingdom and in the plantation. An exemption for twenty-one years, implies a right of imposition after the expiration of the term and there is no distinction between the kingdom and the plantation. By what authority then, in the understanding of the parties, were those impositions to be laid? If any, to support a system, should say by the king, rather than to acknowledge the authority of parliament, yet this could not be the sense of one of our principal patentees, Mr. Samuel Vassal, who, at that instant, 1628, the date of the charter, was suffering the loss of his goods, rather than submit to an imposition laid by the king, without the authority of parliament; and to prove that, a few years after, it could not be the sense of the rest, I need only to refer you to your own records for the year 1642, where you will find an order of the house of commons, conceived in such terms as discover a plain reference to this part of the charter, after fourteen years of the twenty-one were expired. By this order, the house of commons declare, that all goods and merchandise exported to New England, or imported from thence, shall be free from all taxes and impositions, both in the kingdom and New England, until the house shall take further order therein to the contrary. The sense which our predecessors had of the benefit which they took from this order, evidently appears from the vote of the general court, acknowledging their humble thankfulness, and preserving a grateful remembrance of the honorable respect from that high court, and resolving, that the order sent unto them, under the hand of the clerk of the honorable house of commons, shall be entered among their public records, to remain there unto posterity. And, in an address to parliament, nine years after, they acknowledge among other undeserved favors, that of taking off the customs from them.

I am at a loss to know what your ideas could be, when you say that, if the plantations are not part of the realm, they are not part of the kingdom, seeing the two words can properly convey but one idea, and they have one and the same signification in the different languages from whence they are derived. I do not charge you with any design; but the equivocal use of the word realm, in several parts of your answer, makes them perplexed and obscure. Sometimes you must intend the whole dominion, which is subject to the authority of parliament; sometimes only strictly the territorial realm, to which other dominions are, or may be annexed. If you mean that no countries, but the ancient territorial realm, can, constitutionally be subject to the supreme authority of England, which you have very incautiously said is a rule of the common law of England—this is a doctrine which you will never be able to support. That the common law should be controlled and changed by statutes, every day's experience teaches; but that the common law prescribes limits to the extent of the legislative power, I believe has never been said upon any other occasion. That acts of parliaments, for several hundred years past, have respected countries, which are not strictly within the realm, you might easily have discovered by the statute books. You will find acts for regulating the affairs of Ireland, though a separate and distinct kingdom. Wales and Calais, whilst they sent no representatives to parliament, were subject to the like regulations; so are Guernsey, Jersey, Alderney, &c. which send no members to this day. These countries are not more properly a part of the ancient realm, than the plantations, nor do I know they can more properly be said to be annexed to the realm, unless the declaring that acts of parliament shall extend to Wales, though not particularly named, shall make it so, which I conceive it does not, in the sense you intend.

Thus, I think, I have made it appear that the plantations, though not strictly within the realm, have, from the beginning, been constitutionally subject to the supreme authority of the realm, and are so far annexed to it, as

to be, with the realm and the other dependencies upon it, one entire dominion; and that the plantation, or colony of Massachusetts-Bay in particular, is holden as feudatory of the imperial crown of England. Deem it to
be no part of the realm, it is immaterial; for, to use the words of a very great
authority in a case, in some respects analogous, "being feudatory, the conclusion necessarily follows, that it is under the government of the king's laws
and the king's courts, in cases proper for them to interpose, (like counties
Palatine) it has peculiar laws and customs, *jura regalia,* and complete jurisdiction at home."

Your remark upon, and construction of the words, not repugnant to
the laws of England, are much the same with those of the council; but can
any reason be assigned why the laws of England, as they stood just at
that period, should be pitched upon as the standard, more than at any
other period? If so, why was it not recurred to when the second charter
was granted, more than sixty years after the first? It is not improbable, that
the original intention might be a repugnancy in general, and *fortiori,* such
laws as were made more immediately to respect us, but the statute of 7th
and 8th of king William and queen Mary, soon after the second charter,
favors the latter construction only, and the province agent, Mr. Dummer,
in his much applauded defence of the charter, says that, then, a law in the
plantations may be said to be repugnant to a law made in Great Britain,
when it flatly contradicts it, so far as the law made there mentions and relates to the plantations. . . .

The remaining parts of your answer are principally intended to prove
that, under both charters, it hath been the sense of the people that they
were not subject to the jurisdiction of parliament, and, for this purpose,
you have made large extracts from the history of the colony. Whilst you are
doing honor to the book, by laying any stress upon its authority, it would
have been no more than justice to the author, if you had cited some other
passage in my speech to the history. I have said that, except about the time
of the anarchy, which preceded the restoration of king Charles the II, I have
not discovered that the authority of parliament had been called in question,
even by particular persons. It was, as I take it from the principles imbibed
in those times of anarchy, that the persons of influence, mentioned in the
history, disputed the authority of parliament, but the government would not
venture to dispute it. On the contrary, in four or five years after the restoration, the government declared to the king's commissioners, that the act of
navigation had been for some years observed here, that they knew not of
its being greatly violated, and that such laws as appeared to be against it,

were repealed. It is not strange, that these persons of influence should pre-vail upon a great part of the people to fall in, for a time, with their opin-ions, and to suppose acts of the colony necessary to give force to acts of parliament. The government, however, several years before the charter was vacated, more explicitly acknowledged the authority of parliament, and voted that their governor should take the oath required of him, faithfully to do and perform all matters and things enjoined him by the acts of trade. . . .

Inasmuch as you say that I have not particularly pointed out to you the acts and doings of the general assembly, which relate to acts of parlia-ment, I will do it now, and demonstrate to you that such acts have been acknowledged by the assembly, or submitted to by the people.

From your predecessors' removal to America, until the year 1640, there was no session of parliament; and the first short session, of a few days only, in 1640, and the whole of the next session, until the withdraw of the king, being taken up in the disputes between the king and the parliament, there could be no room for plantation affairs. Soon after the king's withdraw, the house of commons passed the memorable order of 1642; and, from that time to the restoration, this plantation seems to have been distinguished from the rest; and the several acts and ordinances, which respected the other planta-tions, were never enforced here; and, possibly, under color of the exemption in 1642, it might not be intended they should be executed.

For fifteen or sixteen years after the restoration, there was no officer of the customs in the colony, except the governor, annually elected by the people, and the acts of trade were but little regarded; nor did the governor take the oath required of governors, by the act of the 12th of king Charles the II until the time which I have mentioned.—Upon the revolution, the force of an act of parliament was evident, in a case of as great importance as any which could happen to the colony. King William and queen Mary were proclaimed in the colony, king and queen of England, France, and Ireland, and the dominions thereunto belonging, in the room of king James; and this, not by virtue of an act of the colony, for no such act ever passed, but by force of an act of parliament, which altered the succession to the crown, and for which the people waited several weeks, with anxious con-cern. By force of another act of parliament, and that only, such officers of the colony as had taken the oaths of allegiance to king James, deemed themselves at liberty to take, and accordingly did take, the oaths to king William and queen Mary. And that I may mention other acts of the like nature together, it is by force of an act of parliament, that the illustrious house of Hanover succeeded to the throne of Britain and its dominions, and by several other acts, the forms of the oaths have, from time to time, been altered; and, by a late act, that form was established which every one of us has complied with, as the charter, in express words, requires, and makes our duty. Shall we now dispute whether acts of parliament have been submitted to, when we find them submitted to, in points which are of the very essence of our constitution? If you should disown that authority, which has power even to change the succession to the crown, are you in no danger of denying the authority of our most gracious sovereign, which I am sure none of you can have in your thoughts?

I think I have before shewn you, gentlemen, what must have been the sense of our predecessors at the time of the first charter; let us now, whilst we are upon the acts and doings of the assembly, consider what it must have been at the time of the second charter. Upon the first advice of the revolution in England, the authority which assumed the government, instructed their agents to petition parliament to restore the first charter, and a bill for that purpose passed the house of commons, but went no further. Was not this owning the authority of parliament? By an act of parliament, passed in the first year of king William and queen Mary, a form of oaths was established, to be taken by those princes, and by all succeeding kings and queens of England, at their coronation; the first of which is, that they will govern the people of the kingdom, and the dominions thereunto belonging, according to the statutes in parliament agreed on, and the laws and customs of the same. When the colony directed their agents to make their humble application to king William, to grant the second charter, they could have no other pretence than, as they were inhabitants of part of the dominions of England; and they also knew the oath the king had taken, to govern them according to the statutes in parliament. Surely, then, at the time of this charter, also, it was the sense of our predecessors, as well as of the king and of the nation, that there was and would remain, a supremacy in the parliament. About the same time, they acknowledge, in an address to the king, that they have no power to make laws repugnant to the laws of England. And, immediately after the assumption of the powers of government, by virtue of the new charter, an act was passed to revive, for a limited time, all the local laws of the colonies of Massachusetts-Bay and New Plymouth, respectively, not repugnant to the laws of England. And, at the same session, an act passed, establishing naval officers, in several ports of the province, for which this reason is given, that all undue trading, contrary to an act of parliament, made in the fifteenth year of king Charles II may be prevented in this, their majesty's province. The act of this province, passed so long ago as the second year of king George the I for stating the fees of the custom house officers, must have relation to the acts of parliament, by which they are constituted; and the provision made in that act of the province, for extending the port of Boston to all the roads, as far as Cape Cod, could be for no other purpose, than for the more effectual carrying the acts of trade into execution. And, to come nearer to the present time, when an act of parliament had passed, in 1771, for putting an end to certain unwarrantable schemes, in this province, did the authority of government, or those persons more immediately affected by it, ever dispute the validity of it? On the contrary, have not a number of acts been passed in the province, the burdens which such persons were subjected, might be equally apportioned; and have not all those acts of the province been very carefully framed, to prevent their militating with the act of parliament? I will mention, also, an act of parliament, made in the first year of queen Anne, although the proceedings upon it more immediately respected the council. By this act no office, civil or military, shall be void, by the death of the king, but shall continue six months, unless suspended, or made void, by the next successor. By force of this act, governor Dudley continued in the administration six months from the demise of queen Anne, and immediately after, the council assumed the administration, and continued it until a proclamation arrived from king George, by virtue of which governor Dudley reassumed the government. It would be tedious to enumerate the addresses, votes and messages, of both the council and house of representatives, to the same purpose. I have said enough to shew that this government has submitted to parliament, from a conviction of its constitutional supremacy, and this not from inconsideration, nor merely from reluctance at the idea of contending with the parent state.

If, then, I have made it appear that, both by the first and second charters, we hold our lands, and the authority of government, not of the king, but of the crown of England, that being a dominion of the crown of England, we are consequently subject to the supreme authority of England. . . .

You ask me, if we have not reason to fear we shall soon be reduced to a worse situation than that of the colonies of France, Spain, or Holland. I may safely affirm that we have not; that we have no reason to fear any evils from a submission to the authority of parliament, equal to what we must feel from its authority being disputed, from an uncertain rule of law and government. For more than seventy years together, the supremacy of parliament was acknowledged, without complaints of grievance. The effect of every measure cannot be foreseen by human wisdom. What can be expected more, from any authority, than when the unfitness of a measure is discovered, to make it void? When, upon the united representations and complaints of the American colonies, any acts have appeared to parliament to be unsalutary, have there not been repeated instances of the repeal of such acts? We cannot expect these instances should be carried so far as to be equivalent to a disavowal, or relinquishment of the right itself. Why, then, shall we fear for ourselves, and our posterity, greater rigor of government for seventy years to come, than what we and our predecessors have felt, in the seventy years past.

You must give me leave, gentlemen, in a few words, to vindicate myself from a charge, in one part of your answer, of having, by my speech, reduced you to the unhappy alternative of appearing, by your silence, to acquiesce in my sentiments, or of freely discussing this point of the supremacy of parliament. I saw, as I have before observed, the capital town of the province, without being reduced to such an alternative, voluntarily, not only discussing but determining this point, and inviting every other town and district in the province to do the like. I saw that many of the principal towns had followed the example, and that there was imminent danger of a compliance in most, if not all the rest, in order to avoid being distinguished. Was not I reduced to the alternative of rendering myself justly obnoxious to the displeasure of my sovereign, by acquiescing in such irregularities, or of calling upon you to join with me in suppressing them? Might I not rather have expected from you an expression of your concern, that any persons should project and prosecute a plan of measures, which would lay me under the necessity of bringing this point before you? It was so far from being my inclination, that nothing short of a sense of my duty to the king, and the obligations I am under to consult your true interest, could have compelled me to it.

Gentlemen of the Council, and Gentlemen of the House of Representatives.

We all profess to be the loyal and dutiful subjects of the king of Great Britain. His majesty considers the British empire as one entire dominion, subject to one legislative power; a due submission to which, is essential to the maintenance of the rights, liberties and privileges of the several parts of this dominion. We have abundant evidence of his majesty's tender and impartial regard to the rights of his subjects; and I am authorized to say, that "his majesty will most graciously approve of every constitutional measure that may contribute to the peace, the happiness, and prosperity of his colony of Massachusetts-Bay, and which may have the effect to shew to the world, that he has no wish beyond that of reigning in the hearts and affections of his people."

THE LEGISLATURE ANSWERS THE GOVERNOR

[Excerpts from the response of the Massachusetts legislature, March 2, 1773]

MAY IT PLEASE YOUR EXCELLENCY,

In your speech, at the opening of the present session, your excellency expressed your displeasure at some late proceedings of the town of Boston, and other principal towns in the province. And, in another speech to both houses, we have your repeated exceptions at the same proceedings, as being "unwarrantable," and of a dangerous nature and tendency; "against which, you thought yourself bound to call upon us to join with you in bearing a proper testimony." This house have not discovered any principles advanced by the town of Boston, that are unwarrantable by the constitution; nor does it appear to us, that they have "invited every other town and district in the province to adopt their principles." We are fully convinced, that it is our duty to bear our testimony against "innovations, of a dangerous nature and tendency;" but it is clearly our opinion, that it is the indisputable right of all, or any of his majesty's subjects, in this province, regularly and orderly to meet together, to state the grievances they labor under; and to propose, and unite in such constitutional measures, as they shall judge necessary or proper, to obtain redress. This right has been frequently exercised by his majesty's subjects within the realm; and we do not recollect an instance, since the happy revolution, when the two houses of parliament have been called upon to discountenance, or bear their testimony against it, in a speech from the throne.

Your excellency is pleased to take notice of some things which we "allege," in our answer to your first speech; and the observation you make, we must confess, is as natural and undeniably true, as any one that could have been made; that, "if our foundation shall fail us in every part of it, the fabric we have raised upon it must certainly fall." You think this foundation will fail us; but we wish your excellency had condescended to a consideration of what we have "adduced in support of our principles." We might then, perhaps, have had some things offered for our conviction, more than bare affirmations; which, we must beg to be excused if we say, are far from being sufficient, though they came with your excellency's authority, for which, however, we have a due regard.

Your excellency says that, "as English subjects, and agreeable to the doctrine of the feudal tenure, all our lands are held mediately, or immediately, of the crown." We trust your excellency does not mean to introduce the feudal system in its perfection; which, to use the words of one of our greatest historians, was "a state of perpetual war, anarchy, and confusion. . . ."

By the struggle for liberty in England, from the days of king John, to the last happy revolution, the constitution has been gradually changing for the better; and, upon the more rational principles that all men, by nature, are in a state of equality in respect of jurisdiction and dominion, power in England has been more equally divided. And thus, also, in America, though we hold our lands agreeably to the feudal principles of the king, yet our predecessors wisely took care to enter into compact with the king, that power here should also be equally divided, agreeably to the original fundamental principles of the English constitution, declared in Magna Charta, and other laws and statutes of England, made to confirm them. . . .

You tell us, that "when any new countries are discovered by English subjects, according to the general law and usage of nations, they become part of the state." The law of nations is, or ought to be, founded on the law of reason. It was the saying of Sir Edwin Sandis, in the great case of the union of the realm of Scotland with England, which is applicable to our present purpose, that "there being no precedent for this case in the law, the law is deficient; and the law being deficient, recourse is to be had to custom; and custom being insufficient, we must recur to natural reason"— the greatest of all authorities, which, he adds, "is the law of nations." The opinions, therefore, and determinations of the greatest sages and judges of the law in the exchequer chamber, ought not to be considered as decisive or binding in our present controversy with your excellency, any further than they are consonant to natural reason. If, however, we were to recur to such opinions and determinations, we should find very great authorities in our favor, to show that the statutes of England are not binding on those who are not represented in parliament there. The opinion of Lord Coke, that Ireland was bound by statutes of England, wherein they were named, if compared with his other writings, appears manifestly to be grounded upon a supposition, that Ireland had, by an act of their own, in the reign of king John, consented to be thus bound; and, upon any other supposition, this opinion would be against reason; for consent only gives human laws their force. We beg leave, upon what your excellency has observed of the colony becoming a part of the state, to subjoin the opinions of several learned civilians, as quoted by a very able lawyer in this country. "Colonies," says Puffendorf, "are settled in different methods; for, either the colony continues a part of the commonwealth it was set out from, or else is obliged to pay a dutiful regard to the mother commonwealth, and to be in readiness to defend and vindicate its honor, and so is united by a sort of unequal confederacy; or, lastly, is erected into a separate commonwealth, and assumes the same rights with the state it descended from." And king Tullius, as quoted by the same learned author from Grotius, says, "we look upon it to be neither truth nor justice, that mother cities ought, of necessity, and by the law of nature, to rule over the colonies."

Your excellency has misinterpreted what we have said, "that no country, by the common law, was subject to the laws or the parliament, but the realm of England;" and are pleased to tell us, "that we have expressed ourselves incautiously." We beg leave to recite the words of the judges of England, in the before mentioned case, to our purpose. "If a king go out of England with a company of his servants, allegiance remaineth among his servants, although he be out of his realm, whereto his laws are confined." We did not mean to say, as your excellency would suppose, that "the common law prescribes limits to the extent of the legislative power," though we shall always affirm it to be true, of the law of reason and natural equity. Your excellency thinks you have made it appear, that the "colony of Massachusetts-Bay is holden as feudatory of the imperial crown of England;" and, therefore, you say, "to use the words of a very great authority in a case, in some respects analogous to it," being feudatory, it necessarily follows that "it is under the government of the king's laws." Your excellency has not named this authority; but we conceive his meaning must be, that, being feudatory, it is under the government of the king's laws absolutely; for, as we have before said, the feudal system admits of no idea of the authority of parliament; and this would have been the case of the colony, but for the compact with the king in the charter. . . .

Your excellency says that, by "our not distinguishing between the crown of England and the kings and queens of England, in their personal or natural capacities, we have been led into a fundamental error." Upon this very distinction we have availed ourselves. We have said, that our ancestors considered the land, which they took possession of in America, as out of the bounds of the kingdom of England, and out of the reach and extent of the laws of England; and that the king also, even in the act of granting the charter, considered the territory as not within the realm; that the king had an absolute right in himself to dispose of the lands, and that this was not disputed by the nation; nor could the lands, on any solid grounds, be claimed by the nation; and, therefore, our ancestors received the lands, by grant, from the king; and, at the same time, compacted with him, and promised him homage and allegiance, not in his public or politic, but natural capacity only. If it be difficult for us to show how the king acquired a title to this country in his natural capacity, or separate from his relation to his subjects, which we confess, yet we conceive it will be equally difficult for your excellency to show how the body politic and nation of England acquired it. Our ancestors supposed it was acquired by neither; and, therefore, they declared, as we have before quoted from your history, that, saving their actual purchase from the natives of the soil, the dominion, the lordship, and sovereignty, they had, in the sight of God and man, no right and title to what they possessed. How much clearer then, in natural reason and equity, must our title be, who hold estates dearly purchased at the expense of our own as well as our ancestors' labor, and defended by them with treasure and blood.

Your excellency has been pleased to confirm, rather than deny or confute, a piece of history, which, you say, we took from an anonymous pamphlet, and by which you "fear we have been too easily misled." It may be gathered from your own declaration, and other authorities, besides the anonymous pamphlet, that the house of commons took exception, not at the king's having made an absolute grant of the territory, but at the claim of an exclusive right to the fishery on the banks and sea coast, by virtue of the patent. At this you say "the house of commons was alarmed, and a bill was brought in for allowing a free fishery." And, upon this occasion, your excellency allows that "one of the secretaries of state declared, that the plantations were not annexed to the crown, and so were not within the jurisdiction of parliament." If we should concede to what your excellency supposes might possibly, or, "perhaps," be the case, that the secretary made this declaration "as his own opinion," the event showed that it was the opinion of the king too, for it is not to be accounted for upon any other principle, that he would have denied his royal assent to a bill, formed for no other purpose, but to grant his subjects in England the privilege of fishing on the sea coasts in America. The account published by Sir Ferdinando Gorges himself, of the proceedings of parliament on this occasion, your excellency thinks will remove all doubt of the sense of the nation, and of the patentees of this patent or charter, in 1620. "This narrative," you say, "has all the appearance of truth and sincerity," which we do not deny; and, to us, it carries this conviction with it, that "what was objected" in parliament, was the exclusive claim of fishing only. His imagining that he had satisfied the house, after divers attendances, that the planting a colony was of much more consequence than a simple disorderly course of fishing, is sufficient for our conviction. We know that the nation was at that time alarmed with apprehension of monopolies; and, if the patent of New England was presented by the two houses as a grievance, it did not show, as your excellency supposes, "the sense they then had of their authority over this new acquired territory," but only their sense of the grievance of a monopoly of the sea.

We are happy to hear your excellency say, that "our remarks upon, and construction of the words, not repugnant to the laws of England, are much the same with those of the council." It serves to confirm us in our opinion, in what we take to be the most important matter of difference between your excellency and the two houses: After saying, that the statute of 7th and 8th of William and Mary favors the construction of the words, as intending such laws of England as are made more immediately to respect us, you tell us, that "the province agent, Mr. Dummer, in his much applauded defence, says that then a law of the plantations may be said to be repugnant to a law made in Great Britain, when it flatly contradicts it, so far as the law made there mentions and relates to the plantations." This is plain and obvious to common sense, and therefore, cannot be denied. But, if your excellency would read a page or two further, in that excellent defence, you will see that he mentions this as the sense of the phrase, as taken from an act of parliament, rather than as the sense he would choose himself to put upon it; and he expressly designs to show, in vindication of the charter, that, in that sense of words, there never was a law made in the plantations repugnant to the laws of Great Britain. He gives another construction, much more likely to be the true intent of the words, namely, "that the patentees shall not presume, under color of their particular charters, to make any laws inconsistent with the great charter, and other laws of England, by which the lives, liberties, and properties of Englishmen are secured." This is the sense in which our ancestors understood the words; and, therefore, they [were] unwilling to conform to the acts of trade, and disregarded them till they made provision to give them force in the colony, by a law of their own; saying, "that the laws of England did not reach America; and those acts were an invasion of their rights, liberties, and properties," because they were not "represented in parliament." The right of being governed by laws, which were made by persons in whose election they had a voice, they looked upon as the foundation of English liberties. . . .

We flatter ourselves that, from the large extracts we have made from your excellency's history of the colony, it appears evidently that, under both charters, it hath been the sense of the people and of the government, that they were not under the jurisdiction of parliament. . . .

You tell us, that "the government, four or five years before the charter was vacated, more explicitly," that is, than by a conversation with the commissioners, "acknowledged the authority of parliament, and voted that their governor should take the oath required of him, faithfully to do and perform all matters and things enjoined him by the acts of trade." But does this, may it please your excellency, show their explicit acknowledgment of the authority of parliament? Does it not rather show directly the contrary? For, what could there be for their vote, or authority, to require him to take the oath already required of him by the act of parliament unless both he and they judged that an act of parliament was not of force sufficient to bind him to take such an oath? We do not deny, but, on the contrary, are fully persuaded, that your excellency's principles in government are still of the same with what they appear to be in the history; for you there say, that "the passing this law, plainly shows that wrong sense they had of relation they stood unto England." But we are from hence convinced, that your excellency, when you wrote the history, was of our mind in this respect that our ancestors, in passing the law, discovered their opinion, that they were without the jurisdiction of parliament; for it was upon this principle alone, they shewed the wrong sense they had, in your excellency's opinion, of the relation they stood unto England.

Your excellency, in your second speech, condescends to point out to us the acts and doings of the general assembly, which relates to acts of parliament, which, you think, "demonstrates that they have been acknowledged by the assembly, or submitted to by the people," neither of which, in our opinion, shows that it was the sense of the nation, and our predecessors, when they first took possession of this plantation, or colony, by a grant and charter from the crown, that they were to remain subject to the supreme authority of the English parliament.

Your excellency seems chiefly to rely upon our ancestors, after the revolution, "proclaiming king William and queen Mary, in the room of king James," and taking the oaths to them, "the alteration of the form of oaths, from time to time," and finally, "the establishment of the form, which every one of us has complied with, as the charter, in express terms, requires and makes our duty." We do not know that it has ever been a point in dispute, whether the kings of England were ipso facto kings in, and over, this colony, or province. The compact was made between king Charles the I, his heirs and successors, and the governor and company, their heirs and successors. It is easy, upon this principle, to account for the acknowledgment of, and submission to, king William and queen Mary, as successors of Charles the I in the room of king James; besides, it is to be considered, that the people in the colony, as well as in England, had suffered under the tyrant James, by which he had alike forfeited his right to reign over both. There had been a revolution here, as well as in England. The eyes of the people here were upon William and Mary; and the news of their being proclaimed in England was, as your excellency's history tells us, "the most joyful news ever received in New England." And, if they were not proclaimed here, "by virtue of an act of the colony," it was, as we think may be concluded from the tenor of your history, with the general or universal consent of the people, as apparently as if "such act had passed." It is consent alone that makes any human laws binding; and, as a learned author observes, a purely voluntary submission to an act because it is highly in our favor and for our benefit, is in all equity and justice, to be deemed as not at all proceeding from the right we include in the legislators, that they thereby obtain an authority over us, and that ever hereafter, we must obey them of duty. We would observe, that one of the first acts of the general assembly of this province, since the present charter, was an act requiring the taking the oaths mentioned in an act of parliament, to which you refer us. For what purpose was this act of the assembly passed, if it was the sense of the legislators that the act of parliament was in force in the province? And, at the same time, another act was made for the establishment of other oaths necessary to be taken, both which acts have the royal sanction, and are now in force. Your excellency says, that when the colony applied to king William for a second charter, they knew the oath the king had taken, which was to govern them according to the statutes in parliament, and (which your excellency here omits,) the laws and customs of parliament, the people of England freely debate and consent to such statutes as are made by themselves or their chosen representatives. This is a law or custom, which all mankind may justly challenge as their inherent right. According to this law, the king has an undoubted right to govern us. Your excellency, upon recollection, surely will not infer from hence, that it was the sense of our predecessors that there was to remain a supremacy in the English parliament, or a full power and authority to make laws binding upon us, in all cases whatever, in that parliament, where we cannot debate and deliberate upon the necessity or expediency of any law, and, consequently, without our consent; and, as it may probably happen, destructive of the first law of society, the good of the whole. You tell us that, "after the assumption of all the powers of government, by virtue of the new charter, an act passed for the reviving, for a limited time, all the local laws of the Massachusetts-Bay and New Plymouth, respectively, not repugnant to the laws of England. And, at the same session, an act passed establishing naval officers, that all undue trading, contrary to an act of parliament, may be prevented." Among the acts that were then revived, we may reasonably suppose was that, whereby provision was made to give force to this act of parliament in the province. The establishment, therefore, of the naval officers, was to aid the execution of an act of parliament, for the observance of which, within the colony, the assembly had before made provision, after free debates, with their own consent, and by their own act.

The act of parliament, passed in 1741, for putting an end to several unwarrantable schemes, mentioned by your excellency, was designed for the general good; and, if the validity of it was not disputed, it cannot be urged as a concession of the supreme authority, to make laws binding on us in all cases whatever. But, if the design of it was for the general benefit of the province, it was, in one respect, at least greatly complained of by the persons more immediately affected by it; and to remedy the inconvenience, the legislature of this province passed an act, directly militating with it; which is the strongest that, although they may have submitted, sub silentio, to some acts of parliament, that they conceived might operate for their benefit, they did not conceive themselves bound by any of its acts which, they judged, would operate to the injury even of individuals. . . .

We shall sum up our own sentiments in the words of that learned writer, Mr. Hooker, in his ecclesiastical policy, as quoted by Mr. Locke.—"The lawful power of making laws to command whole political societies of men, belonging so properly to the same entire societies that for any prince or potentate of what kind soever, to exercise the same of himself, and not from express commission, immediately and personally received from God, is no better than mere tyranny. Laws, therefore, they are not, which public approbation hath not made so; for laws human, of what kind soever, are available by consent." "Since men, naturally, have no full and perfect power to command whole politic multitudes of men, therefore, utterly without our consent, we could in such sort, be at no man's commandment living. And to be commanded, we do not consent, when that society, whereof we be a party, hath at any time before consented." We think your excellency has not proved, either that the colony is a part of the politic society of England, or that it has ever consented that the parliament of England or Great Britain, should make laws binding upon us, in all cases, whether made expressly to refer to us or not.

We cannot help, before we conclude, expressing our great concern, that your excellency had thus repeatedly, in a manner, insisted upon our free sentiments on matters of so delicate a nature and weighty importance. The question appears to us to be no other, than whether we are the subjects of absolute unlimited power, or of a free government, formed on the principles of the English constitution. If your excellency's doctrine be true, the people of this province hold their lands of the crown and people of England; and their lives, liberties, and properties, are at their disposal; and that, even by compact and their own consent, they were subject to the king, as the head alterius populi of another people, in whose legislature they have no voice or interest. They are, indeed, said to have a constitution and a legislature of their own; but your excellency has explained it into a mere phantom; limited, controlled, superseded, and nullified at the will of another. Is this the constitution which so charmed our ancestors, that, as your excellency has informed us, they kept a day of solemn thanksgiving to Almighty God when they received it? And were they men of so little discernment, such children in understanding, as to please themselves with the imagination, that they were blessed with the same rights and liberties which natural born subjects in England enjoyed, when at the same time, they had fully consented to be ruled and ordered by a legislature, a thousand leagues distant from them, which cannot be supposed to be sufficiently acquainted with their circumstances, if concerned for their interest, and in which they cannot be in any sense represented?

(The committee who reported the above, were Mr. Cushing, the speaker, Mr. S. Adams, Mr. Hancock, Mr. Philips, Major Foster, Col. Bowers, Mr. Hobson, Col. Thayer, and Mr. Denny.)

2. MASSACHUSETTS APPOINTS A COMMITTEE OF CORRESPONDENCE

RESOLUTIONS OF THE HOUSE OF REPRESENTATIVES

[Resolutions adopted, on motion of Samuel Adams, by the Massachusetts House of Representatives, May 28, 1773, by a vote of 110 to 4]

Whereas, the speaker hath communicated to this house, a letter from the truly respectable house of Burgesses, in his majesty's ancient colony of Virginia, enclosing a copy of the resolves entered into by them, on the 12th of March last, and requesting that a committee of this house may be appointed to communicate, from time to time, with a corresponding committee, then appointed by the said house of Burgesses in Virginia:

And, whereas this house is fully sensible of the necessity and importance of a union of the several colonies in America, at a time when it clearly appears, that the rights and liberties of all are systematically invaded; in order that the joint wisdom of the whole may be employed in consulting their common safety:

Resolved, That this house have a very grateful sense of the obligations they are under to the house of Burgesses, in Virginia, for the vigilance, firmness and wisdom, which they have discovered, at all times in support of the rights and liberties of the American colonies; and do heartily concur with their said judicious and spirited resolves.

Resolved, That a standing committee of correspondence and enquiry be appointed, to consist of fifteen members, any eight of whom to be a quorum; whose business it shall be, to obtain the most early and authentic intelligence of all such acts and resolutions of the British parliament, or proceedings of administrations as may relate to, or affect the British colonies in America, and to keep up and maintain a correspondence and communication with our sister colonies, respecting these important considerations; and the result of such their proceedings, from time to time, to lay before the house.

Resolved, That it be an instruction to the said committee, that they do, without delay, inform themselves particularly of the principles and authority, on which was constituted a court of enquiry, held in Rhode Island, said to be vested with powers to transport persons, accused of offences committed in America, to places beyond the seas, to be tried.

Resolved, That the said committee be further instructed to prepare and report to this house, a draft of a very respectful answer to the letter, received from the speaker of the honorable house of Burgesses of Virginia, and another, to a letter received from the speaker of the honorable house of representatives, of the colony of Rhode Island: also, a circular letter to the several other houses of assembly, on this continent, enclosing the aforesaid resolves, and requesting them to lay the same before their respective assemblies, in confidence, that they will readily and cheerfully comply with the wise and salutary resolves of the house of Burgesses, in Virginia.

(The committee of correspondence, chosen in pursuance of the resolves aforesaid, were Mr. Cushing, the speaker, Mr. Adams, hon. John Hancock, Mr. William Phillips, captain William Heath, hon. Joseph Hawley, James Warren, esq. R. Derby, jun. esq. Mr. Elbridge Gerry, J. Bowers, esq., Jedediah Foster, esq. Daniel Leonard, esq. captain T. Gardner, capt. Jonathan Greenleaf, and J. Prescott, esq.)

LETTER FROM THE HOUSE TO THE COLONIAL LEGISLATURES

*[Letter sent by the Massachusetts House of Representatives
to the other colonial houses of assembly, June 3, 1773]*

SIR—The house of representatives of this province, being earnestly attentive to the controversy between Great Britain and the colonies, and considering that the authority claimed and exercised by parliament, on the one side, and by the general assemblies of this continent, on the other greatly militates, and is productive of this unhappy contention, think it of the utmost importance to the welfare of both, and particularly of the colonies, that the constitutional powers of each be inquired into, delineated and fully ascertained.

That his majesty's subjects of America, are entitled to the same rights and liberties as those of Great Britain, and that these ought, in justice, by the constitution, to be as well guaranteed and secured, to the one as to the other, are too apparent to be denied.

It is, by this house, humbly conceived, to be likewise undeniable, that the authority assumed, and now forcibly exercised by parliament, over the colonies, is utterly subversive of freedom in the latter; and that, while his majesty's loyal subjects in America have the mortification, daily, to see new abridgments of their rights and liberties, they have not the least security for those which at present remain. Were the colonists only affected by a legislature, subject to their control, they would, even then, have no other security than belongs to them by the laws of nature, and the English constitution; but should the authority, now claimed by parliament, be fully supported by power, submitted to by the colonies, it appears to this house that there will be an end to liberty in America; and that the colonists will then change the name of freemen for that of slaves.

In order to adjust and settle these important concerns, the free and magnanimous Burgesses of Virginia have proposed a method for uniting the councils of its sister colonies; and it appearing to this house to be a measure very wise and salutary, is cheerfully received and heartily adopted.

With great respect for your honorable assembly, and in confidence that a matter, which so nearly affects the safety of each colony, will be assisted by its wise councils, permit this house to enclose a copy of resolutions, lately entered into here, and to request you to communicate the same at a convenient opportunity.

THOMAS CUSHING, Speaker.

3. THE COLONIES RESIST THE TEA ACT

RESOLUTION OF THE NEW YORK SONS OF LIBERTY

[Resolution by the Sons of Liberty, an organization formed to resist the subversion of colonial rights]

NEW YORK, December 15, 1773

The following association is signed by a great number of the principal gentlemen of the city, merchants, lawyers, and other inhabitants of all ranks, and it is still carried about the city, to give an opportunity to those who have not yet signed to unite with their fellow-citizens, to testify their abhorrence to the diabolical project of enslaving America.

The Association of the Sons of Liberty of New York.

It is essential to the freedom and security of a free people, that no taxes be imposed upon them but by their own consent, or their representatives. For "what property have they in that which another may, by right, take when he pleases to himself?" The former is the undoubted right of Englishmen, to secure which they expended millions and sacrificed the lives of thousands. And yet, to the astonishment of all the world, and the grief of America, the commons of Great Britain, after the repeal of the memorable and detestable stamp-act, reassumed the power of imposing taxes on the American colonies; and, insisting on it as a necessary badge of parliamentary supremacy, passed a bill, in the seventh year of his present majesty's reign, imposing duties on all glass, painters' colors, paper and teas, that should, after the 20th of November, 1767, be "imported from Great Britain into any colony or plantation in America."—This bill, after the concurrence of the lords, obtained the royal assent. And thus they who, from time immemorial, have exercised the right of giving to, or withholding from the crown, their aids and subsidies, according to their own free will and pleasure, signified by their representatives in parliament, do, by the act in question, deny us, their brethren in America, the enjoyment of the same right. As this denial, and the execution of that act, involves our slavery, and would sap the foundation of our freedom, whereby we should become slaves to our brethren and fellow subjects, born to no greater stock of freedom than the Americans—the merchants and inhabitants of this city, in conjunction with the merchants and inhabitants of the ancient American colonies, entered into an agreement to decline a part of their commerce with Great Britain, until the above mentioned act should be totally repealed. This agreement operated so powerfully to the disadvantage of the manufacturers of England that many of them were unemployed. To appease their clamors, and to provide the subsistence for them, which the non-importation had deprived them of, the parliament, in 1770, repealed so much of the revenue act as imposed a duty on glass, painters' colors, and paper, and left the duty on tea, as a test of the parliamentary right to tax us. The merchants of the cities of New York and Philadelphia, having strictly adhered to the agreement, so far as it is related to the importation of articles subject to an American duty, have convinced the ministry, that some other measures must be adopted to execute parliamentary supremacy over this country, and to remove the distress brought on the East India company, by the ill-policy of that act. Accordingly, to increase the temptation to the shippers of tea from England, an act of parliament passed the last session, which gives the whole duty on tea, the company were subject to pay, upon the importation of it into England, to the purchasers and exporters; and when the company have ten millions of pounds of tea, in their ware-houses exclusive of the quantity they may want to ship, they are allowed to export tea, discharged from the payment of that duty, with which they were before chargeable. In hopes of aid in the execution of this project, by the influence of the owners of the American ships, application was made by the company to the captains of those ships to take the tea on freight; but they virtuously rejected it. Still determined on the scheme, they have chartered ships to bring the tea to this country, which may be hourly expected, to make an important trial of our virtue. If they succeed in the sale of that tea, we shall have no property that we can call our own, and then we may bid adieu to American liberty.—Therefore, to prevent a calamity which, of all others, is the most to be dreaded—slavery, and its terrible concomitants—we, the subscribers, being influenced from a regard to liberty, and disposed to use all lawful endeavors in our power, to defeat the pernicious project, and to transmit to our posterity, those blessings of freedom which our ancestors have handed down to us; and to contribute to the support of the common liberties of America, which are in danger to be subverted, do, for those important purposes, agree to associate together, under the name and style of the sons of New York, and engage our honor to, and with each other faithfully to observe and perform the following resolutions, viz.

1st. *Resolved,* That whoever shall aid, or abet, or in any manner assist, in the introduction of tea, from any place whatsoever, into this colony, while it is subject, by a British act of parliament, to the payment of a duty, for the purpose of raising a revenue in America. he shall be deemed an enemy to the liberties of America.

2d. *Resolved,* That whoever shall be aiding, or assisting, in the landing, or carting of such tea, from any ship, or vessel, or shall hire any house, store-house, or cellar or any place whatsoever, to deposit the tea, subject to a duty as aforesaid, he shall be deemed an enemy to the liberties of America.

3d. *Resolved,* That whoever shall sell, or buy, or any manner contribute to the sale, or purchase of tea, subject to a duty as aforesaid, or shall aid, or abet, in transporting such tea by land or water, from this city, until the 7th George III chap. 46, commonly called the revenue act, shall be totally and clearly repealed, he shall be deemed an enemy to the liberties of America.

4th. *Resolved,* That whether the duties on tea, imposed by this act, be paid in Great Britain, or in America, our liberties are equally affected.

5th. *Resolved,* That whoever shall transgress any of these resolutions, we will not deal with, or employ, or have any connection with him.

REMINISCENCES OF THE TEA PARTY

[*Submitted to Hezekiah Niles by a Bostonian, c. 1821*]

. . . There was a body meeting on this 16th of December, 1773. This matter of the tea was the occasion of the meeting. The meeting began at Faneuil Hall, but that place not being large enough it was adjourned to the Old South, and even that place could not contain all who came. Jonathan Williams was moderator. Among the spectators was John Rowe . . . among other things, he said,—"Who knows how tea will mingle with salt water"— and this suggestion was received with great applause. Governor Hutchinson was at this time at the house on Milton hill. . . . A committee was sent from the meeting, to request him to order the ships to depart.—While they were gone, speeches were made, for the purpose of keeping the people together. The committee returned about sunset with his answer, that he could not interfere. At this moment the Indian yell was heard from the street. Mr. Samuel Adams cried out that it was a trick of their enemies to disturb their meeting, and requested the people to keep their places—but the people rushed out, and accompanied the Indians to the ships. The number of persons disguised as Indians is variously stated—none put it lower than 60, none higher than 80. It is said by persons who were present, that nothing was destroyed but tea —and this was not done with noise and tumult, little or nothing being said by the agents or the multitude,—who looked on. The impression was that of solemnity, rather than of riot and confusion.—The destruction was effected by disguised persons, and some young men who volunteered; one of the latter collected the tea which fell into the shoes of himself and companions, and put it into a phial and sealed it up; which phial is now in his possession,—containing the same tea.—The contrivers of this measure, and those who carried it into effect, will never be known; some few persons have been mentioned as being among the disguised; but there are many and obvious reasons why secrecy then, and concealment since, were necessary. None of those persons who were confidently said to have been of the party, (except some who were then minors or very young men), have ever admitted that they were so. The persons who appeared to know more than any one, I ever spoke with, refused to mention names. Mr. Samuel Adams is thought to have been in the counselling of this exploit, and many other men who were leaders in the political affairs of the times;—and the hall council is said to have been in the back room of Edes and Gill's printing office, at the corner of the alley leading to Battle street church from Court street. There are very few alive now, who helped to empty the chests of tea, and these few will probably be as prudent as those who have gone before them.

RESOLVES OF THE CITIZENS OF PHILADELPHIA

[Report, dated January 3, 1774, of action taken in Philadelphia against the importation of East India Company tea]

The unanimity, spirit and zeal which have heretofore animated all the colonies, from Boston to South Carolina, have been so eminently displayed in the opposition to the pernicious project of the East India company, in sending tea to America, while it remains subject to a duty, and the Americans at the same time confined by the strongest prohibitory laws to import it only from Great Britain, that a particular account of the transactions of this city cannot but be acceptable to all our readers, and every other friend of American liberty.

Upon the first advice of this measure, a general dissatisfaction was expressed, that, at a time when we were struggling with this oppressive act, and an agreement not to import tea while subject to the duty, our fellow subjects in England should form a measure so directly tending to enforce that act, and again embroil us with our parent state. When it was also considered, that the proposed mode of disposing of the tea, tended to a monopoly, ever odious in a free country, a universal disapprobation shewed itself throughout the city. A public meeting of the inhabitants was held at the state house on the 18th October [1773], at which great numbers attended, and the sense of the city was expressed in the following resolves—

1. That the disposal of their own property is the inherent right of free-men; that there can be no property in that which another can, of right, take from us without our consent; that the claim of parliament to tax America, is, in other words, a claim of right to levy contributions on us at pleasure.

2. That the duty imposed by parliament upon tea landed in America, is a tax on the Americans, or levying contributions on them without their consent.

3. That the express purpose for which the tax is levied on the Americans, namely, for the support of government, administration of justice, and defence of his majesty's dominions in America, has a direct tendency to render assemblies useless, and to introduce arbitrary government and slavery.

4. That a virtuous and steady opposition to this ministerial plan of governing America, is absolutely necessary to preserve even the shadow of liberty, and is a duty which every freeman in America owes to his country, to himself and to his posterity.

5. That the resolution lately entered into by the East India company to send out their tea to America, subject to the payment of duties on its being landed here, is an open attempt to enforce this ministerial plan, and a violent attack upon the liberties of America.

6. That it is the duty of every American to oppose this attempt.

7. That whoever shall, directly or indirectly, countenance this attempt, or in any wise aid or abet in unloading, receiving or vending the tea sent, or to be sent out by the East India company, while it remains subject to the payment of duty here, is an enemy to his country.

8. That a committee be immediately chosen to wait on those gentlemen who, it is reported, are appointed by the East India company to receive and sell the said tea, and request them from a regard to their own character, and the peace and good order of the city and province, immediately to resign their appointment.

In consequence of this appointment, the committee waited upon the gentlemen in this city, who had been appointed consignees of the expected cargo. They represented to them the detestation and abhorrence in which this measure was held by their fellow-citizens, the danger and difficulties which must attend the execution of so odious a trust, and expressed the united desires of the city, that they would renounce the commission, and engage not to intermeddle with the ship or cargo in any shape whatever. Some of the commissioners resigned, in a manner that gave general satisfaction, others in such equivocal terms as required further explanation. However in a few days the resignation was complete. In this situation things remained for a few days. In the meantime, the general spirit and indignation rose to such a height, that it was thought proper to call another general meeting of the principal citizens to consider and resolve upon such farther steps as might give weight, and insure success to the unanimous opposition now formed. Accordingly a meeting was held, for the above purpose, at which a great number of respectable inhabitants attended, and it appeared to be the unanimous opinion that the entry of the ship at the custom-house, or the landing any part of her cargo, would be attended with great danger and difficulty, and would directly tend to destroy that peace and good order which ought to be preserved. An addition of twelve other gentlemen was then made to the former committee, and the general meeting adjourned till the arrival of the tea ship. Information being given of that, the price of tea was suddenly advanced, though it was owing to a general scarcity of that article; yet all the possessors of tea, in order to give strength to the opposition, readily agreed to reduce the price, and sell what remained in their hands at a reasonable rate. Nothing now remained, but to keep up a proper correspondence and connection with the other colonies, and to take all prudent and proper precautions on the arrival of the tea ship.

It is not easy to describe the anxiety and suspense of the city in this interval. Sundry reports of her arrival were received, which proved premature.—But on Saturday evening the 25th ult, an express came up from Chester, to inform the town that the tea ship, commanded by captain Ayres, with her detested cargo, was arrived there, having followed another ship up the river so far.

The committee met early the next morning, and being apprized of the arrival of Mr. Gilbert Barclay, the other consignee, who came passenger in the ship, they immediately went in a body to request his renunciation of the commission. Mr. Barclay politely attended the committee, at the first request; and being made acquainted with the sentiments of the city, and the danger to which the public liberties of America were exposed by this measure, he, after expressing the particular hardship of his situation, also resigned the commission, in a manner which affected every one present.

The committee then appointed three of their members to go to Chester, and two others to Gloucester Point, in order to have the earliest opportunity of meeting captain Ayres, and representing to him the sense of the public, respecting his voyage and cargo. The gentlemen who had set out for Chester, receiving intelligence that the vessel had weighed anchor about 12 o'clock, and proceeded to town, returned. About 2 o'clock she appeared in sight of Gloucester Point, where a number of inhabitants from the town had assembled with the gentlemen from the committee. As she passed along, she was hailed, and the captain requested not to proceed further, but to come on shore. This the captain complied with, and was handed through a lane made by the people, to the gentlemen appointed to confer with him. They represented to him the general sentiments, together with the danger and difficulties that would attend his refusal to comply with the wishes of the inhabitants; and finally desired him to proceed with them to town, where he would be more fully informed of the temper and resolution of the people. He was accordingly accompanied to town by a number of persons, where he was soon convinced of the truth and propriety of the representations which had been made to him—and agreed that, upon the desire of the inhabitants being publicly expressed, he would conduct himself accordingly. Some small rudeness being offered to the captain afterwards in the street, by some boys, several gentlemen interposed, and suppressed it before he received the least injury. Upon an hour's notice on Monday morning, a public meeting was called, and the state house not being sufficient to hold the numbers assembled, they adjourned into the square. This meeting is allowed by all to be the most respectable, both in the numbers and rank of those who attended it, that has been known in this city. After a short introduction, the following resolutions were not only agreed to, but the public approbation testified in the warmest manner:

1. *Resolved,* That the tea, on board the ship Polly, captain Ayres, shall not be landed.

2. That captain Ayres shall neither enter nor report his vessel at the custom-house.

3. That captain Ayres shall carry back the tea immediately.

4. That captain Ayres shall immediately send a pilot on board his vessel, with orders to take charge of her, and proceed to Reedy island next high water.

5. That the captain shall be allowed to stay in town till to-morrow, to provide necessaries for his voyage.

6. That he shall then be obliged to leave the town and proceed to his vessel, and make the best of his way out of our river and bay.

7. That a committee of four gentlemen be appointed to see these resolves carried into execution.

The assembly were then informed of the spirit and resolution of New York, Charleston, South Carolina, and the conduct of the people of Boston, whereupon it was unanimously resolved:

That this assembly highly approve of the conduct and spirit of the people of New York, Charleston, and Boston, and return their hearty thanks to the people of Boston for their resolution in destroying the tea, rather than suffering it to be landed.

The whole business was conducted with a decorum and order worthy the importance of the cause. Captain Ayres being present at this meeting, solemnly and publicly engaged, that he would literally comply with the sense of the city, as expressed in the above resolutions.

A proper supply of necessaries and fresh provisions being then procured, in about two hours the tea ship weighed anchor from Gloucester Point, where she lay within sight of the town, and has proceeded, with her whole cargo, on her return to the East India company.

The public think the conduct of those gentlemen, whose goods are returned on board the tea ship, ought not to pass unnoticed, as they have, upon this occasion, generously sacrificed their private interest to the public good.

Thus this important affair, in which there has been so glorious an exertion of public virtue and spirit, has been brought to a happy issue; by which the force of a law so obstinately persisted in, to the prejudice of the national commerce, for the sake of the principle on which it is founded (a right of taxing the Americans without their consent) has been effectually broken— and the foundations of American liberty more deeply laid than ever.

DESTRUCTION OF THE TEA INSPIRES A BALLAD

[*Written shortly after the Tea Party, reprinted in the*
National Gazette, *September 5, 1821*]

As near beauteous Boston lying,
    On the gently swelling flood,
Without jack or pendant flying,
    Three ill-fated tea-ships rode.

Just as glorious Sol was setting,
    On the wharf, a numerous crew,
Sons of freedom, fear forgetting,
    Suddenly appear'd in view.

Arm'd with hammers, axes, chisels,
   Weapons new for warlike deeds,
Towards the herbage freighted vessels,
   They approach'd with dreadful speed.

Hovering o'er their heads, in mid sky,
   Three bright angel forms were seen;
That was Hampden, this was Sidney,
   With fair Liberty between.

'Soon,' they cried, 'your foes you'll banish,
   'Soon your triumph will be won,
'Scarce shall setting Phoebus vanish,
   'Ere the deathless deed be done.'

Quick as shot the ships were boarded,
   Hatches burst and chests display'd;
Axes, hammers, help afforded,
   What a glorious crash they made!

Captains! once more hoist your streamers,
   Spread your sails and plough the wave!
Tell your masters they are dreamers,
   When they thought to cheat the brave.

4. GOVERNOR HUTCHINSON AND THE LEGISLATURE DEBATE AGAIN

THE GOVERNOR'S MESSAGE

[*Governor Thomas Hutchinson's address to the Council and House of Representatives, January 26, 1774*]

GENTLEMEN OF THE COUNCIL, AND
GENTLEMEN OF THE HOUSE OF REPRESENTATIVES.

The judicial proceedings of the governor and council, as the supreme court of Probate, and as the court for determining in cases of marriage and divorce, having been impeded in many instances, where the opinion of the governor has been different from that of the majority of the councillors present, the governor [has] always considered his consent as necessary to every judicial act. In the year 1771, I stated the arguments, as well against as for the claim of the governor; and his majesty having been pleased to order the case thus stated, to be laid before the lords of his majesty's most honorable privy council, I am now able to inform you, that it has been signified to me, to be his majesty's pleasure, that I do acquiesce in the determination of the majority of the councillors present, voting as a court for proving wills and administration, and deciding controversies concerning marriage and divorce, although I should differ in opinion from that majority. This order more immediately respects the council; nevertheless, the tender regard which his majesty has shown for the interest and convenience of his subjects, in a construction of the charter, different from what had been made by all his governors, ever since its first publication, make it proper for me to communicate the order to both houses.

I am required to signify to you his majesty's disapprobation of the appointment of committees of correspondence in various instances, which sit and act, during the recess of the general court, by prorogation.

ANSWER FROM THE HOUSE OF REPRESENTATIVES

[Reply to the Governor's Message by the Massachusetts House of Representatives, February 5, 1774]

MAY IT PLEASE YOUR EXCELLENCY,

It affords great satisfaction to this house to find, that his majesty has been pleased to put an end to an undue claim, heretofore made by the governors of this province, grounded upon a supposition that the consent of the chair was necessary to the validity of the judicial acts of the governor and council. Whereby their proceedings, when sitting as the supreme court of Probate, and as the court for determining in cases of marriage and divorce, have been so often impeded. The royal order, that the governor shall acquiesce in the determination of the majority of the council, respects not the council only, but the body of the people of this province. And his majesty has herein shewed his regard to justice, as well as the interest and convenience of his subjects, in rescuing a clause in the charter from a construction which, in the opinion of this house, was repugnant to the express meaning and intent of the charter, inconsistent with the idea of a court of justice, and dangerous to the rights and property of the subject.

Your excellency is pleased to inform the two houses, that you are required to signify to them his majesty's disapprobation of the appointment of committees of correspondence, in various instances, which sit and act, during the recess of the general court, by prorogation. You are not pleased to explain to us the grounds and reasons of his majesty's disapprobation; until we shall have such explanation laid before us, a full answer to this part of your speech will not be expected from us. We cannot, however, omit saying, upon this occasion, that while the common rights of the American subjects, continue to be attacked in various instances, and at times when the several assemblies are not sitting, it is highly necessary that they should correspond with each other, in order to unite in the most effectual means for the obtaining a redress of their grievances. And as the sitting of the general assemblies in this, and most of the colonies, depends upon the pleasure of the governors, who hold themselves under the direction of administration, it is to be expected, that the meeting of the assemblies will be so ordered, as that the intention proposed by a correspondence between them, will be impracticable, but by committees, to sit and act in the recess. We would, moreover, observe that, as it has been the practice for years past for the governor and lieutenant governor of this province, and other officers of the crown, at all times, to correspond with ministers of state, and persons of influence and distinction in the nation, in order to concert and carry on such measures of the British administration, as have been deemed by the colonists to be grievous to them, it cannot be thought unreasonable, or improper for the colonists to correspond with their agents, as well as with each other, to the end, that their grievances may be so explained to his majesty, as that, in his justice, he may afford them necessary relief. As this province has heretofore felt the great misfortune of the displeasure of our sovereign, by means of misrepresentations, permit us further to say, there is room to apprehend that his majesty has, in this instance, been misinformed and that there are good grounds to suspect, that those who may have misinformed him, have had in meditation further measures destructive to the colonies, which they were apprehensive would be defeated by means of committees of correspondence sitting and acting in the recess of the respective assemblies.

It must be pleasing to the good people of this province, to find that the heavy debt which had been incurred by their liberal aids, through the course of the late war, for the subduing his majesty's inveterate enemies, and extending his territory and dominion in America, is so nearly discharged. Whenever the house of representatives shall deem it incumbent upon them to provide for any future charges, it will be done, as it ought, by such ways and means as, after due deliberation, to them shall seem meet.

In the meantime, this house will employ the powers with which they are entrusted, in supporting his majesty's just authority in the province, according to the royal charter, and in despatching such public business as now properly lies before us. And, while we pursue such measures as tend, by God's blessing, to the redress of grievances, and to the restoration and establishment of the public liberty, we persuade ourselves, that we shall, at the same time, as far as in us lies, most effectually secure the tranquility and good order of the government, and the great end for which it was instituted, the safety and welfare of the people.

(The committee, by whom the foregoing was reported, were, the speaker, Mr. S. Adams, Mr. Hancock, Col. Warren, Col. Thayer, Col. Bowers, and Captain Derby.)

5. THE RIFT WITH ENGLAND IS REVIEWED

JOHN HANCOCK INVEIGHS AGAINST BRITISH TYRANNY

[Address by John Hancock to the people of Boston on the fourth anniversary of the Boston Massacre, March 5, 1774]

Security to the persons and properties of the governed, is so obviously the design and end of civil government, that to attempt a logical proof of it, would be like burning tapers at noonday, to assist the sun in enlightening the world; and it cannot be either virtuous or honorable, to attempt to support a government, of which this is not the great and principal basis; and it is to the last degree vicious and infamous to attempt to support a government, which manifestly tends to render the persons and properties of the governed insecure. Some boast of being friends to government; I am a friend to righteous government founded upon the principles of reason and justice; but I glory in publicly avowing my eternal enmity to tyranny. Is the present system, which the British administration have adopted for the government of the colonies, a righteous government? or is it tyranny?—Here suffer me to ask (and would to Heaven there could be an answer) what tenderness, what regard, respect or consideration has Great Britain shewn, in their late transactions for the security of the persons or properties of the inhabitants of the colonies? or rather, what have they omitted doing to destroy that security? they have declared that they have, ever had, and of right ought ever to have, full power to make laws of sufficient validity to bind the colonies in all cases whatever: they have exercised this pretended right by imposing a tax upon us without our consent; and lest we should shew some reluctance at parting with our property, her fleets and armies are sent to enforce their mad pretentions. The town of Boston, ever faithful to the British crown, has been invested by a British fleet: the troops of George the III have crossed the wide Atlantic, not to engage an enemy, but to assist a band of traitors in trampling on the rights and liberties of his most loyal subjects in America—those rights and liberties which, as a father, he ought ever to regard, and as a king, he is bound, in honor, to defend from violations, even at the risk of his own life.

Let not the history of the illustrious house of Brunswick inform posterity, that a king descended from that glorious monarch, George the II once sent his British subjects to conquer and enslave his subjects in America, but be perpetual infamy entailed upon that villain who dared to advise his master to such execrable measures; for it was easy to foresee the consequences which so naturally followed upon sending troops into America, to enforce obedience to acts of the British parliament, which neither God nor man ever empowered them to make. It was reasonable to expect that troops, who knew the errand they were sent upon, would treat the people whom they were to subjugate, with a cruelty and haughtiness, which too often buries the honorable character of a soldier in the disgraceful name of an unfeeling ruffian. The troops, upon their first arrival, took possession of our senate-house, and pointed their cannon against the judgment hall, and even continued them there whilst the supreme court of judicature for this province was actually sitting to decide upon the lives and fortunes of the king's subjects. Our streets nightly resounded with the noise of riot and debauchery; our peaceful citizens were hourly exposed to shameful insults, and often felt the effects of their violence and outrage.—But this was not all: as though they thought it not enough to violate our civil rights, they endeavored to deprive us of the enjoyment of our religious privileges; to viciate our morals, and thereby render us deserving of destruction. . . .

But I forbear, and come reluctantly to the transactions of that dismal night, when in such quick succession we felt the extremes of grief, astonishment and rage; when Heaven in anger, for a dreadful moment suffered hell to take the reins; when Satan with his chosen band opened the sluices of New-England's blood, and sacrilegiously polluted our land with the dead bodies of her guiltless sons. Let this sad tale of death never be told without a tear; let not the heaving bosom cease to burn with a manly indignation at the barbarous story, through the long tracts of future time: let every parent tell the shameful story to his listening children 'til tears of pity glisten in their eyes, and boiling passions shake their tender frames; and whilst the anniversary of that ill-fated night is kept a jubilee in the grim court of pandaemonium, let all America join in one common prayer to heaven, that the inhuman, unprovoked murders of the fifth of March, 1770, planned by Hillsborough, and a knot of treacherous knaves in Boston, and executed by the cruel hand of Preston and his sanguinary coadjutors, may ever stand on history without a parallel. . . . Tell me, ye bloody butchers! ye villains high and low! ye wretches who contrived, as well as you who executed the inhuman deed! do you not feel the goads and stings of conscious guilt pierce through your savage bosoms? though some of you may think yourselves exalted to a height that bids defiance to human justice, and others shroud yourselves beneath the mask of hypocrisy, and build your hopes of safety on the low arts of cunning, chicanery and falsehood; yet do you not sometimes feel the gnawings of that worm which never dies? do not the injured shades of Maverick, Gray, Caldwell, Attucks and Carr, attend you in your solitary walks, arrest you even in the midst of your debaucheries, and fill even your dreams with terror? . . .

Ye dark designing knaves, ye murderers, parricides! how dare you tread upon the earth, which has drank in the blood of slaughtered innocents, shed by your wicked hands? . . .

But I gladly quit the gloomy theme of death, and leave you to improve the thought of that important day, when our naked souls must stand before that being, from whom nothing can be hid. I would not dwell too long upon the horrid effects which have already followed from quartering regular troops in this town; let our misfortunes teach posterity to guard against such evils for the future. Standing armies are sometimes (I would by no means say generally, much less universally) composed of persons who have rendered themselves unfit to live in civil society; who have no other motives of conduct than those which a desire of the present gratification of their passions suggests; who have no property in any country; men who have given up their own liberties, and envy those who enjoy liberty; who are equally indifferent to the glory of a George or a Louis; who for the addition of one penny a day to their wages, would desert from the Christian cross, and fight under the crescent of the Turkish sultan, from such men as these, usurping Caesar passed the Rubicon; with such as these he humbled mighty Rome, and forced the mistress of the world to own a master in a traitor. These are the men whom sceptered robbers now employ to frustrate the designs of God and render vain the bounties which his gracious hand pours indiscriminately upon his creatures. By these the miserable slaves in Turkey, Persia, and many other extensive countries, are rendered truly wretched, though their air is salubrious, and their soil luxuriously fertile. By these, France and Spain, though blessed by nature with all that administers to the convenience of life, have been reduced to that contemptible state in which they now appear; and by these Britain —— but if I was possessed of the gift of prophecy, I dare not, except by divine command, unfold the leaves on which the destiny of that once powerful kingdom is inscribed. . . .

The British ministry have annexed a salary to the office of the governor of this province, to be paid out of a revenue, raised in America without our consent. They have attempted to render our courts of justice the instruments of extending the authority of acts of the British parliament over this colony, by making the judges dependent on the British administration for their support. But this people will never be enslaved with their eyes open. The moment they knew that the governor was not such a governor as the charter of the province points out, he lost his power of hurting them. They were alarmed; they suspected him, have guarded against him, and he has found that a wise and a brave people, when they know their danger, are fruitful in expedients to escape it.

The courts of judicature also so far lost their dignity, by being supposed to be under an undue influence, that our representatives thought it absolutely necessary to resolve that they were bound to declare that they would not receive any other salary besides that which the general court should grant them; and if they did not make this declaration, that it would be the duty of the house to impeach them.

Great expectations were also formed from the artful scheme of allowing the East India company to export tea to America, upon their own account. This certainly, had it succeeded, would have effected the purpose of the contrivers, and gratified the most sanguine wishes of our adversaries. We soon should have found our trade in the hands of foreigners, and taxes imposed on every thing which we consumed; nor would it have been strange, if, in a few years, a company in London should have purchased an exclusive right of trading to America. But their plot was soon discovered. The people soon were aware of the poison which, with so much craft and subtilty, had been concealed: loss and disgrace ensued: and, perhaps, this long-concerted master-piece of policy, may issue in the total disuse of tea, in this country, which will eventually be the saving of the lives and the estates of thousands —yet while we rejoice that the adversary has not hitherto prevailed against us, let us by no means put off the harness. Restless malice, and disappointed ambition, will still suggest new measures to our inveterate enemies. Therefore let us also be ready to take the field whenever danger calls; let us be united and strengthen the hands of each other, by promoting a general union among us. Much has been done by the committees of correspondence for this and the other towns of this province, towards uniting the inhabitants; let them still go on and prosper. Much has been done by the committees of correspondence, for the houses of assembly, in this and our sister colonies, for uniting the inhabitants of the whole continent, for the security of their common interest. May success ever attend their generous endeavors. But permit me here to suggest a general congress of deputies, from the several houses of assembly, on the continent, as the most effectual method of establishing such an union, as the present posture of our affairs requires. At such a congress a firm foundation may be laid for the security of our rights and liberties, a system may be formed for our common safety, by a strict adherence to which, we shall be able to frustrate any attempts to overthrow our constitution; restore peace and harmony to America, and secure honor and wealth to Great Britain even against the inclinations of her ministers, whose duty it is to study her welfare; and we shall also free ourselves from those unmannerly pillagers who impudently tell us, that they are licensed by an act of the British parliament to thrust their dirty hands into the pockets of every American.

III

PARLIAMENT DEBATES COLONIAL RIGHTS,

1766-1775

IN THEIR ATTEMPT to define the rights of Englishmen and to clarify the relationship between colonial liberties and imperial authority, the Americans had support from a number of prominent native Englishmen. Most prestigious was William Pitt, after 1766 the Earl of Chatham. On several occasions Chatham argued the American cause in the House of Lords (p. 82), but unfortunately for the American position his influence was never great enough to deter the government's blundering colonial policy. Nor were efforts in the House of Commons by Colonel Isaac Barré, General Henry Conway, and George Johnstone, governor of West Florida from 1763 to 1767 (p. 84). For every champion of the American cause there were a dozen or more advocates of a narrow definition of the rights of Englishmen overseas (p. 89). But for various reasons—some selfish, some altruistic, and most a subtle blend of many motives—the colonial position continued to be supported by articulate spokesmen in Parliament, especially during the drafting of punitive legislation following the Boston Tea Party. Representative of such spokesmen were Bishop Jonathan Shipley of St. Asaph's, who criticized the government's plan to alter the administration of Massachusetts (p. 96), and Edmund Burke, whose famous plea for conciliation between the mother country and her colonies was as memorable for its logic as for its passion (p. 106).

1. THE COLONISTS FIND SUPPORT IN PARLIAMENT

THE EARL OF CHATHAM CONDEMNS TAXATION WITHOUT REPRESENTATION

[Speech against the Declaratory Act, by William Pitt, Earl of Chatham, in the House of Lords, 1766]

When I spoke last on this subject, I thought I had delivered my sentiments so fully, and supported them with such reasons, and such authorities, that I apprehended I should be under no necessity of troubling your lordship again. But I am compelled to rise up and beg your further indulgence. . . .

My position is this—I repeat it—I will maintain it to my last hour—taxation and representation are inseparable: this position is founded on the laws of nature; it is itself an eternal law of nature; for whatever is a man's own, is absolutely his own; no man has a right to take it from him without his consent, either expressed by himself or representative; whoever attempts to do it, attempts an injury; whoever does it, commits a robbery; he throws down and destroys the distinction between liberty and slavery. Taxation and representation are coeval with, and essential to, this constitution. I wish the maxim of Machiavel was followed, that of examining a constitution, at certain periods, according to its first principles; this would correct abuses and supply defects. I wish the times would bear it, and that men's minds were cool enough to enter upon such a task, and that the representative authority of this kingdom was more equally settled. I am sure some histories of late published, have done great mischief; to endeavor to fix the era when the house of commons began in this kingdom, is a most pernicious and destructive attempt; to fix it in an Edward's or Henry's reign, is owing to the idle dreams of some whimsical, ill-judging antiquarians: But, my lord, this is a point too important to be left to such wrong-headed people. When did the house of commons first begin? When! my lord? It began with the constitution, it grew up with the constitution; there is not a blade of grass growing in the most obscure corner of this kingdom, which was not ever represented since the constitution began; there is not a blade of grass which, when taxed, was not taxed by the consent of the proprietor.

There is a history written by one Carte, a history that most people see through; and there is another favorite history, much read and admired. I will not name the author, your lordship must know from whence he pilfered his notions concerning the first beginning of the house of commons. My lord, I challenge any one to point out the time when any tax was laid upon any person by parliament, that person being unrepresented in parliament. The parliament laid a tax upon the palatinate of Chester, and ordered commissioners to collect it there, as commissioners were ordered to collect it in other counties; but the palatinate refused to comply; they addressed the king by petition, setting forth, that the English parliament had no right to tax them; that they had a parliament of their own; they had always taxed themselves, and therefore desired the king to order his commissioners not to proceed. My lord, the king received the petition; he did not declare them either seditious or rebellious, but allowed their plea, and they taxed themselves. Your lordship may see both the petition and the king's answer, in the records in the Tower. The clergy taxed themselves; when the parliament attempted to tax them, they stoutly refused, said they were not represented there; that they had a parliament of their own, which presented the clergy; that they would tax themselves; that they did so. Much stress has been laid upon Wales, before it was united as it now is, as if the king, standing in the place of the former princes of that country, raised money by his own authority; but the real facts are otherwise: For I find that, long before Wales was subdued, the northern counties of that principality had representatives and a parliament or assembly. As to Ireland, my lord, before that kingdom had a parliament, as it now has, if your lordship will examine the old records, you will find that, when a tax was to be laid on that country, the Irish sent over here representatives; and the same records will inform your lordship what wages those representatives received from their constituents. In short, my lord, from the whole of our history, from the earliest period, you will find that taxation and representation were always united; so true are the words of that consummate reasoner and politician Mr. Locke. I before alluded to his book; I have again consulted him; and finding that he writes so applicable to the subject in hand, and so much in favor of my sentiments I beg your lordship's leave to read a little of his book.

"The supreme power cannot take from any man, any part of his property without his own consent;" and B. II. p. 136-139 and particularly 140. Such are the words of this great man, and which are well worth your lordship's serious attention. His principles are drawn from the heart of our constitution, which he thoroughly understood, and will last as long as that shall last: and, to his immortal honor, I know not what, under Providence, the revolution and all its happy effects are more owing than to the principles of government laid down by Mr. Locke. For these reasons, my lord, I can never give my assent to any bill for taxing the American colonies, while they remain unrepresented, for, as to the distinction of a virtual representation, it is so absurd as not to deserve an answer; I therefore pass it over with contempt. The forefathers of the Americans did not leave their native country, and subject themselves to every danger and distress, to be reduced to a state of slavery; they did not give up their rights: they looked for protection, and not for chains, from their mother country; by her they expected to be defended in the possession of their property, and not to be deprived of it: for should the present power continue, there is nothing which they can call their own: or, to use the words of Mr. Locke, "what property have they in that which another may by right take when he pleases to himself?"

GOVERNOR JOHNSTONE CRITICIZES THE BOSTON PORT BILL

[Speech by Governor George Johnstone in the House of Commons, March 25, 1774]

MR. SPEAKER—

It may appear arrogant in a member so inferior as I confess myself to be, to offer objections to a bill so extensive in its consequences under every consideration, especially after it must have been so maturely considered, in every article, by men so distinguished by their talents and high situations in office, besides the general applause which has followed the bill in its rapid progress through this house. Nevertheless though naturally diffident of my opinion, when I had the good or bad fortune (I don't know which to term it) of prognosticating to the chairman of the East-India company, the consequences of sending this tea, on their own account, to America, and that the event has literally fulfilled my words, as it is well known to some members now in my eye, it makes me more confident in warning the house of what I apprehend will be the consequences of this bill.

I told the chairman of the East-India company, first in conversation, on asking my opinion, and afterwards by letter, that the evidence might appear in the progress of things, that I conceived the East-India company exporting tea on their own account was, under every consideration of their situation and institution, wrong, but under the present discontents and disputed matters of government in America, criminally absurd, because they were presenting themselves as the butt in the controversy, where they would probably come off with the loss of the whole. The event has justified my prediction; for whatever re-payment the company may obtain from the town of Boston, under those cruel coercive measures now proposed, (the effect of which I still doubt) yet the company must remain great losers, even if the other provinces, equally culpable, are made to refund the loss arising from their conduct; because it was not supplies of cash at a distant period the company wanted, but an immediate supply to answer a temporary exigency, which a combination of the enemies of the company had produced.

I now venture to predict to this house, that the effect of the present bill must be productive of a general confederacy, to resist the power of this country. It is irritating, tempting, nay, inviting men to those deeds, by ineffectual expedients, the abortions of an undecisive mind, incapable of comprehending the chain of consequences which must result from such a law. I am not one of those who believe, that distant provinces can be retained in their duty by preaching or enchantments; I believe that force of power, conducted with wisdom, are the means of securing regular obedience under every establishment, but that such force should never be applied to any degree of rigor, unless it shall carry the general approbation of mankind in the execution. However much such approbation may prevail at the particular moment in this house, it is impossible to believe the sense of Great Britain, or the sense of America, can go to the punishing a particular town, for resisting the payment of the tea-tax, which is universally odious throughout America, and is held in ridicule and contempt by every thinking man in this country. The question of taxing America is sufficiently nice to palliate resistance, if the subject had never been litigated in this country; but, after the highest characters in the state had declared against the right of this country to impose taxes on America, for the purposes of revenue; after the general voice of the senate had concurred in repealing the stamp-act, upon that principle; after those men, who had maintained these doctrines, had been promoted by his majesty to the first stations in the administration of civil and judicial affairs, there is so much mitigation to be pleaded in favor of the Americans, from those circumstances (allowing them in an error at present) that every man must feel the height of cruelty, by enforcing contrary maxims, with any degree of severity at first, before due warning is given.

It is in vain to say that Boston is more culpable than the other colonies; sending the ships from thence, and obliging them to return to England, is a more solemn and deliberate act of resistance, than the outrage committed by persons in disguise, in the night, when the ship refused to depart.—That the blocking up of the harbor of Boston, to prevent the importation of goods which are to pay for them, is a measure equally absurd as if the parliament here, upon the resistance which was made to their resolution, by the riots of

Brentford, and other disturbances in the county of Middlesex, had decreed, by way of punishment, that the freeholders should have been prohibited from sowing wheat. For whose benefit do the inhabitants of Boston toil and labor! The springs in the circle of commerce bear so nicely on each other, that few men can tell by interrupting one, the degree and extent to which the rest may be exposed. By excluding the importation of molasses, and the exportation of that spirit which is distilled at Boston, the whole Guinea trade will be affected, and in consequence the sugar trade that depends upon it. In extending this kind of punishment to the other colonies, every one must see the danger; and yet, if it can be approved for one, the same arguments will hold good to approve or reject it respecting the other. But let any man figure to himself the consequences to this country, if a similar punishment was applied to the colony of Virginia; £300,000 a year diminution in revenue, besides the loss of all the foreign contracts, and perhaps of that beneficial trade forever. Notwithstanding the general approbation which has been given to this bill, and the loud applauses which have been re-echoed to every word of the noble lord in explaining it, yet no man will be bold enough to say, that this partial punishment is a remedy for the general disease, and yet without knowing what is to follow, no man can be vindicated (even supposing the bill right in part) for giving his assent to it. Those gentlemen who are in the secrets of the cabinet, and know how assuredly every proposition from them is adopted by this house, may be excused for their sanguine acclamations in favor of the measure. But the general mass, who must be equally ignorant with myself of what is to follow, can have no excuse for giving their assent so readily for punishing their fellow subjects in so unprecedented a manner, and their eager zeal serves only to show how ready they are to obey the will of another, without exercising their own judgment in the case. If the government of this country is resisted in America, my opinion is, instead of removing the seat of government in the colony, and forcing the elements to bend to our will, which is impossible, that an effectual force should be carried to the heart of the colony resisting, to crush rebellion in the bud, before a general confederacy can be formed. In the present case we abandon the government, and drive the inhabitants to despair, leaving the multitude a prey to any ambitious spirit that may arise. For my own part I am convinced, from experience in the colonies, that good government may be conducted there upon rational grounds, as well as in this country; but the power and means of governing, rewards and punishments, are taken from your supreme executive magistrate in every sense, and then you are surprised that all order and obedience should cease. The colonies can only be governed by their assemblies, as

England by the house of commons: the patent officers, as well as those in the customs, which were formerly given, at the recommendation of the governors, to men supporting government, and residing in the provinces, are now given in reversion, three or four lives deep, to men living in this country. The command of the military, which was another great source of respect and obedience, is likewise taken from the governor; so that in truth he remains an insignificant pageant of state, fit only to transmit tedious accounts of his own ridiculous situation: or, like the doctor of Sorbonne, to debate with his assembly about abstract doctrines in government.

I am far from wishing to throw any blame upon governor Hutchinson, or to condemn him, like the town of Boston, unheard. The absence of the man, and the general clamor against him, will restrain me from saying many things respecting his conduct, which appear reprehensible. But I cannot admit a passage in the speech of a noble lord to pass unnoticed. His lordship alleges, "that the governor could not apply to the admiral in the harbor, or to the commanding officer of the troops in the castle, for the protection of the custom-house officers, as well as the teas in question, without the advice of his council." But I beg leave to inform the noble lord, as I served in that station myself, that there is a volume of instructions to every governor on this subject, whereby he is commanded, under the severest penalties, "to give all kind of protection to trade and commerce, as well as to the officers of his majesty's customs, by his own authority, without the necessity of acting through his council." Nor can I conceive a possible excuse for the destruction of those teas, while two men of war lay in the harbor, without the least application having been made to the admiral for protection, during so long a transaction.

The first essential point in those disputes which are now likely to become so serious, by the weakness of administration in this country, in following no connected plan, either of force or favor, but constantly vibrating between the two, is to put ourselves in the right, and for this purpose I would recommend the immediate repeal of the tea duty, which can be vindicated upon no principles, either of commerce or policy. Men may allege this would be giving up the point. But if we have no better points to dispute upon, I am ready to yield the argument. Raising taxes in America for the purposes of revenue, I maintain to be unnecessary and dangerous. A stamp act, as a measure of police, varied for the different governments, and leaving the revenue raised thereby to be appropriated by the respective legislatures, I hold to be a measure of the highest efficacy, for maintaining a due obedience to the authority of this country, and prolonging that dependence for ages to come. How far it can be executed after what has already passed, I am rather diffident; but of this I am certain, that in case Great Britain is deprived of executing a measure of that nature, which, by pervading every transaction, secures the execution in itself, she has lost one of the greatest engines for supporting her influence throughout the empire without oppression. Some men, who are for simplifying government to their own comprehensions, will not allow they can conceive that the supreme legislative authority shall not be paramount in all things; and taxation being fully comprehended in legislation, they argue, that the power of the one must necessarily follow that of the other, and yet we find mankind possessed of privileges, which are not to be violated in the most arbitrary countries. The province of Languedoc is a striking example in refutation of the doctrines respecting taxation, which are held by such narrow observers. The kingdom of Ireland is another instance in our dominions. There is not one argument which can apply for exempting Ireland from taxation by the parliament of Great Britain, that does not equally protect the colonies from the power of such partial judges. Every man should now call to his remembrance by what obstinate infatuation Philip the II came to lose the United Provinces. Can it be supposed that, in a nation so wise as Spain was at that time, that no man perceived the injustice and futility of the measure in dispute? But I can easily suppose, from the pride of authority where our vanity is so much flattered, that no man durst venture a proposition for receding from that cruel measure after it had been resisted by violence.

These are the general heads:

The particular objections to the bill are, first, for continuing the punishment "until satisfaction shall be made to the India company," without stating the amount, or what that satisfaction shall be. Next, "until peace and good order shall be certified to be restored," when it is impossible, as to the subject in dispute, that such certificate can [ever] be granted, because the customhouse officers are removed, and all trade and commerce prohibited. The numerous disputes and litigations which must necessarily arise in carrying this law into execution, on contract made by parties before they could be apprised of it, and the despatch of ships in harbor under the limited time, without any exception for the desertion of seamen, or wind and weather, is altogether melancholy to consider! The power given to the admiral, or chief commander, to order the ships returning from foreign voyages to such stations, as he shall direct, is wild, vexatious, indefinite. That of permitting his majesty to alter the value of all the property in the town of Boston, upon restoring the port, by affixing such quays and wharves, as he only shall appoint, for landing and shipping of goods, is liable to such misrepresentation and abuse, that I expect to see every evil follow the exercise of it, and it must create infinite jealousies and distractions among the people.

2. PARLIAMENT ARGUES THE COERCIVE MEASURES

COMMONS DEBATES THE MASSACHUSETTS GOVERNMENT ACT

[*Record of debate in the House of Commons, April 26, 1774*]

MR. FULLER said, he did not rise to make any debate, for he was not enabled as yet to form any opinion whether the bill before the house was a proper bill or not. . . .

SIR GEORGE SAVILE said, he had not troubled the house before on the occasion, but he could not help observing, that the measure now before the house was a very doubtful and dangerous one; doubtful as to the propriety of regulation, and dangerous as to its consequence; that charters by government were sacred things, and are only to be taken away by a due course of law, either as a punishment for an offence, or for a breach of the contract, and that can only be by evidence of the facts; nor could he conceive that in either of those cases there could be any such thing as proceeding without a fair hearing of both parties. "This measure before us seems to be a most extraordinary exertion of legislative power. Let us suppose a lease granted to a man, wherein was a covenant, the breach of which would subject him to a forfeiture of his lease—would not a court of justice require evidence of the fact? Why, then, will you proceed different from the line which is always observed in courts of justice? You are now going to alter the charter because it is convenient. In what manner does the house mean to take away this charter, when in fact they refuse to hear the parties, or to go through a legal course of evidence of the facts. Chartered rights have, at all times, when attempted to be altered or taken away, occasioned much bloodshed and strife; and whatever persons in this house have advanced, that they do not proceed upon this business but with trembling hands, I do also assure them that I have shown my fears upon this occasion; for I have run away from every question, except one, to which I gave my negative. I do not like to be present at a business, which I think inconsistent with the dignity and justice of this house; I tremble when I am, for fear of the consequences; and think it a little extraordinary that Mr. Bollan should be admitted to be heard as an American agent in the house of lords, when in the house of commons he was refused. I believe it is true, that the facts set forth in his petition to this house, were different from those which he presented to the house of lords; in one declaring himself an inhabitant of Boston, in the other omitting it. I cannot conceive it possible to proceed on this bill upon the small ground of evidence which you have had."

MR. WELBORE ELLIS. "I must rise, sir, with great confidence, when I differ from the honorable gentleman who spoke last, whose abilities are so eminently great; but I think, sir, that chartered rights are by no means those sacred things which never can be altered; they are vested in the crown as a prerogative, for the good of the people at large; if the supreme legislature find that those charters so granted, are both unfit and inconvenient for the public utility, they have a right to make them fit and convenient; wherever private property is concerned, the legislature will not take it away without making a full recompense; but wherever the regulation of public matter is the object, they have a right to correct, control, or take it away, as may best suit the public welfare. The crown may sometimes grant improper powers with regard to governments that are to be established; will it not be highly proper and necessary, that the legislature, seeing in what manner the crown has been ill-advised, should take into their consideration, and alter it as far as necessary. It is the legislature's duty to correct the errors that have been established in the infancy of that constitution, and regulate them for the public welfare. Is a charter, not consistent with the public good, to be continued? The honorable gentleman says, much bloodshed has been occasioned by taking away or altering of chartered rights; I grant it; but it has always been where encroachments have been made by improper parties, and the attack has been carried on by improper powers. He also says, this form of government in America ought not to be altered without hearing the parties; the papers on your table, surely, are sufficient evidence of what they have to say in their defence—look only into the letter, dated the 19th November, 1773, wherein the governor applied to the council for advice, and they neglected giving it to him! and also wherein a petition was presented to the council by certain persons who applied for protection to their property during these disturbances, the council, without giving any answer, adjourned for ten days, and the governor was not able to do any thing himself without their opinion. Look again, sir, into the resolution which the council came to when they met again, stating the total insufficiency of their power. This, surely, sir, is an evidence competent to ground this bill upon. We have now got no farther than just to alter these two parts, as stated by themselves. Surely, sir, that form of government which will not protect your property, ought to be altered in such a manner as it may be able to do it."

GENERAL CONWAY. "What I intend to say will not delay the house long. I am very sure what I intend to say will little deserve the attention of the house; but the subject is of that importance, that it requires it. The consequence of this bill will be very important and dangerous. Parliament cannot break into a right without hearing the parties. The question then is simply this:—Have they been heard? What! because the papers say a murder has been committed, does it follow they have proved it? *Audi alteram partem,* is a maxim I have long adhered to; but it is something so inconsistent with parliamentary proceedings not to do it, that I am astonished at it. The council are blamed because they did not give that advice to the governor which he wanted. I think, sir, the governor might have acted alone, without their assistance. Gentlemen will consider, that this is not only the charter of Boston, or of any particular part, but the charter of *all* America. Are the Americans not to be heard?—Do not choose to consent and agree about appointing an agent? I think there is no harm upon this occasion, in stretching a point; and I would rather have Mr. Bollan, as an agent of America (though he is irregular in his appointment) sooner than leave it to be said, that this bill passed without it." —*The house being vociferous,* he said, "I am afraid I tire the house with my weak voice; if that is the case, I will not proceed, but I do think, and it is my sincere opinion, that we are the aggressors and innovators, and not the colonies. We have irritated and forced laws upon them for these six or seven years last past. We have enacted such a variety of laws, with these new taxes, together with a refusal to repeal the trifling duty on tea; all these things have served no other purpose but to distress and perplex. I think the Americans have done no more than every subject would do in an arbitrary state where laws are imposed against their will. In my conscience, I think, taxation and legislation are in this case inconsistent. Have you not a legislative right over Ireland? And yet no one will dare to say we have a right to tax. These acts respecting America, will involve this country and its ministers in misfortunes, and I wish I may not add, in ruin."

LORD NORTH. "I do not consider this matter of regulation to be taking away their charters in such manner as is represented; it is a regulation of government to assist the crown; it appears to me not to be a matter of political expediency, but of necessity. If it does not stand upon that ground, it stands on nothing. The account which has just now been read to you is an authentic paper, transmitted to government here, showing that the council refused in every case their assistance and advice; and will this country sit still when they see the colony proceeding against your own subjects, tarring and feathering your servants, denying your laws and authority, refusing every direction and advice which you send? Are we, sir, seeing all this, to be silent, and give the governor no support? Gentlemen say, let the colony come to your bar, and be heard in their defence; though it is not likely that they will come, when they deny your authority in every instance. Can we remain in this situation long? We must effectually take some measures to correct and amend the defects of that government. I have heard so many different opinions in regard to our conduct in America, I hardly know how to answer them. The honorable gentleman who spoke last, formerly blamed the tame and insipid conduct of government; now he condemns this measure as harsh and severe. The Americans have tarred and feathered your subjects, plundered your merchants, burnt your ships, denied all obedience to your laws and authority; yet so clement and forbearing has our conduct been, that it is incumbent upon us now to take a different course. Whatever may be the consequence, we must risk something; if we do not, all is over. The measure now proposed, is nothing more than taking the election of counsellors out of the hands of those people, who are continually acting in defiance and resistance of your laws. It has also been said by gentlemen—send for the Americans to your bar—give them redress a twelve-month hence. Surely, sir, this cannot be the language that is to give effectual relief to America; it is not, I say again, political convenience, it is political necessity that urges this measure; if this is not the proper method, show me any other which is preferable, and I will postpone it."

SIR GEORGE YOUNG. "It remains to me, sir, that it is unanswered and unanswerable, what has been advanced by the honorable gentleman who spoke second, that the parties should be heard, though even at a twelve-month hence. Nothing, sir, but fatal necessity can countenance this measure. No body of men ought to be proceeded against without being heard, much less ought the regulation of a whole government to take place, without the parties attending in their defence against such alterations."

GOVERNOR [GEORGE] JOHNSTONE. "I see, sir, a great disposition in this house to proceed in this business without knowing any thing of the constitution of America; several inconveniences will arise if the sheriff is to be appointed by the governor; the jury will, of course, be biased by some influence or other; special juries will be most liable to this. (Here the governor gave an account of the different riots which had happened in England, and compared them with what he called the false accounts of those from America.) "I impute . . . all the misfortunes which have happened in America, to the taking away the power of the governor. No man of common sense can apprehend that the governor would ever have gone two or three days into the country, during these disturbances, if he had the command of the military power. The natural spirit of man would be fired, in such a manner, as to actuate himself to shew resistance; but in this governor no power was lodged. I disapprove much of the measure which is before us, and I cannot but think its consequences will be prejudicial."

MR. C. JENKINSON. "I rise, sir, only to observe, that if the colony has not that power within itself to maintain its own peace and order, the legislature should, and ought to have. Let me ask, sir, whether the colony took any step, in any shape, to quell the riots and disturbances? No, they took none. Let me ask again, whether all the checks and control that are necessary, are not put into the commission of the governments? Much has been said about hearing the parties, and taking away their chartered rights; I am of opinion, that where the right is a high political regulation, you are not in that instance bound to hear them; but the hearing of parties is necessary where private property is concerned. It is not only in the late proceedings, but in all former, that they have denied your authority over them; they have refused protection to his majesty's subjects, and in every instance disobeyed the laws of this country; either let this country forsake its trade with America, or let us give that due protection to it which safety requires."

MR. HARRIS. "I cannot see, sir, any reason for so wide a separation between America and England as other gentlemen are apt to think there ought to be; that country, sir, was hatched from this, and I hope we shall always keep it under the shadow of our wings. It has been said, no representation, no taxation. This was the system formerly adopted, but I do not find it authorized in any book of jurisprudence, nor do I deem it to be a doctrine either reasonable or constitutional. I insist upon it, they are bound to obey both the crown and parliament. The last twelve years of our proceedings have been a scene of lenity and inactivity. Let us proceed and mend our method, or else I shall believe, as an honorable gentleman has observed, that we are the aggressors."

SIR EDWARD ASTLEY. "If we have had a twelve years lenity and inactivity, I hope we shall not now proceed to have a twelve years cruelty and oppression. By the resolution and firmness which I perceive in the house, it seems to indicate a perseverance in the measure now proposed, which I deem to be a harsh one, and unworthy of a British legislature."

MR. WARD. (The house was very noisy during the few words which he said.)—He found fault with the charter being left too much, as to the execution of its power, in the people and he could not think the legislature was doing any thing, which it had not a right to do, as he had looked upon all charters to be granted with a particular clause in it expressing that it should not be taken away but by the parliament.

GOVERNOR POWNALL. "I beg leave to set some gentlemen right, who have erred with regard to the charters of America. The appointment of several of the officers is in the governor. The charter of Boston directs, that the governor shall ask the council for advice, but it does not say he shall not act without it, if they refuse to give it. It is said it is criminal to do any thing without advice of the council; I differ greatly, sir, from that doctrine; for I myself have acted without it in putting an end to disturbances, in preserving the peace and good order of the place; if I had been governor during the late disturbances, I would have given an order for the military power to attend, and then let me have seen what officer dare disobey. I think the council are much to blame for not co-operating and assisting the governor, but I think the governor might have acted without the council. The council are inexcusable, though not criminal, as they are not obliged to give it. I, sir, for my part, shall give my last opinion. I have always been in one way of thinking with regard to America, which I have both given here and wrote to America. They have all along tended to one point; but it is now no longer matter of opinion. Things are now come to action; and I must be free to tell the house, that the Americans will resist these measures: they are prepared to do it. I do not mean by arms, but by the conversation of public town meeting; they now send their letter by couriers, instead of the post, from one town to another; and I can say your post office will very soon be deprived of its revenue. With regard to the officers who command the militia of that country, they will have them of their own appointment, and not from government; but I will never more give an opinion concerning America in this house; those I have given have been disregarded."

MR. RIGBY. "Upon my word, sir, what was just now said, is very worthy the consideration of this house; and if, from what the honorable gentleman says, it is true, and I believe he is well informed, it appears, that America is preparing to arms; and that the deliberations of their town meetings tend chiefly to oppose the measures of this country by force. He has told you, sir, that the Americans will appoint other officers than those sent by government to command their troops. He has told you that the post office is established on their account from town to town, in order to carry their traitorous correspondence from one to another. He has told you the post office revenue will soon be annihilated. If these things are true, sir, I find we have been the aggressors, by continually doing acts of lenity for these twelve years last past. I think, sir, and I speak out boldly when I say it, that this country has a right to tax America; but, sir, it is matter of astonishment to me, how an honorable gentleman (Mr. Conway) can be the author of bringing in of declaratory law over all America, and yet saying at one and the same time, that we have no

"The Alternative of Williams-Burg," a British cartoon of 1775 showing a Virginia loyalist signing a patriot resolution against importing British goods. His alternative appears in the background—the gallows, and a barrel of tar and feathers. The keg of tobacco serving as a table is addressed to John Wilkes, one of the few members of Parliament who staunchly defended the colonists' rights.

A contemporary anti-administration British cartoon celebrates the repeal of the Stamp Act in 1766.

John Dickinson, patriot pamphleteer from Delaware and Pennsylvania. Engraved by J. B. Forrest from a portrait by Charles W. Peale in 1770.

The Green Dragon Tavern, Boston, where Samuel Adams, John Hancock, and other New England patriots often met, and where the Boston Tea Party may have been planned.

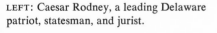

LEFT: Caesar Rodney, a leading Delaware patriot, statesman, and jurist.

CENTER: George Grenville, British Prime Minister who was responsible for the Stamp Act of 1765.

RIGHT: Thomas Hutchinson, Lieutenant Governor, 1758–1771, and Royal Governor, 1771–1774, of Massachusetts, who chose loyalty to the Empire over loyalty to his colony.

A broadside reporting the Boston Massacre of March 5, 1770,
and featuring Paul Revere's famous engraving of the event.

Boston's Old State House, the site of many gatherings of New England patriots and
the scene of the Massacre, on State Street, as it looked some years after the event.

"Destruction of the Tea in Boston Harbour," an early engraving showing the "Indians" of Boston destroying the East India Company's Tea on December 16, 1773.

A New York broadside condemning the Tea Act, 1773.

Paul Revere, Boston silversmith and engraver, who is better remembered for alerting the Massachusetts countryside of the coming of Major Pitcairn's expedition to Lexington and Concord, April 18-19, 1775. Portrait by John Singleton Copley.

A fanciful German version of the destruction of the statue of George III at the foot of Broadway in New York City. Engraved by François Xavier Habermann and first published in Augsburg in 177

Thomas Paine, whose *Common Sense* crystalized sentiment for independence.

A broadside announcing a meeting of the New York So of Liberty, issued on the day of the Boston Tea Part

"New Method of Macarony Making, as Practised
Boston," a British cartoon published in 1774 depict-
a royal customs officer receiving a coat of tar and
thers, and a thorough drenching with tea, for trying
land East India Company tea in the fall of 1773.

John Adams, Massachusetts lawyer,
patriot leader, and diplomat.

A broadside announcing
American casualties at the battles of
Lexington and Concord.

A LIST of the Names of the

PROVINCIALS who were Killed and
Wounded in the late Engagement with
His Majesty's Troops at *Concord*, &c.

KILLED.

Of *Lexington*.

* Mr. Robert Munroe,
* Mr. Jonas Parker,
* Mr. Samuel Hadley,
* Mr. Jona^n Harrington,
* Mr. Caleb Harrington,
* Mr. Isaac Muzzy,
* Mr. John Brown,
Mr. John Raymond,
Mr. Nathaniel Wyman,
Mr. Jedediah Munroe.

Of *Menotomy*.

Mr. Jason Ruffel,
Mr. Jabez Wyman,
Mr. Jason Winship.

Of *Sudbury*.

Deacon Haynes,
Mr. —— Reed.

Of *Concord*.

Capt. James Miles.

Of *Bedford*.

Capt. Jonathan Willson.

Of *Acton*.

Capt. Davis,
Mr. —— Hosmer,
Mr. James Howard.

Of *Woburn*.

* Mr. Azael Porter,
Mr. Daniel Thompson.

Of *Charlestown*.

Mr. James Miller,
Capt. William Barber's Son.

Of *Brookline*.

Isaac Gardner, Esq;

Of *Cambridge*.

Mr. John Hicks,
Mr. Moses Richardson,
Mr. William Maffey.

Of *Medford*.

Mr. Henry Putnam.

Of *Lynn*.

Mr. Abednego Ramsdell,
Mr. Daniel Townsend,
Mr. William Flint,
Mr. Thomas Hadley.

Of *Danvers*.

Mr. Henry Jacobs,
Mr. Samuel Cook,
Mr. Ebenezer Goldthwait,
Mr. George Southwick,
Mr. Benjamin Daland, ju^n.
Mr. Jotham Webb,
Mr. Perley Putnam.

Of *Salem*.

Mr. Benjamin Peirce.

WOUNDED.

Of *Lexington*.

Mr. John Robbins,
Mr. John Tidd,
Mr. Solomon Peirce,
Mr. Thomas Winship,
Mr. Nathaniel Farmer,
Mr. Joseph Comee,
Mr. Ebenezer Munroe,
Mr. Francis Brown,
Prince Easterbrooks,
(A Negro Man.

Of *Framingham*.

Mr. —— Hemenway.

Of *Bedford*.

Mr. John Lane.

Of *Woburn*.

Mr. George Reed,
Mr. Jacob Bacon.

Of *Medford*.

Mr. William Polly.

Of *Lynn*.

Joshua Feit,
Mr. Timothy Munroe.

Of *Danvers*.

Mr. Nathan Putnam,
Mr. Dennis Wallis.

Of *Beverly*.

Mr. Nathaniel Cleaves.

MISSING.

Of *Menotomy*.

Mr. Samuel Frost,
Mr. Seth Ruffell.

Those distinguished with this Mark [*] were killed by the first Fire of the Regulars

Sold in Queen Street.

An early engraving by Amos Doolittle of Connecticut of the Battle of Lexington, April 19, 1775. (1) Major Pitcairn, commander of the British soldiers, (2) redcoats firing at the Minutemen, (3) the Minutemen being driven from the field, (4) British reinforcements, (5) the Lexington church, and (6) the Lexington Inn.

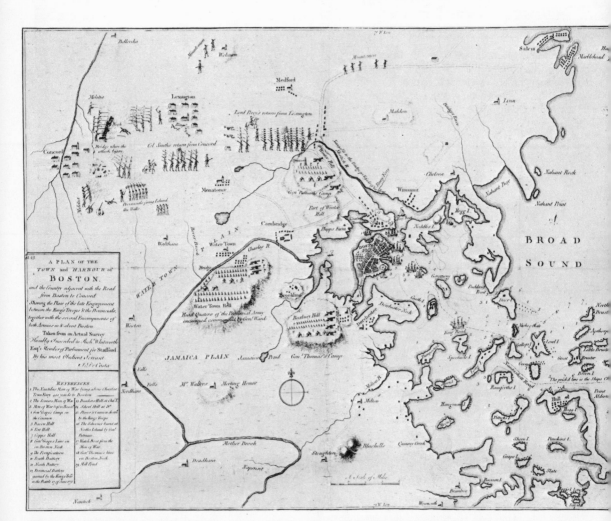

A British map of Boston and vicinity showing the actions at Lexington and Concord. Also pictured are British warships in Boston Harbor and American encampments at Watertown, Cambridge, and Roxbury.

The British troops seize Concord on April 19, 1775, in an engraving made by Amos Doolittle of Connecticut shortly after the event. (1) The British troops entering Concord, (2) the advance troops, formed at attention, (3) a group of redcoats destroying patriot military supplies, (4) Lieutenant Colonel Francis Smith, commander of British reinforcements sent to aid (5) Major John Pitcairn, (6) the Concord Townhouse, and (7) the meetinghouse.

General Thomas Gage, Commander-in-Chief of His Majesty's Forces in America, 1763-1775, and Royal Governor of Massachusetts, 1774-1775.

A British proclamation of the kind that helped bring on the Revolution.

Province of
New-Hampshire.

By the SURVEYOR-GENERAL *of the*
KING's *Woods in* NORTH-AMERICA, &c. &c.

WHEREAS some Persons have formerly gone into the KING's Woods, and thence hauled White Pine Logs into *Connecticut* River, without Licence, and against the Laws made and provided for the Preservation of the KING's Woods; which Timber has been sold to others, who have purchased, not knowing it was unlawful, & thereby exposed themselves to the Penalties of the Law:

THEREFORE, to prevent such fraudulent Practices, and to preserve the Innocent from the Evil, and unjustifiable Impositions of others,---NOTICE is hereby given, That all White Pine Logs cut and hauled out of the King's Woods into *Connecticut* River, or elsewhere, will be seized to his MAJESTY's Use, and Trespassers dealt with according to Law.

Portsmouth, 1st January, 1770.

The Battle of Bunker Hill, June 17, 1775, sketched from Beacon Hill, Boston, by an English officer.

LEFT: "The Able Doctor, or America Swallowing the Bitter Draught," a British cartoon of 1774 depicting a cruel and lascivious Government forcing tea down the throat of the innocent maid, America. Watching on the left are the amused but sly representatives of the French and Spanish governments.

RIGHT: Dr. Joseph Warren, Boston physician and patriot leader, killed at the Battle of Bunker Hill. Portrait by John Singleton Copley.

John Hancock, Boston merchant, patriot, and statesman. Engraved by J. B. Forrest after a painting by John Singleton Copley.

Battle of Bunker Hill.

IT was on the seventeenth by break of day,
 The Yankees did surprize us,
With their strong works they had thrown up
 To burn the town and drive us.
But soon we had an order came,
 An order to defeat them,
Like rebels stout, they stood it out,
 And thought we ne'er could beat them.
About the hour of twelve that day,
 An order came for marching,
With three good flints and sixty rounds,
 Each man hop'd to discharge them,
We marched down to the long wharf,
 Where boats were ready waiting,
With expedition we embark'd,
 Our ships kept cannonading,
And when our boats all filled were,
 With officers and soldiers,
With as good troops as England had
 To oppose, who dare controule us.
And when our boats all filled were,
 And when our boats all filled were,
 We row'd in line of battle,
Where showers of ball like hail did fly,
 Our cannon loud did rattle.
There was Cop's hill battery near Charlestown
 Our twenty fours they played,
And the three frigates in the stream,
 That very well behaved.
The Glasgow frigate clear'd the shore,
 All at the time of landing,
With her grape shot and cannon balls,
 No Yankees e'er could stand them.
And when we landed on the shore,
 We draw'd up altogether,
The Yankees they'd all man'd their works,
 And thought we'd ne'er come thither,
But soon they did perceive brave Howe,
 Brave Howe, our bold commander,
With grenadiers, and infantry,
 We made them to surrender.
Brave William Howe on our right wing
 Cry'd, boys fight on like thunder ;
You soon will see the rebels flee,
 With great amaze and wonder.
Now some lay bleeding on the ground,
 And some fell fast a runnin
O'er hills and dales and mountains high,

Printed and Sold at NO. 35, High Street, PROVIDENCE, where are kept constantly for Sale 200 other kinds of the most excellent Songs and Ballads, by the Hundred, Dozen or Single—great allowance made to Shopkeepers, Pedlers, &c. who buy to sell again—a large assortment of entertaining Books on various subjects, calculated to edify and amuse all classes and characters a long winter evening—a great collection of Picture Books for Children, and a very general assortment of SCHOOL BOOKS and STATIONARY

Crying zounds ! brave Howe's a coming.
Brave Howe is so considerate,
 As to guard against all dangers;
He allow'd each half a gill this day—
 To rum we are no strangers :
They began to play on our left wing,
 Where Pigot he commanded,
But we return'd it back again,
 With courage most undaunted.
To our grape shot and musket balls,
 To which they were but strangers,
They thought to come with sword in hand,
 But soon they found their danger.
And when the works were got into,
 And put them to the flight, sir,
They pepper'd us poor British elves,
 And show'd us they could fight sir.
And when their works we got into
 With some hard knocks and danger,
Their works we found both firm and strong,
 Too strong for British Rangers.
But as for our Artillery,
 They all gave way and run,
For while their ammunition held,
 They gave us Yankee fun
But our commander he got broke,
 For his misconduct sure, sir,
The shot he sent for twelve pound guns,
 Were made for twenty-fours, sir.
There's some in Boston pleas'd to say,
 As we the field were taking,
We went to kill their countrymen,
 While they their hay were making.
For such stout whigs I never saw,
 To hang them all I'd rather,
By making hay with musket balls,
 Lord Howe cursedly did bother !
Bad luck to him by land and sea,
 For he's despis'd by many,
The name of Bunker Hill he dreads,
 Where he was dog'd most plainly.
And now my song is at an end,
 And to conclude my ditty,
'Tis only Britons ignorant
As for our KING and WM. HOWE,
 And Gen GAGE, if they're taken,
The Yankees will hang their heads up high
 On that fine hill call'd Bacon.

Satirical ode on the Battle of Bunker Hill.

"A View of New York in 1775," from an aquatint engraving by Joseph F. W. Desbarres for *The Atlantic Neptune* and published in 1781 for the use of the Royal Navy.

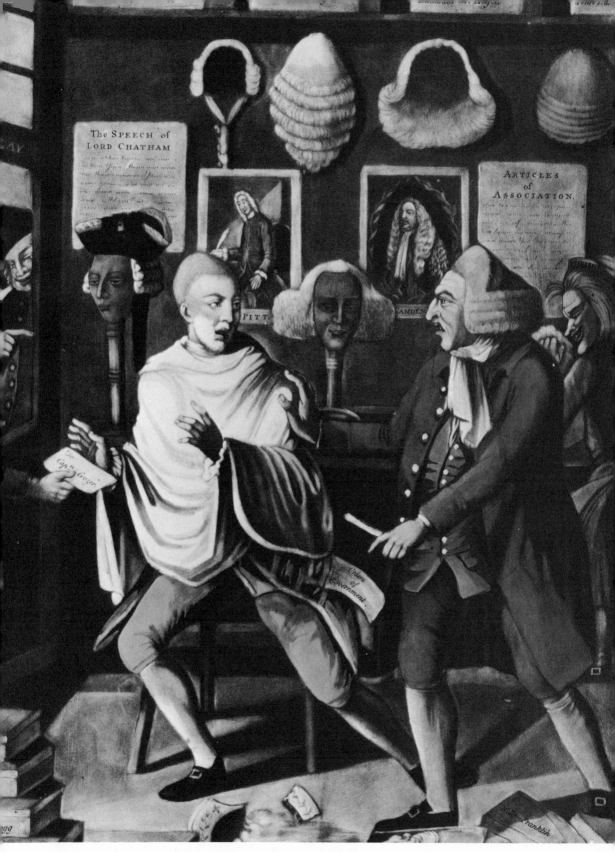

"The Patriotick Barber of New York, or the Captain in the Suds," an anti-administration cartoon printed in London in 1775 and based on an actual incident. A New York barber, razor in hand,
chased a frightened and half-shaved British captain out of his shop upon learning of his custom-
er's occupation. On the wall hang copies of a speech by America's champion, the Earl of Chatham,
and the Articles of Association which imposed a colonial embargo on trade with Great Britain.

George III, King of Great Britain, 1760-1820.

William Pitt, Earl of Chatham, outstanding parliamentary defender of American rights.

Lord North, British Prime Minister, 1770-1782.

The House of Commons as it looked at the time of the Revolution.

Edmund Burke, America's most eloquent friend in Parliament.

William Franklin, son of Benjamin Franklin and the last Royal Governor of New Jersey. He broke with his father in 1776, choosing to remain loyal to Great Britain.

A VIEW OF PART OF THE TOWN OF BOSTON IN NEW ENGLAND AND BRITTISH SHIPS OF WAR LANDING THEIR TROOPS

By his EXCELLENCY
WILLIAM TRYON, Esquire,
Captain General, and Governor in Chief in and over the Province of *New-York*, and the Territories depending thereon in *America*, Chancellor and Vice Admiral of the same.

A PROCLAMATION.

WHEREAS I have received His Majesty's Royal Proclamation, given the Court at *St. James's*, the Twenty-third Day of *August* last, in the Words following:

BY THE KING,
A Proclamation,
For suppressing REBELLION and SEDITION.

GEORGE R.

WHEREAS many of our Subjects in divers Parts of our Colonies and Plantations in *North-America*, misled by dangerous and ill designing Men, and forgetting the Allegiance which they owe to the Power that has protected and sustained them, after various disorderly Acts committed in disturbance of the public Peace, to the Obstruction of lawful Commerce, and to the Oppression of our loyal Subjects carrying on the same, have at length proceeded to an open and avowed Rebellion, by arraying themselves in hostile Manner, to withstand the Execution of the Law, and traitorously preparing, ordering and levying War against us: And whereas there is Reason to apprehend that such Rebellion hath been much promoted and encouraged by the traitorous Correspondence, Counsels, and Comfort of divers wicked and desperate Persons within this Realm:—To the End therefore that none of our Subjects may neglect or violate their Duty through Ignorance thereof, or through any Doubt of the Protection which the Law will afford to their Loyalty and Zeal; we have thought fit, by and with the Advice of our Privy Council, to issue this our Royal Proclamation, hereby declaring, that not only all our Officers Civil and Military, are obliged to exert their utmost Endeavours to suppress such Rebellion, and to bring the Traitors to Justice; but that all our Subjects of this Realm and the Dominions thereunto belonging, are bound by Law to be aiding and assisting in the Suppression of such Rebellion,

In Obedience therefore to his Majesty's Commands to me given, I do hereby publish and make known his Majesty's most gracious Proclamation above recited; earnestly exhorting and requiring all his Majesty's loyal and faithful Subjects within this Province, as they value their Allegiance due to the best of Sovereigns, their Dependance on and Protection from their Parent State, and the Blessings of a mild, free, and happy Constitution; and as they would shun the fatal Calamities which are the inevitable Consequences of Sedition and Rebellion, to pay all due Obedience to the Laws of their Country, seriously to attend to his Majesty's said Proclamation, and govern themselves accordingly.

Given under my Hand and Seal at Arms, in the City of New-York, the Fourteenth Day of November, One Thousand Seven Hundred and Seventy-five, in the Sixteenth Year of the Reign of our Sovereign Lord GEORGE the Third, by the Grace of God of Great-Britain, France and Ireland, King, Defender of the Faith, and so forth.

WM. TRYON.

By his Excellency's Command,
SAMUEL BAYARD, Jun. D. Secry.

GOD SAVE THE KING.

Announcement of
King George III's proclamation
calling for suppression
of the rebellion.

right to tax America? If I was to begin to say that America ought not to be taxed, and that these measures were not proper, I would first desire my own declaratory law to be repealed; but being of opinion that the Americans are the subjects of this country, I will declare freely, that I think this country has a right to tax America; but I do not say that I would put any new tax on at this particular crisis; but when things are returned to a peaceable state, I would then begin to exercise it. And I am free to declare my opinion, that I think we have a right to tax Ireland, if there was a necessity so to do, in order to help the mother country. If Ireland was to rebel and resist our laws, I would tax it. The mother country has an undoubted right and control over the whole of its colonies. Again, sir, a great deal has been said concering requisition. Pray, in what manner is it to be obtained? Is the king to demand it, or are we, the legislative power of this country, to send a very civil polite gentleman over to treat with their assemblies? How and in what manner is he to address that assembly? Is he to tell the speaker that we have been extremely ill used by our neighbors the French; that they have attacked us in several quarters; that the finances of this country are in a bad state; and therefore we desire you will be kind enough to assist us, and give us some money? Is this to be the language of this country to that; and are we thus to go cap in hand? I am of opinion, that if the administration of this country had not been changed soon after passing the stamp-act, that tax would have been collected with as much ease as the land-tax is in Great Britain. I have acted, with regard to America, one consistent part, and shall continue in it, till I hear better reasons to convince me to the contrary."

GOVERNOR POWNALL. . . . "I apprehend I have been totally misunderstood. I did not assert the Americans were now in rebellion, but that they are going to rebel; when that comes to pass, the question will be, who was the occasion of it? Something has been said relative to requisition; I think I gave several instances wherein the same had been complied with in time of war."

MR. C. FOX. "I am glad to hear from the honorable gentleman who spoke last, that now is not the time to tax America; that the only time for that is, when all these disturbances are quelled, and they are returned to their duty; so, I find taxes are to be the reward of obedience; and the Americans, who are considered to have been in open rebellion, are to be rewarded by acquiescing in their measures. When will be the time when America ought to have heavy taxes laid upon it? The honorable gentleman (Mr. Rigby) tells you, that that time will be when the Americans are returned to peace and quietness. The honorable gentleman tells us also, that we have a right to tax Ireland; however, I may agree with him in regard to the principle, it would not be policy to exercise it; I believe we have no more right to tax the one than the other.

I believe America is wrong in resisting against this country, with regard to legislative authority. It was an old opinion, and I believe a very true one, that there was a dispensing power in the crown, but whenever that dispensing power was pretended to be exercised it was always rejected and opposed to the utmost, because it operated to me, as a subject, as a detriment to my property and liberty; but, sir, there has been a constant conduct practised in this country, consisting of violence and weakness; I wish those measures may not continue; nor can I think that the stamp-act would have been submitted to without resistance, if the administration had not been changed; the present bill before you is not tanti to what you want; it irritates the minds of the people, but does not correct the deficiencies of that government."

SIR GILBERT ELLIOT arose to answer Mr. C. Fox, which he did in a very masterly manner, by stating that "there was not the least degree of absurdity in taxing your own subjects, over whom you have declared you had an absolute right; though that tax should, through necessity, be enacted at a time when peace and quietness were the reigning system of the times; you declare you have that right, where is the absurdity in the exercise of it?"

SIR RICHARD SUTTON read a copy of a letter, relative to the government of America, from a governor in America, to the board of trade, shewing that, at the most quiet times, the "dispositions to oppose the laws of this country were strongly ingrafted in them, and that all their actions conveyed a spirit and wish for independence. If you ask an American who is his master? he will tell you he has none, nor any governor but Jesus Christ. I do believe it, and it is my firm opinion, that the opposition to the measures of the legislature of this country, is a determined prepossession of the idea of total independence."

3. CHALLENGES TO THE NORTH MINISTRY CONTINUE

BISHOP SHIPLEY OBJECTS TO THE ADMINISTRATION'S COLONIAL POLICY

[*Speech, prepared by the Reverend Dr. Jonathan Shipley, Bishop of St. Asaph, for delivery in the House of Lords against the bill for altering the charter of the Massachusetts Bay colony; printed in the* Maryland Gazette *on September 29, 1774, though never actually delivered in Parliament*]

It is of such great importance to compose, or even to moderate, the dissensions which subsist at present between our unhappy country and her colonies, that I cannot help endeavoring, from the faint prospect I have of contributing something to so good an end, to overcome the inexpressible reluctance I feel at uttering my thoughts before the most respectable of all audiences.

The true object of all our deliberations on this occasion, which I hope we shall never lose sight of, is a full and cordial reconciliation with North America. Now I own, my lords, I have many doubts whether the terrors and punishments we hang out to them at present are the surest means of producing this reconciliation. Let us at least do this justice to the people of North America, to own that we can all remember a time when they were much better friends than at present to their mother country. They are neither our natural nor our determined enemies. Before the stamp-act, we considered them in the light of as good subjects as the natives of any country in England.

It is worth while to enquire by what steps we first gained their affection, and preserved it so long; and by what conduct we have lately lost it. Such an enquiry may point out the means of restoring peace; and make the use of force unnecessary against a people, whom I cannot yet forbear to consider as our brethren.

It has always been a most arduous task to govern distant provinces, with even a tolerable appearance of justice. The viceroys and governors of other nations are usually temporary tyrants, who think themselves obliged to make the most of their time; who not only plunder the people, but carry away their spoils, and dry up all the sources of commerce and industry. Taxation, in their hands, is an unlimited power of oppression; but in whatever hands the power of taxation is lodged it implies and includes all other powers. Arbitrary taxation is plunder authorized by law: it is the support and the essence of tyranny, and has done more mischief to mankind, than those other three scourges from Heaven, famine, pestilence and the sword. I need not carry your lordship out of your own knowledge, or out of your own dominions, to make you conceive what misery this right of taxation is capable of producing in a provincial government. We need only recollect that our countrymen in India, have, in the space of five or six years, in virtue of this right, destroyed, and driven away more inhabitants from Bengal, than are to be found at present in all our American colonies; more than all those formidable numbers which we have been nursing up for the space of two hundred years, with so much care and success, to the astonishment of all Europe. This is no exaggeration, my lords, but plain matter of fact, collected from the accounts sent over by Mr. Hastings, whose name I mention with honor and veneration. And I must own, such accounts have very much lessened the pleasure I used to feel in thinking myself an Englishman. We ought surely not to hold our colonies totally inexcusable for wishing to exempt themselves from a grievance, which has caused such unexampled devastation; and, my lords, it would be too disgraceful to ourselves, to try so cruel an experiment more than once. Let us reflect, that before these innovations were thought of, by following the line of good conduct which had been marked out by our ancestors, we governed North America with mutual benefit to them and ourselves. It was a happy idea, that made us first consider them rather as instruments of commerce than as objects of government. It was wise and generous to give them the form and the spirit of our own constitution; an assembly, in which a greater equality of representation has been preserved them at home and councils and governors, such as were adapted to their situation, though they must be acknowledged to be very inferior copies of the dignity of this house, and the majesty of the crown.

But what is far more valuable than all the rest, we gave them liberty. We allowed them to use their own judgment in the management of their own interest. The idea of taxing them never entered our heads. On the contrary they have experienced our liberality on many public occasions: we have given them bounties to encourage their industry, and have demanded no return but what every state exacts from its colonies, the advantages of an exclusive commerce, and the regulations that are necessary to secure it. We made requisitions to them on great occasions; in the same manner as our princes formerly asked benevolences of their subjects; and as nothing was asked but what was visibly for the public good, it was always granted; and they sometimes did more than we expected. The matter of right was neither disputed, nor even considered. And let us not forget that the people of New-England were themselves, during the last war, the most forward of all in the national cause; that every year we voted them a considerable sum, in acknowledgment of their zeal and their services; that, in the preceding war, they alone enabled us to make the treaty of Aix-la-Chapelle, by furnishing us with the only equivalent for the towns that were taken from our allies in Flanders; and that, in times of peace, they alone have taken from us six times as much of our woolen manufactures as the whole kingdom of Ireland. Such a colony, my lords, not only from the justice, but from the gratitude we owe them, have a right to be heard in their defence; and if their crimes are not of the most inexpiable kind, I could almost say, they have a right to be forgiven.

But in the times we speak of, our public intercourse was carried on with ease and satisfaction. We regarded them as our friends and fellow-citizens, and relied as much upon their fidelity as on the inhabitants of our own country. They saw our power with pleasure for they considered it only as their protection. They inherited our laws, our language, and our customs; they preferred our manufactures, and followed our fashions with a partiality that secured our exclusive trade with them more effectually than all the regulations and vigilance of the custom-house. Had we suffered them to enrich us a little longer, and to grow a little richer themselves, their men of fortune, like the West-Indians, would undoubtedly have made this country the place of their education and resort. For they looked up to England with reverence and affection, as to the country of their friends and ancestors. They esteemed and they called it their home, and thought of it as the Jews once thought of the land of Canaan.

Now, my lords, consider with yourselves what were the chains and ties that united this people to their mother-country with so much warmth and affection, at so amazing a distance. The colonies of other nations have been discontented with their treatment, and not without sufficient cause; always murmuring at their grievances, and sometimes breaking out into acts of rebellion. Our subjects at home, with all their reasons for satisfaction, have never been entirely satisfied. Since the beginning of this century we have had two rebellions, several plots and conspiracies; and we ourselves been witnesses to the most dangerous excesses of sedition. But the provinces in North America have engaged in no party, have excited no opposition, they have been utter strangers even to the name of whig and tory. In all changes, in all revolutions, they have quietly followed the fortunes and submitted to the government of England.

Now let me appeal to your lordships as to men of enlarged and liberal minds, who have been led by your office and rank to the study of history. Can you find in the long succession of ages, in the whole extent of human affairs, a single instance where distant provinces have been preserved in so flourishing a state, and kept at the same time in such due subjection to their mother-country? My lords, there is no instance; the case never existed before. It is perhaps the most singular phenomenon in all civil history; and the cause of it well deserves your serious consideration. The true cause is, that a mother-country never existed before, who placed her natives and her colonies on the same equal footing; and joined with them in fairly carrying on one common interest.

You ought to consider this, my lords, not as a mere historical fact, but as a most important and invaluable discovery. It enlarges our ideas of the power and energy of good government beyond all former examples; and shews that it can act like gravitation at the greatest distances. It proves to a demonstration that you may have good subjects in the remotest corner of the earth, if you will but treat them with kindness and equity. If you have any doubts of the truth of this kind of reasoning, the experience we have had of a different kind will entirely remove them.

The good genius of our country had led us to the simple and happy method of governing freemen, which I have endeavored to describe. Our ministers received it from their predecessors and for some time continued to observe it; but without knowing its value. At length, presuming on their own wisdom, and the quiet dispositions of the Americans, they flattered themselves that we might reap great advantages from their prosperity by destroying the cause of it. They chose, in an unlucky hour, to treat them as other nations have thought fit to treat their colonies; they threatened, and they taxed them.

I do not now enquire whether taxation is matter of right; I only consider it as matter of experiment; for surely the art of government itself is founded on experience. I need not suggest what were the consequences of this change of measures. The evils produced by it were such as we still remember and still feel. We suffered more by our loss of trade with them, than the wealth flowing in from India was able to recompense. The bankruptcy of the East-India company may be sufficiently accounted for by the rapine abroad and the knavery at home; but it certainly would have been delayed some years, had we continued our commerce with them in the single article of tea. But that and many other branches of trade have been diverted into other channels, and may probably never return entire to their own old course. But what is worst of all, we have lost their confidence and friendship; we have ignorantly undermined the most solid foundation of our own power.

In order to observe the strictest impartiality, it is but just for us to inquire what we have gained by these taxes as well as what we have lost. I am assured that out of all the sums raised in America the last year but one, if the expenses are deducted, which the natives would else have discharged themselves, the net revenue paid into the treasury to go in aid of the sinking fund, or to be employed in whatever public services parliament shall think fit, is eighty-five pounds. Eighty-five pounds, my lords, is the whole equivalent we have received for all the hatred and mischief, and all the infinite losses this kingdom has suffered during that year in her disputes with North America. Money that is earned so dearly as this, ought to be expended with great wisdom and economy. My lords, were you to take up but one thousand pounds more from North America upon the same terms, the nation itself would be a bankrupt. But the most amazing and most alarming circumstances are still behind. It is that our case is so incurable, that all this experience has made no impression upon us. And yet, my lords, if you could but keep these facts, which I have ventured to lay before you, for a few moments in your minds (supposing your right of taxation to be never so clear) yet I think you must necessarily perceive that it cannot be exercised in any manner that can be advantageous to ourselves or them. We have not always the wisdom to tax ourselves with propriety: and I am confident we could never tax a people at that distance, without infinite blunders, and infinite oppression. And to own the truth, my lords, we are not honest enough to trust ourselves with the power of shifting our own burthens upon them. Allow me therefore to conclude, I think unanswerably, that the inconvenience and distress we have felt in this change of our conduct, no less than the ease and tranquility we formerly found in the pursuit of it, will force us, if we have any sense left, to return to the good old path we trod in so long, and found it the way of pleasantness.

I desire to have it understood, that I am opposing no rights legislature may think proper to claim: I am only comparing two different methods of government. By your old rational and generous administration, by treating the Americans as your friends and fellow-citizens, you made them the happiest of human kind; and, at the same time, drew from them, by commerce, more clear profit than Spain has drawn from all its mines; and their growing numbers were a daily increase and addition to your strength. There was no room for improvement or alteration in so noble a system of policy as this. It was sanctified by time, by experience, by public utility. I will venture to use a bold language my lords; I will assert, that if we had uniformly adopted this equitable administration in all our distant provinces as far as circumstances would admit, it would have placed this country, for ages, at the head of human affairs in every quarter of the world. My lords, this is no visionary, or chimerical doctrine. The idea of governing provinces and colonies by force is visionary and chimerical. The experiment has often been tried and it never has succeeded. It ends infallibly in the ruin of the one country or the other, or in the last degree of wretchedness.

If there is any truth, my lords, in what I have said, and I most firmly believe it all to be true, let me recommend to you to resume that generous and benevolent spirit in the discussion of our differences which used to be the source of our union. We certainly did wrong in taxing them: when the stamp-act was repealed we did wrong in laying on other taxes, which tended only to keep alive a claim that was mischievous, impracticable and useless. We acted contrary to our own principles of liberty, and to the generous sentiments of our sovereign, when we desired to have their judges dependent on the crown for their stipends as well as their continuance. It was equally unwise to wish to make the governors independent of the people for their salaries. We ought to consider the governors, not as spies entrusted with the management of our interest, but as the servants of the people, recommended to them by us. Our ears ought to be open to every complaint against the governors, but we ought not to suffer the governors to complain of the people. We have taken a different method, to which no small part of our difficulties are owing. Our ears have been open to the governors and shut to the people. This must necessarily lead us to countenance the jobs of interested men, under the pretence of defending the rights of the crown. But the people are certainly the best judges whether they are well governed; and the crown can have no rights inconsistent with the happiness of the people.

Now, my lords, we ought to do what I have suggested, and many things more, out of prudence and justice, to win their affection, and to do them public service. . . .

My lords, our difficulty lies in the point of honor. We must not let down the dignity of the mother-country; but preserve her sovereignty over all the parts of the British empire. This language has something in it that sounds pleasant to the ears of Englishmen, but is otherwise of little weight. For sure, my lords, there are methods of making reasonable concessions, and yet without injuring our dignity. Ministers are generally fruitful in expedients to reconcile difficulties of this kind to escape the embarrassments of forms, the competitions of dignity and precedency; and to let clashing rights sleep, while they transact their business. Now, my lords, on this occasion can they find no excuse, no pretence, no invention, no happy turn of language, not one colorable argument for doing the greatest service they can ever render to their country? It must be something more than incapacity that makes men barren of expedients at such a season as this. Do, but for once, remove this impracticable stateliness and dignity, and treat the matter with a little common sense and a little good humor, and our reconciliation would not be the work of an hour. But after all, my lords, if there is any thing mortifying in undoing the errors of our ministers, it is a mortification we ought to submit to. If it was unjust to tax them, we ought to repeal it for their sakes; if it was unwise to tax them, we ought to repeal it for our own. A matter so trivial in itself as the three-penny duty upon tea, but which has given cause to so much national hatred and reproach, ought not to be suffered to subsist an unnecessary day. Must the interest, the commerce, and the union of this country and her colonies be all of them sacrificed to save the credit of one imprudent measure of administration? I owe I cannot comprehend that there is any dignity either in being in the wrong, or in persisting in it. I have known friendship preserved, and affection gained, but I never knew dignity lost by the candid acknowledgment of an error. And, my lords, let me appeal to your own experience of a few years backward (I would not mention particulars, because I would pass no censures and revive no unpleasant reflections) but I think every candid minister must own, that administration has suffered in more instances than one, both in interest and credit, by not choosing to give up points that could not be defended.

With regard to the people of Boston, I am free to own that I never approve of their riots nor their punishment: And yet, if we inflict it as we ought with a consciousness that we were ourselves the aggressors, that we gave the provocation, and that their disobedience is the fruit of our own imprudent and imperious conduct, I think the punishment cannot rise to any great degree of severity.

I own, my lords, I have read the report of the lord's committees of this house, with very different sentiments from those with which it was drawn up. It seems to be designed, that we should consider their violent measures and speeches as so many determined acts of opposition to the sovereignty of England, arising from the malignity of their own hearts. One would think the mother country had been totally silent and passive in the progress of the whole affair. I, on the contrary, consider these violences as the natural effects of such measures as ours on the minds of freemen. And this is the most useful point of view in which government can consider them. In their situation, a wise man would expect to meet with the strongest marks of passion and imprudence, and be prepared to forgive them. The first and easiest thing to be done is to correct our own errors: and I am confident we should find it the most effectual method to correct theirs. At any rate let us put ourselves in the right; and then if we must contend with North America, we shall be unanimous at home, and the wise and moderate there will be our friends. At present we force every North American to be our enemy; and the wise and moderate at home, and those immense multitudes which must soon begin to suffer by the madness of our rulers, will unite to oppose them. It is a strange idea we have taken up, to cure their resentments by increasing their provocations; to remove the effects of our own ill conduct by multiplying the instances of it. But the spirit of blindness and infatuation is gone forth. We are hurrying wildly on without any fixed design, without any important object. We pursue a vain phantom of unlimited sovereignty, which was not made for man: and reject the solid advantages of a moderate, useful, and intelligible authority.

That just God, whom we have all so deeply offended, can hardly inflict a severer national punishment than by committing us to the natural consequences of our own conduct. Indeed, in my opinion, a blacker cloud never hung over this island. . . .

Recollect that the Americans are men of like passions with ourselves, and think how deeply this treatment must affect them. They have the same veneration for their charters that we have for our Magna Charta, and they ought in reason to have greater. They are the title deeds to all their rights, both public and private. What! my lords, must these rights never acquire any legal assurance and stability? can they derive no force from the peaceful possession of near two hundred years? and must the fundamental constitution of a powerful state be, forever, subject to as capricious alterations as you think fit to make in the charters of a little mercantile company or the corporation of a borough? this will undoubtedly furnish matter for a more pernicious debate than has yet been moved. Every other colony will make the case its own.—They will complain that their rights can never be ascertained; that every thing belonging to them depends upon our arbitrary will; and may think it better to run any hazard, than to submit to the violence of their mother-country, in a matter in which they can see neither moderation nor end.

But let us coolly enquire, what is the reason of this unheard of innovation. Is it to make them peaceable? my lords, it will make them mad. Will they be better governed if we introduce this change? will they be more our friends? the least that such a measure can do, is to make them hate us. And would to God, my lords, we had governed ourselves with as much economy, integrity and prudence, as they have done. Let them continue to enjoy the liberty our fathers gave them. Gave them, did I say? they are co-heirs of liberty with ourselves; and their portion of the inheritance has been much better looked after than ours. Suffer them to enjoy a little longer that short period of public integrity and domestic happiness, which seems to be the portion allotted by Providence to young rising states. Instead of hoping that their constitution may receive improvement from our skill in government, the most useful wish I can form in their favor, is that Heaven may long preserve them from our vices and our politics.

Let me add further—that to make any changes in their government, without their consent, would be to transgress the wisest rules of policy, and to wound our most important interests. As they increase in numbers and in riches, our comparative strength must lessen. In another age, when our power has begun to lose something of its superiority, we should be happy if we could support our authority by mutual good will and the habit of commanding; but chiefly by those original establishments, which time and public honor might have rendered inviolable. Our posterity will then have reason to lament that they cannot avail themselves of those treasures of public friendship and confidence which our fathers had wisely hoarded up, and we are throwing away. 'Tis hard, 'tis cruel, besides all our debts and taxes, and those enormous expenses which are multiplying upon us every year, to load our unhappy sons with the hatred and curse of North America. Indeed, my lords, we are treating posterity very scurvily. We have mortgaged all the lands; we have cut down all the oaks; we are now trampling down the fences, rooting up the seedlings and samplers, and ruining all the resources of another age. We shall send the next generation into the world, like the wretched heir of a worthless father, without money, credit or friends; with a stripped, incumbered, and perhaps untenanted estate. . . .

My lords I look upon North America as the only great nursery of freemen now left upon the face of the earth. We have seen the liberties of Poland and Sweden swept away, in the course of one year, by treachery and usurpation. The free towns in Germany are like so many dying sparks, that go out one after another; and which must all be soon extinguished under the destructive greatness of their neighbors. Holland is little more than a great trading company, with luxurious manners, and an exhausted revenue; with little strength and with less spirit. Switzerland alone is free and happy within the narrow inclosure of its rocks and valleys. As for the state of this country, my lords, I can only refer myself to your own secret thoughts. I am disposed to think and hope the best of public liberty. Were I to describe her according to my own ideas at present, I should say that she has a sickly countenance, but I trust she has a long constitution.

But whatever may be our future fate, the greatest glory that attends this country, a greater than any other nation ever acquired, is to have formed and nursed up to such a state of happiness those colonies whom we are now so eager to butcher. We ought to cherish them as the immortal monuments of our public justice and wisdom; as the heirs of our better days, of our expiring national virtues. What work of art, or power, or public utility has ever equalled the glory of having peopled a continent without guilt or bloodshed, with a multitude of free and happy commonwealths; to have given them the best arts of life and government; and to have suffered them, under the shelter of our authority, to acquire in peace the skill to use them. In comparison of this, the policy of governing by influence, and even the pride of war and victory, are dishonest tricks and poor contemptible pageantry.

We seem not to be sensible of the high and important trust which Providence has committed to our charge. The most precious remains of civil liberty that the world can now boast of, are now lodged in our hands; and God forbid that we should violate so sacred a deposit. By enslaving your colonies, you not only ruin the peace, the commerce, and the fortunes of both countries; but you extinguish the fairest hopes, shut up the last asylum of mankind. I think, my lords, without being weakly superstitious, that a good man may hope that Heaven will take part against the execution of a plan which seems big not only with mischief, but impiety.

Let us be content with the spoils and the destruction of the east. If your lordships can see no impropriety in it, let the plunderer and oppressor still go free. But let not the love of liberty be the only crime you think worthy of punishment. I fear we shall soon make it a part of our national character, to ruin every thing that has the misfortune to depend upon us. . . .

EDMUND BURKE PLEADS FOR CONCILIATION

[Speech in the House of Commons, March 22, 1775]

. . . The capital leading questions, on which you must this day decide, are these two. First, whether you ought to concede [to the colonists' demands]; and, secondly, what your concession ought to be. On the first of these questions we have gained . . . some ground. But I am sensible that a good deal more is still to be done. Indeed, sir, to enable us to determine both on the one and the other of these great questions, with a firm and precise judgment, I think it may be necessary to consider distinctly the true nature and the peculiar circumstances of the object which we have before us. Because, after all our struggle, whether we will or not, we must govern America according to that nature, and to those circumstances, and not according to our own imaginations; not according to abstract ideas of right; by no means according to mere general theories of government, the resort of which appears to me, in our present situation, no better than arrant trifling. I shall therefore endeavor, with your leave, to lay before you some of the most material of these circumstances, in as full and as clear a manner as I am able to state them.

The first thing that we have to consider with regard to the nature of the object, is the number of people in the colonies. I have taken for some years a good deal of pains on that point. I can by no calculation justify myself in placing the number below two millions of inhabitants of our own European blood and color, besides at least 500,000 others, who form no inconsiderable part of the strength and opulence of the whole. This, sir, is, I believe, about the true number. There is no occasion to exaggerate where plain truth is of so much weight and importance. But whether I put the present numbers too high or too low, is a matter of little moment. Such is the strength with which population shoots in that part of the world, that state the numbers as high as we will whilst the dispute continues, the exaggeration ends. Whilst we are discussing any given magnitude, they are grown to it. Whilst we spend our time in deliberating on the mode of governing two millions, we shall find we have millions more to manage. Your children do not grow faster from infancy to manhood, than they spread from families to communities, and from villages to nations. . . .

But the population of this country, the great and growing population, though a very important consideration, will lose much of its weight if not combined with other circumstances. The commerce of your colonies is out of all proportion beyond the numbers of the people. . . .

The trade to the colonies, taken on the export side, at the beginning of this century, that is, in the year 1704, stood thus:

Exports to North America and the West-Indies, . *£485,265*
To Africa *86,665*
                                        £569,930 [sic]

In the year 1772, which I take as a middle year between the highest and the lowest of those lately laid on your table, the accounts were as follows:

To North America and the West-Indies, ... *£4,791,734*
To Africa, ... *866,398*
To which if you add the export trade to and from
   Scotland, which had in 1704 no existence . . . *364,000*
                                            £6,022,132

From five hundred and odd thousands, it has grown to six millions; it has increased no less than twelvefold. This is the state of the colony trade, as compared with itself at these two periods, within this century; and this is matter for meditation. But this is not all. Examine my second account.

See how the export trade to the colonies alone, in 1772, stood in the other point of view, that is, as compared to the whole trade of England, in 1704.

The whole export trade of England, including that	
to the colonies, in 1704, ...	£6,509,000
Except to the colonies alone, in 1772, ...	6,024,000
Difference	£ 485,000

The trade with America alone is now within less than £500,000 of being equal to what this great commercial nation, England, carried on at the beginning of this century with the whole world! . . .

Mr. Speaker, I cannot prevail upon myself to hurry over this great consideration. It is good for us to be here. We stand where we have an immense view of what is, and what is past. Clouds indeed, and darkness rest upon the future. Let us, however, before we descend from this noble eminence, reflect that this growth of our national prosperity has happened within the short period of the life of man. It has happened within sixty-eight years. There are those alive, whose memory might touch the two extremities! For instance, my lord Bathurst might remember all the stages of the progress. He was, in 1704, of an age at least to be made to comprehend such things. . . . [What if an] angel should have drawn up the curtain, and unfolded the rising glories of his country, and whilst he was gazing with admiration on the then commercial grandeur of England, the genius should point out to him a little speck, scarce visible in the mass of the national interest, a small seminal principle, rather than a formed body, and should tell him—"young man, there is America, which at this day serves for little more than to amuse you with stories of savage men, and uncouth manners; yet shall, before you taste of death, shew itself equal to the whole of that commerce which now attracts the envy of the world. Whatever England has been growing to by a progressive increase of improvements, brought in by variety of people, by succession of civilizing conquests and civilizing settlements in a series of seventeen hundred years, you shall see as much added to her by America, in the course of a single life!" If this state of his country had been foretold to him, would it not require all the sanguine credulity of youth, and all the fervid glow of enthusiasm, to make him believe it?—Fortunate man, he has lived to see it! Fortunate indeed, if he lives to see nothing that shall vary the prospect, and cloud the setting of the day.

Excuse me, sir, if turning from such thoughts I resume this comparative view once more. You have seen it on a large scale; look at it on a small one. I will point out to your attention a particular instance of it in the single province of Pennsylvania. In the year 1704, that province called for £11,459 in value of your commodities, native and foreign. This was the whole. What did it demand in 1772? Why, nearly fifty times as much, for in that year the export to Pennsylvania was £507,909, nearly equal to the export to all the colonies together in the first period. . . .

I pass [now] to the colonies in another point of view—their agriculture. This they have prosecuted with such a spirit, that besides feeding plentifully their own growing multitude, their annual export of grain, comprehending rice, has some years ago exceeded a million [pounds] in value: of their last harvest, I am persuaded they will export much more. At the beginning of the century some of these colonies imported corn from the mother country. For some time past the old world has been fed from the new. The scarcity which you have felt would have been a desolating famine, if this child of your old age, with a true filial piety, with a Roman charity, had not put the full breast of its youthful exuberance to the mouth of its exhausted parent.

As to the wealth which the colonies have drawn from the seas by their fisheries, . . . pray, sir, what in the world is equal to it? Pass by the other parts, and look at the manner in which the people of New England have of late carried on the whale fishery. Whilst we follow them among the tumbling mountains of ice, and behold them penetrating into the deepest frozen recesses of Hudson's Bay and Davis's Straits, whilst we are looking for them beneath the arctic circle, we hear that they have pierced into the opposite region of polar cold; that they are at the antipodes, and engaged under the frozen surface of the south. Falkland island, which seemed too remote and romantic an object for the grasp of national ambition, is but a stage and resting-place in the progress of their victorious industry. Nor is the equinoctial heat more discouraging to them than the accumulated winter of both the poles. We know that whilst some of them draw the line and strike the harpoon on the coast of Africa, others run the longitude, and pursue the gigantic game along the coast of Brazil. No sea but what is vexed by their fisheries; no climate that is not witness to their toils. Neither the perseverance of Holland, nor the activity of France, nor the dextrous and firm sagacity of English enterprise, ever carried this most perilous mode of hardy industry to the extent to which it has been pushed by this recent people; a people who are still, as it were, but in the gristle, and not yet hardened into the bone of manhood. When I contemplate these things; when I know that the colonies in general owe little or nothing to any care of ours, and that they are not squeezed into this happy form by the constraints of watchful and suspicious government, but that, through a wise and salutary neglect, a generous nature has been suffered to take her own way to perfection; when I reflect upon these efforts, when I see how profitable they have been to us, I feel all the pride of power sink, and all presumption in the wisdom of human contrivances melt, and die away within me. My rigor relents. I pardon something to the spirit of liberty.

I am sensible, sir, that all which I have asserted in my detail, is admitted in the gross; but that quite a different conclusion is drawn from it. America, gentlemen, I say, is a noble object. It is an object well worth fighting for. Certainly it is, if fighting a people be the best way of gaining them; gentlemen, in this respect, will be led to their choice of means by their complexion and their habits. Those who understand the military art, will of course have some predilection for it. Those who wield the thunder of the state, may have more confidence in the efficacy of arms. But I confess, possibly for want of this knowledge, my opinion is much more in favor of prudent management than of force; considering force not as an odious but a feeble instrument, for preserving a people, so numerous, so active, so growing, so spirited as this, in a profitable and subordinate connection with us.

First, sir, permit me to observe, that the use of force alone is but temporary; it may subdue for a moment, but it does not remove the necessity of subduing again: and a nation is not governed, which is perpetually to be conquered.

My next object is its uncertainty; terror is not always the effect of force; and an armament is not a victory. If you do not succeed, you are without resource, for, conciliation failing, force remains; but force failing, no farther hope of reconciliation is left. Power and authority are sometimes bought by kindness; but they can never be begged as alms by an impoverished and defeated violence.

A farther objection to force is, that you impair the object by your very endeavors to preserve it. The thing you fought for, is not the thing which you recover; but depreciated, sunk, wasted, and consumed in the contest. Nothing less will content me than whole America. I do not choose to consume its strength along with our own, because in all parts it is the British strength that I consume. I do not choose to be caught by a foreign enemy at the end of this exhausting conflict; and still less in the midst of it. I may escape, but I can make no insurance against such an event. Let me add, that I do not choose wholly to break the American spirit, because it is the spirit that has made the country.

Lastly, we have no sort of experience in favor of force as an instrument in the rule of our colonies. Their growth and their utility has been owing to methods altogether different. Our ancient indulgence has been said to be pursued to a fault. It may be so. But we know, if feeling is evidence, that our fault was more tolerable than our attempt to mend it, and our sin far more salutary than our penitence.

These, sir, are my reasons for not entertaining that high opinion of untried force, by which many gentlemen, for whose sentiments in other particulars I have great respect, seem to be so greatly captivated. But there is still behind a third consideration concerning this object, which serves to determine my opinion on the sort of policy which ought to be pursued in the management of America, even more than its population and its commerce. I mean its temper and character.

In this character of the Americans a love of freedom is the predominating feature, which marks and distinguishes the whole; and as an ardent is always a jealous affection, your colonies become suspicious, restive, and untractable, whenever they see the least attempt to wrest from them by force, or shuffle from them by chicane, what they think [is] the only advantage worth living for. This fierce spirit of liberty is stronger in the English colonies probably than in any other people of the earth, and this from a great variety of powerful causes; which, to understand the true temper of their minds, and the directions which this spirit takes, it will not be amiss to lay open somewhat more largely.

First, the people of the colonies are descendants of Englishmen. England, sir, is a nation which still I hope respects, and formerly adored her freedom. The colonists emigrated from you, when this part of your character was most predominant; and they took this bias and direction the moment they parted from your hands. They are therefore not only devoted to liberty, but to liberty according to English ideas, and on English principles. Abstract liberty, like other mere abstractions, is not to be found. Liberty inheres in some sensible object; and every nation has formed to itself some favorite point which by way of eminence becomes the criterion of their happiness. It happened, you know, sir, that the great contests for freedom in this country, were from the earliest times chiefly upon the question of taxing. Most of the contests in the ancient commonwealths turned primarily on the right of election of magistrates; or on the balance among the several orders of the state. The question of money was not with them so immediate. But in England it was otherwise. On this point of taxes the ablest pens, and most eloquent tongues have been exercised; the greatest spirits have acted and suffered.

In order to give the fullest satisfaction concerning the importance of this point, it was not only necessary for those, who in argument defended the excellence of the English constitution, to insist on this privilege of granting money as a dry point of fact, and to prove that the right had been acknowledged in ancient parchments and blind usages, to reside in a certain body called an house of commons. They went much further; they attempted to prove, and they succeeded, that in theory it ought to be so from the particular nature of a house of commons, as an immediate representative of the people, whether the old records had delivered this oracle or not. They took pains to calculate, as a fundamental principle, that in all monarchies the people must in effect themselves mediately or immediately possess the power of granting their own money, or no shadow of liberty could subsist. The colonies draw from you, as with their life blood, these ideas and principles. Their love of liberty, as with you, fixed and attached on this specific point of taxing. Liberty might be safe, or might be endangered in twenty other particulars, without their being much pleased or alarmed. Here they felt its pulse; and as they found that beat, they found themselves sick or sound. I do not say whether they were right or wrong in applying your general arguments to their own case. It is not easy indeed to make a monopoly of theorems and corollaries. The fact is, that they did thus apply those general arguments; and your mode of governing them, whether through lenity or indolence, through wisdom or mistake, confirm them in the imagination that they, as well as you, had an interest in these common principles.

They were further confirmed in this pleasing error by the form of their provincial legislative assemblies. Their governments are popular in a high degree, some are merely popular; in all, the popular representative is the most weighty; and this share of the people in their ordinary government never fails to inspire them with lofty sentiments, and with a strong aversion from whatever tends to deprive them of their chief importance.

If anything were wanting to this necessary operation of the form of government, religion would have given it a complete effect. Religion, always a principle of energy, in this new people, is no way worn out or impaired; and their mode of professing it is also one main cause of this free spirit. The people are protestants; and of that kind which is the most averse to all implicit submission of mind and opinion.

This is a persuasion not only favorable to liberty but built upon it. I do not think, sir, that the reason of this averseness in the dissenting churches, from all that looks like absolute government, is so much to be sought in their religious tenets, as in their history. Every one knows, that the Roman Catholic religion is at least coeval with most of the governments where it prevails; that it has generally gone hand in hand with them, and received great favor and every kind of support from authority. The church of England too was formed from her cradle under the nursing care of regular government. But the dissenting interests have sprung up in direct opposition to all the ordinary powers of the world; and could justify that opposition only on a strong claim to natural liberty. Their very existence depended on the powerful and unremitted assertion of that claim. All protestantism, even the most cold and passive, is a sort of dissent. But the religion most prevalent in our northern colonies, is a refinement on the principle of resistance, it is the diffidence of dissent; and the protestantism of the protestant religion. This religion, under a variety of denominations agreeing in nothing but in the spirit of liberty, is predominant in most of the northern provinces; where the church of England, notwithstanding its legal rights, is in reality no more than a sort of private sect; not composing most probably the tenth of the people. The colonists left England when this spirit was high: and in the emigrants was the highest of all, and even that strain of foreigners, which has been constantly flowing into these colonies, has for the greatest part, been composed of dissenters from the establishments of their several countries; and have brought with them a temper and character far from alien to that of a people with whom they mixed.

Sir, I can perceive, by their manner, that some gentlemen object to the latitude of this description: because in the southern colonies the church of England forms a large body, and has a regular establishment. It is certainly true. There is, however, a circumstance attending these colonies, which in my opinion, fully counterbalances this difference, and makes the spirit of liberty still more high and haughty than in those to the northward. It is that in Virginia and the Carolinas, they have a vast multitude of slaves. Where this is the case in any part of the world, those who are free, are by far the most proud and jealous of their freedom. Freedom is to them not only an enjoyment, but a kind of rank and privilege. Not seeing there that freedom, as in countries where it is a common blessing, and as broad and general as the air, may be united with much abject toil, with great misery, with all the exterior of servitude, liberty looks amongst them like something that is more noble and liberal. I do not mean, sir, to commend the superior morality of this sentiment, which has at least as much pride as virtue in it, but I cannot alter the nature of man. The fact is so, and these people of the southern colonies are much more strongly, and with a higher and more stubborn spirit, attached to liberty than those of the northward. Such were all the ancient commonwealths; such were our Gothic ancestors; such in our days were the Poles; and such will be all masters of slaves, who are not slaves themselves. In such a people the haughtiness of domination combines with the spirit of freedom, fortifies it, and renders it invincible. . . .

The temper and character, which prevail in our colonies, are, I am afraid, unalterable by any human art. We cannot, I fear, falsify the pedigree of this fierce people, and persuade them, that they are not sprung from a nation, in whose veins the blood of freedom circulates. The language, in which they would hear you tell them this tale, would detect the imposition; your speech would betray you. An Englishman is the unfittest person on earth to argue another Englishman into slavery.

I think it is nearly as little in our power to change their republican religion, as their free descent; or to substitute the Roman Catholic as a penalty, or the church of England as an improvement. The mode of inquisition and dragooning is going out of fashion in the old world, and I should not confide much to their efficacy in the new. The education of the Americans is also on the same unalterable bottom with their religion. You cannot persuade them to burn their books of curious science; to banish their lawyers from their courts of law, or to quench the lights of their assemblies, by refusing to choose those persons who are best read in their privileges. It would be no less impracticable to think of wholly annihilating the popular assemblies, in which these lawyers sit.—The army, by which we must govern in their place would be far more chargeable to us, not quite so effectual, and perhaps in the end, full as difficult to be kept in obedience.

With regard to the high aristocratic spirit of Virginia and the southern colonies, it has been proposed, I know, to reduce it by declaring a general enfranchisement of their slaves. This project has had its advocates and panegyrists: yet I never could argue myself into an opinion of it. Slaves are often much attached to their masters. A general wild offer of liberty would not always be accepted.—History furnishes few instances of it. It is sometimes as hard to persuade slaves to be free, as it is to compel freemen to be slaves, and in this auspicious scheme, we should have both these pleasing tasks on our hands at once. But when we talk of enfranchisement, do we not perceive that the American masters may enfranchise too, and arm servile hands in defence of freedom? A measure to which other people have had recourse more than once, and not without success, is a desperate situation of their affairs.

Slaves, as these unfortunate black people are, and dull as all men are from slavery, must they not a little suspect the offer of freedom from that very nation which has sold them to their present masters? From that nation, one of whose causes of quarrel with those masters, is their refusal to deal any more in that inhuman traffic? An offer of freedom from England would come rather oddly, shipped to them in an African vessel, which is refused an entry into the ports of Virginia and Carolina, with a cargo of three hundred Angola negroes. It would be curious to see the Guinea captain attempting at the same instant to publish his proclamation of liberty, and to advertise his sale of slaves. . . .

If we mean to conciliate and concede, let us see of what nature the concession ought to be? To ascertain the nature of our concession, we must look at their complaint. The colonies complain that they have not the characteristic mark and zeal of British freedom. They complain, that they are taxed in a parliament, in which they are not represented. If you mean to satisfy them at all, you must satisfy them with regard to this complaint. If you mean to please any people, you must give them the boon which they ask; not what you may think better for them, but of a kind totally different. Such an act may be a wise regulation, but it is no concession; whereas our present theme is the mode of giving satisfaction.

Sir, I think you must perceive, that I am resolved this day to have nothing at all to do with the question of the right of taxation. Some gentlemen startle—but it is true. I put it totally out of the question. It is less than nothing in my consideration. I do not indeed wonder, nor will you, sir, that gentlemen of profound learning are fond of displaying it on this profound subject. But my consideration is narrow, confined, and wholly limited to the policy of the question. I do not examine, whether the giving away a man's money be a power excepted and reserved out of the general trust of government, and how far all mankind, in all forms of polity are entitled to an exercise of that right by the charter of nature. Or whether, on the contrary, a right of taxation is necessarily involved in the general principles of legislation, and inseparable from the ordinary supreme power?—These are deep questions, where great names militate against each other; where reason is perplexed, and an appeal to authorities only thickens the confusion. For high and reverend authorities lift up their heads on both sides, and there is no sure footing in the middle. This point is the great Serbonian bog, betwixt Damiata and Mount Cassius old, where armies whole have sunk. I do not intend to be overwhelmed in that bog, though in such respectable company. The question with me is, not whether you have a right to render your people miserable, but whether it is not your interest to make them happy? It is not what a lawyer tells me I may do, but what humanity, reason, and justice tells me I ought to do. Is a politic act the worse for being a generous one? Is no concession proper, but that which is made from your want of right to keep what you grant? Or does it lessen the grace or dignity of relaxing in the exercise of an odious claim, because you have your evidence room full of titles, and all those arms? Of what avail are they, when the reason of the thing tells me, that the assertion of title is the loss of my suit; and that I could do nothing but wound myself by the use of my own weapons?

Such is steadfastly my opinion of the absolute necessity of keeping up the concord of this empire by a unity of spirit, though in a diversity of operations; that, if I were sure the colonists had, at their leaving this country, sealed a regular compact of servitude; that they had solemnly abjured all the rights of citizens; that they had made a vow to renounce all ideas of liberty, for them and their posterity, to all generations; yet I should hold myself obliged to conform to the temper I found universally prevalent in my own day, and to govern two millions of men, impatient of servitude, on the principles of freedom. I am not determining a point of law; I am restoring tranquility, and the general character and situation of a people must determine what sort of government is fitted for them. That point nothing else can or ought to determine.

My idea, therefore, without considering whether we yield as matter of right, or grant as matter of favor, is to admit the people of our colonies into an interest in the constitution; and by recording that admission in the journals of parliament, to give them as strong an assurance as the nature of the thing will admit, that we mean forever to adhere to that solemn declaration of sympathetic indulgence. . . .

One fact is clear and indisputable. The public and avowed origin of this quarrel was on taxation. This quarrel has indeed brought on new disputes, on new questions; but certainly the least bitter, and the fewest of all, on the trade laws [that is, the various laws passed during the eighteenth century to control colonial trade]. To judge which of the two be the real radical cause of quarrel, we have to see whether the commercial dispute did, in order of time, precede the dispute on taxation? There is not a shadow of evidence for it. Next, to enable us to judge whether at this moment a dislike to the trade laws be the real cause of quarrel, it is absolutely necessary to put the taxes out of the question by a repeal. See how the Americans act in this position, and then you will be able to discern correctly what is the true object of the controversy, or whether any controversy at all will remain? Unless you consent to remove this cause of difference, it is impossible, with decency, to assert that the dispute is not upon what it is avowed to be. And I would, sir, recommend to your serious consideration whether it be prudent

to form a rule for punishing people, not on their own acts, but on your con-
jectures. Surely it is preposterous at the very best. It is not justifying your
anger by their misconduct, but it is converting your ill-will into their delin-
quency. . . .

You will now, sir, perhaps, imagine that I am on the point of proposing
to you a scheme for a representation of the colonies in parliament. Perhaps
I might be inclined to entertain some such thought; but a great flood stops
me in my course. *Opposuit natura*—I cannot remove the eternal barriers
of the creation. The thing in that mode, I do not know to be possible. As I
meddle with no theory, I do not absolutely assert the impracticability of
such a representation. But I do not see my way to it; and those who have
been more confident, have not been more successful. However, the arm of
public benevolence is not shortened, and there are often several means to the
same end. What nature has disjoined in one way, wisdom may unite in another. When we cannot give the benefit as we would wish, let us not refuse
it altogether. If we cannot give the principal, let us find a substitute. But
how? Where? What substitute?

Fortunately I am not obliged, for the ways and means of this substitute,
to tax my own unproductive invention. I am not even obliged to go to the
rich treasury of the fertile framers of imaginary commonwealths; not to the
republic of Plato, not to the Utopia of Moore, not to the oceans of Harrington. It is before me. It is at my feet, and the rude swain treads daily on it
with his clouted shoon. I only wish you to recognize, for the theory, the
ancient constitutional policy of this kingdom with regard to representatives,
as that policy has been declared in acts of parliament; and as to the practice,
to return to that mode which a uniform experience has marked out to you
as best; and in which you walked with security, advantage, and honor, until
the year 1763.

My resolutions, therefore, mean to establish the equity and justice of a
taxation of America by grant and not by imposition. To mark the legal
competency of the colony assemblies for the support of their government in
peace, and for public aids in time of war. To acknowledge that this legal
competency has had a dutiful and beneficial exercise; and that experience
has shown the benefit of their grants, and the futility of parliamentary taxation as a method of supply.

These solid truths compose six fundamental propositions. There are
three more resolutions corollary to these. If you admit the first set you can
hardly reject the others. But if you admit the first, I shall be far from solicitous whether you accept or refuse the last. I think these six massive pillars

will be of strength sufficient to support the temple of British concord. I have no more doubt than I entertain of my existence, that if you admitted these, you would command an immediate peace; and with but tolerable future management, a lasting obedience in America. I am not arrogant in this confident assurance. The propositions are all mere matters of fact; and if they are such facts as draw irresistible conclusions even in the stating, that is the power of truth, and not any management of mine.

Sir, I shall open the whole plan to you together, with such observations on the motions as may tend to illustrate them where they may want explanation. The first is a resolution—"That the colonies and plantations of Great Britain in North America, consisting of fourteen separate governments, and containing two million and upwards of free inhabitants, have not the liberty and privilege of electing and sending any knights and burgesses, or others, to represent them in the high court of parliament."—This is a plain matter of fact, necessary to be laid down, and (excepting the description) it is laid down in the language of the constitution; it is taken nearly verbatim from acts of parliament.

The second is like unto the first—"That the said colonies and plantations have been liable to, and bounden by, several subsidies, payments, rates, and taxes, given and granted by parliament, though the said colonies and plantations have not their knights and burgesses, in the said high court of parliament, of their own election, to represent the condition of their country; by lack whereof they have been oftentimes touched and grieved by subsidies given, granted, and assented to, in the said court, in a manner prejudicial to the commonwealth, quietness, rest, and peace, of the subjects inhabiting within the same."

Is this description too hot, or too cold, too strong, or too weak? Does it arrogate too much to the supreme legislature? Does it lean too much to the claims of the people? If it runs into any of these errors, the fault is not mine. It is the language of your own ancient acts of parliament. *Non meus hic sermo, sed qua proecepit, ofella, rusticus, abnormis sapiens,* it is the general produce of the ancient, rustic, manly, home-bred sense of this country. I did not dare to rub off a particle of the venerable rust that rather adorns and preserves than destroys the metal. It would be a profanation to touch with a tool the stones which construct the sacred altar of peace. I would not violate, with modern polish, the ingenious and noble roughness of these truly constitutional materials. Above all things, I was resolved not to be guilty of tampering—the odious vice of restless and unstable minds. I put my foot in the tracks of our forefathers, where I can neither wander nor stumble. Determining to fix articles of peace, I was resolved not to be wise beyond what was written; I was resolved to use nothing else than the form of sound words to let others abound in their own sense; and carefully to abstain from all expressions of my own. What the law has said, I say. In all things else I am silent. I have no organ but for her words. This if it be not ingenious, I am sure is safe.

There are, indeed, words expressive of grievance in this second resolution, which those who are resolved always to be in the right, will deny to contain matter of fact, as applied to the present case; although parliament thought them true with regard to the counties of Chester and Durham.—— They will deny that the Americans were ever "touched and grieved" with the taxes. If they consider nothing in taxes but their weight as pecuniary impositions, there might be some pretence for this denial. But men may be sorely touched and deeply grieved in their privileges as well as in their purses. Men may lose little in property by the act which takes away all their freedom. When a man is robbed of a trifle on the highway, it is not the twopence lost that constitutes the capital outrage. This is not confined to privileges; even ancient indulgences withdrawn, without offence on the part of those who enjoyed such favors, operate as grievances. But were the Americans then not touched and grieved by the taxes, in some measure, merely asked? If so, why were they all either wholly repealed or exceedingly reduced? Were they not touched and grieved even by the regulating duties of the sixth of George the II? Else why were the duties first reduced to one third in 1764, and afterwards to a third of that third in the year 1766? were they not touched and grieved by the stamp act? I shall say they were until that tax is revived. Were they not touched and grieved by the duties of 1767, which were likewise repealed, and which lord Hillsborough tells you (for the ministry) were laid contrary to the true principle of commerce? Is not the assurance given by that noble person to the colonies of a resolution to lay no more taxes on them, an admission that taxes would touch and grieve them? Is not the resolution of the noble lord in the blue riband, now standing on your journals, the strongest of all proofs that parliamentary subsidies really touched and grieved them? Else why all these changes, modifications, repeals, assurances and resolutions?

The next proposition is, "That, from the distance of the said colonies, and from other circumstances, no method has hitherto been devised for procuring a representation in parliament for the said colonies." This is an assertion of a fact. I go no farther on the paper, though in my private judgment, an useful representation is impossible; I am sure it is not desired by them, nor ought it perhaps by us; but I abstain from opinions.

The fourth resolution is, "That each of the said colonies hath within itself a body chosen in part, or in the whole, by the freemen, freeholders, or other free inhabitants thereof, commonly called the general assembly, or general court, with powers legally to raise, levy, and assess, according to the several usage of such colonies, duties and taxes towards defraying all sorts of public service."

This competence in the colony assemblies is certain. It is proved by the whole tenor of their acts of supply in all the assemblies, in which the constant style of granting is, "An aid to his majesty;" and acts, granting to the crown, has regularly, for near a century, passed the public offices without dispute. Those who have been pleased paradoxically to deny this right, holding that none but the British parliament can grant to the crown, are wished to look to what is done, not only in the colonies, but in Ireland, in one uniform un-broken tenor every session. . . .

The sixth and last resolution, which is—"That it hath been found, by experience, that the manner of granting the said supplies and aids, by the said general assemblies, hath been more agreeable to the said colonies, and more beneficial and conducive to the public service, than the mode of giving and granting aids in parliament, to be raised and paid in the same colonies." This makes the whole of the fundamental part of the plan. The conclusion is irre-sistible. You cannot say that you were driven by any necessity to an exercise of the utmost rights of legislature. You cannot assert that you took on your-selves the task of imposing colony taxes, from the want of another legal body, that is competent to the purpose of supplying the exigencies of the state, with-out wounding the prejudices of the people. Neither is it true that the body so qualified, and having that competence had neglected the duty. . . .

I wish, sir, to repeal the Boston port bill, because (independently of the dangerous precedent of suspending the rights of the subjects during the king's pleasure) it was passed, as I apprehend, with less regularity, and on more partial principles than it ought. The corporation of Boston was not heard, before it was condemned. Other towns full as guilty as she was, have not had their ports blocked up. Even the restraining bill of the present session does not go to the length of the Boston port act. The same ideas of prudence, which induced you not to extend equal punishment to equal guilt, even when you were punishing, induce me, who mean not to chastise, but to reconcile, to be satisfied with the punishment already partially inflicted.

Ideas of prudence, and accommodation to circumstances, prevent you from taking away the charters of Connecticut and Rhode Island, as you have taken away that of Massachusetts colony, though the crown has far less power in the above two former provinces than it enjoyed in the latter; and though the abuses have been full as great, and as flagrant, in the exempted as in the punished. The same reasons of prudence and accommodation have weight with me in restoring the charter of the Massachusetts Bay. Besides, sir, the act which changes the charter of the Massachusetts Bay is in many particulars so exceptionable, that if I did not wish absolutely to repeal, I would by all means desire to alter it, as several of its provisions tend to the subversion of all public and private justice. Such, among others, is the power in the governor to change the sheriff at his pleasure, and to make a new returning officer for every special cause. It is shameful to behold such a regulation standing among English laws.

The act for bringing persons, accused of committing murder, under the order of government, to England, for trial, is but temporary. That act has calculated the probable duration of our quarrel with the colonies, and is accommodated to that supposed duration. I would hasten the happy moment of reconciliation: and therefore must, on my principle, get rid of that most justly obnoxious act. . . .

The Americans will have no interest contrary to the grandeur and glory of England, when they are not oppressed by the weight of it, and they will rather be inclined to respect the acts of a superintending legislature, when they see in them the acts of that power, which is itself the security, not the rival of their secondary importance. In this assurance, my mind most perfectly acquiesces; and I confess I feel not the least alarm, from the discontents which are to arise from putting people at their ease; nor do I apprehend the destruction of this empire, from giving, by an act of free grace and indulgence, to two millions of my fellow citizens, some share of those rights upon which I have always been taught to value myself.

It is said indeed that this power of granting, vested in American assemblies, would dissolve the unity of the empire, which was preserved entire, although Wales, Chester, and Durham were added to it. Truly, Mr. Speaker, I do not know what this unity means; nor has it ever been heard of, that I know, in the constitutional policy of this country. The very idea of subordination of parts excludes this notion of simple and undivided unity. England is the head; but she is not the head and the members too. Ireland has ever had, from the beginning, a separate, but not an independent, legislature: which, far from distracting, promoted the union of the whole. Every thing was sweetly and harmoniously disposed through both islands for the conservation of English dominion, and the comminution of English liberties. I do not see that the same principles might not be carried into twenty islands, and with the same good effect. This is my model with regard to America, as far as the internal circumstances of the two countries are the same. I know no other unity of this empire, than I can draw from its example during these periods when it seemed, to my poor understanding, more united than it is now, or than it is likely to be by the present methods. . . .

My hold of the colonies is in the close affection which grows from common names, from kindred blood, from similar privileges, and equal protection. These are ties which though light as air, are as strong as links of iron. Let the colonies always keep the idea of their civil rights associated with your government; they will cling and grapple to you; and no force under Heaven will be of power to tear them from their allegiance. But let it once be understood, that your government may be one thing, and their privileges another, that these two things may exist without any mutual relation, the cement is gone; the cohesion is loosened; and every thing hastens to decay and dissolution. As long as you have wisdom to keep the sovereign authority of this country as the sanctuary of liberty, the sacred temple consecrated to our common faith, wherever the chosen race and sons of England worship freedom, they will turn their faces towards you.

The more they multiply, the more friends you will have; the more ardently they love liberty, the more perfect will be their obedience. Slavery they can have any where. It is a weed that grows in every soil. They may have it from Spain, they may have it from Prussia. But until you become lost to all feeling of your true interest, and your natural dignity, freedom they can have from none but you. This is the commodity of price, of which you have the monopoly. This is the true act of navigation, which binds to you the commerce of the colonies, and through them secures to you the wealth of the world. Deny them this participation of freedom and you break that sole bond, which originally made, and must still preserve, the unity of the empire. Do not entertain so weak an imagination, as that your registers and your bonds, your affidavits and your suffrances, your cockets and clearances, are what form the great securities of your commerce. Do not dream, that your letters of office, and your instructions, and your suspending classes are the things that hold together the great contexture of this mysterious whole. These things do not make your government. Dead instruments, passive tools as they are, it is the spirit of English communion that gives all their life and efficacy to them. It is the spirit of the English constitution which, infused through the mighty mass, pervades, feeds, invigorates, vivifies, every part of the empire, even down to the minutest members.

Is it not the same virtue which does everything for us here in England?

Do you imagine then, that it is the land tax act which raises your revenue? that it is the annual vote in the committee of supply, which gives you your army? or that it is the mutiny bill which inspires it with bravery and discipline? No! surely no! It is the love of the people, it is their attachment to their government, from the sense of the deep stake they have in such a glorious institution, which gives you your army and your navy, and infuses into both that liberal obedience, without which your army would be a base rabble, and your navy nothing but rotten timber.

All this, I know well enough, will sound wild and chimerical to the profane herd of those vulgar and mechanical politicians, who have no place among us; a sort of people who think that nothing exists but what is gross and material; and who therefore, far from being qualified to be directors of the great movement of empire, are not fit to turn a wheel in the machine. But to men truly initiated and rightly taught, these ruling and master principles, which, in the opinion of such men as I have mentioned, have no substantial existence, are in truth everything, and all in all. Magnanimity in politics is not seldom the truest wisdom; and a great empire and little minds go ill together. If we are conscious of our situation, and glow with zeal to fill our place as becomes our station and ourselves, we ought to auspicate all our public proceedings on America, with the old warning of the church, *sursum corda!* We ought to elevate our minds to the greatness of that trust to which the order of Providence has called us. By adverting to the dignity of this high calling, our ancestors have turned a savage wilderness into a glorious empire; and have made the most extensive, and the only honorable conquests; not by destroying, but by promoting, the wealth, the number, the happiness, of the human race. Let us get an American revenue as we have got an American empire. English privileges have made it all that it is; English privileges alone will make it all it can be. In full confidence of this unalterable truth, I now lay the first stone of the temple of peace; and I move to you,

"That the colonies and plantations of Great Britain, in North America, consisting of fourteen separate governments and containing two millions and upwards of free inhabitants, have not had the right and privilege of electing and sending their knights and burgesses, or others, to represent in the high court of parliament."

PART TWO

Defending the Rights of Englishmen

1774-1776

PART TWO

Defending the Rights of Englishmen

1774-1776

DESPITE THE BEST efforts of Chatham, Burke, and other friends of America, Parliament in the spring of 1774 enacted a series of measures that alarmed the colonists as no previous legislation had. Fundamental constitutional questions had been paramount since 1763, but they had usually come singly or, at worst, as in the case of the Townshend duties, in a fairly limited package. But now, with the Boston Port Bill, the Administration of Justice Act, the Massachusetts Government Act, and a new Quartering Act—known collectively as the "Coercive Acts"—the colonists thought they saw the total subversion of their rights as Englishmen. The issue was no longer a particular tax bill or a specific readjustment in imperial administration. The Coercive Acts threatened the system that the colonists had come to think of as their natural right.

The Boston Port Act, which became effective on June 1, 1774, closed Boston's harbor to regular trade until the East India Company and the Customs Service received compensation for the losses sustained in the Tea Party. It seemed unfair to many Americans that an entire town must suffer for the acts of a few. But a more serious threat to liberty was posed by the Administration of Justice Act, which permitted under certain circumstances the transference of important trials from Massachusetts to England—an insult as well as an injury to the colony's system of justice. The Massachusetts Government Act went even further toward a revamping of colonial institutions: the colony's Council would henceforth be appointed by the King rather than be elected by the House of Representatives, certain judges and law enforcement officers would now be appointed and removed by the Governor, and

[127]

town meetings were to be held only with the consent of the Governor. While these provisions did not affect colonies other than Massachusetts, each colony was well aware that it might now suffer similar reorganization at the whim of Parliament. And the last of the Coercive Acts, the new Quartering Act, did apply to all mainland colonies: it authorized the quartering of troops in occupied dwellings—an invasion of privacy certain to antagonize most Americans. The colonists decided to resist.

But it soon became apparent that the mother country was as intent on enforcing its new policy as the colonies were on thwarting it. Resistance by the colonists brought more and more redcoated British regulars into American towns. The bolder colonists armed themselves; the officers of the imperial troops tried to prevent rebel armaments from becoming a threat to imperial authority. Had the first clash not come at Lexington in mid-April 1775 it would surely have occurred elsewhere—in Virginia, in New York, in South Carolina—not long after. While Americans still toasted the King, still proclaimed loyalty to Great Britain, and still considered themselves Englishmen, the day of defining the rights of Englishmen was largely over. Most men now knew what they thought those rights to be, and they were ready to fight to preserve them.

For almost a year, war raged in the colonies between American rebels and British troops before there was serious talk of independence. Armies advanced and retreated; cities were besieged and often captured; soldiers enlisted, fought, and died; but still the question was rights, not political separation. Not until January 1776.

With the publication of Thomas Paine's *Common Sense* in the first month of 1776, the struggle between the government of George III and its American dependencies entered a new phase. During the next six months the events of war seemed secondary to the deliberations of local, colonial, and intercolonial congresses. By June, the colonies—outside of areas actively occupied by British forces—had achieved *de facto* independence. Within another month the Continental Congress, representing thirteen mainland colonies from New Hampshire to Georgia, had pledged their lives, fortunes, and sacred honor to a determination that "these United Colonies are, and of right ought to be free and independent states."

IV

THE COLONIES DEFY THE INTOLERABLE ACTS,

1774-1775

THE COERCIVE ACTS together with the Quebec Act of May 1774 were soon dubbed the "Intolerable Acts." Each of the five Parliamentary measures brought determined opposition from various segments of the population; collectively they were condemned by the colonial governments. The Boston Port Bill, for example, seemed so harsh a retribution for the Tea Party that town, county, and colonial governments rallied to the aid of the Bostonians (pp. 130, 131, and 133). Even Americans in England felt the implications of the Intolerable Acts to be so serious that they petitioned the Crown to reject the Administration of Justice Bill and the Massachusetts Government Act, both recently approved by Parliament (p. 134).

By midsummer 1774 resistance to the Intolerable Acts had expanded into a general resistance to British authority, pending repeal of the detested legislation. In Virginia the House of Burgesses adopted a resistance program, as broad as it was bold, that included a general boycott of British goods (p. 135). Meanwhile the contempt for British authority in Massachusetts made that colony virtually self-governing, except for the occupied city of Boston (pp. 139, 140, 142).

With opposition to the Intolerable Acts so widespread, it could not be long before intercolonial cooperation would pick up where the Stamp Act Congress had left off. In June 1774 the Massachusetts House of Representatives proposed a colonial congress; by September the First Continental Congress was in session. All thirteen colonies except Georgia were represented, and most of the delegates bore instructions that allowed them to promote united resistance to imperial authority (pp. 144, 146, 152, 154).

The fifty-six delegates met in Philadelphia from early September to late October 1774. After heated debate they endorsed the strongly worded Suffolk Resolves advocating civil and military resistance to the Coercive Acts (p. 154), while rejecting the more moderate compromise proposals of Joseph Galloway, a delegate from Pennsylvania. The Congress also issued a Declaration and Resolves against the Intolerable Acts and several other measures of Parliament passed since 1763. To back its demands the Congress framed a plan of intercolonial boycott of British goods, known as the Continental Association, modeled after the scheme already proposed by Virginia. The strong stand taken by the First Continental Congress received widespread approval from the colonies (pp. 158, and 161).

1. THE BOSTON PORT BILL PROVIDES WIDESPREAD RESISTANCE

QUEEN ANNE'S COUNTY PLEDGES COMMON CAUSE WITH BOSTON

[Report of a meeting held in Queen Anne's County, Maryland, May 30, 1774]

At a meeting of a considerable number of the magistrates, and other the most respectable inhabitants of Queen-Anne's county, at Queen's town, on the thirtieth day of May, 1774, in order to deliberate upon the tendency and effect of the act of parliament for blocking up the port and harbor of Boston.

Duly considering and deeply affected with the prospect of the unhappy situation of Great Britain and British America, under any kind of disunion, this meeting think themselves obliged, by all the ties which ever ought to preserve a firm union among Americans, as speedily as possible to make known their sentiments to their distressed brethren of Boston; and therefore publish to the world.

That they look upon the cause of Boston in its consequences to be the common cause of America.

That the act of parliament for blocking up the port and harbor of Boston, appears to them a cruel and oppressive invasion of their natural rights as men, and constitutional rights as English subjects, and if not repealed, will be a foundation for the utter destruction of American freedom.

That all legal and constitutional means ought to be used by all America, for procuring a repeal of the said act of parliament.

That the only effectual means of obtaining such repeal, they are at present of opinion, is an association, under the strongest ties, for breaking off all commercial connections with Great Britain, until the said act of parliament be repealed, and the right assumed by parliament for taxing America, in all cases whatsoever, be given up, and American freedom ascertained and settled upon a permanent constitutional foundation.

That the most practicable mode of forming such an effectual association, they conceive to be a general meeting of the gentlemen, who are already or shall be appointed committees, to form an American intercourse and correspondence upon this most interesting occasion.

That in the mean time they will form such particular associations as to them shall seem effectual; yet professing themselves ready to join in any reasonable general one that may be devised as aforesaid.

That these sentiments be immediately forwarded to be printed in the Maryland and Pennsylvania Gazettes.

That Edward Tilghman, Solomon Wright, Turbut Wright, John Browne, Richard Tilghman Earle, James Hollyday, Thomas Wright, William Hemsley, Adam Gray, Clement Sewell, Richard Tilghman, James Kent, John Kerr, James Bordley, and William Bruff, be a committee of correspondence and intercourse, until some alteration is made in this appointment by a more general meeting.

Attested by—

JAMES EARLE, Clk. Com.

BALTIMORE COUNTY PROPOSES TRADE REPRISALS

[Report of a meeting held in Baltimore, Maryland, May 31, 1774]

At a general meeting of the freeholders, gentlemen, merchants, tradesmen, and other inhabitants of Baltimore county, held at the court house of the said county, on Tuesday the 31st day of May 1774, Captain CHARLES RIDGELY, Chairman—

I. *Resolved,* That it is the opinion of this meeting, that the town of Boston is now suffering in the common cause of America, and that it is the duty of every colony in America to unite in the most effectual means to obtain a repeal of the late act of parliament for blocking up the harbor of Boston.— Dissentient three.

II. That it is the opinion of this meeting, that if the colonies come into a joint resolution to stop importations from, and exportations to Great Britain and the West-Indies, until the act for blocking up the harbor of Boston be repealed, the same may be the means of preserving North America in her liberties. Dissentient three.

III. That therefore the inhabitants of this county will join in an association with the several counties in this province and the principal colonies in America, to put a stop to exports to Great Britain and the West-Indies, after the first day of October next, or such other day as may be agreed on, and to put a stop to the imports from Great Britain after the first day of December next, or such other day as may be agreed upon until the said act shall be repealed, and that such association shall be upon oath.— Dissentient nine.

IV. Unanimously.—That it is the opinion of this meeting, that as the most effectual means of uniting all parts of this province in such association, as proposed, a general congress of deputies from each county be held at Annapolis at such times as may be agreed upon and that if agreeable to the sense of our sister colonies, delegates shall be appointed from this province to attend a general congress of delegates from the other colonies, at such time and place as shall be agreed on, in order to settle and establish a general plan of conduct for the important purposes aforementioned.

V. Unanimously.—That the inhabitants of this county will, and it is the opinion of this meeting, that this province ought to break off all trade and dealings with that colony, province or town, which shall decline or refuse to come into similar resolutions with a majority of the colonies.

VI. That Capt. Charles Ridgely, Charles Ridgely, son of John, Walter Tolley, jun. Thomas Cockey Dye, William Lux, Robert Alexander, Samuel Purviance, jun. John Moale, Andrew Buchanan, and George Risteau, be a committee to attend a general meeting at Annapolis. And that the same gentlemen, together with John Smith, Thomas Harrison, William Buchanan, Benjamin Nicholson, Thomas Sollars, William Smith, James Gittings, Richard Moale, Jonathan Plowman, and William Spear, be a committee of correspondence to receive and answer all letters, and on any emergency, to call a general meeting, and that any six of the number have power to act.

VII. That a copy of the proceedings be transmitted to the several counties of this province, directed to their committee of correspondence, and be also published in the Maryland Gazette, to evince to all the world the sense they entertain of the invasion of their constitutional rights and liberties.

VIII. That the chairman be desired to return the thanks of this meeting to the gentlemen of the committee of correspondence from Annapolis, for their polite personal attendance in consequence of an invitation by the committee of correspondence for Baltimore town.

Signed per order,
WILLIAM LUX, Clerk.

PHILADELPHIA RECOMMENDS A GENERAL CONGRESS

*[Resolutions passed against the Boston Port Bill in Philadelphia,
June 18, 1774]*

Philadelphia, Saturday, June 18, 1774

I. *Resolved,* That the act of parliament, for shutting up the port of Boston, is unconstitutional; oppressive to the inhabitants of that town; dangerous to the liberties of the British colonies; and that therefore, we consider our brethren, at Boston, as suffering in the common cause of America.

II. That a congress of deputies from the several colonies, in North America, is the most probable and proper mode of procuring relief for our suffering brethren, obtaining redress of American grievances, securing our rights and liberties, and re-establishing peace and harmony between Great Britain and these colonies on a constitutional foundation.

III. That a large and respectable committee be immediately appointed for the city and county of Philadelphia, to correspond with their sister colonies and with the several counties in this province, in order that all may unite in promoting and endeavoring to attain the great and valuable ends, mentioned in the foregoing resolution.

IV. That the committee nominated by this meeting shall consult together, and on mature deliberation determine, what is the most proper mode of collecting the sense of this province, and appointing deputies for the same, to attend a general congress; and having determined thereupon, shall take such measures, as by them shall be judged most expedient, for procuring this province to be represented at the said congress, in the best manner that can be devised for promoting the public welfare.

V. That the committee be instructed immediately to set on foot a subscription for the relief of such poor inhabitants of the town of Boston, as may be deprived of the means of subsistence by the operation of the act of parliament, commonly styled the Boston port-bill. The money arising from such subscription to be laid out as the committee shall think will best answer the ends proposed.

VI. That the committee consist of forty-three persons, viz. John Dickinson, Edward Pennington, John Nixon, Thomas Willing, George Clymer, Samuel Howell, Joseph Reade, John Roberts, (miller) Thomas Wharton, jun. Charles Thomson, Jacob Barge, Thomas Barclay, William Rush, Robert Smith, (carpenter,) Thomas Fitzimons, George Roberts, Samuel Ervin, Thomas Mifflin, John Cox, George Gray, Robert Morris, Samuel Miles, John M. Nesbit, Peter Chevalier, William Moulder, Joseph Moulder, Anthony Morris, jun. John Allen, Jeremiah Warder, jun. rev. D. William Smith, Paul Engle, Thomas Penrose, James Mease, Benjamin Marshall, Reuben Haines, John Bayard, Jonathan B. Smith, Thomas Wharton, Isaac Howell, Michael Hillegas, Adam Hubley, George Schlosser, and Christopher Ludwick.

THOMAS WILLING, JOHN DICKINSON, Esquires, Chairmen.

AMERICANS IN LONDON PETITION THE KING

[*Petition to the King by a number of Americans, including Benjamin Franklin, 1774*]

TO THE KING'S MOST EXCELLENT MAJESTY,

The petition of several natives of America, most humbly sheweth:

That your petitioners, being your majesty's most faithful subjects, are obliged to implore your gracious interposition, to protect them in the enjoyment of those privileges which are the right of all your people.

Your majesty's petitioners, have already seen, with unspeakable grief, their earnest prayers rejected, and heavy penalties inflicted, even on the innocent among their countrymen, to the subversion of every principle of justice, without their being heard. By this alarming procedure all property was rendered insecure; and they now see in two bills (for altering the government of the Massachusetts Bay, and the impartial administration of justice there) the intended subversion of the two other grand objects of civil society and constitutional protection, to wit, liberties and life.

Your petitioners most humbly represent to your majesty, that, to destroy or assume their chartered rights, without a full and fair hearing, with legal proof of forfeiture, and the abrogating of their most valuable laws, which had duly received the solemn confirmation of your majesty's royal predecessors, and were thence deemed unchangeable, without the consent of the people, is such a proceeding as renders the enjoyment of every privilege they possess totally uncertain and precarious. That an exemption of the soldiery from being tried in the Massachusetts Bay, for murder or other felony, committed upon your majesty's subjects there, is such an encouragement to licentiousness and incentive to outrage, as must subject your majesty's liege people to continued danger.

Your petitioners and their countrymen have been ever most zealously attached to your majesty's person and family. It is therefore with inexpressible affliction that they see an attempt, in these proceedings against them, to change the principle of obedience to government, from the love of the subjects towards their sovereign, founded on the opinion of his wisdom, justice and benevolence, into the dread of absolute power and laws of extreme rigor, unsupportable to a free people.

Should the bills above mentioned receive your royal sanction, your majesty's faithful subjects will be overwhelmed with grief and despair.

It is therefore our most earnest prayer that your majesty will be graciously pleased to suspend your royal assent to the said bills. . . .

VIRGINIA DRAFTS A BROAD PROGRAM OF RESISTANCE

*[Resolutions of county delegates assembled at Williamsburg,
Virginia, August 1, 1774]*

At a very full meeting of the delegates from the different counties in the colony and dominion of Virginia, begun in Williamsburg, the first day of August, in the year of our Lord 1774, and continued by several adjournments to Saturday the 6th of the said month, the following association was unanimously resolved upon and agreed to.

We, his majesty's dutiful and loyal subjects, the delegates of the freeholders of Virginia, deputed to represent them at a general meeting in the city of Williamsburg, avowing our inviolable and unshaken fidelity and attachment, to our most gracious sovereign, our regard and affection for all our friends and fellow subjects in Great Britain and elsewhere, protesting against every act or thing, which may have the most distant tendency to interrupt, or in any wise disturb his majesty's peace, and the good order of government, within this his ancient colony, which we are resolved to maintain and defend, at the risk of our lives and fortunes, but at the same time affected with the deepest anxiety, and most alarming apprehensions, of those grievances and distresses by which his majesty's American subjects are oppressed, and having taken under our most serious deliberation, the state of the whole continent, find that the present unhappy situation of our affairs is chiefly occasioned by certain ill-advised regulations, as well of our trade as internal policy, introduced by several unconstitutional acts of the British parliament, and at length, attempted to be enforced by the hand of power; solely influenced by these important and weighty consider-ations, we think it an indispensable duty, which we owe to our country, ourselves, and latest posterity, to guard against such dangerous and exten-sive mischiefs, by every just and proper means.

If, by the measures adopted, some unhappy consequences and incon-veniences should be derived to our fellow subjects, whom we wish not to injure in the smallest degree, we hope and flatter ourselves, that they will impute them to their real cause—the hard necessity to which we are driven.

That the good people of this colony may, on so trying an occasion, continue steadfastly directed to their most essential interests, in hopes that they will be influenced and stimulated by our example to the greatest indus-try, the strictest economy, and frugality, and the execution of every public virtue, persuaded that the merchants, manufacturers, and other inhabitants of Great Britain, and, above all, that the British parliament will be con-vinced how much the true interest of that kingdom must depend on the restoration and continuance of that mutual friendship and cordiality, which so happily subsisted between us, we have unanimously, and, with one voice, entered into the following resolutions and association, which we do oblige ourselves, by those sacred ties of honor and love to our country, strictly to observe; and further declare, before God and the world, that we will reli-giously adhere to and keep the same inviolate, in every particular, until re-dress of all such American grievances as may be defined and settled at the general congress of delegates from the different colonies, shall be fully ob-tained, or until this association shall be abrogated or altered by a general meeting of the deputies of this colony, to be convened, as is herein after directed. And we do, with the greatest earnestness, recommend this our asso-ciation, to all gentlemen, merchants, traders, and other inhabitants of this colony, hoping that they will cheerfully and cordially accede thereto.

1st. We do hereby resolve and declare that we will not, either directly or indirectly, after the first day of November next, import from Great Britain, any goods, wares, or merchandises, whatever, (medicines excepted), nor will we, after that day, import any British manufactures, either from the West-Indies or any other place, nor any article whatever, which we shall know, or have reason to believe, was brought into such countries from Great Britain, nor will we purchase any such articles so imported, of any person or persons whatsoever, except such as are now in the country, or such as may arrive on or before the said first day of November, in consequence of orders already given, and which cannot now be countermanded in time.

2dly. We will neither ourselves import, nor purchase any slave, or slaves, imported by any person after the first day of November next, either from Africa, the West-Indies, or any other place.

3dly. Considering the article of tea as the detestable instrument which laid the foundation of the present sufferings of our distressed friends in the town of Boston, we view it with horror, and therefore, resolve that we will not from this day, either import tea of any kind whatever, nor will we use or suffer, even such of it as is now at hand, to be used in any of our families.

4thly. If the inhabitants of the town of Boston, or any other colony, should, by violence or dire necessity, be compelled to pay the East-India company for destroying any tea, which they have lately, by their agents, unjustly attempted to force into the colonies, we will not, directly or indirectly, import or purchase any British East-India commodity whatever, till the company, or some other person, on their behalf, shall refund and fully restore to the owners, all such sum or sums of money as may be so extorted.

5thly. We do resolve, that unless American grievances be redressed before the 10th day of August, 1775, we will not, after that day, directly or indirectly, export tobacco or any other article whatever, to Great Britain; nor will we sell any such articles as we think can be exported to Great Britain with a prospect of gain, to any person or persons whatever, with a design of putting it into his or their power to export the same to Great Britain, either on our own, his or their account. And that this resolution may be the more effectually carried into execution, we do hereby recommend it to the inhabitants of this colony, to refrain from the cultivation of tobacco as much as conveniently may be, and in lieu thereof that they will, as we resolve to do, apply their attention and industry, to the cultivation of all such articles, as may form a proper basis for manufactures of all sorts, which we will endeavor to encourage throughout this colony to the utmost of our abilities.

6thly. We will endeavor to improve our breed of sheep, and increase their number to the utmost extent, and to this end, we will be as sparing as we conceivably can in killing of sheep, especially those of the most profitable kind, and if we should at any time be overstocked and can conveniently spare any we will dispose of them to our neighbors, especially the poorer sort of people, upon moderate terms.

7thly. Resolved, that the merchants and others, venders of goods and merchandises within this colony, ought not to take advantage of the scarcity of goods that may be occasioned by this association, but that they ought to sell the same at the rates they have been accustomed to for twelve months past, and if they shall sell any such goods on higher terms, or shall in any manner or by any device whatever, violate or depart from this resolution, we will not, and are of opinion that no inhabitant of this colony ought, at any time thereafter, to deal with any such persons, their factors, or agents, for any commodity whatever; and it is recommended to the deputies of the several counties, that committees be chosen in each county, by such persons as accede to this association, to take effectual care that these resolves be properly observed, and for corresponding occasionally with the general committee of correspondence in the city of Williamsburg. Provided that, if exchange should rise, such advance may be made in the prices of goods as shall be approved by the committee of each county.

8thly. In order the better to distinguish such worthy merchants and traders, who are well wishers to this colony, from those who may attempt, through motives of self-interest, to obstruct our views, we do hereby resolve, that we will not, after the first day of November next, deal with any merchant or trader, who will not sign this association, nor until he hath obtained a certificate of his having done so from the county committee, or any three members thereof. And if any merchant, trader, or other persons, shall import any goods or merchandise, after the first day of November, contrary to this association, we give it as our opinion, that such goods and merchandise should be either forthwith re-shipped, or delivered up to the county committee, to be stored at the risk of the importer, unless such importer shall give a proper assurance to the said committee, that such goods or merchandises shall not be sold within this colony during the continuance of this association; and if such importer shall refuse to comply with one or the other of these terms, upon application and due caution given to him or her, by the said committee, or any three members thereof, such committee is required to publish the truth of the case in the Gazettes, and in the county where he or she resides, and we will thereafter consider such person or persons as inimical to this country, and break off every connection and all dealings with them.

9thly. Resolved, That if any person or persons shall export tobacco, or any other commodity, to Great Britain, after the 10th day of August, 1775, contrary to this association, we shall hold ourselves obliged to consider such person or persons as inimical to the community, and as an approver of American grievances; and give it as our opinion, that the public should be advertised of his conduct, as in the 8th article is desired.

10thly. Being fully persuaded that the united wisdom of the general congress may improve these our endeavors to preserve the rights and liberties in British America, we decline enlarging at present, but do hereby resolve that we will conform to, and strictly observe, all such alterations, or additions, assented to by the delegates for this colony, as they may judge it necessary to adopt, after the same shall be published and made known to us.

11thly. Resolved, That we think ourselves called upon by every principle of humanity and brotherly affection, to extend the utmost and speediest relief to our distressed fellow subjects in the town of Boston, and therefore most earnestly recommend it to all the inhabitants of this colony, to make such liberal contributions as they can afford; to be collected and remitted to Boston, in such manner as may best answer so desirable a purpose.

12thly, and lastly. Resolved, That the moderator of this meeting, and, in case of his death, Robert Carter Nicholas, esquire, be empowered, on any future occasion, that may in his opinion require it, to convene the several delegates of this colony, at such time and place as he may judge proper; and in case of the death or absence of any delegate, it is recommended that another be chosen in his place.

2. ROYAL AUTHORITY DISINTEGRATES IN MASSACHUSETTS

An Anecdote Reveals the Impotence of the British Army

[Extract of a letter from John Trumbull to John Adams, from Boston, August 20, 1774]

In the county of Worcester, the people, at a general meeting, have resolved that no court shall be held there, according to the new regulation of juries, and that judge Oliver shall not take his seat. Upon a report that a regiment would be sent to protect the court, they declared that they were ready to meet it. It is to be hoped, however, that no violent measures will be taken, till the sense of the whole continent is known; as the people have great dependence upon the determinations of congress, and expect them to chalk out the line for their conduct. As to the soldiers here, they are no more feared than if they were the troops of Lilliput. Indeed, they are much more disposed to flight than combat, and have more inclination to desert to us than to fight us—above two hundred having already left them. To put a stop to these frequent desertions, the officers are obliged to treat them with great severity—death or 1000 lashes, is the only choice offered to those who are retaken. There is a humorous story told about the town of one of the deserters, though I cannot say it is absolutely to be depended upon as a fact: a soldier, whose name is Patrick, deserted sometime ago and settled in a country town at some distance, and there undertook to instruct a company of about fifty men in military exercises. A sergeant and eight men were sent to apprehend deserters, got intelligence of him, and agreed with a countryman, for a couple of guineas, to conduct them to him. Patrick, it seems, was at that time exercising his company; however, being called by the sergeant and his men, he immediately came up to them. The sergeant demanded what he did there, told him he was his prisoner, and ordered him to return and join his regiment. Sir, said Patrick, I beg your pardon, but I don't think it possible for me to obey you at present. The sergeant repeated his orders in a very peremptory style. Patrick still assured him of the great improbability of his being able to comply with the command; but told him, as it was not absolutely certain, he would see what could be done about it. You must know, said he, that we determine every thing here by a vote—and turning to his company, which had by this time come up,—gentlemen, says he, if it be your mind that I should leave the town and return to my regiment, please to manifest it. Not a single hand appeared in favor of the motion. He then desired that those who were contrary-minded should manifest it, which passed nem con. The sergeant and his men, finding themselves in so small a minority, and seeing it in vain to oppose the general voice of the meeting, were about to return again in peace, when one or two of his men were desirous to have it put to vote whether they should not stay also. Patrick, as moderator, immediately put the question, which it was not difficult to carry in such an assembly, and the sergeant, knowing it vain to resist, returned with six men to his regiment.

BOSTON GRAND JURORS REFUSE TO SIT

[Statement by twenty-two Boston residents, including Paul Revere, in Suffolk County (Boston), August 30, 1774]

We, who are returned by the several towns in this county, to serve as grand jurors at the superior court for this present term, being actuated by a zealous regard for peace and good order, and a sincere desire to promote justice, righteousness and good government, as being essential to the happiness of the community, would now most glady proceed to the discharge of the important duty required in that department, could we persuade ourselves that, by doing thus, it would add to our own reputation, or promote the welfare of our country. But when we consider the dangerous inroads that have been made upon our civil constitution, the violent attempts now making to alter and annul the most essential parts of our charter, granted by the most solemn faith of kings, and repeatedly recognized by British kings and parliaments; while we see the open and avowed design of establishing the most complete system of despotism in this province, and thereby reducing the freeborn inhabitants thereof to the most abject state of slavery and bondage; we feel ourselves necessarily constrained to decline being impanelled, for reasons that we are ready to offer to the court, if permitted, which are as follows:

1st. Because Peter Oliver, esq. who sits as chief judge of this court, has been charged with high crimes and misdemeanors, by the late honorable house of representatives, the grand inquest of this province; of which charge he has never been legally acquitted, but has been declared by that house, unqualified to act as judge of this court.

2d. Because, by a late act of the British parliament, for altering the constitution of this province, the continuance of the present judges of this court, as well as the appointment of others, from the 1st of July last, is made to depend solely on the king's pleasure, vastly different from the tenure of the British judges; and as we apprehend they now hold their places, only in consequence of that act, all the judicial proceedings of the court will be taken as concessions to the validity of the same, to which we dare not assent.

3d. Because three of the judges, being the major part of the court, namely, the said Peter Oliver, esq. Foster Hutchinson, esq. and William Brown, esq. by taking the oath of counsellors under authority of the aforementioned act, are (as we are informed) sworn to carry into execution all the late grievous acts of the British parliament, among the last of which, is one, made ostensively for the impartial administration of justice in this province, but, as we fear, really for the impunity of such persons as shall, under pretext of executing those acts, murder any of the inhabitants thereof, which acts appear to us to be utterly repugnant to every idea of justice and common humanity, and are justly complained of, throughout America, as highly injurious and oppressive to the good people of this province, and manifestly destructive of their natural as well as constitutional rights.

4th. Because we believe, in our consciences, that our acting in concert with a court so constituted, and under such circumstances, would be so far betraying the just and sacred rights of our native land, which were not the gift of kings, but were purchased solely with the toil, the blood, and treasure, of our worthy and revered ancestors, and which we look upon ourselves under the most sacred obligations to maintain, and to transmit the same, whole and entire to our posterity.

Therefore, we, the subscribers, unanimously decline serving as grand jurors at this court.

THE PROVINCIAL CONGRESS ADMONISHES GENERAL THOMAS GAGE

[Address from the Provincial Congress of Massachusetts to the new Royal Governor, General Gage, at Concord, October 1774]

MAY IT PLEASE YOUR EXCELLENCY,

The delegates, from the several towns in the province of Massachusetts-Bay, convened in congress, beg leave to address you. The distressed and miserable state of the province, occasioned by the intolerable grievances and oppressions to which the people are subjected, and the danger and destruction to which they are exposed, of which your excellency must be sensible, and the want of a general assembly, have rendered it indispensably necessary to collect the wisdom of the province, by their delegates, in this congress, to concert some adequate remedy for preventing impending ruin, and providing for the public safety.

It was with the utmost concern we see your hostile preparations, which have spread such alarm through the province and the whole continent, as threaten to involve us in all the confusion and horrors of civil war: and, while we contemplate an event so deeply to be regretted by every good man, it must occasion the surprise and astonishment of all mankind, that such measures are pursued, against a people whose love of order, attachment to Britain, and loyalty to their prince, have ever been truly exemplary. Your excellency must be sensible, that the sole end of government is the protection and security of the people: whenever, therefore, that power, which was originally instituted to effect these important and valuable purposes, is employed to harass and enslave the people, in this case it becomes a curse, rather than a blessing.

The most painful apprehensions are excited in our minds, by the measures now pursuing; the rigorous execution of the (Boston) port bill, with improved severity, must certainly reduce the capital and its numerous dependencies to a state of poverty and ruin. The acts for altering the charter, and the administration of justice in the colony, are manifestly designed to abridge this people of their rights, and to license murders: and, if carried into execution, will reduce them to slavery. The number of troops in the capital, increased by daily accessions drawn from the whole continent, together with the formidable and hostile preparations which you are now making on Boston Neck, in our opinion, greatly endanger the lives, liberties, and property, not only of our brethren in the town of Boston, but of this province in general. Permit us to ask your excellency, whether an inattentive and unconcerned acquiescence to such alarming, such menacing measures, would not evidence a state of insanity? Or, whether the delaying to take every possible precaution for the security of this province, would not be the most criminal neglect in a people, heretofore rigidly and justly tenacious of their constituted rights?

Penetrated with the most poignant concern, and ardently solicitous to preserve union and harmony between Great Britain and the colonies, necessary to the well being of both, we entreat your excellency to remove that brand of contention, the fortress at the entrance of Boston. We are much concerned that you should have been induced to construct it, and thereby causelessly excite such a spirit of resentment and indignation as now generally prevails.

We assure you, that the good people of this colony never have had the least intention to do any injury to his majesty's troops; but on the contrary, most earnestly desire, that every obstacle to treating them as fellow subjects may be immediately removed: but are constrained to tell your excellency, that the minds of the people will never be relieved, till those hostile works are demolished. And we request, you, as you regard his majesty's honor and interest, the dignity, and happiness of the empire, and the peace and welfare of this province, that you immediately desist from the fortress, now constructing at the south entrance into the town of Boston, and restore the pass to its natural state.

3. RESISTANCE IS CENTRALIZED IN A CONTINENTAL CONGRESS

VIRGINIA INSTRUCTS ITS DELEGATES

*[Instructions from the Provincial legislature of Virginia,
meeting at Williamsburg, to its delegates to the First
Continental Congress, 1774]*

The unhappy disputes between Great Britain and her American colonies, which began about the third year of the reign of his present majesty, and since continually increasing, have proceeded to lengths so dangerous and alarming as to excite just apprehensions, in the minds of his majesty's faithful subjects of this colony, that they are in danger of being deprived of their natural, ancient, constitutional, and chartered rights, have compelled them to take the same into their most serious consideration; and being deprived of their usual and accustomed mode of making known their grievances, have appointed us their representatives to consider what is proper to be done in this dangerous crisis of American affairs. It being our opinion that the united wisdom of North America should be collected in a general congress of all the colonies, we have appointed the honorable Peyton Randolph, esquire, Richard Henry Lee, George Washington, Patrick Henry, Richard Bland, Benjamin Harrison, and Edmund Pendleton, esquires, deputies to represent this colony in the said congress, to be held at Philadelphia on the first Monday in September next.

And that they may be the better informed of our sentiments, touching the conduct we wish them to observe on this important occasion, we desire they will express, in the first place, our faith and true allegiance to his majesty, king George the third, our lawful and rightful sovereign; and that we are determined with our lives and fortunes, to support him in the legal exercise of all his just rights and prerogatives; and however misrepresented, we sincerely approve of a constitutional connection with Great Britain, and wish most ardently a return of that intercourse of affection and commercial connection that formerly united both countries, which can only be effected by a removal of those causes of discontent which have of late unhappily divided us.

It cannot admit of a doubt but that British subjects in America, are entitled to the same rights and privileges as their fellow subjects possess in

Britain; and therefore, that the power assumed by the British parliament to bind America by their statutes, in all cases whatsoever, is unconstitutional, and the source of these unhappy differences.

The end of government would be defeated by the British parliament exercising a power over the lives, the property, and the liberty of the American subject; who are not, and from their local circumstances cannot, be there represented. Of this nature we consider the several acts of parliament for raising a revenue in America, for extending the jurisdiction of the courts of admiralty, for seizing American subjects and transporting them to Britain to be tried for crimes committed in America, and the several late oppressive acts respecting the town of Boston, and province of the Massachusetts-Bay.

The original constitution of the American colonies possessing their assemblies with the sole right of directing their internal polity, it is absolutely destructive of the end of their institution that their legislatures should be suspended, or prevented, by hasty dissolutions, from exercising their legislative power.

Wanting the protection of Britain, we have long acquiesced in their acts of navigation restrictive of our commerce, which we consider as an ample recompense for such protection; but as those acts derive their efficacy from that foundation alone, we have reason to expect they will be restrained, so as to produce the reasonable purposes of Britain, without being injurious to us.

To obtain a redress of those grievances, without which the people of America can neither be safe, free, nor happy, they are willing to undergo the great inconvenience that will be derived to them from stopping all imports whatsoever from Great Britain, after the first day of November next, and also to cease exporting any commodity whatsoever, to the same place, after the 10th day of August, 1775. The earnest desire we have, to make as quick and full payment, as possible, of our debts to Great Britain, and to avoid the heavy injury that would arise to this country from an earlier adoption of the non-exportation plan, after the people have already applied so much of their labor to the perfecting of the present crop, by which means they have been prevented from pursuing other methods of clothing and supporting their families, have rendered it necessary to restrain you in this article of non-exportation; but it is our desire that you cordially co-operate with our sister colonies, in general congress, in such other just and proper methods, as they, or the majority, shall deem necessary for the accomplishment of these valuable ends.

The proclamation issued by general Gage, in the government of the province of the Massachusetts-Bay, declaring it treason for the inhabitants of that province to assemble themselves to consider of their grievances, and form associations for their common conduct on the occasion, and requiring the civil magistrates and officers to apprehend all such persons to be tried for their supposed offences, is the most alarming process that ever appeared in a British government; that the said general Gage hath thereby assumed and taken upon himself power denied by the constitution to our legal sovereign; that he, not having condescended to disclose by what authority he exercises such extensive and unheard of powers we are at a loss to determine whether he intends to justify himself as the representative of the king, or as the commander in chief of his majesty's forces in North America. If he considers himself as acting in the character of his majesty's representative, we would remind him, that the statute 25th Edward III, has expressed and defined all treasonable offences, and that the legislature of Great Britain hath declared that no offence shall be construed to be treason but such as is pointed out by that statute, and that this was done to take out of the hands of tyrannical kings, and of weak and wicked ministers, that deadly weapon which constructive treason had furnished them with, and which had drawn the blood of the best and honestest men in the kingdom, and that the king of Great Britain hath no right, by his proclamation, to subject his people to imprisonment, pains, and penalties.

That, if the said general Gage conceives he is empowered to act in this manner, as the commander in chief of his majesty's forces in America, this odious and illegal proclamation must be considered as a plain and full declaration that this despotic viceroy will be bound by no law, nor regard the constitutional rights of his majesty's subjects, whenever they interfere with the plan he had formed for oppressing the good people of the Massachusetts-Bay; and therefore, that the executing or attempting to execute, such proclamation, will justify *resistance* and *reprisal*.

PENNSYLVANIA INSTRUCTS ITS DELEGATES

*[Instructions from a representative committee of Pennsylvanians,
meeting in Philadelphia, to its delegates to the First
Continental Congress, July 23, 1774]*

PHILADELPHIA, July 23, 1774
The committee chosen by the several counties in Pennsylvania, having brought in a draught of instructions, the same were debated and amended,

and being agreed to, were ordered to be signed by the chairman. The committee in a body then waited on the assembly, and presented the same.

GENTLEMEN—The dissensions between Great Britain and her colonies on this continent, commencing about ten years ago, since continually increasing, and at length grown to such an excess as to involve the latter in deep distress and danger, have excited the good people of this province to take into their serious consideration, the present situation of public affairs. . . .

To us . . . it appears, at this alarming period, our duty to God, to our country, to ourselves, and to our posterity, to exert our utmost abilities, in promoting and establishing harmony between Great Britain and these colonies, *on a constitutional foundation.*

For attaining this great and desirable end, we request you as soon as you meet, to appoint a proper number of persons to attend a congress of deputies from the several colonies, appointed, or to be appointed, by the representatives of the people of the colonies respectively, in assembly or convention, or by delegates chosen by the counties generally in the respective colonies, and met in provincial committee, at such time and place as shall be generally agreed on: and that the deputies from this province may be induced and encouraged to concur in such measures, as may be devised for the common welfare, we think it proper, particularly to inform you how far, we apprehend, they will be supported in their conduct by their constituents.

The assumed parliamentary power of internal legislation, and the power of regulating trade, as of late exercised, and designed to be exercised, we are thoroughly convinced, will prove unfailing and plentiful sources of dissensions to our mother country and these colonies, unless some expedients can be adopted to render her secure of receiving from us every emolument that can, in justice and reason, be expected, and as secure in our lives, liberties, properties, and an equitable share of commerce.

Mournfully revolving in our minds the calamities that, arising from these dissensions, will most probably fall on us or our children, we will now lay before you the particular points we request of you to procure, if possible, to be finally decided; and the measures that appear to us most likely to produce such a desirable period of our distresses and dangers. We therefore desire of you—

First. That the deputies you appoint may be instructed by you strenuously to exert themselves at the ensuing congress, to obtain a renunciation, on the part of Great Britain, of all powers under the statute of the 35th of Henry the eighth, chapter the 2d—of all powers of internal legislation—of imposing taxes or duties, internal or external—and of regulating trade, except with respect to any new articles of commerce, which the colonies may hereafter raise, as silk, wine, etc., reserving a right to carry these from one colony to another—a repeal of all statutes for quartering troops in the colonies, or subjecting them to any expense on account of such troops—of all statutes imposing duties to be paid in the colonies, that were passed at the accession of his present majesty or before this time: which ever period shall be judged most advisable—of the statutes giving the courts of admiralty in the colonies greater power than courts of admiralty have in England—of the statutes of the 5th of George the second, chapter the 22d, and of the 23d, of George the second, chapter the 29th—of the statute for shutting up the port of Boston—and of every other statute particularly affecting the province of Massachusetts-Bay, passed in the last session of parliament.

In case of obtaining these terms, it is our opinion, that it will be reasonable for the colonies to engage their obedience to the acts of navigation, and to every other act of parliament declared to have force, at this time, in these colonies, other than those above mentioned, and to confirm such statutes by acts of the several assemblies. It is also our opinion, that, taking example from our mother country, in abolishing the "courts of wards and liveries, tenures in capite, and by knights service and purveyance," it will be reasonable for the colonies, in case of obtaining the terms before mentioned, to settle a certain annual revenue on his majesty, his heirs and successors, subject to the control of parliament, and to satisfy all damages done to the East-India company.

This our idea of settling a revenue, arises from a sense of duty to our sovereign and esteem for our mother country. We know and have felt the benefits of subordinate connection with her. We neither are so stupid as to be ignorant of them, nor so unjust as to deny them. We have also experienced the pleasures of gratitude and love, as well as advantages from that connection. The impressions are not yet erased. We consider her circumstances with tender concern. We have not been wanting, when constitutionally called upon, to assist her to the utmost of our abilities; insomuch that she has judged it reasonable to make us recompenses for our overstrained exertions: and we now think we ought to contribute more than we do, to the alleviation of her burthens.

Whatever may be said of these proposals on either side of the Atlantic, this is not a time, either for timidity or rashness. We perfectly know that, the great cause now agitated, is to be conducted to a happy conclusion, only by that well tempered composition of councils, with firmness, prudence, loyalty to our sovereign, respect to our parent state, and affection to our native country, united must form.

By such a compact, Great Britain will secure every benefit, that the parliamentary wisdom of ages has thought proper to attach to her. From her alone we shall still continue to receive manufactures. To her alone we shall continue to carry the vast multitude of enumerated articles of commerce, the exportation of which her policy has thought fit to confine to herself. With such parts of the world only, as she has appointed us to deal, we shall continue to deal, and such commodities only, as she has permitted us to bring from them, we shall continue to bring. The executive and controling power of the crown will retain their present full force and operation. We shall contentedly labor for her as affectionate friends, in time of tranquility: and cheerfully spend for her, as dutiful children, our treasure and our blood, in time of war. She will receive a certain income from us, without the trouble or expense of collecting it—without being constantly disturbed by complaints of grievances which she cannot justify and will not redress. In case of war, or in any emergency of distress to her, we shall also be ready and willing to contribute all aids within our power: and we solemnly declare, that on such occasions, if we or our posterity shall refuse, neglect, or decline thus to contribute, it will be a mean and manifest violation of a plain duty, and a weak and wicked desertion of the true interests of this province, which ever have been and must be bound up in the prosperity of our mother country. Our union, founded on mutual compacts and mutual benefits, will be indissoluble, at least more firm, than an union perpetually disturbed by disputed right and reported injuries.

Secondly. If all the terms above mentioned cannot be obtained, it is our opinion, that the measures adopted by the congress for our relief should never be relinquished or intermitted, until those relating to the troops—internal legislation—imposition of taxes or duties hereafter—the 35th of Henry the 8th, chapter the 2d—the extension of admiralty courts,—the ports of Boston, and the province of Massachusetts Bay, are obtained.—Every modification or qualification of these points, in our judgment, shall be inadmissible. To obtain them, we think it may be prudent to settle a revenue as above mentioned, and to satisfy the East India company.

Thirdly. If neither of those plans should be agreed to, in congress, but some other of a similar nature shall be framed, though on the terms of a revenue and satisfaction to the East India company, and though it shall be agreed by the congress to admit no modification or qualification in the terms they shall insist on, we desire your deputies may be instructed to concur with the other deputies in it; and we will accede to, and carry it into execution as far as we can.

Fourthly. As to the regulation of trade—we are of opinion, that by making some few amendments, the commerce of the colonies might be settled on a firm establishment, advantageous to Great Britain and them, requiring and subject to no future alterations, without mutual consent. We desire to have this point considered by the congress; and such measures taken, as they may judge proper.

In order to obtain redress of our common grievances, we observe a general inclination among the colonies of entering into agreements of non-importation and non-exportation. We are fully convinced, that such agreements would withhold very large supplies from Great Britain, and no words can describe our contempt and abhorrence of these colonies, if any such there are, who, from a sordid and ill-judged attachment to their own immediate profit, would pursue that, to the injury of their country, in this great struggle for all the blessings of liberty. It would appear to us a most wasteful frugality, that would lose every important possession by too strict an attention to small things, and lose also even these at the last. For our part, we will cheerfully make any sacrifice, when necessary, to preserve the freedom of our country. But other considerations have weight with us. We wish every mark of respect to be paid to his majesty's administration. We have been taught from our youth to entertain tender and brotherly affections for our fellow subjects at home. The interruption of our commerce must distress great numbers of them. This we earnestly desire to avoid. We therefore request, that the deputies you shall appoint may be instructed to exert themselves, at the congress, to induce the members of it to consent to make a full and precise statement of grievances, and a decent yet firm claim of redress, and to wait the event before any other step is taken. It is our opinion, that persons should be appointed and sent home to present this state and claim, at the court of Great Britain.

If the congress shall choose to form agreements of non-importation and non-exportation immediately, we desire the deputies from this province will endeavor to have them so formed as to be binding upon all, and that they may be permanent, should the public interest require it. They cannot be efficacious, unless they can be permanent, and it appears to us, that there will be a danger of their being infringed, if they are not formed with great caution and deliberation. We have determined in the present situation of public affairs to consent to a stoppage of our commerce with Great Britain only; but in case any proceedings of parliament, of which notice shall be received on this continent, before or at the congress, shall render it necessary, in the opinion of the congress, to further steps, the inhabitants of this province will adopt such steps, and do all in their power to carry them into execution.

This extensive power we commit to the congress, for the sake of preserving that unanimity of counsel and conduct, that alone can work out the salvation of these colonies, with a strong hope and trust, that they will not draw this province into any measure judged by us, who must be better acquainted with its state than strangers, highly inexpedient. Of this kind, we know any other stoppage of trade, but of that with Great Britain, will be. Even this step we should be extremely afflicted to see taken by the congress, before the other mode above pointed out is tried. But should it be taken, we apprehend that a plan of restrictions may be so framed, agreeably to the respective circumstances of the several colonies, as to render Great Britain sensible of the imprudence of her counsels, and yet leave them a necessary commerce. And here it may not be improper to take notice, that if redress of our grievances cannot be wholly obtained, the extent or continuance of our restrictions may, in some sort, be proportioned to the rights we are contending for, and the degree of relief afforded us. This mode will render our opposition as perpetual as our oppression, and will be a continual claim and assertion of our rights. We cannot express the anxiety, with which we wish the consideration of these points to be recommended to you. We are persuaded, that if these colonies fail of unanimity, or prudence in forming their resolutions, or of fidelity in observing them, the opposition by non-importation and non-exportation agreements will be ineffectual; and then we shall have only the alternative of a more dangerous contention, or of a tame submission.

Upon the whole, we shall repose the highest confidence in the wisdom and integrity of the ensuing congress: and though we have, for the satisfaction of the good people of this province, who have chosen us for this express purpose, offered you such instructions as have appeared expedient to us, yet it is not our meaning, that by these or by any you may think proper to give them the deputies appointed by you should be restrained from agreeing to any measure that shall be approved by a majority of the deputies in congress. We should be glad the deputies chosen by you could, by their influence, procure our opinions hereby communicated to you, to be as nearly adhered to, as may be possible: but to avoid difficulties, we desire that they may be instructed by you, to agree to any measure that shall be approved by the congress, in the manner before mentioned; the inhabitants of this province having resolved to adopt and carry them into execution. Lastly—we desire the deputies from this province, may endeavor to procure an adjournment of the congress, to such a day as they shall judge proper, and the appointment of a standing committee.

Agreed, that John Dickinson, Joseph Reade, and Charles Thomson, be a committee to write to the neighboring colonies, and communicate to them these resolves and instructions.

Agreed, that the committee for the city and county of Philadelphia, or any fifteen of them, be a committee of correspondence for the general committee of this province.

Extract from the minutes,

CHARLES THOMSON, Secretary.

NEW YORK INSTRUCTS ITS DELEGATES

[Resolutions by a public gathering in New York City, July 6, 1774]

At a numerous meeting of the inhabitants of the city of New York, convened in the fields, by public advertisement, on Wednesday the 6th of July, 1774.

MR. ALEXANDER M'DOUGALL, Chairman—

The business of the meeting being fully explained by the chairman, and the dangerous tendency of the numerous and vile arts used by the enemies of America, to divide and distract her councils, as well as the misrepresentations of the virtuous intentions of the citizens of this metropolis, in this interesting and alarming state of the liberties of America, the following resolutions were twice read, and the question being separately put on each of them, they were passed without one dissentient.

1st. *Resolved, nem. con.* That the statute commonly called the Boston port act, is oppressive to the inhabitants of that town, unconstitutional in its principles and dangerous to the liberties of British America; and that therefore, we consider our brethren at Boston as now suffering in the common cause of these colonies.

2d. *Resolved, nem. con.* That any attack or attempt to abridge the liberties, or invade the constitution of any of our sister colonies is immediately an attack upon the liberties and constitution of all the British colonies.

3d. *Resolved, nem. con.* That the shutting up of any of the ports in America, with intent to exact from Americans, a submission to parliamentary taxations, or extort a reparation of private injuries, is highly unconstitutional, and subversive of the commercial rights of the inhabitants of this continent.

4th. *Resolved, nem. con.* That it is the opinion of this meeting, that if the principal colonies on this continent, shall come into a joint resolution, to stop all importation from, and exportation to Great Britain, till the act of parliament for blocking up the harbor of Boston be repealed, the same will prove the salvation of North America and her liberties, and that, on the other hand, if they continue their exports and imports, there is great reason to fear that fraud, power, and the most odious oppression, will arise triumphant over right, justice, social happiness, and freedom:—Therefore,

5th. *Resolved, nem. con.* That the deputies who shall represent this colony in the congress of American deputies, to be held at Philadelphia, about the first of September next, are hereby instructed, empowered, and directed to engage with a majority of the principal colonies, to agree, for this city, upon a non-importation from Great Britain, of all goods, wares and merchandises, until the act for blocking up the harbor of Boston be repealed, and American grievances be redressed; and also to agree to all such other measures as the congress shall, in their wisdom, judge advansive of these great objects, and a general security of the rights and privileges of America.

6th. *Resolved, nem. con.* That this meeting will abide by, obey, and observe all such resolutions, determinations, and measures, which the congress aforesaid shall come into, and direct or recommend to be done, for obtaining and securing the important ends mentioned in the foregoing resolutions. And that an engagement to this effect be immediately entered into and sent to the congress, to evince to them, our readiness and determination to co-operate with our sister colonies, for the relief of our distressed brethren of Boston, as well as for the security of our common rights and privileges.

7th. *Resolved, nem. con.* That it is the opinion of this meeting, that it would be proper for every county in the colony, without delay, to send two deputies, chosen by the people, or from the committee, chosen by them in each county, to hold in conjunction with deputies for this city and county, a convention for the colony (on a day to be appointed) in order to elect a proper number of deputies, to represent the colony in the general congress: but that, if the counties shall conceive this mode impracticable, or inexpedient, they be requested to give their approbation to the deputies who shall be chosen for this city and county, to represent the colony in congress.

8th. *Resolved, nem. con.* That a subscription should immediately be set on foot, for the relief of such poor inhabitants of Boston as are, or may be deprived of the means of subsistence, by the operation of the act of parliament for stopping up the port at Boston. The money which shall arise from such subscription, to be laid out as the city committee of correspondence shall think will best answer the end proposed.

9th. *Resolved, nem. con.* That the city committee of correspondence be, and they are hereby instructed to use their utmost endeavors to carry these resolutions into execution.

Ordered, That these resolutions be printed in the public newspapers of this city, and transmitted to the different counties in this colony, and to the committees of correspondence, for the neighboring colonies.

New York, July 7, 1774.

On Monday evening the committee met and nominated five gentlemen as delegates at the grand congress on the first of next September, who are to be proposed to the citizens summoned to assembly this day at 12 o'clock, at the city hall, for their approbation; or to make such alterations as may be agreed upon.

JOHN ADAMS RECALLS ADVICE GIVEN TO THE MASSACHUSETTS DELEGATION

[Letter from John Adams to Hezekiah Niles, Quincy, Massachusetts, February 5, 1819]

DEAR SIR,—I enclose you the "broken hints to be communicated to the committee of congress for the Massachusetts," by Major Joseph Hawley, of Northampton.

This is the original paper that I read to Patrick Henry in the fall of the year 1774, which produced his rapturous burst of approbation, and solemn asseveration "I am of that man's mind."

I pray you to send it back to me. I would not exchange this original for the show book of Harvard college, and printed it shall be at my own expense in a hand-bill.

BROKEN HINTS TO BE COMMUNICATED TO THE COMMITTEE OF CONGRESS FOR THE MASSACHUSETTS.

We must fight, if we can't otherwise rid ourselves of British taxation, all revenues, and the constitution or form of government enacted for us by the British parliament. It is evil against right—utterly intolerable to every man who has any idea or feeling of right or liberty.

It is easy to demonstrate that the regulation act [that is, the Massachusetts Government Act] will soon annihilate every thing of value in the charter, introduce perfect despotism, and render the house of representatives a mere form and ministerial engine.

It is now or never, that we must assert our liberty. Twenty years will make the number of tories on this continent equal to the number of whigs. They who shall be born will not have any idea of a free government.

It will necessarily be a question, whether the new government of this province shall be suffered to take place at all,—or whether it shall be immediately withstood and resisted?

A most important question this—I humbly conceive it not best forcibly or wholly to resist it, immediately.

There is not heat enough yet for battle. Constant and a sort of negative resistance of government, will increase the heat and blow the fire. There is not military skill enough. That is improving, and must be encouraged and improved, but will daily increase.

Fight we must finally, unless Britain retreats.

But it is of infinite consequence that victory be the end and issue of hostilities. If we get to fighting before necessary dispositions are made for it, we shall be conquered, and all will be lost forever.

A certain clear plan, for a constant, adequate and lasting supply of arms and military stores, must be devised and fully contemplated. This is the main thing. This, I think, ought to be a capital branch of the business of congress —to wit: to devise and settle such a plan; at least, clearly to investigate how such supplies can be extensively had in case of need. While this is effecting —to wit: while the continent is providing themselves with arms and military stores, and establishing a method for a sure and unfailing and constant supply, I conceive we had best to negotiate with Britain. If she will cede our rights and restore our liberties all is well—every good man will rejoice; if she will not agree to relinquish and abolish all American revenues, under every pretence and name, and all pretensions to order and regulate our internal policy and constitution—then, if we have got any constant and sufficient supply of military stores, it will be time to take our arms. I can't quit this head—it ought to be immediately and most seriously attended to. It can't be any other than madness to commence hostilities before we have established resources on a sure plan for certain and effectual military supplies. Men, in that case, will not be wanting.

But what considerate man will ever consent to take arms and go to war, where he has no reasonable assurance but that all must be given over and he fall a prey to the enemy, for want of military stores and ammunition, in a few weeks?

Either an effectual non-consumption agreement or resistance of the new government will bring on hostilities very soon.

1. As to a non-consumption agreement—it appears to me that ought to

be taken for certain truth, that no plan of importation or consumption of tea, British goods in general, or enumerated articles, which is to rest and depend on the virtue of all the individuals, will succeed; but must certainly prove abortive.

The ministry may justly call such a plan futile—futile it will turn out. A plan of that sort may safely rest and be founded on the virtue of the majority: but then the majority, by the plan, must be directed to control the minority, which implies force. The plan, therefore, must direct and prescribe how that force shall be exercised.

Those, again, who exercise that force, under the direction and by order of the majority, must by that majority be defended and indemnified.

Dispositions must therefore necessarily be made to resist or overcome that force which will be brought against you—which will directly produce war and bloodshed.

From thence it follows, that any other non-consumption or non-importation plan, which is not perfectly futile and ridiculous, implies hostilities and war.

2. As to the resistance of the new government, that also implies war: for in order to resist and prevent the effect of the new government, it is indispensably necessary that the charter government, or some other, must be maintained—constitutionally exercised and supported.

The people will have some government or other—they will be drawn in by a seeming mild and just administration, which will last awhile; legislation and executive justice must go on in some form or other, and we may depend on it they will,—therefore the new government will take effect until the old is restored.

The old cannot be restored until the council take on them the administration, call assemblies, constitute courts, make sheriffs, etc. The council will not attempt this without good assurance of protection. This protection can't be given without hostilities.

Our salvation depends upon an established persevering union of the colonies.

The tools of administration are using every device and effort to destroy that union, and will certainly continue so to do—

Thereupon, all possible devices and endeavors must be used to establish, improve, brighten and maintain such union.

Every grievance of any one colony must be held and considered by the whole as a grievance to the whole and must operate on the whole as a grievance to the whole. This will be a difficult matter to effect: but it must be done.

Quere, therefore—whether is it not absolutely necessary that some plan be settled for a continuation of congresses?—But here we must be aware that congresses will soon be declared and enacted by parliament to be high treason.

Is the India company to be compensated or not?

If to be compensated—each colony to pay the particular damage she has done, or is an average to be made on the continent?

The destruction of the tea was not unjust—therefore to what good purpose is the tea to be paid for, unless we are assured that by so doing, our rights will be restored and peace obtained?

What future measures is the continent to preserve with regard to imported dutied tea, whether it comes as East India property or otherwise, under the pretence and lie that the tea is imported from Holland, and the goods imported before a certain given day? Dutied tea will be imported—your non-importation agreement eluded, rendered contemptible and ridiculous—unless all teas used, and all goods, are taken into some public custody which will be inviolably faithful.

(The foregoing is a literal copy of the venerable paper before me, except its frequent abbreviations of *the* and *that,* with the addition only of a few commas, etc. to make it read.)

CAESAR RODNEY REPORTS ON THE CONGRESS

[*Letter from Caesar Rodney to Thomas Rodney, Philadelphia,*
September 17, 1774]

SIR—By express, which arrived here yesterday from the committee of the town of Boston, to the continental congress, we are informed the county of Suffolk, of which the town of Boston is the capital, had entered into certain resolutions, a copy of which was enclosed us, generally to the purport of not suffering the commander in chief to execute the act of parliament, changing their government, by persuading, protecting, and compelling officers under the new regulation to resign, and by a refusal in jurymen to serve, etc. That they have ordered all those able to bear arms to keep in readiness to defend their inherent rights, even with loss of blood and treasure; that they are determined not to injure the general or any of the king's troops, unless compelled thereto by an attack made by the troops on them. They complain of the general seizing of the powder at Cambridge, which they say was private property; and also that he is now fortifying the only pass that leads from the town of Boston into the country, from whence the inhabitants of the town are daily supplied: this pass is a narrow neck of land about 120 yards wide, at which he has placed a number of troops and 28 cannon; that the country people passing and repassing this place are suffered to be insulted by the soldiery—and that the inhabitants feared, (from those movements of the general), he had designs of apprehending and sending to England those persons who have stood foremost in the great cause of liberty—that in consequence of his conduct, and those their suspicions, the inhabitants of Suffolk sent (by a committee appointed for that purpose) an address to the general, enquiring the cause of his stopping up and fortifying the pass, seizing and securing the magazines, etc. and their disapprobation of his conduct—and that they had no intention to assault either him or his soldiers;—but that, if he continued to block up the pass, and thereby prevent them of the only means of supplying the town with necessaries, they should look upon it as a commencement of hostilities: Upon the whole, they sent an express to the general congress here for their instructions as to their future conduct. The congress met on that business this day, and have resolved thereon—which you will see in the "Packet" of Monday, being ordered immediately to be printed, as well that the general as the people might know what they thought of the matter.

I am yours, etc.,
CAESAR RODNEY.

4. THE COLONIES ENDORSE THE ACTIONS OF CONGRESS

MARYLAND ENDORSES RESISTANCE

[Report of a meeting held at Annapolis, Maryland, December 1774]

At a meeting of the deputies appointed by the several counties of the province of Maryland, at the city of Annapolis, by adjournment, on the 8th day of December, 1774, and continued till the 12th day of the same month, were present, eighty-five members.

MR. JOHN HALL in the Chair, and
MR. JOHN DUCKETT, Clerk.

The proceedings of the continental congress were read, considered, and unanimously approved. *Resolved,* That every member of this convention will, and every person in the province ought strictly and inviolably to observe and carry into execution the association agreed on by the said continental congress.

On motion, unanimously *resolved,* That the thanks of this convention be given, by the chairman, to the gentlemen who represented this province as deputies in the late continental congress for their faithful discharge of that important trust: And the same was done accordingly.

To increase our flocks of sheep, and thereby promote the woolen manufacture in this province, *Resolved,* That no person ought to kill any lamb, dropt before the first day of May yearly, or other sheep, after the first day of January next, under four years of age.

To increase the manufacture of linen and cotton, *Resolved,* That every planter and farmer ought to raise as much flax, hemp, and cotton, as he conveniently can; and the cultivation thereof is particularly recommended to such inhabitants of this province, whose lands are best adapted to that purpose—And *resolved,* That no flax-seed, of the growth of the present year, ought to be purchased for exportation, after the twelfth day of this month.

It being represented to this convention, that many merchants and traders of this province, from a scarcity of cash to make their remittances, and other causes, had sold their goods, within twelve months next before the twentieth day of October last, at, and sometimes even below, the prime cost; and that, in many different parts of this province, merchants had vended their goods at a very different advance on the prime cost; and it appearing to this convention to be unjust to compel such merchants to sell their goods at prime cost, and that one general rule, allowing a reasonable profit to the trader, and preventing him from taking advantage of the scarcity of goods which may be occasioned by the non-importation, would give great satisfaction to the merchants and people of this province, *resolved* unanimously, That no merchant ought to sell his goods, at wholesale, for more than $112\frac{1}{2}$ per cent—at retail, for cash, for more than 13 per cent—on credit, for more than 150 per cent, advance on the prime cost; and that no merchant, or other person, ought to engross any goods, wares, or merchandise whatsoever.—And in case any question should arise, respecting the prime cost of goods, every merchant or factor possessing or owning such goods, ought to ascertain the same on oath, if requested to do it by the committee.

As a further regulation to enforce an observance of the late continental association—*Resolved* unanimously, That in all cases, where breaches of the continental association, or the resolves of this convention, shall happen and be declared such by any committee of a county, no gentleman of the law ought to bring or prosecute any suit whatever for such offender. And if any factor shall commit any breach of the said association or resolves, that no gentleman of the law ought to bring or prosecute any suit for any debt due to the store of which the said factor has the management, after notice as aforesaid.

Resolved, That it is earnestly recommended, by this convention, to the people of this province, that the determinations of the several county committees be observed and acquiesced in. That no persons, except members of the committees, undertake to meddle with or determine any question respecting the construction of the association entered into by the continental congress. And that peace and good order be inviolably maintained throughout this congress.

Resolved unanimously, That if the late acts of parliament, relative to the Massachusetts-Bay, shall be attempted to be carried into execution by force in that colony, or if the assumed power of parliament to tax the colonies shall be attempted to be carried into execution by force, in that colony or any other colony, that in such case, this province will support such colony to the utmost of their power.

Resolved unanimously, That a well regulated militia, composed of the gentlemen, freeholders, and other freemen, is the natural strength and only stable security of a free government, and that such militia will relieve our mother country from any expense in our protection and defence; will obviate the pretence of a necessity for taxing us on that account, and render it unnecessary to keep any standing army (ever dangerous to liberty) in this province. And therefore, it is recommended to such of the said inhabitants of this province as are from sixteen to fifty years of age, to form themselves into companies of sixty-eight men; to choose a captain, two lieutenants, an ensign, four sergeants, four corporals, and one drummer, for each company; and use their utmost endeavors to make themselves masters of the military exercise. That each man be provided with a good firelock and bayonet fitted thereon, half a pound of powder, two pounds of lead, and a cartouch-box, or powder-horn and bag for ball, and be in readiness to act on any emergency.

Resolved unanimously, That it is recommended to the committees of each county to raise by subscription, or in such other voluntary manner as they think proper, and will be most agreeable to their respective counties.

NEW HAMPSHIRE PRAISES CONGRESS

*[Report of a convention of 144 deputies from the towns of
New Hampshire held at Exeter, January 25, 1775]*

At the convention of the deputies appointed by the several towns in the province aforesaid, held at Exeter, on the 25th day of January, 1775. Present 144 members.

HON. JOHN WENTWORTH, esq., President.

Voted unanimously, That we heartily approve of the proceedings of the late grand continental congress respecting the just state of the rights and liberties of the British colonies; and of the means recommended to restore, secure, and protect the same; and that we return our most unfeigned thanks to late members of that congress in general, and to those of this province in particular, for the faithful discharge of the important trust reposed in them.

Voted, That John Sullivan, and John Langdon, esqrs., be delegates to represent this province in the continental congress, proposed to be held at Philadelphia, on the tenth day of May next, and that they and each of them in the absence of the other, have full and ample power, in behalf of this province, to consent and agree to all measures, which said congress shall deem necessary to obtain redress of American grievances.

Voted, That two hundred and fifty pounds, lawful money, be raised for defraying the expenses of said delegates.

Voted, That the hon. John Wentworth, col. Nath. Folsom, hon. Meseach Weare, esq. col. Josiah Bartlet, col. Christopher Toppan, Ebenezer Thompson, and William Whipple, esqrs. be a committee, in behalf of this province, to call a provincial convention of deputies, when they shall judge the exigencies of public affairs require it: And that they, together with Samuel Cutts and John Pickering, esqrs. be a committee of correspondence for this province,

Voted, the following address:

To the inhabitants of the province of New Hampshire.

Brethren—when we consider the unhappy condition to which you and your American brethren are reduced! when we reflect that, for near ten months past, you have been deprived of any share in your own government, and of those advantages, which flow to society from legislative assemblies; when we view the lowering clouds, charged with ministerial vengeance, fast spreading over this extensive continent, ready to burst on the heads of its inhabitants and involve the whole British empire in one common ruin—at this alarming juncture, duty to Almighty God, to our country, ourselves, and posterity, loudly demands our most strenuous exertions to avoid the impending danger.

Such are the measures adopted by the British ministry, for enslaving you, and with such incessant vigilance has their plan been prosecuted, that tyranny already begins to wave its banners in your borders, and to threaten these once happy regions with infamous and detestable slavery!

Shall we, knowing the value of freedom, and nursed in the arms of liberty, make a base and ignominious surrender of our rights, thereby consigning succeeding generations to a condition of wretchedness, from which perhaps, all human efforts will be insufficient to extricate them?

Duty to ourselves, and regard for our country, should induce us to defend our liberties, and to transmit the fair inheritance unimpaired to posterity.

Should our restless enemies drive us to arms in defence of every thing we hold dear, we should be reduced to a state, dreadful even in contemplation; for should we prove victorious, the blood of our brethren, shed in the unhappy contest, would cause the laurels to wither on our brows, and make the conquerors mourn with the vanquished: but should our enemies be successful, they will thereby rivet the chains of slavery upon us and our posterity.

Thus surrounded with dangers and distresses on every side, it behoves us to adopt and pursue such peaceable measures as, under God, will be most likely to prevent those dreadful calamities with which we are threatened.

Fully sensible that to point out, with any degree of certainty, the methods by which you may shun the threatening evils, would require more than human wisdom, we can only recommend such measures as appears to us most likely to answer that desirable end, best calculated to restore to you that peace and harmony, so ardently wished for by every good and honest American.

We therefore earnestly recommend,

1st. That you discountenance and discourage all trespasses and injuries against individuals, and their property, and all disorders of every kind; and that you cultivate and maintain peace and harmony among yourselves.

2d. That you yield due obedience to the magistrates within this government; and carefully endeavor to support the laws thereof.

3d. That you strictly adhere to the association of the late continental congress, and deal with the violators of it, in the manner therein recommended.

4th. That you endeavor particularly to enforce the laws of the province against hawkers, pedlars, and petty chapmen.

5th. That you abstain from the use of East India tea, whenever and by whatever means it has, or may be imported.

6th. That you encourage and support your several committees of correspondence and inspection, in discharging the very important trust you have reposed in them.

7th. That in case any inhabitant of the colonies should be seized in order to be transported to Great Britain, or other parts beyond seas, to be tried for offences supposed to be committed in America, you conduct yourselves agreeable to the advice of the late continental congress.

8th. That, in your several stations you promote and encourage the manufactures of this country; and endeavor, both by precept and example, to induce all under you, and with whom you are connected, to practice economy and industry, and to shun all kinds of extravagance.

9th. That the officers of the several regiments strictly comply with the laws of this province for regulating a militia—And as the militia upon this continent, if properly disciplined, would be able to do great service in its defence, should it ever be invaded by his majesty's enemies, that you acquaint yourselves with the manual exercise, particularly that recommended and enjoined by the captain general—the motions being natural, easy, and best calculated to qualify persons for real action; and also to improve themselves in those evolutions which are necessary for infantry in time of engagement.

10th. That, as your enemies are using every art to impoverish and distress you, in order to induce submission to their arbitrary mandates, you carefully shun those measures which may have a tendency to distress your brethren and fellow sufferers, and avoid all unnecessary law-suits, and endeavor to settle disputes between you in the most amicable and least expensive manner. —That all debtors exert themselves in discharging their just debts, and creditors exercise such lenity as their circumstances will admit of.

11th. That as the inhabitants of the town of Boston, in the province of Massachusetts-Bay, are now laboring under a load of ministerial vengeance, laid upon them to enforce obedience to certain arbitrary and unconstitutional acts, which, if once submitted to, must involve all America in slavery and ruin; conscious that all these colonies are largely indebted to the virtue and fortitude of those patriotic asserters of freedom, we heartily recommend a continuation of your contributions for the relief of that oppressed people;

and that you keep yourselves in constant readiness to support them in their just opposition, whenever necessity may require.

Lastly, We earnestly entreat you, at this time of tribulation and distress, when your enemies are urging you to despair; when every scene around is full of gloom and horror; that, in imitation of your pious forefathers, with contrition of spirit, and penitence of heart, you implore the Divine Being, who alone is able to deliver you from your present unhappy and distressing situation, to espouse your righteous cause, secure your liberties, and fix them on a firm and lasting basis. And we fervently beseech him to restore to you and your American brethren, that peace and tranquility, so ardently desired, and earnestly sought for, by every true friend to liberty and mankind.

By order of the convention,

J. WENTWORTH, President.

V

DEBATE GIVES WAY TO WARFARE,

1775-1776

Wɪᴛʜ ʙᴏᴛʜ ᴀᴅᴠᴇʀsᴀʀɪᴇs heavily armed and unwilling to retreat from the positions they had taken, it was only a matter of time before debate would give way to open warfare. The crisis came in the early spring of 1775 when General Thomas Gage, commander of His Majesty's forces in North America and Royal Governor of Massachusetts, received orders to seize rebel military supplies. His first attempt, at Salem in late March, was fruitless; his second attempt was met by the Minute Men at Lexington and Concord (p. 167). War had come at last.

Although Gage succeeded in destroying some American military equipment at Concord, his foray into the countryside resulted in heavy British losses. It also brought Boston under virtual siege by the patriot forces that now gathered at the approaches to the city. The Governor of Massachusetts was almost a prisoner in his own capital, powerless against the barrage of denunciations and protests that descended upon him (p. 168). General Gage found even the population of Boston difficult to control (p. 169).

The other colonies rapidly came to the aid of Massachusetts (pp. 171, 173, 175, and 178). Within a month after the battle of Lexington, the other New England colonies had voted to send ten thousand troops to reinforce the Massachusetts forces, and the colonies to the south also promised military aid. At the same time, spokesmen for both sides confidently justified their use of force (pp. 178, 181, and 188).

As spring wore into summer, the contest between colonial and imperial forces took on an air of permanency. The theater of war expanded to include

[165]

Fort Ticonderoga on Lake Champlain and St. John's in Canada. It spread in the Boston area as well, when British regulars stormed the American positions at Breed's Hill and Bunker Hill on the Charlestown peninsula. By September a colonial army was invading Canada, and by mid-November 1775 it had seized Montreal.

Such extensive operations called for an intercolonial military establishment. This was accomplished during the summer and fall of 1775: in June the Second Continental Congress transformed the scattered colonial forces outside Boston into a continental army and appointed George Washington to be its Commander-in-Chief. In the following months a plan of military organization was developed, funds were raised, and fresh units were authorized to supplement the forces already in the field (pp. 189, 190, and 191).

Throughout the fall of 1775 and into the spring of 1776, the fortunes of war shifted unpredictably back and forth. In the south the war took on a particularly bitter quality when Virginia's Governor Dunmore offered freedom to any slave who would desert his master (pp. 194, and 195), but the net effect of Dunmore's maneuver was a heightening of colonial animosity toward imperial authority (p 197). British strategy proved sounder in Canada, where the American attempt under Benedict Arnold to capture Quebec ended in disaster. But the most dramatic victory of the year went to American troops at Boston, where guns hauled from Fort Ticonderoga forced the British to evacuate the Massachusetts capital on St. Patrick's Day, 1776 (pp. 199, and 201). General Washington was the hero of the day (pp. 202, and 203).

Not every American, however, rejoiced at the victories of the Continental Army. Throughout the colonies many remained loyal to the King's government and refused to join the growing tide of rebellion. The American "patriots," fearful that active dissension would doom their cause, imposed restrictions and hardships on any of their neighbors bold enough to espouse the imperial cause (pp. 205, 206, and 207). The war now pitted colonist against colonist as well as colonies against mother country.

1. THE FIRST CLASH COMES AT LEXINGTON

REPORT OF THE MASSACHUSETTS PROVINCIAL CONGRESS

*[Address by the Massachusetts Provincial Congress, sitting
at Watertown, to the "Inhabitants of Great Britain,"
April 26, 1775]*

FRIENDS AND FELLOW SUBJECTS—Hostilities are at length commenced in this colony by the troops under the command of General Gage, and it being of the greatest importance, that an early, true, and authentic account of this inhuman proceeding should be known to you, the congress of this colony have transmitted the same, and from want of a session of the hon. continental congress, think it proper to address you on the alarming occasion.

By the clearest depositions relative to this transaction, it will appear that on the night preceding the nineteenth of April instant, a body of the king's troops, under command of colonel Smith, were secretly landed at Cambridge, with an apparent design to take or destroy the military and other stores, provided for this colony, and deposited at Concord—that some inhabitants of the colony, on the night aforesaid, whilst travelling peaceably on the road, between Boston and Concord, were seized and greatly abused by armed men, who appeared to be officers of General Gage's army; that the town of Lexington, by these means, was alarmed, and a company of the inhabitants mustered on the occasion—that the regular troops on their way to Concord, marched into the said town of Lexington, and the said company, on their approach, began to disperse—that, notwithstanding this, the regulars rushed on with great violence and first began hostilities, by firing on said Lexington company, whereby they killed eight, and wounded several others—that the regulars continued their fire, until those of said company, who were neither killed or wounded had made their escape—that colonel Smith, with the detachment then marched to Concord, where a number of provincials were again fired on by the troops, two of them killed and several wounded, before the provincials fired on them, and that these hostile measures of the troops, produced an engagement that lasted through the day, in which many of the provincials and more of the regular troops were killed and wounded.

To give a particular account of the ravages of the troops, as they retreated from Concord to Charlestown, would be very difficult, if not impracticable; let it suffice to say, that a great number of the houses on the road were plundered and rendered unfit for use, several were burnt, women in child-bed were driven by the soldiery naked into the streets, old men peaceably in their houses were shot dead, and such scenes exhibited as would disgrace the annals of the most uncivilized nation.

These, brethren, are marks of ministerial vengeance against this colony, for refusing, with her sister colonies, a submission to slavery; but they have not yet detached us from our royal sovereign. We profess to be his loyal and dutiful subjects, and so hardly dealt with as we have been, are still ready, with our lives and fortunes, to defend his person, family, crown and dignity. Nevertheless, to the persecution and tyranny of his cruel ministry we will not tamely submit—appealing to Heaven for the justice of our cause, we determine to die or be free.

We cannot think that the honor, wisdom and valor of Britons will suffer them to be longer inactive spectators of measures in which they themselves are so deeply interested—measures, pursued in opposition to the solemn protests of many noble lords, and expressed sense of conspicuous commoners, whose knowledge and virtue have long characterized them as some of the greatest men in the nation—measures, executed contrary to the interest, petitions and resolves of many large, respectable and opulent counties, cities and boroughs in Great Britain—measures highly incompatible with justice, but still pursued with a specious pretence of easing the nation of its burthens—measures which, if successful, must end in the ruin and slavery of Britain, as well as the persecuted American colonies.

We sincerely hope that the Great Sovereign of the universe, who hath so often appeared for the English nation, will support you in every rational and manly exertion with these colonies, for saving it from ruin, and that, in a constitutional connection with the mother country, we shall soon be altogether a free and happy people.

By order, JOSEPH WARREN, President P.T.

THE MASSACHUSETTS PROVINCIAL CONGRESS
DENOUNCES GENERAL GAGE

[Resolutions of the Massachusetts Provincial Congress,
May 5, 1775]

WATERTOWN, May 5, 1775

Whereas his excellency, general Gage, since his arrival in this colony, hath conducted, as an instrument in the hands of an arbitrary ministry, to enslave this people; and a detachment of the troops under his command, has of late been by him ordered to the town of Concord, to destroy the public stores, deposited in that place for the use of that colony; and whereas, by this clandestine and perfidious measure, a number of respectable inhabitants of this colony, without any provocation given by them, have been illegally, wantonly, and inhumanly slaughtered by his troops:

Therefore, resolved, that the said general Gage hath, by these and many other means, utterly disqualified himself to serve to this colony as a governor, and in every capacity; and that no obedience ought, in future, to be paid by the several towns and districts in this colony to his writs for calling an assembly, or to his proclamations, or any other of his acts or doings; but that, on the other hand, he ought to be considered and guarded against, as an unnatural and inveterate enemy to the country.

JOSEPH WARREN, President P.T.

A BOSTONIAN RECALLS THE AFTERMATH OF LEXINGTON

[Reminiscences of a Bostonian after the Battle of Lexington, 1775]

There are very few of the present generation, who have any idea of the humiliation to which their ancestors were subjected, while under a colonial government, from the contumely and insolence of upstart officers, who, in their own country, had been as servile as the spaniel, but on their arrival here, aped the port and authority of the lion. Not only humiliations, but other severe sufferings and privations were endured by them, with patience and fortitude, and with a moral rectitude, which would have done honor to Greece or Rome, in their most virtuous days.

After the battle of Lexington, the egress of a part of the inhabitants of Boston was prohibited by a breach of faith on the part of gen. Gage, and those who were permitted to depart, were obliged to obtain passports, as mentioned in my last communication.

It was not until the fifth of June that my father became determined to leave the town. On that day he directed me to make out a schedule of the family, agreeably to the rules instituted by general Gage, and demand a pass of major Cain, of the army, who was empowered to perform that service. Such was the crowd of citizens, eagerly pressing to obtain passports, that it was not until several hours of exertion that I was enabled to reach the door of the major's apartment, and when it was opened, I was so forcibly urged on by the crowd behind, that, on entering the chamber, I lost my balance, which caused me to rush violently into the room, and though he must have perceived that the act was involuntary, yet he had the brutality to exclaim (in broad Scotch) "hoot, hoot mon! are you going to murder me?" I was obliged to bear this insolence in silence, though my countenance must have exhibited marks of indignation, and I walked to a window which looked into the court yard, where my feelings were still more excited by a view of my fellow citizens, who, with countenances almost bordering despair, were waiting for a favorable moment to obtain admission. The first reflection which presented itself to my mind was, what must be the indignation of our king, if he knew how his faithful, loyal, and affectionate subjects, were abused, insulted and driven into acts of reluctant resistance. Which brought to my recollection a part of Warren's oration, on the preceding 5th of March, in which he observes, that "The royal ear, far distant from this western world, has been assaulted by the tongue of slander, and villains, traitorous alike to king and country, have prevailed upon a gracious prince to clothe his countenance with wrath.". . .

After waiting nearly an hour the major accosted me with, "Well, young man, what do you want?" I handed him a schedule of my father's family, including that of his sister's (the widow of a clergyman). He examined a small book which contained what the tories called the "black list," when slowly raising his scowling eyes, he said with great asperity, "Your father, young man, is a damn'd rebel, and cannot be accommodated with a pass." Not at all intimidated by his brutality, I asserted with much vehemence, that my father was no rebel, that he adored the illustrious house of Hanover, and had fought for good king George the 2d, in forty-five. Whether it was, that he himself had been a real rebel in Scotland, in 1745, or whether my mentioning that number reminded him of Wilkes' North Briton No. 45, a paper published in London, and peculiarly obnoxious to the house of Hanover, was intended as an insinuation against his own loyalty, (which it really was),—whatever may have been the cause of his irritation—the moment I had finished speaking he rose from his chair, and with a countenance foaming with rage, he ordered me out of the room with abusive language. The sentinel at the door had an English countenance, and, with apparent sympathy, very civilly opened it for my departure, which I made without turning my back on my adversary.

On inquiry it was afterwards ascertained, that what constituted the crime of my father and caused him to be denominated a rebel, was his having been a member of the Whig club!

The Whig club, in consequence of the perturbed state of the times, had not assembled or met for more than a year. The gentlemen that had composed it, were James Otis, Dr. Warren, Dr. Church, Dr. Young, Richard Derby, of Salem, Benjamin Kent, Nathaniel Barber, William Mackay, Col. Bigelow, of Worcester, and about half a dozen more. Through the instrumentality of my father, I was sometimes admitted to hear their deliberations. There was always at each meeting, a speech or dissertation by one of the members, on the principles of civil liberty, and the British constitution. They professed loyalty to the king, but were in violent opposition to the encroachments of the parliament, and their discussions tended to a consideration of what would be the duty of Americans if those encroachments were continued. For this purpose they corresponded with some society in London, the name of which I have forgotten, (probably the Revolution society). Among the names of their correspondents I recollect, Wilkes, Savile, Barré and Sawbridge. A few years previous to the revolution, they sent the London society two green turtles, one of which weighed 45 and the other 92 pounds. Those who are acquainted with the history of those times, will easily understand to what those numbers alluded. On their arrival in London, a grand dinner was prepared, which Col. Barré presided, and among other distinguished guests I recollect hearing the names of earl Temple, lord Cambden, and the lord mayor; and among the toasts, "The Whig club of Boston," and "The ninety-two patriots of Massachusetts Bay," were drank with three times three cheers.

2. THE COLONIES RALLY BEHIND MASSACHUSETTS

REACTION OF A PHILADELPHIAN TO THE BATTLE OF LEXINGTON

[Letter from a woman in Philadelphia to a British officer in Boston, 1775]

SIR—We received a letter from you—wherein you let Mr. S. know that you had written after the battle of Lexington, particularly to me—knowing my martial spirit—that I would delight to read the exploits of heroes. Surely, my friend, you must mean the New England heroes, as they alone performed exploits worthy fame—while the regulars, vastly superior in numbers, were obliged to retreat with a rapidity unequalled, except by the French at the battle of Minden. Indeed, general Gage gives them their due praise in his letter home, where he says lord Percy was remarkable for his activity. You will not, I hope, take offence at any expression that, in the warmth of my heart, should escape me, when I assure you, that though we consider you as a public enemy, we regard you as a private friend; and while we detest the cause you are fighting for, we wish well to your own personal interest and safety. Thus far by way of apology. As to the martial spirit you suppose me to possess, you are greatly mistaken. I tremble at the thoughts of war; but of all wars, a civil one: our all is at stake; and we are called upon by every tie that is dear and sacred to exert the spirit that Heaven has given us in this righteous struggle for liberty.

I will tell you what I have done. My only brother I have sent to the camp with my prayers and blessings; I hope he will not disgrace me; I am confident he will behave with honor, and emulate the great examples he has before him; and had I twenty sons and brothers they should go. I have retrenched every superfluous expense in my table and family; tea I have not drank since last Christmas, nor bought a new cap or gown since your defeat at Lexington, and what I never did before, have learnt to knit, and am now making stockings of American wool for my servants, and this way do I throw in my mite to the public good. I know this, that as free I can die but once, but as a slave I shall not be worthy of life. I have the pleasure to assure you that these are the sentiments of all my sister Americans. They have sacrificed both assemblies, parties of pleasure, tea drinking and finery to that great spirit of patriotism, that actuates all ranks and degrees of people throughout this extensive continent. If these are the sentiments of females, what must glow in the breasts of our husbands, brothers and sons? They are as with one heart determined to die or be free. It is not a quibble in politics, a science which few understand, which we are contending for; it is this plain truth, which the most ignorant peasant knows, and is clear to the weakest capacity, that no man has a right to take their money without their consent. The supposition is ridiculous and absurd, as none but highwaymen, and robbers attempt it. Can you, my friend, reconcile it with your own good sense, that a body of men in Great Britain, who have little intercourse with America, and of course know nothing of us, nor are supposed to see or feel the misery they would inflict upon us, shall invest themselves with a power to command our lives and properties, at all times and in all cases whatsoever? You say you are no politician. Oh, sir, it requires no Machiavelian head to develop this, and to discover this tyranny and oppression. It is written with a sun beam. Every one will see and know it because it will make them feel, and we shall be unworthy of the blessings of Heaven, if we ever submit to it.

All ranks of men amongst us are in arms.—Nothing is heard now in our streets but the trumpet and drum; and the universal cry is "Americans to arms.". . . We have five regiments in the city and county of Philadelphia, complete in arms and uniform, and very expert at their military manoeuvres. We have companies of lighthorse, light infantry, grenadiers, riflemen, and Indians, several companies of artillery, and some excellent brass cannon and field pieces. Add to this, that every county in Pennsylvania, and the Delaware government, can send two thousand men to the field. Heaven seems to smile on us, for in the memory of man never were known such quantities of flax, and sheep without number.—We are making powder fast, and do not want for ammunition. In short, we want for nothing but ships of war to defend us, which we could procure by making alliances; but such is our attachment to Great Britain, that we sincerely wish for reconciliation, and cannot bear the thoughts of throwing off all dependence on her, which such a step would assuredly lead to. The God of mercy will, I hope, open the eyes of our king that he may see, while in seeking our destruction, he will go near to complete his own. It is my ardent prayer that the effusion of blood may be stopped. We hope yet to see you in this city, a friend to the liberties of America, which will give infinite satisfaction to,

Your sincere friend,
C.S.

CONNECTICUT BACKS HER NEIGHBOR'S STAND

[Letter from Governor Jonathan Trumbull of Connecticut to the British general Thomas Gage, Hartford, April 28, 1775]

SIR—The alarming situation of public affairs in this country, and the late unfortunate transactions in the province of Massachusetts Bay, have induced the general assembly of this colony, now sitting in this place, to appoint a committee of their body to wait upon your excellency, and to desire me, in their name, to write to you relative to these very interesting matters.

The inhabitants of this colony are intimately connected with the people of your province, and esteem themselves bound, by the strongest ties of friendship, as well as of common interest, to regard with attention, whatever concerns them. You will not, therefore, be surprised, that your first arrival at Boston, with a body of his Majesty's troops, for the declared purpose of carrying into execution certain acts of parliament, which, in their apprehension, were unconstitutional and oppressive, should have given the good people of this colony a very just and general alarm; your subsequent proceedings in fortifying the town of Boston, and other military preparations, greatly increased their apprehensions for the safety of their friends and brethren; they could not be unconcerned spectators of their sufferings, in that which they esteemed the common cause of this country; but the late hostile and secret inroads of some of the troops under your command into the heart of the country, and the violences they have committed, have driven them almost into a state of desperation. They feel now not only for their friends, but for themselves, and their dearest interests and connections. We wish not to exaggerate; we are not sure of every part of our information; but, by the best intelligence that we have yet been able to obtain, the late transaction was a most unprovoked attack upon the lives and property of his majesty's subjects; and it is represented to us, that such outrages have been committed, as would disgrace even barbarians, and much more Britons, so highly famed for humanity, as well as bravery. It is feared, therefore, that we are devoted to destruction, and that you have it in command and intention, to ravage and desolate the country. If this is not the case, permit us to ask, why have these outrages been committed? Why is the town of Boston now shut up? And to what end are all the hostile preparations that are daily making, and why do we continually hear of fresh destination of troops for this country? The people of this colony, you may rely upon it, abhor the idea of taking arms against the troops of their sovereign, and dread nothing so much as the horrors of civil war; but, at the same time, we beg leave to assure your excellency, that as they apprehend themselves justified by the principles of self defence, so they are most firmly resolved to defend their rights and privileges to the last extremity; nor will they be restrained from giving aid to their brethren, if any unjustifiable attack is made upon them. Be so good, therefore, as to explain yourself upon this most important subject, as far as is consistent with your duty to our common sovereign. Is there no way to prevent this unhappy dispute from coming to extremities? Is there no alternative but absolute submission, or the desolations of war? By that humanity which constitutes so amiable a part of your character; for the honor of our sovereign, and by the glory of the British empire, we entreat you to prevent it, if it be possible; surely, it is to be hoped that the temperate wisdom of the empire might, even yet, find expedients to restore peace, that so all parts of the empire may enjoy their particular rights, honors, and immunities: Certainly, this is an event most devoutly to be wished for; and will it not be consistent with your duty to suspend the operation of war on your part, and enable us on ours, to quiet the minds of the people, at least, till the result of some further deliberations may be known? The importance of the occasion will, we doubt not, sufficiently apologize for the earnestness with which we address you, and any seeming impropriety, which may attend it, as well as induce you to give us the most explicit and favorable answer in your power.

I am, with great esteem and respect, in behalf of the general assembly, sir, &c.

(Signed) JONATHAN TRUMBULL.

NEW YORK EXPLAINS ITS CASE TO LONDON

[From a committee of citizens of New York, to the lord mayor, aldermen, and common council of London, May 5, 1775]

MY LORD AND GENTLEMEN—Distinguished as you are, by your noble exertions in the cause of liberty, and deeply interested in the expiring commerce of the empire, you necessarily command the most respectful attention. The general committee of association, for the city and county of New York, beg leave, therefore, to address you, and the capital of the British empire, through its magistrates, on the subject of American wrongs. Born to the bright inheritance of English freedom, the inhabitants of this extensive continent, can never submit to the ignominious yoke, nor move in the galling fetters of slavery. The disposal of their own property, with perfect spontaneity, and in a manner wholly divested of every appearance of constraint, is their indefeasible birthright. This exalted blessing, they are resolutely determined to defend with their blood, and transfer it, uncontaminated, to their posterity.

You will not then, wonder at their early jealousy of the design, to erect in this land of liberty, a despotism scarcely to be paralleled in the pages of antiquity, or the volumes of modern times; a despotism, consisting in power, assumed by the representatives of a part of his majesty's subjects, at their sovereign will and pleasure, to strip the rest of their property:—and what are the engines of administration to execute this destructive project? The duty on tea; oppressive restraints on the commerce of the colonies; the blockade of the port of Boston; the change of internal police in the Massachusetts, and Quebec, the establishment of popery in the latter; the extension of its bounds; the ruin of our Indian commerce, by regulations calculated to aggrandize that arbitrary government; unconstitutional admiralty jurisdiction throughout the colonies; the invasion of our right to a trial, in the most capital cases, by a jury of the vicinage [vicinity]; the horrid contrivance to screen from punishment the bloody executioners of ministerial vengeance; and not to mention the rest of the black catalogue of our grievances, the hostile operations of an army, who have already shed the blood of our countrymen. The struggles excited by the detestable stamp act, have so lately demonstrated to the world that Americans will not be slaves; that we stand astonished at the gross impolicy of the minister.—Recent experience had evinced, that the possessors of this extensive continent would never submit to a tax, by pretext of legislative authority in Britain; disguise, therefore, became the expedient. In pursuit of the same end, parliament declared their absolute supremacy in attempting to raise a revenue, under the specious pretence of providing for their good government and defence. Administration, to exhibit a degree of moderation, purely ostensible and delusory, while they withdrew their hands from our most necessary articles of importation, determined with an eager grasp to hold the duty on tea, as a badge of their taxative power. Zealous on our part, for an indissoluble union with the parent state, studious to promote the glory and happiness of the empire, impressed with a just sense of the necessity of a controlling authority to regulate and harmonize the discordant commercial interests of its various parts; we cheerfully submit to a regulation of commerce, by the legislature of a parent state, excluding, in its nature, every idea of taxation.

Whither, therefore, the present machinations of arbitrary power infallibly tend, you may easily judge; if unremittedly pursued, as they were inhumanly devised, they will, by a fatal necessity, terminate in a total dissolution of the empire.

The subjects of the country will not, we trust, be deceived by any measures conciliatory in appearance, while it is evident that the minister aims at a sordid revenue, to be raised by grievous and oppressive acts of parliament, and by fleets and armies employed to enforce the execution. They never will, we believe, submit to an auction on the colonies, for the more effectual augmentation of the revenue, by holding it up as a temptation to them, that the highest bidder shall enjoy the greatest share of government favor. This plan, as it would tend to sow the seeds of discord, would be far more dangerous than hostile force, in which we hope the king's troops will ever be, as they have already been, unsuccessful. Instead of those unusual, extraordinary, and unconstitutional modes of procuring levies from the subjects, should his majesty graciously be pleased, upon suitable emergencies, to make requisitions in ancient form, the colonies have expressed their willingness to contribute to the support of the empire—but to contribute of their voluntary gift, as Englishmen; and when our unexampled grievances are redressed, our prince will find his American subjects testifying, on all proper occasions, by as ample aids as their circumstances will permit, the most unshaken fidelity to their sovereign, and inviolable attachment to the welfare of his realm and dominions. Permit us further to assure you that America is grown so irritable by oppression, that the least shock, in any part, is by the most powerful and sympathetic affection, instantaneously felt through the whole continent. That Pennsylvania, Maryland, and New York, have already stopped their exports to the fishing islands, and those colonies, which at this dangerous juncture, have refused to unite with their brethren in the common cause; and all supplies to the navy and army at Boston; and that probably the day is at hand, when our continental congress will totally shut up our ports.

The minions of power here, may now inform administration, if they can ever speak the language of truth, that this city is as one man in the cause of liberty; that to this end, our inhabitants are almost unanimously bound by the inclosed association; that it is continually advancing to perfection, by additional subscriptions; that they are resolutely bent on supporting their committee, and the intended provincial and continental congresses; that there is not the least doubt of the efficacy of their example in the other colonies; in short, that while the whole continent are ardently wishing for peace on such terms as can be acceded to by Englishmen, they are indefatigible in preparing for the last appeal. That such are the language and conduct of our fellow-citizens, will be further manifested by a representation of the lieutenant governor and council of the 1st inst. to general Gage, at Boston, and to his majesty's ministers by the packet. Assure yourselves, my lord and gentlemen, that we speak the real sentiments of the confederated colonies on the continent, from Nova Scotia to Georgia, when we declare, that all the horrors of a civil war, will never compel America to submit to taxation by authority of parliament.

A sincere regard to the public weal, and the cause of humanity; in hearty desire to spare the further effusion of human blood; our loyalty to our prince, and the love we bear to all our fellow subjects in his majesty's realm and dominions; a full conviction of the warmest attachment in the capital of the empire, to the cause of justice and liberty, have induced us to address you on this momentous subject, confident that the same cogent motives will induce the most vigorous exertions of the city of London to restore union, mutual confidence, and peace to the whole empire.

We have the honor to be, my lord and gentlemen, your most obedient and affectionate fellow-subjects, and humble servants,

ISAAC LOW, Chairman.

SOUTH CAROLINA PLEDGES RESISTANCE BY FORCE

[Resolutions of a meeting of citizens in South Carolina, June 1775]

The actual commencement of hostilities against this continent, by the British troops, in the bloody scene on the 19th of April last, near Boston; the increase of arbitrary impositions, from a wicked and despotic ministry, and the dread of instigated insurrections in the colonies, are causes sufficient to drive an oppressed people to the use of arms:—We, therefore, the subscribers, inhabitants of South Carolina, holding ourselves bound, by that most sacred of all obligations, the duty of good citizens towards an injured country, and thoroughly convinced, that, under our present distressed circumstances, we shall be justified before God and man, in resisting force by force, do unite ourselves under every tie of religion and honor, and associate as a band in her defence, against every foe; hereby solemnly engaging that whenever our continental and provincial councils shall decree it necessary, we will go forth, and be ready to sacrifice our lives, and fortunes, to secure her freedom and safety.—This obligation to continue in full force until a reconciliation shall take place between Great Britain and America, upon constitutional principles; an event which we most ardently desire. And we will hold all those persons inimical to the liberties of the colonies, who shall refuse to subscribe to this association.

Subscribed by every member present, and certified by

HENRY LAURENS, President

3. EACH SIDE JUSTIFIES ITS STAND

GOVERNOR GAGE STATES HIS POSITION

[Proclamation of Gov. Thomas Gage, June 12; 1775, as reported by a Cambridge, Mass., newspaper]

BY HIS EXCELLENCY THE HON. THOMAS GAGE, ESQ.

Governor and commander in chief in and over his majesty's Province of Massachusetts Bay, and vice-admiral of the same.

A PROCLAMATION.

Whereas the infatuated multitudes, who have long suffered themselves to be conducted by certain well-known incendiaries and traitors, in a fatal progression of crimes, against the constitutional authority of that state, have at length proceeded to avowed rebellion; and the good effects which were expected to arise from the patience and lenity of the king's government, have been often frustrated, and are now rendered hopeless, by the influence of the same evil counsels; it only remains for those who are entrusted with supreme rule, as well for the punishment of the guilty, as the protection of the well affected, to prove they do not bear the sword in vain.

The infringements which have been committed upon the most sacred rights of the crown and people of Great Britain, are too many to enumerate on one side, and are too atrocious to be palliated on the other. All unprejudiced people who have been witnesses of the late transactions, in this and neighboring provinces, will find, upon a transient review, marks of premeditation and conspiracy that would justify the fullness of chastisement: And even those who are least acquainted with facts, cannot fail to receive a just impression of their enormity, in proportion as they discover the arts and assiduity by which they have been falsified or concealed. The authors of the present unnatural revolt, never daring to trust their cause or their actions to the judgment of an impartial public, or even to the dispassionate reflection of their followers, have uniformly placed their chief confidence in the suppression of truth: And while indefatigable and shameless pains have been taken to obstruct every appeal to the real interest of the people of America, the grossest forgeries, calumnies and absurdities that ever insulted human understanding, have been imposed upon their credulity. The press, that distinguished appendage of public liberty, and when fairly and impartially employed, its best support, has been invariably prostituted to the most contrary purposes: the animated language of ancient and virtuous times, calculated to vindicate and promote the just rights and interests of mankind, have been applied to countenance the most abandoned violation of those sacred blessings; and not only from the flagitious prints, but from the popular harangues of the times, men have been taught to depend upon activity in treason for the security of their persons and properties; till, to complete the horrible profanation of terms and of ideas, the name of God has been introduced in the pulpits to excite and justify devastation and massacre.

The minds of men having been thus gradually prepared for the worst extremities, a number of armed persons, to the amount of many thousands, assembled on the 19th of April last, and from behind walls and lurking holes, attacked a detachment of the king's troops who, not expecting so consummate an act of frenzy, unprepared for vengeance and willing to decline it, made use of their arms only in their own defence. Since that period the rebels, deriving confidence from impunity, have added insult to outrage; have repeatedly fired upon the king's ships and subjects, with cannon and small arms; have possessed the roads and other communications by which the town of Boston was supplied with provisions; and, with a preposterous parade of military arrangement, they affect to hold the army besieged; while part of their body make daily indiscriminate invasions upon private property, and, with a wantonness of cruelty ever incident to lawless tumult, carry depredation and distress wherever they turn their steps. The actions of the 19th of April are of such notoriety, as must baffle all attempts to contradict them, and the flames of buildings and other property, from the islands and adjacent country, for some weeks past, spread a melancholy confirmation of the subsequent assertions.

In this exigency of complicated calamities, I avail myself of the last effort within the bounds of my duty to spare the effusion of blood; to offer, and I do hereby in his majesty's name, offer and promise his most gracious pardon to all persons who shall forthwith lay down their arms, and return to the duties of peaceable subjects, excepting only from the benefit of such pardon, Samuel Adams and John Hancock, whose offences are of too flagitious a nature to admit of any other consideration than that of condign punishment.

And to the end that no person within the limits of this proffered mercy may plead ignorance of the consequences of refusing it, I by these presents proclaim, not only the persons above-named and excepted, but also all their adherents, associates and abettors, meaning to comprehend in those terms all and every person, and persons of what class, denomination or description soever, who have appeared in arms against the king's government, and shall not lay down the same as afore-mentioned; and likewise all such as shall so take arms after the date hereof, or who shall in anywise protect and conceal such offenders or assist them with money, provision, cattle, arms, ammunition, carriages, or any other necessary for subsistence or offence; or shall hold secret correspondence with them by letter, message, signal, or otherwise, to be rebels and traitors, and as such to be treated.

And whereas, during the continuance of the present unnatural rebellion, justice cannot be administered by the common law of the land, the course whereof, has, for a long time past, been violently impeded, and wholly interrupted; from whence results a necessity for using and exercising the law martial; I have therefore thought fit, by the authority vested in me, by the royal charter to this province, to publish, and I do hereby publish, proclaim and order the use and exercise of the law martial, within and throughout the province, for so long time as the present unhappy occasion shall necessarily require; whereof all persons are hereby required to take notice, and govern themselves, as well to maintain order and regularity among the peaceable inhabitants of the province, as to resist, encounter and subdue the rebels and traitors above described by such as shall be called upon for those purposes.

To these inevitable, but I trust salutary measures, it is a far more pleasing part of my duty to add the assurances of protection and support, to all who, in so trying a crisis, shall manifest their allegiance to the king, and affection to the parent state. So that such persons as may have been intimidated to quit their habitations in the course of this alarm, may return to their respective callings and professions, and stand distinct and separate from the parricides of the constitution, till God, in his mercy, shall restore to his creatures, in this distracted land, that system of happiness from which they have been seduced, the religion of peace, and liberty founded upon law.

GIVEN at Boston, this twelfth day of June, in the fifteenth year of the reign of his majesty GEORGE the third, by the grace of GOD, of Great Britain, France and Ireland, KING, defender of the Faith, etc. Annoque Domini, 1775.

THOMAS GAGE

By his excellency's command:

THO'S FLUCKER, Secretary
GOD SAVE THE KING

GENERALS LEE AND BURGOYNE DEBATE COLONIAL RESISTANCE

[Excerpts from the correspondence of the American general Charles Lee and his old friend British general John Burgoyne, 1775]

PHILADELPHIA, June 7, 1775

MY DEAR SIR—We have had twenty different accounts of your arrival at Boston, which have been regularly contradicted the next morning; but as I now find it certain that you are arrived, I shall not delay a single instant addressing myself to you. It is a duty I owe to the friendship I have long and sincerely professed for you; a friendship to which you have the strongest claim from the first moments of our acquaintance. There is no man from whom I have received so many testimonies of esteem and affection; there is no man whose esteem and affection could in my opinion, have done me greater honor. I entreat and conjure you, therefore, my dear sir, to impute these few lines not to a petulant itch of scribbling, but to the most unfeigned solicitude for the future tranquility of your mind, and for your reputation. I sincerely lament the infatuation of the times, when men of such a stamp as Mr. Burgoyne and Mr. [William] Howe can be seduced into so impious and nefarious a service by the artifice of a wicked and insidious court and cabinet. You, sir, must be sensible that these epithets are not unjustly severe. You have yourself experienced the wickedness and treachery of this court and cabinet. . . . I shall not trouble you with my opinion of the right of taxing America without her own consent, as I am afraid, from what I have seen of your speeches, that you have already formed your creed on this article; but I will boldly affirm, had this right been established by a thousand statutes, had America admitted it from time immemorial, it would be the duty of every good Englishman, to exert his utmost to divest parliament of this right, as it must inevitably work the subversion of the whole empire. The malady under which the state labors is indisputably derived from the inadequate representation of the subject, and the vast pecuniary influence of the crown. To add to this pecuniary influence and incompetency of representation, is to insure and precipitate our destruction. To wish any addition, can scarcely enter the heart of a citizen, who has the least spark of public virtue, and who is at the same time capable of seeing consequences the most immediate. I appeal, sir, to your own conscience, to your experience and knowledge of our court and parliament, and I request you to lay your hand upon your heart, and then answer with your usual integrity and frankness, whether, on the supposition America should be abject enough to submit to the terms imposed, you think a single guinea, raised upon her, would be applied to the purpose (as it is ostentatiously held out to deceive the people at home) of easing the mother country? or whether you are not convinced that the whole they could extract would be applied solely to heap up still further the enormous fund for corruption, which the crown already possesses, and of which a most diabolical use is made. On these principles I say, sir, every good Englishman, abstracted of all regard for America, must oppose her being taxed by the British parliament; for my own part, I am convinced that no argument (not totally abhorrent from the spirit of liberty and the British constitution) can be produced in support of this right.

But it will be impertinent to trouble you upon a subject which has been so amply and in my opinion, so fully discussed. I find by a speech given as yours in the public papers, that it was by the king's positive command you embarked in this service. I am somewhat pleased that it is not an office of your own seeking, though, at the same time, I must confess that it is very alarming to every virtuous citizen, when he sees men of sense and integrity, (because of a certain profession) lay it down as a rule implicitly to obey the mandates of a court, be they ever so flagitious. It furnishes, in my opinion, the best arguments for the total reduction of the army. But I am running into a tedious essay, whereas I ought to confine myself to the main design and purpose of this letter, which is to guard you and your colleagues from those prejudices which the same miscreants, who have infatuated general Gage and still surround him, will labor to instil into you against a brave, loyal and most deserving people. The avenues of truth will be shut up to you. I assert, sir, that even general Gage will deceive you as he has deceived himself; I do not say he will do it designedly. I do not think him capable; but his mind is totally poisoned, and his understanding so totally blinded by the society of fools and knaves, that he no longer is capable of discerning facts as manifest as the noon day sun. I assert, sir, that he is ignorant, that he has from the beginning been consummately ignorant of the principles, temper, disposition and force of the colonies. I assert, sir, that his letters to the ministry, (at least such as the public have seen) are one continued tissue of misrepresentation, injustice, and tortured inferences from misstated facts. I affirm, sir, that he has taken no pains to inform himself of the truth; that he has never conversed with a man who has had the courage or honesty to tell him the truth—I am apprehensive that you and your colleagues may fall into the same trap, and it is the apprehension that you may be inconsiderately hurried by the vigor and activity you possess, into measures which may be fatal to many innocent individuals, may hereafter wound your own feelings, and which cannot possibly serve the cause of those who sent you, that has promoted me to address these lines to you. I most devoutly wish, that your industry, valor and military talents, may be reserved for a more honorable and virtuous service against the natural enemies of your country, (to whom our court are so basely complaisant) and not be wasted in ineffectual attempts to reduce to the wretchedest state of servitude, the most meritorious part of your fellow subjects. I say, sir, that any attempts to accomplish this purpose, must be ineffectual. You cannot possibly succeed. No man is better acquainted with the state of this continent than myself. I have run through almost the whole colonies, from the North to the South, and from the South to the North. I have conversed with all orders of men, from the first estated gentlemen, to the lowest planters and farmers, and can assure you, that the same spirit animates the whole.

Not less than a hundred and fifty thousand gentlemen, yeomen and farmers, are now in arms, determined to preserve their liberties or perish.—As to the idea that the Americans are deficient in courage, it is too ridiculous and glaringly false to deserve a serious refutation.—I never could conceive upon what this notion was founded.—I served several campaigns in America the last war, and cannot recollect a single instance of ill behavior in the provincials, where the regulars acquitted themselves well. Indeed we well remember some instances of the reverse, particularly where the late colonel Grant, (he who lately pledged himself for the general cowardice of America) ran away with a large body of his own regiment, and was saved from destruction by the valor of a few Virginians. Such preposterous arguments are only proper for the Rigbys and Sandwichs, from whose mouths never issued, and to whose breasts, truth and decency are utter strangers. You will much oblige me in communicating this letter to general Howe, to whom I could wish it should be considered in some measure addressed, as well as to yourself. . . . These, sir, are my principles; this is my persuasion, and consequentially I am determined to act. I have now, sir, only to entreat that whatever measures you pursue, whether those which your real friends (myself amongst them) would wish, or unfortunately those which our accursed misrulers shall dictate, you will still believe me to be, personally, with the greatest sincerity and affection,

Yours, &c.   C. LEE.

[Burgoyne's reply, dated July 9, 1775]

DEAR SIR—When we were last together in service, I should not have thought it within the vicissitude of human affairs that we should meet at any time, or in any sense as foes; the letter you have honored me with, and my own feelings combine to prove we are still far from being personally such. . . .

I have, like you, entertained from my infancy a veneration for public liberty. I have likewise regarded the British constitution as the best safeguard of that blessing, to be found in the history of mankind. The vital principle of the constitution in which it moves and has its being, is the supremacy of the king in parliament; a compound, indefinite, indefeasible power, coeval with the origin of the empire, and coextensive over all its parts—I am no stranger to the doctrines of Mr. Locke and other of the best advocates for the rights of mankind, upon the compact always implied between the governing and governed, and the right of resistance in the latter, when the compact shall be so violated as to leave no other means of redress. I look with reverence, almost amounting to idolatry, upon those immortal whigs who adopted and applied such doctrine during part of the reign of Charles the 1st, and in that of James the IId—Should corruption pervade the three estates of the realm, so as to pervert the great ends of their institution, and make the power, vested in them for the good of the whole people, operate like an abuse of the prerogative of the crown, to general oppression, I am ready to acknowledge, that the same doctrine of resistance applies as forcibly against the abuses of the collective body of power, as against those of the crown, or either of the component branches separately: still always understood that no other means of redress can be obtained.—A case, I contend, much more difficult to suppose when it relates to the whole than when it relates to parts. But in all cases that have existed, or can be conceived, I hold that resistance, to be justifiable, must be directed against the usurpation or undue exercise of power, and that it is most criminal when directed against any power itself inherent in the constitution.

And here you will discern immediately why I drew a line in the allusion I made above to the reign of Charles the first. Towards the close of it the true principle of resistance was changed, and a new system of government projected accordingly. The patriots, previous to the long parliament and during great part of it, as well as the glorious revolutionists of 1688, resisted to vindicate and restore the constitution; the republicans resisted to subvert it.

Now, sir, lay your hand upon your heart, as you have enjoined me to do on mine, and tell me, to which of these purposes do the proceedings of America tend? Is it the weight of taxes imposed, and the impossibility of relief, after due representation of her burthens, that has induced her to take arms? Or is it a denial of the legislative right of Great Britain to impose them, and consequently a struggle for total independency?—For the idea of a power that can tax externally and not internally, and all the sophistry that attends it, though it may catch the weakness and prejudices of the multitude, in a speech or a pamphlet, is too preposterous to weigh seriously with a man of your understanding, and I am persuaded you will admit the question fairly put.

Is it then for a relief from taxes—or from the control of parliament, "in all cases whatsoever," that we are in war? If for the former the quarrel is at an end—There is not a man of sense and information in America, who does not see it is in the power of the colonies to obtain a relinquishment of the exercise of taxation immediately and forever.—I boldly assert it, because sense and information must also suggest to every man, that it can never be the interest of Britain to make a second trial.

But if the other ground is taken, and it is intended to wrest from Great Britain, a link of that substantial, and I hope perpetual chain, by which the empire holds—think it not a ministerial mandate; think it not more professional ardor; think it not prejudice against any part of our fellow subjects, that induces men of integrity, and among such you have done me the honor to class me, to act with vigor:—But be assured it is conviction that the whole of our political system depends upon preserving entire its great and essential parts, and none is so great and essential as the supremacy of legislation—It is conviction that as a king of England never appears in so glorious a capacity as when he employs the executive power of the state to maintain the laws, so in the present exertions of that power, his majesty is particularly entitled to our zeal and grateful obedience, not only as soldiers but as citizens.

These principles, depend upon it, actuate the army and fleet throughout. And let me, at the same time add, there are few, if any, gentlemen among us who would have drawn his sword in the cause of slavery. But, why do I confine myself to the fleet and army: I affirm the sentiments I here touched, to be those of the great bulk of the nation. I appeal even to those trading towns which are sufferers by the dispute, and the city of London at the head of them, notwithstanding the petitions and remonstrances that the arts of parties and factions have extorted from some individuals; and last, because least in your favor, I appeal to the majorities of the last year upon American questions in parliament. The most licentious news writer wants assurance to call these majorities ministerial; much less will you, when you impartially examine the characters of which they were in a great degree composed—men of the most independent principles and fortunes, and many of them professedly in opposition in their general line of conduct.

Among other supporters of British rights against American claims, I will not speak positively, but I firmly believe, I may name the men of whose integrity and judgment you have the highest opinion, and whose friendship is nearest your heart: I mean lord Thanet, from whom my aid de camp has a letter for you, with another from Sir C. Davers. I do not enclose them, because the writers, little imagining how difficult your conduct would render our intercourse, desired they might be delivered into your own hands.

For this purpose, as well as to renew "the rights of our fellowship," I wish to see you; and above all I should think an interview happy if it induced such explanations as might tend in their consequences to peace. I feel, in common with all around me, for the unhappy deluded bulk of this country—they fore-see not the distress that is impending. I know Great Britain is ready to open her arms upon the first reasonable overtures of accommodation; I know she is equally resolute to maintain her original rights: and I also know, that if the war proceeds, your hundred and fifty thousand men will be no match for her power. I put my honor to these assertions, as you have done to others, and I claim the credit I am willing to give.

The place I would propose for our meeting is the house on Boston Neck, just within our advanced sentries, called Brown's house. I will obtain author-ity to give you my parole of honor for your secure return: I shall expect the same on your part, that no insult be offered to me. If the proposal is agree-able to you, name your day and hour—And, at all events, accept a sincere re-turn of the assurances you honor me with, and believe me affectionately yours,

J. BURGOYNE.

P.S. I have been prevented by business answering your letter sooner.—I obeyed your commands in regard to general Howe and [Henry] Clinton; and I likewise communicated to lord Percy the contents of your letter and my answer.—They all join with me in compliments, and authorize me to as-sure you they do the same in principles.

[*Lee's answer, July 11, 1775*]

GENERAL LEE'S COMPLIMENTS TO GENERAL BURGOYNE.—Would be extremely happy in the interview he so kindly proposed. But as he perceives that General Burgoyne has already made up his mind on this great subject; and that it is impossible that he [Gen. Lee] should ever alter his opinion, he is apprehensive that the interview might create those jealousies and suspi-cions, so natural to a people struggling in the dearest of all causes, that of their liberty, property, wives, children and their future generations. He must, therefore, defer the happiness of embracing a man whom he most sincerely loves until the subversions of the present tyrannical ministry and system, which he is persuaded must be in a few months, as he knows Great Britain cannot stand the contest.—He begs General Burgoyne will send the letters which his aid de camp has for him. If Gardiner is his aid de camp, he desires his love to him.

NORTH CAROLINA ADDRESSES THE BRITISH EMPIRE

*[Address adopted by the Provincial Congress of North Carolina,
September 3, 1775]*

Mr. Hooper laid before the house an address to the inhabitants of the British empire; and the same being read was unanimously received, and is as follows, viz.

FRIENDS AND FELLOW-CITIZENS—The fate of the contest which at present subsists between these American colonies and the British ministers who now sit at the helm of public affairs, will be one of the most important epochs which can mark the annals of the British history.

Foreign nations with anxious expectation wait the result, and see with amazement the blind infatuated policy which the present administration pursues to subjugate these colonies, and reduce them from being loyal and useful subjects, to an absolute dependence and abject slavery; as if the descendants of those ancestors who have shed rivers of blood, and expended millions of treasure, in fixing upon a lasting foundation of the liberties of the British constitution, saw with envy the once happy state of this western region, and strove to exterminate the patterns of those virtues which shone with a lustre which bids fair to rival and eclipse their own.

To enjoy the fruits of our own honest industry; to call that our own which we earn with the labor of our hands, and the sweat of our brows; to regulate that internal policy by which we, and not they, are to be affected; these are the mighty boons we ask. And traitors, rebels, and every harsh appellation that malice can dictate, or the violence of language express, are the returns which we receive to the most humble petitions and earnest supplications. We have been told that independence is our object; that we seek to shake off all connection with the parent state. Cruel suggestion! do not all our professions, all our actions, uniformly contradict this?

We again declare, and we invoke that Almighty Being who searches the recesses of the human heart and knows our most secret intentions, that it is our most earnest wish and prayer to be restored with the other United Colonies, to the state in which we and they were placed before the year 1763, disposed to glance over any regulations which Britain had made previous to this, and which seem to be injurious and oppressive to these colonies, hoping that at some future day she will benignly interpose, and remove from us every cause of complaint. . . .

These expressions flow from an affection, bordering upon devotion, to the succession of the house of Hanover, as by law established, from subjects who view it as a monument that does honor to human nature; a monument capable of teaching kings how glorious it is to reign over a free people.— These are the heartfelt effusions of men ever ready to spend their blood and treasure, when constitutionally called upon, in support of that succession of his majesty King George the third, his crown and dignity, and who fervently wish to transmit his reign to future ages as the era of common happiness to people. Could these our sentiments reach the throne, surely our sovereign would forbid the horrors of war and desolation to intrude into this once peaceful and happy land, and would stop that deluge of human blood which now threatens to overflow this colony; blood too precious to be shed but in a common cause, against the common enemy of Great Britain and her sons.

This declaration we hold forth as a testimony of loyalty to our sovereign, and affection to our parent state, and as a sincere earnest of our present and future intentions.

We hope, thereby, to remove those impressions which have been made by the representation of weak and wicked men to the prejudice of this colony, who thereby intended that the rectitude of our designs might be brought into distrust, and sedition, anarchy, and confusion, spread through this loyal province.

We have discharged a duty which we owe to the world, to ourselves, and posterity; and may the Almighty God give success to the means we make use of, so far as they are aimed to produce just, lawful, and good purposes, and the salvation and happiness of the whole British empire.

4. CREATING AN AMERICAN ARMY

General Gates' Instructions to Recruiters

*[Instructions issued by General Horatio Gates of the
Continental Army, July 10, 1775]*

Instructions for the officers of the several regiments of the Massachusetts Bay forces, who are immediately to go upon the recruiting service.

You are not to enlist any deserter from the ministerial army, nor any stroller, negro, or vagabond, or person suspected of being an enemy to the liberty of America, nor any under eighteen years of age.

As the cause is the best that can engage men of courage and principle to take up arms, so it is expected that none but such will be accepted by the recruiting officer; the pay, provision, etc., being so ample, it is not doubted but the officers set upon this service, will without delay complete their respective corps, and march the men forthwith to the camp.

You are not to enlist any person who is not an American born, unless such person has a wife and family, and is a settled resident in this country.

The person you enlist, must be provided with good and complete arms.

Given at the head-quarters at Cambridge, this 10th day of July, 1775.

HORATIO GATES, Adj. Gen.

A REGIMENT IS FORMED IN PENNSYLVANIA

[The formation of a Pennsylvania Regiment as reported by the Pennsylvania Gazette, June 1775]

The ladies in Bristol township have evidenced a laudable regard to the interest of their country. At their own expense, they have furnished the regiment of that county with a suit of colors and drums, and are now making a collection to supply muskets to such of the men as are not able to supply themselves. We hear the lady, who was appointed to present the colors to the regiment, gave in charge to the soldiers, never to desert the colors of the ladies, if they ever wish that the ladies should list under their banners.

The spirit of opposition to the arbitrary and tyrannical acts of the ministry and parliament of Britain, hath diffused itself so universally throughout this province, that the people, even to its most extended frontiers, are indefatigable in training themselves to military discipline. The aged, as well as the young, daily march out under the banners of liberty and discover a determined resolution to maintain her cause even until death. In the town of Reading, in Berks county, there had been some time past three companies formed, and very forward in their exercise; since, however, we are well informed, a fourth company have associated under the name of the Old Man's company. It consists of about eighty Germans, of the age of forty and upwards. Many of them have been in the military service in Germany. The person who, at their first assembling, led them to the field, is 97 years of age, has been 40 years in the regular service, and in 17 pitched battles, and the drummer is 84. In lieu of a cockade, they wear in their hats a black crape, as expressive of their sorrow for the mournful events which have occasioned them, at their late time of life, to take arms against our brethren, in order to preserve that liberty which they left their native country to enjoy.

EXPENSES OF THE CONTINENTAL ARMY

[Budget—in sterling money—for the Continental Army, dated May 1776]

STAFF	per diem.					
	£.	s.	d.			
Commander in chief, general						
Washington, (for table)	2	0	0			
4 Aids-de-camp, 4s.6d. each		18	0			
1 Adjutant general.		18				
1 Quarter master general,		12				
1 Assistant quarter master general,		4	6			
1 Pay master general,		13	6			
6 Majors brigade, 4s.6d.	[sic]	7				
Secretary to commander in chief		9				
Directors of hospitals		18		8	0	6

4 Surgeons, 6s.		1	4			
1 Apothecary			6			
2 Mates, and one clerk, 3s.			9			
1 Commissary general,			12			
2 Major generals under commander in chief, 24s.9d.		2	9	6		
4 Aid-de-camps, 4s.6d.			18			
6 Brigadier generals, 18s. 9d.		5	12	6		
1 Engineer,			9			
4 Sub-engineers, 4s.6d.			18			
4 Major generals, commanding separate armies, 49s.6d.		9	18			
8 Aid-de-camps, 4s.6d.		1	16			
8 Majors brigade, 4s.6d.		1	16			
4 Secretaries, 4s.9d.			19			

STAFF	per diem.					
	£.	s.	d.			
4 Deputy adjutant generals, 9s.4d ½ .	1	17	6			
4 Deputy quarter master generals, 6s.	1	4				
4 Deputy commissary generals, 6s.	1	4				
8 Sub-engineers, 4s.6d.	1	16				
9 Brigadier generals, 18s.9d.*	8	8	5	41	17	0

* Including Thompson, who is prisoner.

60 REGIMENTS.

	£	s.			
60 Colonels, 13s.6d.	40	10			
60 Lieutenant colonels, 9s.	27				
60 Majors, 6s.	18				
540 Captains, 4s.6d.	121	10			
1080 Lieutenants, 3s.	162				
540 Ensigns, 2s.	54				
2160 Sergeants, 1s.3d.	135				
2160 Corporals, 1s.1d.	117				
540 Drums, 1s.1d. and 540 fifes, 1s.1d.	58	10			
30600 Privates, 1s.	1530				
(Chaplains, Surgeons, and Surgeon's mates, not included)			2263	10	0

FLYING CAMP.

	£	s.	d.			
14 Colonels, 13s.6d.	9	9				
14 Lieutenant colonels, 9s.	6	6				
14 Majors, 6s.	4	4				
128 Captains, 4s.6d.	28	16				
256 Lieutenants, 3s.	38	8				
128 Ensigns, 2s.	12	16				
512 Sergeants, 1s.3d.	32					
512 Corporals, 1s.1d.	27	14	8			
256 Drums and fifes, 1s.1d.	13	7	4			
8692 Privates, 1s.	434	12		520	10	0

JERSEY BRIGADE.

	£	s.	d.
5 Colonels, 13s.6d.	3	7	6
5 Lieutenant colonels, 9s.	2	5	

STAFF

		per diem.					
		£.	s.	d.			
5	Majors, 6s.	1	10				
42	Captains, 4s.6d.	9	9				
84	Lieutenants, 3s.	12	12				
42	Ensigns, 2s.	4	4				
168	Sergeants, 1s.3d.	10	10				
168	Corporals, 1s.1d.	9	2				
84	Drums and fifes, 1s.1d.	4	11				
2856	Privates, 1s.	142	16		200	6	6

MILITIA (in pay.)

		£.	s.	d.			
44	Colonels, 18s.6d.	29	14				
44	Lieutenant colonels, 9s.	19	16				
400	Captains, 4s.6d.	90					
800	Lieutenants, 3s.	120					
400	Ensigns, 2s.	40					
1600	Sergeants, 1s.3d.	100					
1600	Corporals, 1s.1d.	86	13	4			
800	Drums and fifes, 1s.1d.	43	6	8			
27000	Privates 1s.	1350			1892	14	0
					5014	12	0

DAILY ALLOWANCE OF PROVISIONS.

1 lb. fresh beef, or 1 lb. salt fish; ¾ lb. pork, or 20 oz. salt beef; 1 lb. bread, flour, 1 pint milk, 1 quart cider or spruce beer, per diem each—3 lb. candles, 8 lb. hard soap, per week for 100 men—3 pints pease, 1 pint Indian meal, 6 oz. butter, per man a week. This is about 10d. sterling ration per day.

		£.	s.	d.			
Rations on an average 3 per day, for general and other officers, 4898 at 2s. 6d.		612	5	0			
Non-commissioned officers, and privates, 80,248, at 10d.		3343	13	4	3955	18	4
					8970	10	4

STAFF

per diem.

£.   s.   d.

Clothing for continental army, flying camp, and Jersey brigade, 49,248, 2d. per day

410   8

Daily expenses,

9380   18   4

Nothing of the navy contingencies, or army extraordinaries, are included

5. LORD DUNMORE "FREES" THE SLAVES

DUNMORE'S PROCLAMATION OF NOVEMBER 7, 1775

[A proclamation by Governor Dunmore of Virginia, November 7, 1775, in an attempt to intimidate the rebels]

By his excellency, the right honorable JOHN EARL OF DUNMORE, his majesty's lieutenant and governor general of the colony of Virginia, and vice admiral of the same.

A PROCLAMATION

As I have ever entertained hopes that an accommodation might have taken place between Great Britain and this colony, without being compelled by my duty to do this most disagreeable, but now absolutely necessary duty, rendered so by a body of men, unlawfully assembled, firing on his majesty's tenders, and the formation of an army, and an army now on its march to attack his majesty's troops, and destroy the well disposed subjects of this colony. To defeat such treasonable purposes, and that all such traitors, and their abettors may be brought to justice, and that the peace and good order of this colony may be again restored, which the ordinary course of the civil law is unable to effect, I have thought fit to issue this my proclamation, hereby declaring that, until the aforesaid good purposes can be obtained, I do, in virtue of the power and authority to me given, by his majesty, determine to execute martial law, and cause the same to be executed throughout this colony; and to the end that peace and good order may the sooner be restored, I do require every person capable of bearing arms to resort to his majesty's standard, or be looked upon as traitors to his majesty's crown and government, and thereby become liable to the penalty the law inflicts upon such offences; such as

forfeiture of life, confiscation of lands, etc., etc. And I do hereby further declare all indented servants, negroes, or others (appertaining to rebels) free,
that are able and willing to bear arms, they joining his majesty's troops as
soon as may be, for the more speedily reducing his colony to a proper sense
of their duty to his majesty's crown and dignity. I do further order and require
all his majesty's liege subjects, to retain their quit-rents or other taxes due, or
that may become due in their own custody, till such a time may again be restored to this at present most unhappy country, or demanded of them for their
former salutary purposes, by officers properly authorized to receive the same.

Given under my hand, on board the ship William, off Norfolk, the 7th
day of November, in the 16th year of his majesty's reign.

DUNMORE.

God Save the King

DUNMORE DESCRIBES THE SITUATION TO GENERAL HOWE

[*Extract from a letter by Governor Dunmore to General Howe,
November 30, 1775*]

I must inform you, that with our little corps I think we have done won-
ders. We have taken and destroyed above fourscore pieces of ordnance, and
by landing in different parts of the country, we keep them in continual hot
water. . . . Among the prisoners, we have taken one Oliver Porter, and
—— Deane, two natives of Boston, bringing in gunpowder to North Carolina. The latter was sent from Boston to influence the minds of the people, in
which he has been but too successful. He was taken from on board a schooner
going from this place to the Western Islands, to bring powder to this colony;
and the others have carried arms against his majesty in this province. I have
sent them more with a view of intimidating others than to punish them, as
they expect here that, so sure as they are sent to Boston, they are to be hanged.
Robinson is a delegate of our convention. Matthews was a captain of their
minute-men. Perhaps they may be of some use to you, in exchanging them for
good men.

The sloop not sailing so soon as I expected, I have to inform you that, on
the 14th inst. I had information that a party of about a hundred of the North
Carolina rebels had marched to the assistance of those in this colony, and
were posted at a place called the Great-Bridge, a very essential pass in the
country. I accordingly embarked our little corps in boats, in the night of the
14th, with between twenty and thirty volunteers from Norfolk. We landed

within four miles of the bridge, and arrived there a little after daylight; but, to our great mortification, found the birds had flown the evening before. But hearing that a body, between 2 and 300, of our rebels were within about ten miles of us, we determined to beat up their quarters, and accordingly proceeded about eight miles, when they fired on our advanced guards from the woods: on which I immediately ordered our people to rush upon them, and at the same time sent a party of the regulars, with the volunteers, to out-flank them. The enemy immediately fled on all quarters, and our people pursued them for a mile or more, killed a few, drove others to a creek, where they were drowned, and took nine prisoners, among whom is one of their colonels. We only had one man wounded, who is recovering. I immediately upon this issued the enclosed proclamation; which has had a wonderful effect, as there are no less than 300 who have taken and signed the enclosed oath. The blacks are also flocking from all quarters, which I hope will oblige the rebels to disperse, to take care of their families and property, and had I but a few more men here, I would immediately march to Williamsburg, my former place of residence, by which I should soon compel the whole colony to submit.

We are in great want of small arms; and if two or three field pieces and their carriages could be spared, they would be of great service to us; also some cartridge paper, of which not a sheet is to be got in this country, and all our cartridges are expended.—Since the 19th of May last I have not received a single line from any one in administration, though I have wrote volumes to them, in each of which I have prayed to be instructed, but to no purpose. I am therefore determined to go on doing the best of my power for his majesty's service. I have accordingly ordered a regiment, called the Queen's own loyal regiment, of 500 men, to be raised immediately, consisting of a lieutenant-colonel commandant, major, and ten companies, each of which is to consist of one captain, two lieutenants, one ensign, and fifty privates, with non-commissioned officers in proportion.

You may observe, by my proclamation, that I offer freedom to the blacks of all rebels that join me, in consequence of which there are between 2 and 300 already come in, and those I form into corps as fast as they come in, giving them white officers and non-commissioners in proportion. And from these two plans, I make no doubt of getting men enough to reduce this colony to a proper sense of their duty. My next distress will be the want of arms, accoutrements and money, all of which you may be able to relieve me from. The latter I am sure you can, as there are many merchants here who are ready to supply me, on my giving them bills on you, which you will have to withdraw, and give your own in their room. I hope this mode will be agreeable to you; it is the same that general Gage proposed. I have now, in order to carry on the recruiting business, victualling, clothing, etc. drawn on you for 5000 sterling, and have appointed a paymaster, who will keep exact accounts. I wish you would inform me, by the return of the sloop, what bounty money may be given to those who enlist.— Having heard that 1000 chosen men belonging to the rebels, a great part of whom were riflemen, were on their march to attack us here, or to cut off our provisions, I determined to take possession of the pass at the Great-Bridge, which secures us the greatest part of two counties, to supply us with provisions. I accordingly ordered a stockade to be erected there, which was done in a few days; and I put an officer and 25 men to garrison it, with some volunteers and ——, who have defended it against all the efforts of the rebels for these eight days past. We have killed several of their men, and I make no doubt we shall now be able to maintain our ground there; but should we be obliged to abandon it, we have thrown up an intrenchment on the land side of Norfolk, which I hope they never will be able to force. Here we are contending, with only a very small part of a regiment, against the extensive colony of Virginia. If you could but spare me, for a few months, the 64th regiment now in the castle, and the remaining part of the 14th, I really believe we should reduce this colony to a proper sense of their duty.

REACTION OF THE VIRGINIA CONVENTION

[*Resolution of the Virginia Convention at Williamsburg,*
January 25, 1776]

WILLIAMSBURG, VIRGINIA, January 25, 1776
Resolved, unanimously, that this convention do highly approve of col. Woodford's conduct, manifested, as well in the success of the troops under his command, as in the humane treatment of, and kind attention to, the unfortunate, though brave officers and soldiers, who were made prisoners in the late action near the Great Bridge, and that the president communicate to col. Woodford the sense of his country on this occasion.

Whereas lord Dunmore, by his proclamation, dated on board the ship William, the 7th day of November, 1775, hath presumed, in direct violation of the constitution, and the laws of this country, to declare martial law in force, and to be executed throughout this colony, whereby our lives, our liberty, and our property, are arbitrarily subjected to his power and direction: and whereas the said lord Dunmore, assuming powers which the king himself cannot exercise, to intimidate the good people of this colony into a compliance with his arbitrary will, hath declared those who do not immediately repair to his standard, and submit it in all things to a government not warranted by the constitution, to be in actual rebellion, and thereby to have incurred the penalties inflicted by the laws for such offences; and hath offered freedom to the servants and slaves of those he is pleased to term rebels, arming them against their masters, and destroying the peace and happiness of his majesty's good and faithful subjects, whose property is rendered insecure, and whose lives are exposed to the dangers of a general insurrection. We, as guardians of the lives and liberty of the people, our constituents, conceived it to be indispensably our duty to protect them against every species of despotism, and to endeavor to remove those fears with which they are so justly alarmed. . . .

Whereas lord Dunmore, by his proclamation, dated on board the ship William off Norfolk, the 7th day of November, 1775, hath offered freedom to such able bodied slaves as are willing to join him, and take up arms against the good people of this colony, giving thereby encouragement to a general insurrection, which may induce a necessity of inflicting the severest punishments upon those unhappy people already deluded by his base and insidious arts, and whereas, by an act of the general assembly now in force in this colony, it is enacted, that all negro, or other slaves, conspiring to rebel or make insurrection, shall suffer death, and be excluded all benefit of clergy —we think it proper to declare, that all slaves who have been, or shall be, seduced by his lordship's proclamation, or other arts, to desert their master's service, and take up arms against the inhabitants of this colony, shall be liable to such punishment as shall hereafter be directed by the convention. And to the end that all such, who have taken this unlawful and wicked step, may return in safety to their duty, and escape the punishment due to their crimes, we hereby promise pardon to them, they surrendering themselves to colonel William Woodford or any other commander of our troops, and not appearing in arms after the publication hereof. And we do further earnestly recommend it to all humane and benevolent persons in this colony, to explain and make known this our offer of mercy to those unfortunate people.

And whereas, notwithstanding the favorable and kind dispositions shewn by the convention and the natives of this colony, and the extraordinary and unexampled indulgence by them held out to the natives of Great

Britain, residing in this colony, (the Scotch who gave themselves this title in their petition) many of these have lately become strict adherents to the lord Dunmore and the most active promoters of all his cruel and arbitrary persecutions of the good people of this colony, not only by violating the continental association, to which they had solemnly subscribed, in many the most flagrant instances; not merely by giving intelligence to our enemies and furnishing them with provisions, but by propagating, as well in Great Britain as in this colony, many of the most mischievous falsehoods, to the great prejudice and dishonor of this country: And moreover, many of these natives of Great Britain, instead of giving their assistance in suppressing insurrections, have contrary to all faith, solemnly plighted in their petition, excited our slaves to rebellion, and some of them have daringly led those slaves in arms against our inhabitants; the committee having these things in full proof, and considering their alarming and dangerous tendency, do give it as their opinion, and it is accordingly resolved, that the former resolution in their favor ought from henceforth to be totally abrogated and rescinded; that none of the freemen, inhabitants of this country, wherever born, ought to be exempted from any of the burthens or dangers to which the colony is exposed: but that, as good citizens, it is incumbent on them to use every exertion of their power and abilities in the common defence; and should any persons of ability decline or shrink from so necessary a duty to the community, that all such, except those who have taken up arms against our inhabitants, or shewn themselves to us, may be permitted, under a license of the committee of safety, to leave the country.

6. THE BRITISH EVACUATE BOSTON

REMINISCENCES OF A BOSTONIAN

[*Reminiscences of the evacuation of Boston published in the*
Boston Centinal, *1821-1822*]

The British army evacuated Boston on the forenoon of Sunday, the 17th March, 1776. On the afternoon of that day I landed (in company with a surgeon who was ordered in by general Washington) at the bottom of the common, near the high bluff, which was taken away a few years ago to make Charles-street. The first object that I observed on landing was a thirteen-inch iron mortar on the beach of extraordinary dimensions and weight, which the British had thrown down from a battery they had erected on the height above. I was told that another of the same size was sunk at the long-wharf, which was afterwards raised. One of them is now at the navy-yard in Charleston, and the other was a few years since on the grand battery at New-York, where it was carried in the same year.

On crossing the common we found it very much disfigured with ditches and cellars, which had been dug by the British troops for their accommodation when in camp. To our great regret, we saw several large trees lying in the mall, which had been cut down that morning. We were informed that the tories were so exasperated at being obliged to leave the town, that they were determined to do all the mischief possible, and had commenced destroying that beautiful promenade; but it being told to some of the selectmen, they went in haste to general Howe and represented the circumstance, who kindly sent one of his aids to forbid the further destruction of the trees, and to reprimand the tories for their conduct. General Howe could not but feel some degree of grateful regard and sympathy for the people of Massachusetts, as they had erected a monument in Westminster Abbey to the memory of his brother, whose urbane and gentlemanly deportment had gained the esteem and respect of the Massachusetts forces, and who was killed in a battle with the French and Indians in 1758.

The mall was originally laid out with only two rows of trees, a third was added a few years before the war, which we found were all cut down for fuel, together with the entire fence which surrounded the common as was also a large magnificent tree which stood on the town's land, near the school house, in West-street, of equal size with that which now stands in the middle of the common, both of which I suppose to be aboriginal.

On passing into the town, it presented an indescribable scene of desolation and gloominess, for notwithstanding the joyous occasion of having driven our enemies from our land, our minds were impressed with an awful sadness at the sight of the ruins of many houses which had been taken down for fuel—the dirtiness of the streets—the wretched appearance of the very few inhabitants who remained during the siege—the contrast between the Sunday we then beheld, compared with those we formerly witnessed, when well dressed people, with cheerful countenances, were going to, and returning from church, on which occasion, Boston exhibits so beautiful a scene—but more especially when we entered the Old South church, and had ocular demonstration that it had been turned into a *riding school,* for the use of general Burgoyne's regiment of cavalry, which formed a part of the garrison, but which had never ventured to pass the barriers of the town. The pulpit and all the pews were taken away and burnt for fuel, and many hundred loads of dirt and gravel were carted in, and spread upon the floor. The south door was closed, and a bar was fixed, over which the cavalry were taught to leap their horses at full speed. A grog shop was erected in the gallery, where liquor was sold to the soldiery, and consequently produced scenes of riot and debauchery in that holy temple. All these circumstances conspired to fill the mind with sombre reflections. But amidst the sadness of the scene, there was a pleasing satisfaction in the hope that men capable of such atrocities, could not have the blessing of Heaven in their nefarious plan of subjugating our beloved country. The English soldiers were generally Episcopalians, and viewed this act with indifference, but the Scotch, who were mostly dissenters, and much more moral and pious looked upon it with horror, and not without some feelings of superstition. . . .

WASHINGTON'S PROCLAMATION

[Proclamation of General Washington on taking possession of Boston, March 21, 1776]

By his excellency, GEORGE WASHINGTON, Esq., general commander in chief of the thirteen united colonies.

Whereas the ministerial army has abandoned the town of Boston, and the forces of the united colonies, under my command, are in possession of the same: I have therefore thought it necessary for the preservation of peace, good order and discipline, to publish the following orders, that no persons offending therein, may plead ignorance as an excuse for their misconduct.

All officers and soldiers are hereby ordered to live in the strictest amity with the inhabitants; and no inhabitant, or other person, employed in his lawful business in the town, is to be molested in his person or property, on any pretence whatever.

If any officer or soldier shall presume to strike, imprison, or otherwise ill-treat any of the inhabitants they may depend on being punished with the utmost severity; and if any officer or soldier shall receive any insult from any of the inhabitants, he is to seek redress in a legal way, and no other.

Any non-commissioned officer or soldier or others under my command, who shall be guilty of robbing or plundering in the town, are to be immediately confined, and will be most rigidly punished. All officers are therefore ordered to be very vigilant in the discovery of such offenders, and report their names and crime to the commanding officer in the town as soon as may be.

The inhabitants and others, are called upon to make known to the quarter-master-general, or any of his deputies, all stores belonging to the ministerial army, that may be remaining or secreted in the town: any person or persons whatever, that shall be known to have concealed any of the said stores, or to appropriate them to his or their use, will be considered an enemy to America, and treated accordingly.

The selectmen and other magistrates of the town, are desired to return to the commander-in-chief, the names of all or any person or persons, they may suspect of being employed as spies upon the continental army, that they may be dealt with accordingly.

All officers of the continental army, are enjoined to assist the civil magistrates in the execution of their duty, and to promote peace and good order. They are to prevent, as much as possible the soldiers from frequenting tippling-houses, and strolling from their posts. Particular notice will be taken of such officers as are inattentive and remiss in their duty; and on the contrary, such only as are active and vigilant will be entitled to future favor and promotion.

Given under my hand, at head-quarters, in Cambridge, the 21st day of March, one thousand seven hundred and seventy-six.

GEORGE WASHINGTON

THE MASSACHUSETTS GOVERNMENT THANKS WASHINGTON

[*Address of the Council and House of Representatives of Massachusetts to George Washington, March 29, 1776*]

MAY IT PLEASE YOUR EXCELLENCY—

When the liberties of America were attacked by the violent hand of oppression—when troops, hostile to the rights of humanity, invaded this colony, seized our capital, and spread havoc and destruction around it; when our virtuous sons were murdered, and our houses destroyed by the troops of Britain, the inhabitants of this and the other American colonies, impelled by self-preservation and the love of freedom, forgetting their domestic concerns, determined resolutely and unitedly to oppose the sons of tyranny.

Convinced of the vast importance of having a gentleman of great military accomplishments to discipline, lead, and conduct the forces of the colonies, it gave us the greatest satisfaction to hear that the honorable congress of the united colonies had made choice of a gentleman thus qualified; who, leaving the pleasure of domestic and rural life was ready to undertake the arduous task. And your nobly declining to accept the pecuniary emoluments annexed to this high office, fully evidenced to us that a warm regard to the sacred rights of humanity, and sincere love to your country, solely influenced you in the acceptance of this important trust.

From your acknowledged abilities as a soldier, and your virtues in public and private life, we had the most pleasing hopes; but the fortitude and equanimity so conspicuous in your conduct; the wisdom of your counsels; the mild, yet strict government of the army; your attention to the civil constitution of this colony; the regard you have at all times shewn for the lives and health of those under your command; the fatigues you have with cheerfulness endured; the regard you have shewn for the preservation of our metropolis, and the great address with which our military operations have been conducted, have exceeded our most sanguine expectations, and demand the warmest returns of gratitude.

The Supreme Ruler of the universe having smiled on our arms, and crowned your labors with remarkable success, we are now, without that effusion of blood we so much wished to avoid, again in the quiet possession of our capital; the wisdom and prudence of those movements, which have obliged the enemy to abandon our metropolis, will ever be remembered by the inhabitants of this colony.

May you still go on approved by Heaven, revered by all good men, and dreaded by those tyrants who claim their fellow men as their property. May the united colonies be defended from slavery by your victorious arms. May they still see their enemies flying before you: and (the deliverance of your country being effected) may you, in retirement enjoy that peace and satisfaction of mind, which always attends the good and great: and may future generations in the peaceful enjoyment of that freedom, the exercise of which your sword shall establish, raise the richest and most lasting monuments to the name of a *Washington*.

HARVARD AWARDS WASHINGTON AN HONORARY DEGREE

[*An honorary degree of Doctor of Laws conferred upon General Washington shortly after the recapture of Boston*]

In Cambridge, in New England, to all faithful in Christ, to whom these presents shall come, Greeting. Boston, April 3, 1776.

Whereas academical degrees were originally instituted for this purpose, that men, eminent for knowledge, wisdom and virtue, who have highly merited of the republic of letters, should be rewarded with the honor of these laurels, there is the greatest propriety in conferring such honor on that very illustrious gentleman, George Washington, esq., the accomplished general of the confederated colonies in America; whose knowledge and patriotic ardor are manifest to all; who, for his distinguished virtues, both civil and military, in the first place being elected by the suffrages of the Virginians one of their delegates, exerted himself with fidelity and singular wisdom in the celebrated congress in America, for the defense of liberty, when in the utmost danger of being forever lost, and for the salvation of his country, and then at the earnest request of that grand council of patriots, without hesitation, left all the pleasures of his delightful seat in Virginia, and the affairs of his own estate, that, through all the fatigues and dangers of camp, without accepting any reward, he might deliver New England from the unjust and cruel arms of Great Britain, and defend the other colonies; and who, by the most signal smiles of Divine Providence on his military operations, drove the fleet and troops of the enemy with disgraceful precipitation from the town of Boston, which for eleven months had been shut, fortified and defended by a garrison of above 7,000 regulars; so that the inhabitants, who suffered a great variety of hardships and cruelties while under the power of their oppressors, now rejoice in their deliverance; the neighboring towns are also freed from the tumult of arms, and our university has the agreeable prospect of being restored to its ancient seat.

Know ye, therefore, that we, the president and fellows of Harvard College in Cambridge, (with the consent of the honored and reverend overseers of our academy) have constituted and created the aforesaid gentleman, George Washington, who merits the highest honor, doctor of laws, the law of nature and nations, and the civil law; and have given and granted him at the same time all rights, privileges and honors to the said degree pertaining.

In testimony whereof, we have affixed the common seal of our university to these letters, and subscribed them with our handwriting, this third day of April, in the year of our Lord one thousand seven hundred and seventy-six.

SAMUEL LANGDON, S. T. D. Preses.
NATHANIEL APPLETON, S. T. D.
JOHANNES WINTHROP, Mat. et. Phi. P.
ANDREAS ELLIOT, S. T. D. (Hol.) LL.D.

SAMUEL COOPER, S. T. D.
JOHANS WADSWORTH, Log. et. Eth. Pre.

7. THE PATRIOTS SUPPRESS LOYALIST OPINION

MARYLAND BANISHES A TORY

*[Resolutions passed by the Maryland Provincial Convention
against a merchant of Baltimore, August 7, 1775]*

Resolved that . . . James Christie, hath manifested a spirit and principle altogether inimical to the rights and liberties of America; That the said James Christie, by insinuating the necessity of introducing a military force into this province, has manifested an inveterate enmity to the liberty of this province in particular, and of British America in general.

Therefore, *resolved,* That the said James Christie is and ought to be considered as an enemy to America, and that no person trade, deal, or barter with him hereafter, unless for necessaries and provisions, or for the sale or purchase of any part of his real or personal estate, of which he may be at this time seized or possessed.

Resolved, That the said James Christie be expelled and banished this province forever, and that he depart the province before the first day of September next.

Resolved, That the said James Christie deposite in the hands of this convention, or into the hands of such person or persons as they shall appoint, the sum of five hundred pounds sterling, to be expended occasionally towards his proportion of all charges and expenses incurred or to be incurred for the defence of America, during the present contest with Great Britain; the overplus if any, after a reconciliation shall happily be effected, to be restored to the said James Christie.

Resolved, That no punishment be inflicted on the said James Christie, other than what is now directed by this convention.

Resolved, That the five hundred pounds sterling is to be paid in sterling, or other money at par.

Resolved, That the resolutions of the committee of Baltimore county are, by the determinations of this convention superseded, and that therefore the said James Christie may negotiate his bills of exchange; and that he may assign, or he, or any person for him, may collect the debts due to him, in the same manner as other persons may negotiate their bills of exchange, assign or collect their debts.

Signed by order of the convention,

G. DUVALL, Clerk.

A LOYALIST ENCOUNTERS DELAWARE JUSTICE

[Letter from Samuel M'Masters of Lewes, Delaware, to Dr. James Tilton of Dover, November 14, 1775]

SIR—This informs you, that an indictment was found by the grand jury of Sussex county, against a number of zealous friends to their country, for, as is said, insulting a certain J.C. The particulars are as follows: J.C., some time in the month of September, came to Lewes, and in an open, profane manner, cursed the honorable continental congress, and all those that would not curse it; calling upon the supreme Being in a most solemn manner to d—n the congress, and all that would not d—n it; that d—d set would ruin the country. For which expressions and such like, it was thought proper he should be had up before the committee of inspection, as guilty of treason against the liberties of America, and also the congress; for the congress acting suitable to the power delegated, that body ought to be esteemed as king, and therefore whatever is said against that body should be deemed treason. C. being had up before the committee, and the facts before mentioned sufficiently proved, one of the audience said "it sounded like a death warrant." C. in an insulting, swearing way, said, "put it in execution." However, upon mature consideration of the committee, some of which was no better than C. a sort of recantation was drawn up and signed by C. but by no means satisfactory to the people. Upon which, some concluded we should proceed in the new mode of making converts, by bestowing upon C. a coat of tar and feathers; but after some hesitation, and much persuasion, were prevented from using any violent measures, unless beating the drum a few rods, and two boys throwing an egg a piece unknown to the men—which, as soon as they were observed, was immediately stopped. No threatening or abusive language was made use of to intimidate or affright him. . . .

Rhode Island Imposes a Loyalty Oath

*[An oath extracted from the citizens of Rhode Island by General
Lee of the Continental Army, December 1775]*

I—here in the presence of Almighty God, as I hope for ease, honor and comfort in this world, and happiness in the world to come, most earnestly, devoutly and religiously swear; that I will neither directly nor indirectly assist the wicked instruments of ministerial tyranny and villainy, commonly called the king's troops and navy, by furnishing them with provisions and refreshments of any kind, unless authorized by the continental congress or legislature at present established in this particular colony of Rhode Island: I do also swear by the Tremendous and Almighty God, that I will neither directly or indirectly convey any intelligence, nor give any advice to the aforesaid enemies described; and that I pledge myself, if I should by any accident get knowledge of such treasons, to inform immediately the committee of safety: and as it is justly allowed that when the rights and sacred liberties of a nation or community are invaded, neutrality is not less base and criminal than open and avowed hostility: I do further swear and pledge myself, as I hope for eternal salvation, that I will whenever called upon by the voice of the continental congress, or by that of the legislature of this particular colony under their authority, to take arms and subject myself to military discipline in defence of the common rights and liberties of America. So help me God.

VI

TOWARD A DECLARATION OF INDEPENDENCE,

1775-1776

As CIVIL WAR spread in scope and intensity in the months following the Battle of Lexington, so too did the idea of American independence. A few colonials may have wanted to separate from the British Empire as early as 1763—perhaps a very few even earlier—but the bulk of the colonial population did not begin to think seriously of political independence until the fall of 1775. By that time it had become apparent that the British administration was not going to meet American demands. While Parliament continued to debate its colonial stand (p. 209), the situation in the colonies became less and less conducive to a peaceful settlement.

The turn of events in America deeply disturbed some Englishmen as it did many Americans (pp. 213, and 218), but their voices were lost in the avalanche of votes that again and again endorsed the administration's determination to punish the rebels. Here and there a British officer felt so sympathetic to the American position that he refused to serve against the colonists (p. 222). But the ministry of Lord North had plenty of other men ready and willing to suppress the colonists.

Of course, it was one thing to send an army to America and quite another to establish effective control over thirteen rebellious colonies. Massachusetts had been almost totally self-governing since 1774; other colonies now followed suit. During the spring of 1776 most features of royal authority vanished, to be replaced by governments of the people's own choice (pp. 224, 225, 226, and 227). This move coincided with the growing sentiment for independence, a sentiment that had spread rapidly since warfare began in April 1775 and that had gained strength from the actions of the British government. Especially galling was its act of December 21, 1775, which declared the colonies outside the protection of the Crown—interpreted by many colonists as a severing of the imperial tie. Beginning in January 1776 with Thomas Paine's clarion call for independence, a steady flow of pamphlets, broadsides, newspaper articles, and speeches advocated—implicitly or explicitly—a total separation of the American colonies from the British Empire (pp. 228, 229, and 235).

Steps toward independence came in rapid succession in the spring of 1776. In April, North Carolina authorized its delegates in Congress to vote for a declaration of independence. A month later Virginia instructed its delegates to take the initiative and move in Congress for independence (p. 236), a decision well received by the citizens of Williamsburg (p. 238). Other colonies quickly signified their own desire for independence (pp. 238 and 240). On June 7, Virginia's Richard Henry Lee proposed to Congress a resolution of independence; on June 11 a committee of five was appointed to draft a declaration of independence. Congress received Thomas Jefferson's version on the 28th, on July 2 it voted unanimously for independence, and by the 4th it had approved an amended draft of the Declaration of Independence. The thirteen colonies were now thirteen states.

1. LONDON TURNS A DEAF EAR TO PROTESTS

PARLIAMENT INTERROGATES GOVERNOR PENN

*[Report of the examination of Governor Penn of Pennsylvania
before the House of Lords, November 11, 1775]*

Saturday, November 11, 1775

HOUSE OF LORDS. The lords were yesterday assembled for the purposes of examining governor Penn, and of discussing a motion which the duke of Richmond proposed to ground on such information as that gentleman should afford the house. . . .

The duke of Richmond having finished his preliminary remarks, Mr. Penn was called to the bar, and interrogated nearly to the following purport:

Q. How long had he resided in America?

A. Four years. Two of those years in the capacity of governor of Pennsylvania.

Q. Was he acquainted with any of the members of the continental congress?

A. He was personally acquainted with all the members of that congress.

Q. In what estimation was the congress held?

A. In the highest veneration imaginable by all ranks and orders of men.

Q. Was an implicit obedience paid to the resolutions of that congress throughout all the provinces?

A. He believed this to be the case.

Q. How many men had been raised throughout the province of Pennsylvania?

A. Twenty thousand effective men had voluntarily enrolled themselves to enter into actual service if necessity required.

Q. Of what rank, quality and condition were these persons?

A. Men of the most respectable character in the province.

Q. Were not a considerable number of them entirely destitute of property?

A. It was presumed that, subtracted from so large a number as 20,000 there were some necessitous, but the major part were in flourishing situations.

Q. Besides those 20,000 who voluntarily enrolled themselves to act as exigencies might require, what other forces had the provincials of Pennsylvania raised?

A. Four thousand minute-men, whose duty was pointed out by their designation. They were to be ready for service at a minute's warning.

Q. Did the province of Pennsylvania grow corn sufficient for the supply of its inhabitants?

A. Much more than sufficient, there was a surplus for exportation if required.

Q. Were they capable of making gunpowder in Pennsylvania?

A. They perfectly well understood the art, and had effected it.

Q. Could salt-petre be made in the province?

A. It could; mills and other instruments for effecting such an undertaking had been erected with success.

Q. Could cannon be cast in Pennsylvania?

A. The art of casting cannon had been carried to great perfection; they were amply furnished with iron for that purpose.

Q. Could small arms be made to any degree of perfection?

A. To as great a degree of perfection as could be imagined. The workmanship employed in finishing the small arms was universally admired for its excellence.

Q. Were the Americans expert in ship-building?

A. More so than the Europeans.

Q. To what extent of tonnage did the largest of their shipping amount?

A. A ship of about three hundred tons was the largest they were known to build.

Q. Circumstanced as things at present were, did the witness think, that the language of the congress expressed the sense of the people in America in general?

A. As far as the question applied to Pennsylvania, he was sure this was the case; for the other provinces, he replied in the affirmative from information only.

Q. Did he suppose that the congress contained delegates fairly nominated by the choice of the people?

A. He had no doubt but that the congress did contain delegates chosen under this description.

Q. By what mode were the delegates in congress appointed?

A. By the votes of assemblies in some places, by ballot in others.

Q. In what light had the petition, which the witness had presented to the king, been considered by the Americans?

A. The petition had been considered as an olive branch, and the witness had been complimented by his friends, as the messenger of peace.

Q. On the supposition that the prayer of this petition should be rejected, what did the witness imagine would be the consequence?

A. That the Americans, who placed much reliance on the petition, would be driven to desperation by its non-success.

Q. Did the witness imagine, that sooner than yield to what were supposed to be unjust claims of Great Britain, the Americans would take the desperate resolution of calling in the aid of foreign assistance?

A. The witness was apprehensive that this would be the case.

Q. What did the witness recollect of the stamp act?

A. That it caused great uneasiness throughout America.

Q. What did the witness recollect, concerning repeal of that act?

A. The anniversary of that memorable day is kept throughout America, by every testimony of public rejoicing, such as bonfires, illuminations, and other exhibitions of gladness.

Q. Would not the neglect with which the last petition was treated induce the Americans to resign all hopes of pacific negotiations?

A. In the opinion of the witness it would.

Q. When the witness presented the petition to the secretary of state, was he asked any questions relative to the state of America?

A. Not a single question.

CROSS EXAMINED BY THE LORDS DENBIGH AND SANDWICH

[Q.] As the witness had acted in the capacity of governor, was he well acquainted with the charter of Pennsylvania?

A. He had read the charter, and was well acquainted with its contents.

Q. Did he know that there was a clause which specifically subjected the colony to taxation by the British legislature?

A. He was well apprised that there was such a clause.

Q. Were the people of Pennsylvania content with their charter?

A. Perfectly content.

Q. Then did they not acquiesce in the right of the British parliament to enforce taxation?

A. They acquiesced in a declaration of the right so long as they experienced no inconvenience from the declaration.

QUERIES FROM LORD SANDWICH

Q. Had the witness ever heard of an act entitled, "The declaratory act?"

A. He had heard of such an act.

Q. Did he ever peruse, and was he sufficiently acquainted with the contents of that act?

A. He never had perused it. It never had been much discussed whilst he resided in America.

Q. Did the witness apprehend that the congress acquiesced in an act which maintained the authority of the British parliament in all cases whatsoever?

Objected to, and the witness was desired to withdraw; but being called in again, the question was put, and he replied:

[A.] That, except in the case of taxation, he apprehended the Americans would have no objection to acknowledge the sovereignty of Great Britain.

Q. Had the witness any knowledge of certain resolutions passed by the county of Suffolk?

A. He had not attended to them.

Q. Had the witness any knowledge of an answer given by the continental congress, to what had been commonly called lord North's conciliatory motion?

A. The witness knew nothing of the proceedings of the congress, they were generally transacted under the seal of secrecy.

Q. Was the witness personally acquainted with Mr. Harrison, a member of the congress?

A. The witness knew him well.

Q. What character did he bear?

A. A very respectable one.

Q. Had the witness ever heard of any persons who had suffered persecutions, for declaring sentiments favorable to the supremacy of the British parliament?

A. He had heard of such oppressions in other provinces, but never met with them during his residence in Pennsylvania.

Q. In the opinion of the witness, were the Americans now free?

A. They imagined themselves to be so.

Q. In case a formidable force should be sent to America, in support of government, did the witness imagine there were many who would openly profess submission to the authority of parliament?

A. The witness apprehended the few who would join on such occasion would be too trivial a number to be of any consequence.

Mr. Penn was then ordered to withdraw, and the duke of Richmond, after descanting with singular propriety on the necessity of immediate conciliation, proposed the last petition from the continental congress to the king, as a basis for a plan of accommodation. His grace of Richmond moved, "That the preceding paper furnished grounds of conciliation of the unhappy differences at present subsisting between Great Britain and America, and that some mode should be immediately adopted, for the effectuating so desirable a purpose."

This produced a debate supported on both sides with infinite ingenuity. The numbers were:

For the motion 27—Proxies 6——33

Against the motion 50—Proxies 36——86

Majority against the motion 52 [sic]

A CLERGYMAN GIVES HIS VIEWS TO LORD DARTMOUTH

[Letter from a Maryland minister to Lord Dartmouth, Britain's Secretary of State for American Affairs, December 20, 1775]

MARYLAND, December 20, 1775

MY LORD—If constitutional allegiance to my king, a warm attachment to my country, and the most sanguine emotions for peace and permanent union between the parent state and her colonies, will sufficiently expiate for epistolary freedom, permit a minister of the king of kings to address a minister of the king of Great Britain, France, Ireland, and North America. . . .

Since the battle of Lexington, I have been twice in eight of the thirteen united colonies, namely, Massachusetts-Bay, Rhode Island, Connecticut, New-York, New-Jersey, Pennsylvania, New-Castle, etc, and Maryland, all which, except New-York, are almost unanimous in the voice of liberty. Indeed none (save a few officers under the crown) are willing to be bound by the British parliament, in all cases whatsoever. The Americans declare a master can lay no greater burden on a slave than to bind him in all cases whatsoever.—These things the united colonies have imbibed, and before this can reach your lordship, Canada will, in all human probability, be added to the thirteen, for St. John's and Montreal have, upon capitulation, surrendered, and the rest of the province in every other respect, bids fair for a general surrender, or subjection to the American side. In New-York city and province, although there are, I verily believe, more friends to government (as they call themselves) than all the rest of the colonies together can produce, yet in the city and province there is, on the other side of the question, a majority large enough to subdue them at any time: for instance, a few weeks ago some of these friends appeared in the province in opposition to the American voice; whereon a small party went out immediately, who subdued and disarmed them. These friends, my lord are not worthy of the appellation; they are only sycophants; they flatter with their lips and pens, and deceive (I fear) your lordship and others in administration, from packet to packet. They have repeatedly insinuated, that the New England governments have nothing else in view but independence. It is totally repugnant to truth. Before the sword was drawn, there could not possibly be greater loyalists. In the year 1769, I arrived first in America, and they daily manifested what loving subjects they were: and the dissenting clergy also, in every opportunity, were particularly anxious to invoke the Great Jehovah in behalf of their dread sovereign, of whom they spake in terms the most pathetic; also for all his governors and officers, as well as for others, that peace and happiness, truth and justice, religion and piety, might still be and flourish under his sceptre. Add to this, I justly may, the several conversations I have had with, and the private prayers I have heard by those gentlemen concerning his majesty, his crown and dignity; with all which every loyalist could but be perfectly well pleased. To these facts, my lord, I have not only been an eye witness in one colony, but in many, nay even in Massachusetts-Bay, and her capital.

Now, my lord, for Christ's sake, attend faithfully.

About two months ago I viewed the camps, Roxbury and Cambridge.

The lines of both are impregnable; with forts (many of which are bomb proof) and redoubts, supposing them to be all in a direction, are about 20 miles; the breastworks of a proper height, and in many places 17 feet in thickness, the trenches wide and deep in proportion, before which lay forked impediments, and many of the forts, in every respect, are perfectly ready for battle; the whole, in a word, an admiration to every spectator; for verily their fortifications appear to be the works of seven years, instead of about as many months. At these camps are about 20,000 men, well disciplined. The generals and other officers, in all their military undertakings, solid, discreet, and courageous, the men daily raving for action, and seemingly void of fear. There are many floating batteries, and also batteaus in abundance; besides this strength, 10,000 militia are ordered in that government to appear on the first summons. Provisions and money there are very plenty, and the soldiers faithfully paid. The army in great order, and very healthy, and about six weeks ago lodged in comfortable barracks.—Chaplains constantly attend the camps, morning and night. Prayers are often offered up for peace and reconciliation, and the soldiers very attentive. The roads, at the time I viewed the camps, were almost lined with spectators, and thousands with me can declare the above, respecting the camps, to be a just description; but, my lord, I have more facts to mention.

Continental and provincial currencies, to facilitate this great undertaking, are emitted, which circulate freely, and are daily exchanged for silver and gold. Their harbors, by spring, will swarm with privateers; an admiral is appointed, a court established, and on the 3d instant the continental flag, on board the Black Prince, opposite Philadelphia, was hoisted. Many of the captains of those vessels, in the last war, proved their intrepidity to the world by their prizes, and some of them have already taken many valuable prizes which government had ordered to Boston, and thereby must have much distressed the troop; all which the prints will particularize.

The appointment of the continental and provincial congresses and committees, your lordship, without doubt, before now, must be fully acquainted with. These sets of gentlemen, by virtue of the great privileges with which the colonies have entrusted them, claim now the following prerogatives over the united colonies: The continental congress is over all, under the king; the provincials over the committees, and the committees over the counties. The congresses and committees have so raised and regulated the militia and minutemen, whom they have raised almost in every county, that they make, in every city and town, the most warlike appearance. Salt-petre is made in abundance, and powder-mills constantly employed in many provinces; and many believe that there is now in the possession of the Americans, powder enough for three years. This to me is very obvious. Soon after General Gage collected the troops from the several provinces into one body at Boston, the congresses ordered all the shop-keepers not to sell their powder to fowlers and hunters, but to keep the same for the use of the colonies, which in general was faithfully observed. Before this, a person might get a large quantity of powder almost at every large store, or merchant's shop, in every city, town, and county on the continent. Now all this collected together, and what the mills have made, together with the great quantities taken at St. John's, Montreal, other forts, and on the seas, must make an immense quantity: add to this, the constant employment of the mills, and a great number of privateers faithfully looking out for yours. And, my lord, how is it possible for all store ships to escape a fleet so large, which, at this time, I firmly believe, is composed of 50 sail, and by next spring I shall not marvel if their fleet be doubled.

Iron guns of the best quality have been made in America, and as they have plenty of iron and lead mines, they can make what quantity of cannon, shot, and bullets they please; but administration have lately supplied them with a very valuable assortment of such stores. Rifles, infinitely better than those imported. are daily made in many places in Pennsylvania, and all the gunsmiths everywhere constantly employed. In this country, my lord, the boys, as soon as they can discharge a gun, frequently exercise themselves therewith, some a fowling, and others a hunting. The great quantities of game, the many kinds and the great privileges of killing, making the Americans the best marksmen in the world, and thousands support their families principally by the same, particularly riflemen on the frontiers, whose objects are deer and turkeys. In marching through woods, one thousand of these riflemen would cut to pieces ten thousand of your best troops. I don't, my lord, speak at random, or write partially; I have travelled too much among these men to be insensible of their abilities.—Oh, my lord! if your lordship knew but one half what I know of America your lordship would not persist, but be instantly for peace, or resign. . . . My lord, administration have not one friend they can call theirs, in every respect, that is a resident among the Americans; they have several, it is true, who, for sordid gain, act under the rose, but woe to them if they should be discovered.—Many examples have been already made, and this may be relied on, that in a few months (as ways and means are now under consideration) administration will in every respect in America be friendless. The destroying of Falmouth, and Lord Dunmore's proclamation, proclaiming a jubilee to the slaves and convicts in Virginia,

"The Horse America, Throwing his Master," a British cartoon of about 1777 portraying George III being tossed from his saddle by his horse — symbolic of the rebellious American colonies. A French soldier approaches on the right, ready to take advantage of England's distress.

XVII

An early engraving of General Washington's successful retreat
from Long Island to Manhattan on the night of August 29-30, 1776.

Modern representations of Revolutionary uniforms, from watercolors by
Charles M. Lefferts. Shown here are: (1) Officer of Grenadier Company, (2)
Private, Pennsylvania State Regiment, and (3) British Tenth Regiment of Foot.

In PROVINCIAL CONGRESS for the Colony of *New-York*, the _Twentieth_ Day of *Feby* —— 1776.

To *Abraham Haasbrook* —————— *Esquire* Greeting:

BY virtue of the authority repofed in us, We do hereby nominate, authorize, conftitute and appoint you *the said Abraham Haasbrook* ———— *Colonel* ———————————— of the *Northern Regiment* *of Militia of foot in Ulster County.* ———————————— hereby requiring you, before you enter into the exercife of your faid office, to make in writing, and fubfcribe in prefence of the Chairman of the Committee of the City, Town, Diftrict, or Precinct wherein you refide, the Declaration appointed and directed by the eleventh Section of the feventh Refolve contained in the rules and orders for regulating the Militia of the Colony of New-York, recommended by this Congrefs on the 22d day of Auguft, 1775, and authorizing you fully to execute all the powers belonging to your faid office, by virtue of the faid rules and orders, and the faid declaration : And we do hereby require all perfons under your command, to pay due obedience to you, according to the faid rules and orders, and fuch further rules and orders as fhall be made and recommended for the Militia of this Colony, by the prefent, or any future Continental Congrefs, or Provincial Congrefs of this Colony.

Atteft.   By Order,   *Nath. Woodhull Prosidt*

Robt Benson Secy

A colonel's commission in the New York militia.

Baron von Steuben, the Prussian officer
who volunteered his services to the
American army in 1777 and soon became
its leading disciplinarian, drillmaster,
and military organizer.

An American cartoon mocking the British Army's
use of Indian allies. The two Indians in the fore-
ground are selling the scalps of American soldiers
to the British officer. In the background, Indians
and redcoats dance around a campfire.

Landing of the British troops under General Cornwallis along the palisades in New Jersey, November 20, 1776. Drawing attributed to Lord Rawdon, a member of Cornwallis's staff, but more probably made by Captain Thomas Davies of the Royal Regiment of Artillery.

A Lefferts watercolor of
Sir William Howe,
Commander-in-Chief of British Forces
in America, 1775-1778.

Black Watch Highlanders break before the American attack at the Battle of Harlem Heights, September 16, 1776.

A Lefferts watercolor of the officers of the Massachusetts Regiment of Artillery.

Brigadier General Anthony Wayne, Pennsylvania patriot and military hero, most noted for his victory at Stony Point, New York, in 1779.

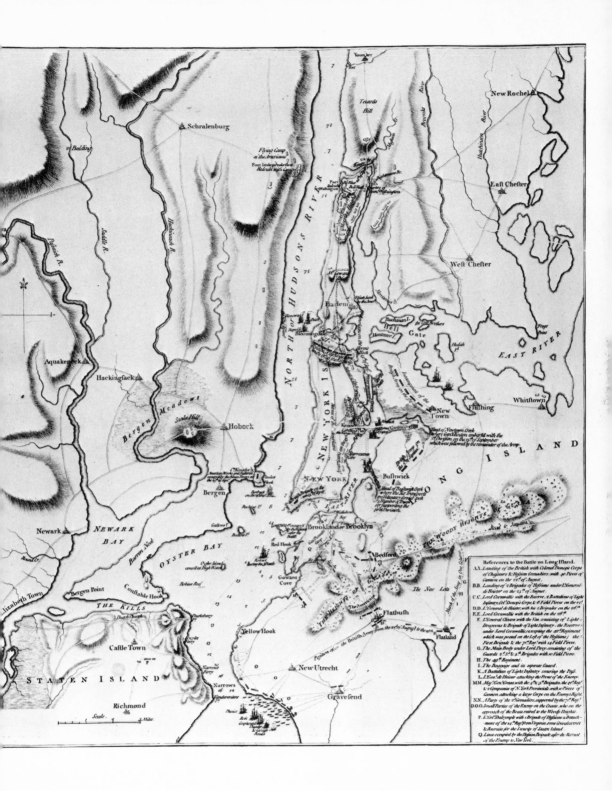

A British map of October 1776 showing
the battles on Long Island and Manhattan
during the previous August and September.

British troops triumphantly parade through the streets of New York in mid-September 1776. From a contemporary but imaginary drawing by François Xavier Habermann published in Augsburg, Germany, later the same year.

LEFT: Major General John Burgoyne, whose surrender to American forces at Saratoga, New York, on October 17, 1777, marked the turning point in the war.

RIGHT: A French version of the surrender of General Burgoyne to the American forces under General Horatio Gates.

A British cartoon parodies the surrender of General Burgoyne.

American vessels attack two British warships in the Hudson River, August 16, 1776. This engraving, published in 1778, was one of the few naval prints of the Revolutionary period and the first to show American ships in action.

America's favorite Frenchman:
Marie Joseph Paul Yves Roch Gilbert du Motier, Marquis de Lafayette.

Benjamin Franklin, Pennsylvania's universal man: scientist, inventor, publisher, diplomat, and statesman.

John Paul Jones, America's greatest naval hero in the War for Independence.

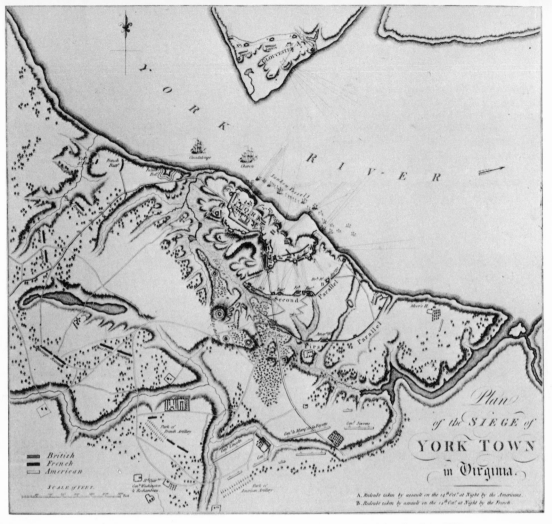

A British map of 1787 showing the siege of Yorktown, Virginia, October 1781.

Charles Wentworth, Marquis of Rocking-ham, who as Prime Minister in 1776 pre-sided over the repeal of the Stamp Act. En-graving from a portrait by Sir Joshua Reynolds.

William Livingston, New York patriot, lawyer, statesman, and first governor of the state of New Jersey, 1776-1790.

An American political cartoon shows a two-faced effigy of Benedict Arnold being paraded through Philadelphia, September 30, 1780. A figure of the Devil stands behind Arnold, according to the caption that appeared with the original picture, "shaking a purse of money at the general's left ear, and in his right hand a pitchfork, ready to drive him into hell as the reward due for [his] many crimes."

David Ramsay, M.D., South Carolina patriot, legislator, and historian. From a portrait by Charles Wilson Peale.

Three Virginia leaders: Patrick Henry, General Washington, and Edmund Pendleton shown riding to the First Continental Congress in Philadelphia.

Benjamin Rush, Pennsylvania physician, patriot spokesman, and social reformer. Engraving by R. W. Dodson
from a painting by Thomas Sully.

John Jay, New York patriot leader, statesman, and jurist.

George Mason, Virginia planter, statesman, and author of many of his state's
revolutionary documents, including the
Declaration of Rights in 1776.

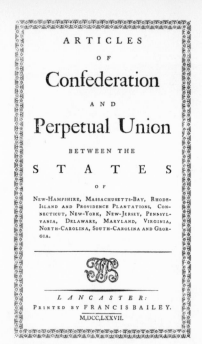

ARTICLES

OF

Confederation

AND

Perpetual Union

BETWEEN THE

S T A T E S

OF

NEW-HAMPSHIRE, MASSACHUSETTS-BAY, RHODE-
ISLAND AND PROVIDENCE PLANTATIONS, CON-
NECTICUT, NEW-YORK, NEW-JERSEY, PENNSYL-
VANIA, DELAWARE, MARYLAND, VIRGINIA,
NORTH-CAROLINA, SOUTH-CAROLINA AND GEOR-
GIA.

LANCASTER:
PRINTED BY FRANCIS BAILEY.
M,DCC,LXXVII.

Title page of the Articles of Confederation, drafted in 1777, and observed
as our federal constitution, 1781-1788.

The second earliest known map of the United States of America. Published in London in early February, 1783, less than a month after the signing of the Treaty of Paris ended the War for Independence.

Philadelphia, the nation's seat of government throughout most of the Revolutionary period. Shown here is the intersection of Second and High streets.

The poet of the Revolution, Joel Barlow of Connecticut. Engraving by A. B. Durand from a painting by Robert Fulton.

William Henry Drayton, South Carolina patriot leader and jurist.

FEDERAL HALL

The Seat of Congress

Printed & Sold by A. Doolittle New-Haven 1790

The inauguration of President Washington, at Federal Hall, New York, on April 30, 1789, as depicted in the only known contemporary representation of the event. Drawn by Pierre Lacour, a French visitor to the United States, and engraved and published by Amos Doolittle of Connecticut.

provided they repair to the royal standard in due time, have exasperated the Americans beyond description, and made the breach infinitely wider.— A few days ago his lordship's party was repulsed with great loss. His lordship, my lord, can do nothing but cause the men and treasure now under his command to be sacrificed and expended in vain; for he is surrounded by hundreds of the best riflemen, who have driven his troops out of their intrenchments, etc. Most, if not all, by this time, of his majesty's governors are afloat and rendered incapable of fulfilling your lordship's commands. . . .

The Americans may be led with a hair; but they have too much English blood in them, are too well disciplined, and too numerous to be driven, even by an hundred thousand of the best forces government can raise. Where government can produce one thousand on the continent, America, with as much ease and expense, can produce ten thousand in opposition: for men, women and children are against the proceedings of administration throughout the united colonies to a wonderful majority. The women, both old and young, being greatly irritated at the inflexibility of administration, are not only willing their sons and brothers should turn out in the field, but also declare that they will give them up and themselves likewise as a sacrifice before they will bow to Pharaoh's task-masters; this makes the raising of troops on the continent very easy. Let a person go into any province, city, town, or county, and ask the females, "Are you willing your sons or brothers should go for soldiers and defend their liberties?" they would severally answer, "Yes, with all my soul, and if they won't go I won't own them as my sons, or brothers; for I'll help myself if there should be any need of mine: if I can't stand in the ranks, I can help forward with powder, balls, and provisions.". . . This, my lord, is the language of the American women; your lordship knows it is generally the reverse with the English, the mothers' and sisters' lives are bound up in the boys; but I am afraid I shall trespass on your lordship's patience: Therefore,

In the great name, and for the sake of the ever blessed Trinity, I now beseech your lordship to weigh thoroughly, and with patience, impartiality, and love, this narrative of facts; and may that ever blessed adorable person, Jesus Christ, the wonderful counsellor and prince of peace, give your lordship a right judgment and understanding in all things, and counsel and influence administration to act wisely, and repeal the acts in dispute, and so make peace. I am, my lord, your lordship's ready and willing servant, for Christ's sake,

B.P.

CHATHAM PLEADS FOR REMOVAL OF THE TROOPS

[Speech by William Pitt, Earl of Chatham, to the House of Lords,
December 20, 1775]

On a motion for an address to his majesty to give immediate orders for removing his troops from Boston, forthwith, in order to quiet the minds and take
away the apprehensions of his good subjects in America.

MY LORDS—. . . . The measures of last year . . . which have produced the present alarming state of America, were founded upon misrepresentation—they were violent, precipitate and vindictive. The nation was told,
that it was only a faction in Boston, which opposed all lawful government;
that an unwarrantable injury had been done to private property, for which
the justice of parliament was called upon, to order reparation;—that the
least appearance of firmness would awe the Americans into submission. . . .

But now, my lords, we find, that instead of suppressing the opposition
of the faction at Boston, these measures have spread it over the whole continent. They have united that whole people, by the most indissoluble of all
bands—intolerable wrongs. The just retribution is an indiscriminate, un-
merciful proscription of the innocent with the guilty, unheard and untried.
The bloodless victory, is an impotent general, with his dishonored army,
trusting solely to the pick-axe and the spade, for security against the just indignation of an injured and insulted people.

My lords, I am happy that a relaxation of my infirmities permits me to
seize this earliest opportunity of offering my poor advice to save this unhappy
country, at this moment tottering to its ruin. But as I have not the honor of
access to his majesty, I will endeavor to transmit to him, through the constitutional channel of this house my ideas on American business, to rescue him
from the misadvice of his present ministers. . . . When I state the importance of the colonies to this country, and the magnitude of danger hanging
over this country from the present plan of mis-administration practised
against them, I desire not to be understood to argue for a reciprocity of indulgence between England and America: I contend not for indulgence, but
justice, to America; and I shall ever contend that the Americans owe obedience to us, in a limited degree; they owe obedience to our ordinances of trade
and navigation; but let the line be skilfully drawn between the objects of those
ordinances, and their private, internal property: Let the sacredness of their
property remain inviolate; let it be taxable only by their own consent, given
in their provincial assemblies, else it will cease to be property: As to the meta-

physical refinements attempting to show that the Americans are equally free from obedience to commercial restraints, as from taxation for revenue, as being unrepresented here, I pronounce them futile, frivolous and groundless.— Property is, in its nature, single as an atom. It is indivisible, can belong to one only, and cannot be touched but by his own consent. The law that attempts to alter this disposal of it annihilates it.

When I urge this measure for recalling the troops from Boston, I urge it on this pressing principle—that it is necessarily preparatory to the restoration of your prosperity. It will then appear that you are disposed to treat amicably and equitably, and to consider, revise and repeal, if it should be found necessary, as I affirm it will, those violent acts and declarations which have disseminated confusion throughout your empire. Resistance to your acts, was as necessary as it was just; and your vain declarations of the omnipotence of parliament, and your imperious doctrines of the necessity of submission, will be found equally impotent to convince or enslave your fellow subjects in America, who feel that tyranny, whether ambitioned by an individual part of the legislature, or by the bodies which compose it, is equally intolerable to British principles.

As to the means of enforcing this thraldom, they are found to be as ridiculous and weak in practice, as they were unjust in principle: Indeed I cannot but feel, with the most anxious sensibility, for the situation of general Gage and the troops under his command; thinking him, as I do, a man of humanity and understanding, and entertaining, as I ever shall, the highest respect, the warmest love, for the British troops. Their situation is truly unworthy, pent up, pining in inglorious inactivity. They are an army of impotence. You may call them an army of safety and of guard; but, they are in truth an army of impotence and contempt—and to render the folly equal to the disgrace, they are an army of irritation. I do not mean to censure the inactivity of the troops. It is prudent and necessary inaction. But it is a miserable condition, where disgrace is prudence; and where it is necessary to be contemptible. This tameness, however disgraceful, ought not to be blamed, as I am surprised to hear is done by these ministers. The first drop of blood, shed in a civil and unnatural war, would be an immedicabile vulnus. It would entail hatred and contention between the two people, from generation to generation. Woe be to him who sheds the first the unexpiable drop of blood in an impious war, with a people contending in the great cause of public liberty. I will tell you plainly, my lords, no son of mine nor any one over whom I have influence, shall ever draw his sword upon his fellow subjects.

I therefore urge and conjure your lordships immediately to adopt this conciliatory measure. I will pledge myself for its immediately producing conciliatory effects, from its being well timed: But if you delay, till your vain hope of triumphantly dictating the terms shall be accomplished—you delay forever. And, even admitting that this hope, which in truth is desperate, should be accomplished, what will you gain by a victorious imposition of amity? You will be untrusted and unthanked. Adopt then the grace, while you have the opportunity of reconcilement, or at least prepare the way; allay the ferment prevailing in America, by removing the obnoxious hostile corps. . . .

His majesty is advised that the union of America cannot last.—Ministers have more eyes than I, and should have more ears, but from all the information I have been able to procure, I can pronounce it a union solid, permanent and effectual. Ministers may satisfy themselves and delude the public with the reports of what they call commercial bodies in America. They are not commercial. They are your packers and factors; they live upon nothing, for I call commission nothing; I mean the ministerial authority for their American intelligence. The runners of government, who are paid for their intelligence. But these are not the men, nor this the influence to be considered in America, when we estimate the firmness of their union. Even to extend the question, and to take in the really mercantile circle, will be totally inadequate to the consideration. Trade indeed increases the wealth and glory of a country; but its real strength and stamina are to be looked for among the cultivators of the land. In their simplicity of life is founded the simplicity of virtue, the integrity and courage of freedom. Those true genuine sons of the earth are invincible: and they surround and hem in the mercantile bodies; even if those bodies, which supposition I totally disclaim, could be supposed disaffected to the cause of liberty. Of this general spirit existing in the American nation, for so I wish to distinguish the real and genuine Americans from the pseudo traders I have described; of this spirit of independence, animating the nation of America, I have the most authentic information. It is not new among them; it is, and ever has been their established principle, their confirmed persuasion; it is their nature and their doctrine. I remember some years ago when the repeal of the stamp act was in agitation, conversing in a friendly confidence with a person of undoubted respect and authenticity on this subject; and he assured me with a certainty which his judgment and opportunity gave him, that these were the prevalent and steady principles of America: That you might destroy their towns, and cut them off from the superfluities, perhaps the conveniencies of life, but that they were prepared to despise your power, and would not lament their loss whilst they had, what, my lords?— Their woods and liberty. The name of my authority, if I am called upon, will authenticate the opinion irrefragably.

If illegal violences have been, as it is said committed in America, prepare the way, open a door of possibility, for acknowledgment and satisfaction. But proceed not to such coercion, such proscription. Cease your indiscriminate inflictions, amerce not thirty thousands, oppress not three millions, for the faults of forty or fifty. Such severity of injustice must forever render incurable the wounds you have given your colonies; you irritate them to unappeasable rancor. What though you march from town to town, and from province to province?—Though you should be able to force a temporary and local submission, which I only suppose, not admit, how shall you be able to secure the obedience of the country you leave behind you in your progress? To grasp the dominion of 1,800 miles of continent, populous in valor, liberty and resistance? This resistance to your arbitrary system of taxation might have been foreseen; it was obvious from the nature of things and of mankind; and above all, from the whiggish spirit flourishing in that country. The spirit which now resists your taxation in America is the same which formerly opposed, and with success opposed, loans, benevolences, and ship money in England—the same spirit which called all England on its legs, and by the bill of rights vindicated the English constitution—the same spirit which established the great fundamental and essential maxim of your liberties, that no subject shall be taxed, but by his own consent. . . .

This glorious spirit of whiggism animates three millions in America, who prefer poverty with liberty, to golden chains and sordid affluence; and who will die in defence of their rights, as men—as freemen. What shall oppose this spirit? aided by the congenial flame glowing in the breast of every whig in England, to the amount, I hope, of at least double the American numbers! Ireland they have to a man. In that country, joined as it is with the cause of the colonies, and placed at their head, the distinction I contend for, is and must be observed.

My lords—This country superintends and controls their trade and navigation; but they tax themselves. And this distinction between external and internal control, is sacred and insurmountable; it is involved in the abstract nature of things. Property is private, individual, absolute. Trade is an extended and complicated consideration; it reaches as far as ships can sail or winds can blow. It is a great and various machine—To regulate the numberless movements of its several parts, and combine them into effect for the good of the whole, requires the superintending wisdom and energy of the supreme power in the empire. But this supreme power has no effect towards internal taxation—for it does not exist in that relation. There is no such thing, no such idea in this constitution, as a supreme power operating upon property.

Let this distinction then remain forever ascertained. Taxation is theirs, commercial regulation is ours. As an American, I would recognize to England her supreme right of regulating commerce and navigation. As an Englishman, by birth and principle, I recognize to the Americans their supreme, unalienable right to their property; a right which they are justified in the defence of, to the extremity. . . .

When your lordships look at the papers transmitted us from America, when you consider their decency, firmness and wisdom, you cannot but respect their cause, and wish to make it your own—for myself I must declare and avow that, in all my reading and observation, and it has been my favorite study—I have read Thucydides, and have studied and admired the master statesmen of the world—that for solidity and reasoning, force of sagacity, and wisdom of conclusion, under such a complication of different circumstances, no nation or body of men can stand in preference to the general congress at Philadelphia.—I trust it is obvious to your lordships, that all attempts to impose servitude on such men, to establish despotism over such a mighty continental nation—must be vain—must be futile.—We shall be forced ultimately to retract, whilst we can, not when we must. I say we must necessarily undo these violent and oppressive acts:—they must be repealed—you will repeal them: I pledge myself for it you will in the end repeal them. I stake my reputation on it: I will consent to be taken for an idiot if they are not finally repealed. Avoid then this humiliating, disgraceful necessity.—With a dignity becoming your exalted situation, make the first advances to concord, to peace and happiness, for that is your true dignity to act with prudence and with justice. . . .

To conclude, my lords, if the ministers thus persevere in misadvising and misleading the king, I will not say that they can alienate his subjects from his crown, but I will affirm that they will make the crown not worth his wearing. I shall not say that the king is betrayed, but I will pronounce that the kingdom is undone.

LORD EFFINGHAM RESIGNS HIS COMMISSION

[Letter to Lord Barrington, Secretary at War, conveying Lord Effingham's resignation from military service, April 12, 1775]

MY LORD.—I beg the favor of your lordship to lay before his majesty the peculiar embarrassment of my present situation.

Your lordship is no stranger to the conduct which I have observed in the unhappy disputes with our American colonies.

The king is too just and too generous not to believe, that the votes I have given in parliament have been given according to the dictates of my conscience. Whether I have erred or not, the course of future events must determine. In the mean time, if I were capable of such duplicity, as to be any way concerned in enforcing those measures of which I have so publicly and solemnly expressed my disapprobation, I should ill deserve what I am most ambitious of obtaining, the esteem and favorable opinion of my sovereign.

My request therefore to your lordship is this, that after having laid those circumstances before the king, you will assure his majesty, that he has not a subject who is more ready than I am with the utmost cheerfulness to sacrifice his life and fortune in support of the safety, honor, and dignity of his majesty's crown and person. But the very same principles which have inspired me with these unalterable sentiments of duty and affection to his majesty, will not suffer me to be instrumental in depriving any part of his people of those liberties which form the best security for their fidelity and obedience to his government. As I cannot, without reproach from my own conscience, consent to bear arms against my fellow subjects in America, in what, to my weak discernment, is not a clear cause; and as it seems now to be finally resolved, that the 22d regiment is to go upon American service, I desire your lordship to lay me in the most dutiful manner at his majesty's feet, and humbly beg that I may be permitted to retire.

Your lordship will also be so obliging to entreat, that as I wave what the custom of the service would entitle me to the right of selling what I bought, I may be allowed to retain my rank in the army, that whenever the envy or ambition of foreign powers should require it, I may be enabled to serve his majesty and my country in that way, in which alone I can expect to serve them with any degree of effect.

Your lordship will easily conceive the regret and mortification I feel at being necessitated to quit the military profession, which has been that of my ancestors for many generations, to which I have been bred almost from my infancy, to which I have devoted the study of my life; and to perfect myself in which, I have sought instruction and service in whatever part of the world they were to be found.

I have delayed this to the last moment, lest any wrong construction should be given to a conduct which is influenced only by the purest motives. I complain of nothing; I love my profession, and should think it highly blameable to quit any course of life, in which I might be useful to the public, so long as my constitutional principles, and my notions and honor, permitted me to continue in it.

I have the honor to be, with great respect, your lordship's most obedient, and most humble servant,

EFFINGHAM.

2. THE COLONIES OUST THEIR ROYAL GOVERNORS

PROCLAMATION OF THE GENERAL COURT OF MASSACHUSETTS

[Proclamation issued by the General Court, January 23, 1776, and ordered by the Council to be read in every court, town meeting, and pulpit]

It is a maxim that in every government, there must exist, somewhere, a supreme, sovereign, absolute, and uncontrolable power; but this power resides always in the body of the people; and it never was, or can be delegated to one man, or a few; the great Creator has never given to men a right to vest others with authority over them, unlimited either in duration or degree.

When kings, ministers, governors, or legislators, therefore, instead of exercising the powers entrusted with them, according to the principles, forms and proportions stated by the constitution, and established by the original compact, prostitute those powers to the purposes of oppression—to subvert, instead of supporting a free constitution;—to destroy, instead of preserving the lives, liberties and properties of the people;—they are no longer to be deemed magistrates vested with a sacred character, but become public enemies, and ought to be resisted. . . . As our enemies have proceeded to such barbarous extremities, commencing hostilities upon the good people of this colony, and with unprecedented malice exerting their power to spread the calamities of fire, sword and famine through the land, and no reasonable prospect remains of a speedy reconciliation with Great Britain, the congress have resolved:

"That no obedience being due to the act of parliament for altering the charter of the colony of Massachusetts-Bay, nor to a governor or lieutenant-governor, who will not observe the directions of, but endeavor to subvert that charter, the governor and lieutenant-governor of that colony are to be considered as absent, and their offices vacant. And as there is no council there, and inconveniences arising from the suspension of the powers of government are intolerable, especially at a time when general Gage hath actually levied war, and is carrying on hostilities against his majesty's peaceable and loyal subjects of that colony: that, in order to conform as near as may be to the spirit and substance of the charter, it be recommended to the provincial convention to write letters to the inhabitants of the several places which are entitled to representation in assembly, requesting them to choose such representatives; and that the assembly, when chosen, do elect counsellors; and that such assembly and council exercise the powers of government, until a governor of his majesty's appointment will consent to govern the colony according to its charter."

In pursuance of which advice, the good people of this colony have chosen a full and free representation of themselves, who, being convened in assembly, have elected a council; who, as the executive branch of government, have constituted necessary officers through the colony. The present generation, therefore, may be congratulated on the acquisition of a form of government more immediately, in all its branches, under the influence and control of the people; and therefore more free and happy than was enjoyed by their ancestors. But as a government so popular can be supported only by universal knowledge and virtue in the body of the people, it is the duty of all ranks to promote the means of education, for the rising generation, as well as true religion, purity of manners, and integrity of life, among all orders and degrees. . . .

That piety and virtue, which alone can secure the freedom of any people, may be encouraged, and vice and immorality suppressed, the great and general court have thought fit to issue this proclamation, commanding and enjoining it upon the good people of this colony, that they lead sober, religious and peaceable lives, avoiding all blasphemies, contempt of the holy scriptures, and of the lord's day, and all other crimes and misdemeanors, all debauchery, profaneness, corruption, venality, all riotous and tumultuous proceedings, and all immoralities whatsoever; and that they decently and reverently attend the public worship of God, at all times acknowledging with gratitude his merciful interposition in their behalf, devoutly confiding in him, as the God of armies, by whose favor and protection alone they may hope for success, in their present conflict. . . .

SOUTH CAROLINA INSTALLS A PATRIOT GOVERNOR

[*Address of the South Carolina Assembly to John Rutledge,
April 3, 1776*]

To His Excellency John Rutledge, Esq. president and commander in chief in and over the colony of South Carolina.

The address of the legislative council and general assembly.

MAY IT PLEASE YOUR EXCELLENCY—
    We, the legislative council and general assembly of South Carolina, convened under the authority of the equitable constitution of government established by a free people in congress, on the 26th ult. beg leave, most respectfully, to address your excellency. . . .
    By the suffrages of a free people you, sir, have been chosen to hold the reins of government, an event as honorable to yourself as beneficial to the public. We firmly trust that you will make the constitution the great rule of your conduct; and, in the most solemn manner, we do assure your excellency that, in the discharge of your duties, under that constitution which looks forward to an accommodation with Great Britain (an event which though traduced and treated as rebels, we still earnestly desire,) we will support you with our lives and fortunes.
    In the legislative council, the 3d day of April, 1776.
                                    GEORGE GABRIEL POWELL, Speaker
    In the general assembly, the 3d day of April, 1776.
                            By order of the house,
                                    JAMES PARSONS, Speaker

THE GOVERNOR OF GEORGIA CHRONICLES HIS DECLINE

[Excerpts from letters by Governor James Wright to a correspondent in England]

    "14th October, 1775. . . . I wrote your lordship before in what manner the command of the militia was wrested from me; they have not yet attempted to obstruct the court of Chancery, but except that I have scarce any power left, but proving wills and granting letters of administration."
    "3d January, 1776. . . . They say that now they have gone so far, that neither fortune or lives are to be regarded, and that they will go every length. But still if we had proper support and assistance, I think numbers would join the king's standard; but no troops, no money, no orders or instructions, and a wild multitude gathering fast, what can any man do in such a situation? No arms, no ammunition, not so much as a ship of war of any kind, and the neighboring Province at the same time threatening vengeance against the friends of government, and to send 1000 men to assist the liberty people if they want assistance, all these things my Lord are really too much.

They have also publicly declared that every man shall sign the association or leave the Province; that is, private persons, but that no King's officer shall be suffered to go: they will take care to prevent any of them from stirring. Surely my lord, His Majesty's officers and dutiful and loyal subjects will not be suffered to remain under such cruel tyranny and oppression.

"10th March, 1776. . . . Your Lordship will judge of the cruel state and situation we are reduced to; the rebels encouraged and exulting; their numbers in and about town increased, according to the best information I can get, to about 800 men in arms; about 200 of their regiment or battalion already enlisted and daily increasing; a considerable part of my property seized upon, and the negroes employed in throwing up and making military works in and about the town; the King's officers and friends to government, some seized upon and kept prisoners, and others hiding and obliged to desert their families and property to save their lives and liberties, and some threatened to be shot whenever met with: which distresses my Lord I humbly conceive would not have happened, had no King's ships or troops come here, until there was sufficient to reduce the rebels at once."

NEW JERSEY REPUDIATES GOVERNOR FRANKLIN

[*Resolutions of the Provincial Congress of New Jersey,
meeting at Burlington, June 14, 1776*]

Resolved, That in the opinion of this congress, the proclamation of William Franklin, esq. late governor of New Jersey, bearing date the thirtieth day of May last, in the name of the king of Great Britain, appointing a meeting of the general assembly, to be held on the twentieth of this instant, June, ought not to be obeyed.

Resolved, That, in the opinion of this congress, all payments of money on account of salary or otherwise, to the said William Franklin, esq. as governor, ought from henceforth, to cease; and that the treasurer or treasurers of this province, shall account for the monies in their hands to this congress, or to the future legislation of this colony.

By order of the congress,

SAMUEL TUCKER, President

3. AMERICANS BEGIN TO ADVOCATE SEPARATION

A PATRIOT ENUMERATES AMERICA'S GRIEVANCES

[An anonymous item published in Philadelphia, March 1776]

MEMENTO TO AMERICANS

Remember the stamp act, by which immense sums were to be yearly extorted from you.

Remember the declaratory act, by which a power was assumed of binding you, in all cases whatsoever, without your consent.

Remember the broken promise of the ministry, never again to attempt a tax on America.

Remember the duty act.

Remember the massacre at Boston, by British soldiers.

Remember the ruin of that once flourishing city by their means.

Remember the massacre at Lexington.

Remember general Gage's infamous breach of faith with the people of Boston.

Remember the cannonading, bombarding, and burning of Falmouth.

Remember the shrieks and cries of the women and children.

Remember the cannonading of Stonington and Bristol.

Remember the burning of Jamestown, Rhode Island.

Remember the frequent insults of Newport.

Remember the broken charters.

Remember the cannonade of Hampton.

Remember the act for screening and encouraging your murderers.

Remember the cannonade of New York.

Remember the altering your established jury laws.

Remember the hiring foreign troops against you.

Remember the rejection of lord Chatham's, Mr. Hartley's and Mr. Burke's plans of conciliation.

Remember the treatment of Franklin and Temple.

Remember the rejection of all your numerous humble petitions.

Remember the contempt with which they spoke of you in both houses.

Remember the cowardly endeavor to prevent foreign nations supplying you with arms and ammunition, when they themselves knew they intended coming to cut your throats.

Remember their hiring savages to murder your farmers with their families.

Remember the bribing negro slaves to assassinate their masters.

Remember the burning of Norfolk.

Remember their obliging you to pay treble duties, when you came to trade with the countries you helped them to conquer.

Remember their depriving you of all share in the fisheries, you equally with them spent your blood and treasure to acquire.

Remember their old restrictions on your woolen manufactories, your hat-making, your iron and steel forges and furnaces.

Remember their arbitrary admiralty courts.

Remember the inhuman treatment of the brave colonel Allen, and the irons he was sent in to England.

Remember the long, habitual, base venality of British parliaments.

Remember the corrupt, putrified state of that nation, and the virtuous, sound, healthy state of your own young constitution.

Remember the tyranny of Mezentius, who bound living men, face to face, with dead ones, and the effect of it.

Remember the obstinacy and unforgiving spirit of the —, evident in the treatment of his own b—s.

Remember that an honorable death is preferable to an ignominious life; and never forget what you owe to yourselves, your families, and your posterity.

JUDGE DRAYTON DRAWS A HISTORICAL PARALLEL

[*Charge to South Carolina grand jury by Chief Justice William
Henry Drayton, April 1776*]

GENTLEMEN OF THE GRAND JURY. . . . I proceed to lay before you, the principal causes leading to the late revolution of our government. . . .

The house of Brunswick was yet scarcely settled in the British throne, to which it had been called by a free people, when, in the year 1719, our ancestors in this country, finding that the government of the lords proprietors operated to their ruin, exercised the rights transmitted to them by their forefathers of England; and casting off the proprietary authority, called upon the house of Brunswick to rule over them—a house elevated to royal dominion, for no other purpose than to preserve to a people their unalienable rights. The king accepted the invitation, and thereby indisputably admitted the legality of that revolution. And in so doing, by his own act, he vested in those our forefathers, and us their posterity, a clear right to effect another revolution, if ever the government of the house of Brunswick should operate to the ruin of the people.—So the excellent Roman, emperor, Trajan, delivered a sword to Saburanus, his captain of the Praetorian guard, with this admired sentence. "Receive this sword, and use it to defend me if I govern well, but against me, if I behave ill."

With joyful acclamations our ancestors, by act of assembly passed on the 18th day of August, 1721, recognized the British monarch: The virtues of the second George are still revered among us—He was the father of his people: And it was with ecstacy we saw his grandson George the Third, mount the throne possessed of the hearts of his subjects.

But alas! almost with the commencement of his reign, his subjects felt causes to complain of government. The reign advanced—the grievances became more numerous and intolerable—the complaints more general and loud—the whole empire resounded with the cries of injured subjects! At length, grievances being unredressed and ever increasing; all patience being borne down; all hope destroyed; all confidence in royal government blasted! —Behold! the empire is rent from pole to pole! perhaps to continue asunder forever.

The catalogue of our oppressions, continental and local, is enormous. Of such oppressions, I will mention only some of the most weighty.

Under color of law, the king and parliament of Great Britain have made the most arbitrary attempts to enslave America:

By claiming a right to bind the colonies "in all cases whatsoever."

By laying duties at their mere will and pleasure upon all the colonies;

By suspending the legislature of New York;

By rendering the American charters of no validity, having annulled the most material parts of the charter of the Massachusetts Bay;

By divesting multitudes of the colonists of their property, without legal accusation or trial;

By depriving whole colonies of the bounty of Providence on their own proper coasts, in order to coerce them by famine;

By restricting the trade and commerce of America;

By sending to, and continuing in America, in time of peace, an armed force without and against the consent of the people;

By granting impunity to a soldiery instigated to murder the Americans;

By declaring, that the people of Massachusetts Bay are liable for offences, or pretended offences, done in that colony, to be sent to, and tried for the same in England; or in any colony anywhere they cannot have the benefit of a jury of the vicinage.

By establishing in Quebec the Roman Catholic religion, and an arbitrary government; instead of the Protestant religion and a free government. . . .

If I turn my thoughts to recollect in history, a change of government upon more cogent reasons, I say I know of no change upon principles so provoking—compelling—justifiable. And in this respect, even the famous revolution in England, in the year 1688, is much inferior.—However we need no better authority than that illustrious precedent; and I will therefore compare the causes of, and the law upon the two events.

On the 7th of February, 1688, the lords and commons of England, in convention, completed the following resolution.

"*Resolved* that king James the second, having endeavored to subvert the constitution of the kingdom, by breaking the original contract between king and people; and, by the advice of Jesuits and other wicked persons, having violated the fundamental laws, and having withdrawn himself out of this kingdom; has abdicated the government, and that the throne is thereby vacant."

That famous resolution deprived James of his crown; and became the foundation on which the throne of the present king of Great Britain is built —it also supports the edifice of government which we have erected.

In that resolve, there are but three facts stated to have been done by James; I will point them out, and examine whether those facts will apply to the present king of Great Britain, with regard to the operations of government, by him or his representative, immediately or by consequence affecting this colony.

The first fact is, the having endeavored to subvert the constitution of the kingdom by breaking the original contract.

The violation of the fundamental laws is the second fact; and in support of these two charges, the lords spiritual and temporal and commons, assembled at Westminster, on the 12th day of February, 1688, declared that James was guilty.

"By assuming, and exercising a power of dispensing with, and suspending of laws, and the execution of laws, without consent of parliament:

"By committing and persecuting divers worthy prelates, for humbly petitioning to be excused from concurring to the said assumed power:

"By issuing and causing to be executed a commission, under the great seal, for erecting a court, called the court of commissioners for ecclesiastical causes:

"By levying money for, and to the use of the crown, by pretence of prerogative, for other time, and in other manner, than the same was granted by parliament:

"By raising and keeping a standing army within this kingdom in time of peace, without consent of parliament; and quartering soldiers contrary to law:

"By causing several good subjects, being protestants, to be disarmed, at the same time when papists were both armed and employed contrary to law:

"By violating the freedom of election of members to serve in parliament:

"By prosecutions in the court of king's bench, for matters and causes cognizable only in parliament; and by divers and other arbitrary and illegal courses.". . .

James the second suspended the operations of laws—George the third caused the charter of the Massachusetts Bay to be in effect annihilated; he suspended the operation of the law which formed a legislature in New York, vesting it with adequate powers; and thereby he caused the very ability of making laws in that colony to be suspended.

King James levied money without the consent of the representatives of the people called upon to pay it—King George has levied money upon America, not only without, but expressly against the consent of the representatives of the people in America.

King James violated the freedom of election of members to serve in parliament—King George, by his representative, lord William Campbell, acting for him and on his behalf, broke through a fundamental law of this country, for the certain holding of general assemblies; and thereby, as far as in him lay, not only violated but annihilated the very ability of holding a general assembly.

King James in time of peace kept a standing army in England, without consent of the representatives of the people among whom that army was kept—king George hath in time of peace invaded this continent with a large standing army without the consent, and he hath kept it within this continent, expressly against the consent of the representatives of the people among whom that army is posted.

All which doings by king George the third respecting America are as much contrary to our interests and welfare; as much against law, and tend as much, at least, to subvert and extirpate the liberties of this colony, and of America, as the similar proceedings, by James the second, operated respecting the people of England. For the same principle of law, touching the premises, equally applies to the people of England in the one case, and to the people of America in the other. And this is the great principle. Certain acts done, over, and affecting a people, against and *without their consent expressed by themselves, or by representatives of their own election.*—Upon this *only* principle was grounded the complaints of the people of England— upon the *same* is grounded the complaints of the people of America. And hence it clearly follows, that if James the second violated the fundamental laws of England, George the third hath also violated the fundamental laws of America.

Again—

King James broke the original contract by not affording due protection to his subjects, although he was not charged with having seized their towns and with having held them against the people—or with having laid them in ruins by his arms—or with having seized their vessels—or with having pursued the people with fire and sword—or with having declared them rebels, for resisting his arms levelled to destroy their lives, liberties and properties—But George the third hath done all those things against America; and it is therefore undeniable that he hath not afforded the due protection to the people. Wherefore, if James the second broke the original contract, it is undeniable that George the third has also broken the original contract between king and people; and that he made use of the most violent measures by which it could be done—Violences, of which James was guiltless—Measures, carrying conflagration, massacre and open war amidst a people, whose subjection to the king of Great Britain, the law holds to be due only as a return for protection. And so tenacious and clear is the law upon this very principle, that it is laid down, subjection is not due even to a king, *de jure,* or of right, unless he be also king *de facto,* or in possession of the executive powers dispensing protection.

Again—

The third fact charged against James is, that he withdrew himself out of the kingdom—And we know that the people of this country have declared, that lord William Campbell, the king of Great Britain's representative, "having used his utmost efforts to destroy the lives, liberties, and properties of the good people here, whom by the duty of his station he was bound to protect, withdrew himself out of the colony."—Hence it will appear that George the third hath withdrawn himself out of this colony, provided it be established that exactly the same natural consequence resulted from the withdrawing in each case respectively: king James personally out of England, and king George out of Carolina, by the agency of his substitute and representative, lord William Campbell.——By king James withdrawing, the executive magistrate was gone, thereby, in the eye of the law, the executive magistrate was dead, and of consequence royal government actually ceased in England—— So by king George's representative's withdrawing, the executive magistrate was gone, the death, in law, became apparent, and of consequence royal government actually ceased in this colony. Lord William withdrew as the king's representative, carrying off the great seal and royal instructions to governors, and acting for and on the part of his principal, by every construction of law, that conduct became the conduct of his principal; and thus, James the second withdrew out of England and George the third withdrew out of South Carolina; and by such a conduct, respectively, the people in each country were exactly in the same degree injured.

The three facts against king James being thus stated and compared with similar proceedings by king George, we are now to ascertain the result of the injuries done by the first, and the law upon that point; which being ascertained, must naturally constitute the judgment in law, upon the result of similar injuries done by the last: And I am happy that I can give you the best authority upon this important point.

Treating upon this great precedent in constitutional law, the learned judge Blackstone declares that the result of the facts "amounted to an abdication of the government, which abdication did not affect only the person of the king himself, but also, all his heirs; and rendered the throne absolutely and completely vacant." Thus it clearly appears that the government was not abdicated, and the throne vacated by the resolution of the lords and commons; but that the resolution was only declaratory of the law of nature and reason, upon the result of the injuries proceeding from the three combined facts of mal-administration. And thus, as I have on the foot of the best authorities made it evident, that George the third, king of Great Britain has endeavored to subvert the constitution of this country, by breaking the original contract between king and people; by the advice of wicked persons, has violated the fundamental laws, and has withdrawn himself, by withdrawing the constitutional benefits of the kingly office, and his protection out of this country: From such a result of injuries, from such a conjuncture of circumstances—the law of the land authorizes me to declare, and it is my duty boldly to declare the law, that George the third, king of Great Britain, has abdicated the government, and that the throne is thereby vacant; that is, HE HAS NO AUTHORITY OVER US AND WE OWE NO OBEDIENCE TO HIM. . . .

A Soldier Predicts American Independence

[*Speech by a farmer of Philadelphia on joining the Continental Army, May 1776*]

My Friends and Countrymen—I have observed that some of you are a little surprised that I, with so many inducements as I have to remain at home, should have resolved to quit my family, and my farm for the fatigues and dangers of war. I mean you should be perfectly satisfied as to my motives. I am an American: and am determined to be free. I was born free: and have never forfeited my birth-right; nor will I ever, like the infatuated son of Isaac, sell it for a mess of pottage. I will part with my life sooner than my liberty, for I prefer an honorable death to the miserable and despicable existence of a slave. . . .

Had we begun this quarrel, had we demanded some new privileges, unknown to the constitution, or some commercial licenses, incompatible with the general interest of the empire, had we presumed to legislate for Great Britain, or plotted with the Bourbon family, to reinstate the execrable race of the Stuarts, and fled to arms unprovoked to accomplish these designs, there would then be some plausible apology for the severest hostile treatment we have received. But what have we done? when alarmed, ere we had yet rested from the toils of the last war, by new unconstitutional demands of revenue, we asserted our rights and petitioned for justice. Was this a crime? as unconstitutional statutes of different forms were repeatedly enacted, we repeated our petitions for redress; was this a crime? we suffered ourselves to be insulted by the introduction of an armed force to dragoon us into obedience; we suffered them to take possession of our towns and fortifications, still waiting with decent and anxious expectation from the wonted justice, humanity, and generosity of Britons: was this a crime? disposed to try every pacific measure which might probably procure our relief, we agreed to withhold our commerce from them, in hopes that, feeling the effects of their injustice, they might see how ruinous their proceedings were to their own interests, and return in time to wisdom and peace: was this a crime? nor did we once lift the sword even in our defence, until provoked to it by a wanton commencement of hostilities on their part. . . .

I will not however fight as one who beateth the air. I speak plainly; I consider this year as the grand and final period of British administration in this American world; I see no probability of their proffering such terms as we can accept of consistently with our safety, honor, and peace; nay, should they grant all that our public councils have heretofore claimed, we should still be in a most dangerous situation, liable to renewed encroachments and renewed hostilities. What else can be supposed from such a situation, and from the views, temper, and prejudices that must, and will, prevail in the British court and parliament: besides who in that case will reimburse our losses: or how shall our public debts be paid? I do solemnly declare, and that with respect to the best reconciliation that can reasonably be expected, with so corrupt, treacherous, and tyrannical an administration, that if I thought we should again revert to a dependence on Britain, I should, from this day, lay down my sword, and weep that I was born in America. But far other prospects are before us: glory, empire, liberty and peace, are, I am persuaded, unless we are lost to ourselves, very near at hand. And, on every consideration of the present state and progress of our public affairs, compared with the spirit of Britain, and the spirit, the interest, and the internal advantages of America, methinks I hear a voice, as if an angel from Heaven should proclaim, "come out from among them, and be ye separate from them. Come out of her my people, that ye be not partakers of her sins, and ye receive not of her plagues."

4. THE COLONIES CALL FOR INDEPENDENCE

VIRGINIA INSTRUCTS ITS DELEGATES TO TAKE THE INITIATIVE

*[Instructions issued by the Virginia Convention at Williamsburg
to its delegates in the Continental Congress, May 15, 1776]*

In the Virginia Convention—present 112 members.

WILLIAMSBURG, Wednesday, May 15, 1776

Forasmuch as all the endeavors of the United Colonies, by the most decent representations and petitions to the king and parliament of Great Britain, to restore peace and security to America under the British government, and a re-union with that people upon just and liberal terms, instead of a redress of grievances, have produced, from an imperious and vindictive administration, increased insult, oppression, and a vigorous attempt to effect our total destruction. By a late act, all these colonies are declared to be in rebellion, and out of the protection of the British crown, our properties subject to confiscation, our people, when captivated, compelled to join in the murder and plunder of their relations and countrymen, and all former rapine and oppression of Americans declared legal and just. Fleets and armies are raised, and the aid of foreign troops engaged to assist these destructive purposes. The king's representative in this colony hath not only withheld all the powers of government from operating for our safety, but, having retired on board an armed ship, is carrying on a practical and savage war against us, tempting our slaves, by every artifice, to resort to him, and training and employing them against their masters. In this state of extreme danger, we have no alternative left but an abject submission to the will of those over-bearing tyrants, or a total separation from the crown and government of Great Britain, uniting and exerting the strength of all America for defence, and forming alliances with foreign powers for commerce and aid in war. Wherefore, appealing to the Searcher of hearts for the sincerity of former declarations, expressing our desire to preserve the connection with that nation, and that we are driven from that inclination by their wicked councils and the eternal laws of self-preservation:

Resolved, unan. That the delegates appointed to represent this colony in general congress be instructed to propose to that respectable body to declare the United Colonies free and independent states, absolved from all allegiance to, or dependence upon, the crown or parliament of Great Britain; and that they give the assent of this colony to such declaration, and to whatever measures may be thought proper and necessary by the congress for forming foreign alliances, and a Confederation of the Colonies, at such time, and in the manner, as to them shall seem best. Provided, that the power of forming government for, and the regulations of the internal concerns of each colony, be left to the respective colonial legislatures.

Resolved, unan. That a committee be appointed to prepare a Declaration of Rights, and such a plan of government as will be most likely to maintain peace and order in this colony, and secure substantial and equal liberty to the people.

Edmund Pendleton, President.

VIRGINIANS RESPOND TO THE IDEA OF INDEPENDENCE

*[Account of the reception of the Convention's resolutions
by the people of Williamsburg, May 15, 1776]*

WILLIAMSBURG, May 15, 1776

In consequence of the above resolution, universally regarded as the only door which will lead to safety and prosperity, some gentlemen made a handsome collection for the purpose of treating the soldiery, who next day were paraded in Waller's grove, before brigadier general Lewis attended by the gentlemen of the committee of safety, the members of the general convention, the inhabitants of this city, etc., etc. The resolution being read aloud to the army, the following toasts were given, each of them accompanied by a discharge of the artillery and small arms, and the acclamations of all present:

1. The American independent states.

2. The grand congress of the United States, and their respective legislatures.

3. General Washington, and victory to the American arms.

The Union Flag of the American states waved upon the capitol during the whole of this ceremony, which being ended, the soldiers partook of the refreshment prepared for them by the affection of their countrymen, and the evening concluded with illuminations, and other demonstrations of joy; every one seeming pleased that the domination of Great Britain was now at an end, so wickedly and tyrannically exercised for these twelve or thirteen years past, notwithstanding our repeated prayers and remonstrances for redress.

A MASSACHUSETTS TOWN URGES INDEPENDENCE

*[Instructions of the inhabitants of Malden, Massachusetts, to their
representative in Congress, May 27, 1776]*

SIR—A resolution of the hon. house of representatives, calling upon the several towns in this colony to express their minds with respect to the important question of American independence, is the occasion of our now instructing you. The time was, sir, when we loved the king and the people of Great Britain with an affection truly filial; we felt ourselves interested in their glory; we shared their joys and sorrows; we cheerfully poured the fruit of all our labors into the lap of our mother-country, and without reluctance expended our blood and our treasure in their cause.

These were our sentiments towards Great Britain while she continued to act the part of a parent state; we felt ourselves happy in our connection with her, nor wished it to be dissolved; but our sentiments are altered, it is now the ardent wish of our souls that America may become a free and independent state.

A sense of unprovoked injuries will arouse the resentment of the most peaceful. Such injuries these colonies have received from Britain. Unjustifiable claims have been made by the king and his minions to tax us without our consent; these claims have been prosecuted in a manner cruel and unjust to the highest degree. The frantic policy of administration hath induced them to send fleets and armies to America; that, by depriving us of our trade and cutting the throats of our brethren, they might awe us into submission, and erect a system of despotism in America, which should so far enlarge the influence of the crown as to enable it to rivet their shackles upon the people of Great Britain.

This plan was brought to a crisis upon the ever memorable nineteenth of April. We remember the fatal day! the expiring groans of our countrymen yet vibrate on our ears! and we now behold the flames of their peaceful dwellings ascending to heaven! we hear their blood crying to us from the ground for vengeance! charging us, as we value the peace of their manes, to have no further connection with ——, who can unfeelingly hear of the slaughter of ——, and composedly sleep with their blood upon his soul. The manner in which the war had been prosecuted hath confirmed us in these sentiments; piracy and murder, robbery and breach of faith, have been conspicuous in the conduct of the king's troops: defenceless towns have been attacked and destroyed: the ruins of Charlestown, which are daily in our view, daily reminds us of this: the cries of the widow and the orphan demand our attention; they demand that the hand of pity should wipe the tear from their eye, and that the sword of their country should avenge their wrongs. We long entertained hopes that the spirit of the British nation would once more induce them to assert their own and our rights, and bring to condign punishment the elevated villains who have trampled upon the sacred rights of men, and affronted the majesty of the people. We hoped in vain; they have lost their love to freedom: they have lost their spirit of just resentment; we therefore renounce with disdain our connection with a kingdom of slaves; we bid a final adieu to Britain.

Could an accommodation be now effected, we have reason to think that it would be fatal to the liberties of America; we should soon catch the contagion of venality and dissipation, which hath subjected Britons to lawless domination. Were we placed in the situation we were in 1763: were the powers of appointing to offices, and commanding militia, in the hands of governors, our arts, trade and manufactures would be cramped; nay, more than this, the life of every man who has been active in the cause of his country would be endangered.

For these reasons, as well as many others which might be produced, we are confirmed in the opinion, that the present age will be deficient in their duty to god, their posterity and themselves, if they do not establish an American republic. This is the only form of government which we wish to see established; for we can never be willingly subject to any other King than he who, being possessed of infinite wisdom, goodness and rectitude, is alone fit to possess unlimited power.

We have freely spoken our sentiments upon this important subject, but we mean not to dictate; we have unbounded confidence in the wisdom and uprightness of the continental congress; with pleasure we recollect that this affair is under their direction and we now instruct you, sir, to give them the strongest assurance that, if they should declare America to be a free and independent republic, your constituents would support and defend the measure, to the last drop of their blood, and the last farthing of their treasure.

Attest.

SAM MERRIT, Town-clerk.

PENNSYLVANIA FOLLOWS SUIT

[*Declaration of the Deputies of Pennsylvania, in the Provincial Congress, Philadelphia, June 24, 1776*]

Whereas George the third, king of Great Britain, etc., in violation of the principles of the British constitution, and of the laws of justice and humanity, hath by an accumulation of oppressions, unparalleled in history, excluded the inhabitants of this, with the other American colonies, from his protection; and whereas he hath paid no regard to any of our numerous and dutiful petitions for redress of our complicated grievances, but hath lately purchased foreign troops to assist in enslaving us, and hath excited the savages of this country to carry on a war against us, as also the negroes, to embrue their hands in the blood of their masters, in a manner unpractised by civilized nations; and moreover hath lately insulted our calamities by declaring, that he will shew us no mercy, until he has subdued us; and whereas, the obligations of allegiance (being reciprocal between a king and his subjects) are now dissolved, on the side of the colonists, by the despotism and declaration of the said king, insomuch that it appears that loyalty to him is treason against the good people of this country; and whereas not only the parliament, but there is reason to believe too many of the people of Great Britain, have concurred in the aforesaid arbitrary and unjust proceedings against us; and whereas the public virtue of this colony (so essential to its liberty and happiness) must be endangered by a future political union with, or dependence upon a crown and nation, so lost to justice, patriotism, and magnanimity: We, the deputies of the people of Pennsylvania, assembled in full provincial conference, for forming a plan for executing the resolve of congress of the 15th of May last, for suppressing all authority in this province, derived from the crown of Great Britain, and for establishing a government upon the authority of the people only, do, in this public manner, in behalf of ourselves, and with the approbation, consent, and authority of our constituents, unanimously declare our willingness to concur in a vote of the congress, declaring the United Colonies free and independent states; provided, the forming the government and the regulation of the internal police of this colony, be always reserved to the people of the said colony. And we do further call upon the nations of Europe, and appeal to the Great Arbiter and governor of the empires of the world, to witness for us, that this declaration did not originate in ambition, or in an impatience of lawful authority, but that we were driven to it in obedience to the first principles of nature, by the oppressions and cruelties of the aforesaid king and parliament of Great Britain, as the only possible measure that was left us to preserve and establish our liberties, and to transmit them inviolate to posterity.

Signed, by order of the conference,

THOMAS M'KEAN, President.

PART THREE

Securing the Rights of Americans

1776-1789

PART THREE

Securing the Rights of Americans

1776-1789

THE INDEPENDENCE DECLARED so boldly by the American colonies in 1776 was not acknowledged by most European nations for seven long years. Only after the Americans demonstrated their determination and their strength on the field of battle did George III and other monarchs of Europe concede that thirteen former British colonies were totally independent of their mother nation. Wringing such a concession from the courts of Europe proved an arduous and often agonizing task, one that might have been impossible without timely aid from Britain's old rival, France.

But winning the military contest was only half of the challenge the American patriots had undertaken. Independence would bring with it very real problems of government: the creation of state governments to replace the old colonial system, the development of an interstate authority to replace the old imperial structure, and the evolution of an American political theory to fill the role once played by the British Constitution. In all these tasks the Americans would have the precedents and practices of their long colonial experience, and these in large part account for the substantial success of America's venture into nationhood.

But in 1776 all this was in the future. Nothing seemed certain except hardship. On the field of battle and in the halls of assembly a whole generation would have to toil and sacrifice to secure the rights of Americans.

VII

KEEPING SPIRITS HIGH,

1776-1781

"THESE ARE THE times that try men's souls," wrote Thomas Paine in the fall of 1776. Washington's army was in rapid retreat after a series of defeats in southern New York; troops, munitions, and funds were in low supply. And worst of all, an air of discouragement had settled over the land. To win the war Americans would need not only the tools of war but an attitude of hope and determination as well. In short, part of the story of the American Revolution is the effort to keep spirits high.

The task of upholding morale fell in part on the newly formed state governments, a task that was met principally through public pronouncements by governor or legislature (pp. 247, 249, and 251). And although there was no official federal government until 1781, the Second Continental Congress remained in operation throughout the war and did its share to boost the people's spirits (pp. 255, and 257). Private citizens lent a hand as well. Clergymen, educators, and jurists, among others, accepted the responsibility of encouraging the people to greater efforts and of honoring those who had made the ultimate sacrifice (p. 252).

Nevertheless, it proved impossible to drown completely the voices of discouragement and dissent. Even General Washington, a bulwark of hope and confidence, succumbed to long and frequent periods of discouragement—though he was careful to reveal them only in private communications (p. 260). Less discreet were a group of Philadelphians—possibly more in sympathy with the tory than the patriot side of the conflict—who publicly protested against their treatment by the government of Pennsylvania (p. 262). Still more harmful to American morale were the occasional open criticisms of

[246]

the patriot cause or its leaders, as can be seen in a petition by American loyalists (p. 264) and in an attack on Washington for his role in the execution of the British spy Major John André (p. 266).

Fortunately for the Americans, their sense of humor did not desert them entirely, even in the darkest moments of the war. "The History of John Bull's Children" may have come from an Englishman's pen, but it found its warmest reception in the former colonies (p. 267). And in the rare moments when Americans had no parodies of George III and his ministers to amuse them, they found an equally susceptible subject for buffoonery even closer to home. General John Burgoyne, commander of the army that in 1777 attempted to split the states along the Hudson River–Lake Champlain line, became the principal target of American wit, no less after his surrender at Saratoga than before it (pp. 269, and 271). At times, however, American humor took on a grimmer visage, as demonstrated by the Philadelphians who paraded and then burned an effigy of the infamous traitor Benedict Arnold (p. 274).

1. THE STATES UPHOLD THE SPIRIT OF '76

ENCOURAGEMENT FOR THE PATRIOTS OF MASSACHUSETTS

[*An address to the "Independent Sons in Massachusetts State,"*
Boston, November 14, 1776]

> *"Our bless'd forefathers," is the grateful sound,*
> *From age to age, the world will echo round!*
> *And every future tongue that speaks your name,*
> *Will brighten the hours with your growing fame.*

Our losses this year are small, when compared with the advantages we have gained, and it would be extreme folly, even in the weakest American, to suppose our cause did not continue to rise.—The complete triumph of liberty undoubtedly draws nearer every hour. When we review the state of America, and that of our enemy, we behold eminent and growing advantages on the part of our country. The valor and discipline of our troops are constantly improving, as every late action with the enemy testifies; this circumstance, considered with that of our superior numbers, affords a bright prospect of success. It was always supposed, that the enemy would have the greatest advantage in the beginning of the war, and it must be acknowledged, (with gratitude to Heaven) that they have done much less, and our success has been much greater, than might have been expected. At this period, we have so many experienced men of tried valor, such magazines of warlike stores, such a military system formed, such a disciplined militia, (as no other nation can produce), and such a union and fervor of spirit in support of the righteous cause of our country, as must damp the malevolent spirit of our enemies, and give vigor to every virtuous mind. When we survey our naval department, such are our preparations, such our amazing progress in fitting out armed vessels, and so wonderful our success in taking the ships, the persons, and the riches of the enemy, that even our antagonists are almost ready to exclaim, "God is on that side!"

Another happy circumstance in our favor, is the fruitful season and plentiful harvest with which Heaven hath blessed our country. In truth, so numerous are the favors of Providence, and so encouraging our prospect of success, that we have much greater cause for thanksgiving than for petitioning; and it is unmanly, unchristian, and unworthy of any free mind, to discover the least degree of timidity. Our difficulties and sufferings, in supporting the great cause of liberty, have been little, if compared with what other nations have suffered in defence of their freedom. The Switzers fought sixty battles in defending their liberties, and finally, drove all the murdering tyrants out of their country, set up independent states, and have flourished in freedom to this day, in spite of all the tyrants in Europe. They are a striking proof of the superior virtue and strength of a free people, for their whole country is not larger than the Massachusetts state, not half so fruitful, nor any ways comparable for happiness of situation, and commercial advantages. What then may not the United States of America accomplish? We may rationally suppose, upon a survey of the present state of all nations, that these United States will make swifter progress in arts and arms, and in all that adorns and dignifies human society, than any people or nation ever yet have done.

The tyrants of Britain, and the abject slaves whom they can hire, are all the enemies we have to encounter; the rest of the world will be our friends. As we wish to injure no people, other nations will naturally be our friends, some from interest, and others, whose interest is no ways concerned, from motives of humanity. As America is so very extensive, capable of supporting so many millions of inhabitants, more than she has at present; and as the virtuous part of mankind love freedom, they will transplant themselves from the slavish dominions of Europe, to this land of liberty, whereby the industry, the virtue, and the wisdom of the world will centre in these free and independent states. Such being our field of hope, such our prospect of happiness, not only for ourselves, but for millions of others, by what name shall we call that folly which would abate your ardor, and discourage your efforts, to maintain the entire independence of America?

GOVERNOR LIVINGSTON EXHORTS THE NEW JERSEY LEGISLATURE

[Address by Governor William Livingston to the legislature of New Jersey, meeting at Haddonfield, February 25, 1777]

GENTLEMEN . . . [There are some] who, terrified by the power of Britain, have persuaded themselves that she is not only formidable, but irresistible. That her power is great, is beyond question; that it is not to be despised, is the dictate of common prudence. But then we ought also to consider her, as weak in council, and ingulfed in debt—reduced in her trade—reduced in her revenue—immersed in pleasure—enervated with luxury—and, in dissipation and venality, surpassing all Europe. We ought to consider her as hated by a potent rival, her natural enemy and particularly exasperated by her imperious conduct in the last war, as well as her insolent manner of commencing it; and thence inflamed with resentment, and only watching a favorable juncture for open hostilities. We ought to consider the amazing expense and difficulty of transporting troops and provisions above three thousand miles, with the impossibility of recruiting their army at a less distance, save only with such recreants, whose conscious guilt must at the first approach of danger, appeal the stoutest heart. Those insuperable obstacles are known and acknowledged by every virtuous and impartial man in the nation. Even the author of this horrid war is incapable of concealing his own confusion and distress. Too great to be wholly suppressed, it frequently discovers itself in the course of his speech—a speech terrible in word, and fraught with contradiction—breathing threatenings, and betraying terror—a motley mixture of magnanimity and consternation—of grandeur and abasement.—With troops invincible he dreaded a defeat, and wants reinforcements. Victorious in America, and triumphant on the ocean, he is an humble dependent on a petty prince; and apprehends an attack upon his metropolis; and, with full confidence in the friendship and alliance of France, he trembles upon his throne, at her secret designs and open preparations.

With all this, we ought to contrast the numerous and hardy sons of America, inured to toil—seasoned alike to heat and cold—hale—robust—patient of fatigue—and, from their ardent love of liberty, ready to face danger and death—the immense extent of continent, which our infatuated enemies have undertaken to subjugate—the remarkable unanimity of its inhabitants, notwithstanding the exception of a few apostates and deserters—their unshaken resolution to maintain their freedom, or perish in the attempt— the fertility of our soil in all kinds of provisions necessary for the support of war —our inexhaustible internal resources for military stores and naval armaments—our comparative economy in public expenses—and the millions we save by having reprobated the farther exchange of our valuable staples for the worthless baubles and finery of English manufacture. Add to this, that in a cause so just and righteous on our part, we have the highest reason to expect the blessing of Heaven upon our glorious conflict. For who can doubt the interposition of the supremely just, in favor of a people forced to recur to arms in defence of every thing dear and precious. . . .

Let us not, however, presumptuously rely on the interposition of Providence, without exerting those efforts which it is our duty to exert, and which our bountiful Creator has enabled us to exert. Let us do our part to open the next campaign with redoubled vigor; and until the United States have humbled the pride of Britain, and obtained an honorable peace, cheerfully furnish our proportion for continuing the war—a war, founded on our side of the immutable obligation of self-defence and in support of freedom, of virtue, and everything tending to ennoble our nature, and render a people happy—on their part, prompted by boundless avarice, and a thirst for absolute sway, and built on a claim repugnant to every principle of reason and equity—a claim subversive of all liberty, natural, civil, moral, and religious; incompatible with human happiness, and usurping the attributes of deity, degrading man, and blaspheming God.

Let us all, therefore, of every rank and degree, remember our plighted faith and honor, to maintain the cause with our lives and fortunes. Let us inflexibly persevere in prosecuting to a happy period, what has been so gloriously begun, and hitherto so prosperously conducted. And let those in more distinguished stations use all their influence and authority, to rouse the supine; to animate the irresolute; to confirm the wavering; and to draw from his lurking hole, the skulking neutral, who leaving to others the heat and burden of the day, means in the final result to reap the fruits of that victory, for which he will not contend. Let us be peculiarly assiduous in bringing to condign punishment, those detestable parricides who have been openly active against their native country. And may we, in all our deliberations and proceedings, be influenced and directed by the Great Arbiter of the fate of nations, by whom empires rise and fall, and who will not always suffer the sceptre of the wicked to rest on the lot of the righteous, but in due time avenge an injured people on their unfeeling oppressor, and his bloody instruments.

The Government of Virginia Lauds Its Citizen Soldiers

[Proclamation by Governor Patrick Henry to the people
of Virginia on the arrival of a British fleet in
Chesapeake Bay, May 14, 1779]

Friends and Countrymen—When our country is invaded by the avowed enemies to the common rights of mankind; when it is threatened with all those calamities which barbarity and cruelty can inflict, it is no longer time to pause. We have not an enemy to oppose who can claim the common pretension for war. We have to combat those who seek not for a retaliation of injuries done them, but who would be our tyrants. Tyrants of the blackest nature, who would rob us not only of those privileges which are dearest to us, but would bring our grey hairs down with sorrow to the grave. To be the base slaves of arbitrary power, to be insulted, trampled under foot by a soldiery, the outcasts of jails, to be stripped of your property, to behold your wives and children the victims of brutal lust, or nobly to resist the torrent of despotism, nobly to stand forth and to wreak your vengeance upon an enemy the most barbarous and cruel, is the only alternative which now awaits you. They have already commenced the horrid war. Your houses are already devoted to the flames; your wives have been driven with the flocks and herds to their ships. To the Hessian, and the still more barbarous Highlander, let them now offer up their prayers for mercy. But what mercy are they to hope from those whose avowed design is conquest, ruin, and misery! Indignation usurps the place of reflection. Indignation should hurry us to action, should fire our souls with the noble emulation, who first should have the immortal glory of plunging his dagger in the breast of such an enemy.

Fortunately for us, we have men to command, beloved, respected, and admired for their intrepidity, activity, and good conduct; men who, if supported by their fellow citizens, will soon baffle the designs of our enemy; will soon rescue this country from the disgrace of being plundered and ravaged by a merciless banditti. Virginia stands foremost for public spirit. Her sons have now the most glorious opportunity of gaining immortal fame. They have a commander to lead them to the field, whose experience and bravery will ensure them victory. They may now have that satisfaction not only of saving their country but of revenge—of revenge for attempts, which, if carried into execution, will entail shame and ruin upon us to the latest ages.

Activity, vigor, a determination to conquer or to die, will soon expel those invaders of our rights; torpor and inactivity will confirm them in their conquest. Example will create heroes. The body of the people must be put in motion by the influence of those whom they respect and esteem. Follow then the conduct of our brave brethren to the north, remember what gave a favorable cast to the melancholy prospect they had before them. Men of fortune and distinction were the first to oppose the enemy. Success crowned their efforts, and patriotism received eternal honor. Similar example here will ensure similar success. The progress of the enemy in our country may carry along with it the most dangerous consequences. What accessions will they not gain from those among us who feel every day the yoke of slavery! We shall supply them with the certain means of our own destruction, unless our activity and vigor arrest them in their progress. The possession of sufficient ground for their encampment is not only disgraceful to us, but ruinous. It will be an asylum for our slaves; they will flock to their standards, and form the flower of their army. They will rival the Hessian or Highlander, if possible, in cruelty and desolation. It is said that at present their army does not consist of more than two thousand. This circumstance, which may lull us into security, seems big with the most fatal consequences, unless we resolve to anticipate the evil. They doubtless expect reinforcements from our slaves; not to mention from tories and the disaffected.

In a word, the means of our salvation are difficult, but certain and glorious, if we will seize them in time. Delay and inactivity will bring along with them infamy, disgrace, and certain perdition.

A Eulogy to Those Who Lost Their Lives

[*Speech by Judge Henry Brackenridge in the German Calvinist Church, Philadelphia, July 5, 1779*]

. . . Heroes then arose;
Who, scorning coward self, for others liv'd,
Toll'd for their case, and for their safety bled.
THOMSON.

It is the high reward of those who have risked their lives in a just and necessary war, that their names are sweet in the mouths of men, and every age shall know their actions. I am happy in having it in my power, before a polite assembly, to express what I think of those who have risked their lives in the war of America. I know my abilities rise not to a level with so great a subject, but I love the memory of the men, and it is my hope, that the affection which I feel, will be to me instead of genius, and give me warm words to advance their praises.

I conceive it as the first honor of these men that, before they engaged in the war, they saw it to be just and necessary. They were not the vassals of a proud chieftain rousing them, in barbarous times, by the blind impulse of attachment to his family, or engaging them to espouse his quarrel, by the music and entertainment of his hall. They were themselves the chieftains of their own cause, highly instructed in the nature of it, and from the best principles of patriotism, resolute in defence. They had heard the declaration of the court and parliament of Great Britain, claiming the authority of binding them in all cases whatsoever. They had examined this claim, and found it to be, as to its foundation, groundless; as to its nature tyrannical, and in its consequences, ruinous to the peace and happiness of both countries. On this clear apprehension and decided judgment of the cause, ascertained by their own reason, and collected from the best writers, it was the noble purpose of their minds to stand forth and assert it, at the expense of fortune, and the hazard of their lives.

These brave men were not soldiers by profession, bred to arms, and from a habit of military life attached to it. They were men in the easy walks of life; mechanics of the city, merchants of the counting house, youths engaged in the literary studies, and husbandmen, peaceful cultivators of the soil. Happy in the sociability and conversation of the town, the simplicity and innocence of the country village, or the philosophic ease of academic leisure, and the sweets of rural life, they wished not a change of these scenes of pleasure, for the dangers and calamities of war. It was the pure love of virtue and of freedom, burning bright within their minds, that alone could engage them to embark in an undertaking of so bold and perilous a nature.

These brave men were not unacquainted with the circumstances of their situation, and their unprepared state of war. Not a bayonet was anvilled out, not a fire-arm was in their possession. No redoubt was cast up to secure the city, no fort was erected to resist invasion, no gun mounted on the battery, and no vessel launched upon the stream.

The power of Britain, on the other hand, was well known, and by the lightning of her orators, in a thousand writings and harangues, had been thrown, in full force, upon their minds. They were taught to believe her, (what indeed she was) old in arts and in arms, and enriched with the spoils of a thousand victories. Embraced with the ocean as her favorite, her commerce was extensive, and she sent her ships to every sea. Abounding in men, her armies were in full force, her fleets were completely manned, her discipline was regular, and the spirit of her enterprise, by sea and land, had, in most cases, insured her successes.

The idea of resistance to the power of Britain was indeed great—but the mighty soul of the patriot drank it in, and, like the eagle on the mountain top, collected magnanimity from the very prospect of the height from which he meant to soar: Like the steed who swallows the distant ground with his fierceness, he attempts the career, and poured himself upon the race.

The patriot quits his easy independent walk of life, his shop, his farm, his office and his counting house, and with every hope and every anxious thought, prepares himself for war. The materials of gun powder are extracted from the earth: the bayonet is anvilled out; the firearm is manufactured in the shop; the manual exercise is taught; the company is formed in battalion; the battalion is instructed to manoeuvre on the field; the brigade is drawn forth; and the standard of defiance is planted on the soil.

Shall I mention the circumstances of the day when the sword was drawn, and the first blood was shed; and shall I trace the progress of the war in the course of five campaigns? The narration would require the space of an entire day: I can mention but the sum of things; and only tell you, that the inroad of the foe has been sustained upon the plain, and the forward and impetuous bands have been driven over the disdaining ground which they had measured in advance. The hill has been defended, and the repulsed and rallying foe has been taught to understand, that the valor of America was worthy of the cause which her freemen have espoused. The wilderness has been surmounted in the march. It has been fought, foot to foot, and point to point, in skirmishes, and night surprises, and in pitched battles, with alternate hope and dubious success. The enemy, beaten in one state has retired to a second, and beaten in the second, he has returned to the first; beaten in every state he has sought the water and like a sea monster rolling to the deep, has washed his wounds in the brine of ocean. Rising from the ocean he has sought the land, and advanced with a slow and suspicious step upon the hostile territory. War is again arisen, and it has been fought from spring to autumn and from autumn to spring, through the heat of summer and the inclemencies of winter, with unabated ardor, and unshaken perseverance. What tract of country has not been marked with the vestiges of war? What ground has not been cut with trenches?—What hill has not been covered with redoubts?—What plain has not been made the scene of the engagement? What soil of our whole earth has not been sowed with ball?

These have been the toils of the heroes of our army; but the brave men whom we this day celebrate, have added to their toils the loss of life. They have fallen in the contest: These of them in the long and laborious march: These by the fever of the camp: These have fallen when, advancing on the enemy, they have received the bayonet in their breast: or high in hope, and anxious of victory, they have dropt by the cannon or the musket ball.

For what cause did these brave men sacrifice their lives? For that cause which, in all ages, has engaged the hopes, the wishes, and endeavors of the breast of men—the cause of liberty. Liberty! thou art indeed valuable; the source of all that is good and great upon the earth!—For thee, the patriot of America has drawn his sword, and has fought and has fallen. . . .

When after times shall speak of those who have risen to renown, I will charge it to the golden winged and silver tongued bards, that they recollect and set in order every circumstance; the causes of the war; early and just exertions, the toils, hazardous achievements, noble resolution, unshaken perseverance, unabated ardor; hopes in the worst of times; triumphs of victory; humanity to an enemy; All these will I charge it, that they recollect and set in order, and give them bright and unsullied to the coming ages. The bards I know will hear me, and you my gallant countrymen, shall go down to posterity with exceeding honor. Your fame shall ascend on the current of the stream of time: It shall play with the breezes of the morning. Men at rest, in the cool age of life, from the fury of a thousand wars finished by their fathers, shall observe the spreading ensign. They shall hail it, as it weaves with variegated glories: and feeling all the warm rapture of the heart, shall give their plaudit from the shores.

2. CONGRESS TRIES TO BOOST MORALE

A Manifesto from Congress

*[Address by the Continental Congress to the people
of the United States, October 30, 1778]*

By the Congress of the United States of America—

A Manifesto.

These United States having been driven to hostilities by the oppressive and tyrannous measures of Great Britain; having been compelled to commit the essential rights of man to the decision of arms; and having been, at length, forced to shake off a yoke which had grown too burdensome to bear, they declared themselves free and independent.

Confiding in the justice of their cause; confiding in him who disposes of human events, although weak and unprovided, they set the power of their enemies at defiance.

In this confidence they have continued through the various fortune of three bloody campaigns, unawed by the power, unsubdued by the barbarity of their foes. Their virtuous citizens have borne, without repining, the loss of many things which makes life desirable. Their brave troops have patiently endured the hardships and dangers of a situation, fruitful in both beyond former example.

The congress considering themselves bound to love their enemies, as children of that being who is equally the father of all; and desirous, since they could not prevent, at least to alleviate, the calamities of war, have studied to spare those who were in arms against them, and to lighten the chains of captivity.

The conduct of those serving under the king of Great Britain hath, with some few exceptions, been diametrically opposite. They have laid waste the open country, burned the defenceless villages, and butchered the citizens of America. Their prisons have been the slaughter-houses of her soldiers; their ships, of her seamen, and the severest injuries have been aggravated by the grossest insults.

Foiled in their vain attempt to subjugate the unconquerable spirit of freedom, they have meanly assailed the representatives of America with bribes, with deceit, and the servility of adulation. They have made a mock of religion, by impious appeals to God whilst in the violation of his sacred commands; they have made a mock even of reason itself, by endeavoring to prove that the liberty and happiness of America could safely be entrusted to those who have sold their own, unawed by the sense of virtue or of shame.

Treated with the contempt, which such conduct deserved, they have applied to individuals; they have solicited them to break the bonds of allegiance and embrue their souls with the blackest of crimes: but, fearing none could be found through these United States equal to the wickedness of their purpose, to influence weak minds they have threatened more wide devastation.

While the shadow of hope remained, that our enemies could be taught by our example to respect those laws which are held sacred among civilized nations, and to comply with the dictates of a religion, which they pretend in common with us to believe and to revere, they have been left to the influence of that religion and that example. But since their incorrigible dispositions cannot be touched by kindness and compassion, it becomes our duty by other means to vindicate the rights of humanity.

We, therefore, the congress of the United States of America, do solemnly declare and proclaim, that if our enemies presume to execute their threats, or persist in their present career of barbarity, we will take such exemplary vengeance as shall deter others from a like conduct. We appeal to that God who searcheth the hearts of men, for the rectitude of our intentions; and, in his holy presence, we declare, that as we are not moved by any light and hasty suggestions of anger and revenge, so through every possible change of fortune we will adhere to this our determination.

Done in Congress, by unanimous consent, the thirtieth day of October, one thousand seven hundred and seventy eight.

(Signed) HENRY LAURENS, President

CONGRESS ADDRESSES THE AMERICAN PEOPLE

*[Address by the Continental Congress to the people
of the United States, May 26, 1779]*

TO THE INHABITANTS OF THE UNITED STATES OF AMERICA.

FRIENDS AND COUNTRYMEN—The present situation of public affairs demands your most serious attention, and particularly the great and increasing depreciation of your currency requires the immediate, strenuous, and united efforts of all true friends to their country, for preventing an extension of the mischiefs that have already flowed from that source. . . .

For defraying the expenses of this uncommon war, your representatives in congress were obliged to emit paper money; an expedient that you knew to have been before generally and successfully practised on this continent.

They were very sensible of the inconveniences with which too frequent emissions would be attended, and endeavored to avoid them. For this purpose they established loan-offices so early as in October, 1776, and have, from that time to this, repeatedly and earnestly solicited you to lend them money on the faith of the United States. The sums received on loan have nevertheless proved inadequate to the public exigencies. Our enemies prosecuting the war by sea and land with implacable fury and with some success, taxation at home and borrowing abroad, in the midst of difficulties and dangers, were alike impracticable. Hence the continued necessity of new emissions.

But to this cause alone we do not impute the evil before mentioned. We have too much reason to believe it has been in part owing to the artifices of men who have hastened to enrich themselves by monopolizing the necessaries of life, and to the misconduct of inferior officers employed in the public service. . . .

We are sorry to hear that some persons are so slightly informed of their own interests, as to suppose that it is advantageous to them to sell the produce of their farms at enormous prices, when a little reflection might convince them that it is injurious to those interests and the general welfare. If they expect thereby to purchase imported goods cheaper, they will be egregiously disappointed; for the merchants, who know they cannot obtain returns in gold, silver, or bills of exchange, but that their vessels, if loaded here at all, must be loaded with produce, will raise the price of what they have to sell, in proportion to the price of what they have to buy, and consequently the landholder can purchase no more foreign goods, for the same quantity of his produce, than he could before.

The evil, however, does not stop at this point. The landholder, by acting on this mistaken calculation, is only laboring to accumulate an immense debt, by increasing the public expenses, for the payment of which his estate is engaged, and to embarrass every measure adopted for vindicating his liberty, and securing his posterity. . . .

In vain will it be for your delegates to form plans of economy; to strive to stop a continuation of emissions by taxation or loan, if you do not zealously co-operate with them in promoting their designs, and use your utmost industry to prevent the waste of money in the expenditure, which your respective situations, in the several places where it is expended, may enable you to do. A discharge of this duty, a compliance with recommendations for supplying money might enable congress to give speedy assurances to the public that no more emissions shall take place, and thereby close that source of depreciation. . . .

Think not we despair of the commonwealth, or endeavor to shrink from opposing difficulties. No. Your cause is too good, your objects too sacred, to be relinquished. We tell you truths, because you are freemen who can bear to hear them, and may profit by them; and when they reach your enemies, we fear not the consequences, because we are not ignorant of their resources or our own. . . .

Your enemies, despairing however, as it seems, of the success of their united forces against our main army, have divided them, as if their design was to harass you by predatory, desultory, operations. If you are assiduous in improving opportunities, Saratoga may not be the only spot on this continent to give a new denomination to the baffled troops of a nation, impiously priding herself in notions of her omnipotence.

Rouse yourselves, therefore, that this campaign may finish the great work you have so nobly carried on for several years past. What nation ever engaged in such a contest under such a complication of disadvantages; so soon surmounted many of them, and in so short a period of time had so certain a prospect of a speedy and happy conclusion? We will venture to pronounce, that so remarkable an instance exists not in the annals of mankind. We well remember what you said at the commencement of this war. You saw the immense difference between your circumstances and those of your enemies, and you knew the quarrel must decide on no less than your lives, liberties and estates. All these you greatly put to every hazard, resolving rather to die freemen than to live slaves; and justice will oblige the impartial world to confess you have uniformly acted on the same generous principle. Consider how much you have done, how comparatively little remains to be done, to crown you with success. Persevere, and you ensure peace, freedom, safety, glory, sovereignty, and felicity to yourselves, your children, and your children's children.

Encouraged by favors already received from infinite goodness, gratefully acknowledging them, earnestly imploring their continuance, constantly endeavoring to draw them down on your heads by an amendment of your lives, and a conformity to the Divine Will, humbly confiding in the protection so often and wonderfully experienced, vigorously employ the means placed by Providence in your hands, for completing your labors.

Fill up your battalions—be prepared in every part to repel the incursions of your enemies—place your several quotas in the continental treasury— lend money for public uses—sink the emissions of your respective states— provide effectually for expediting the conveyance of supplies for your armies and fleets, and for your allies—prevent the produce of the country from being monopolized—effectually superintend the behavior of public officers, —diligently promote piety, virtue, brotherly love, learning, frugality, and moderation—and may you be approved before Almighty God worthy of those blessings we devoutly wish you to enjoy.

Done in congress, by unanimous consent,
    this twenty-sixth day of May, one thousand
    seven hundred and seventy-nine.
      Attest.   JOHN JAY, President.
CHARLES THOMPSON, Secretary.

3. VOICES OF DISCOURAGEMENT

WASHINGTON LAMENTS THE HARDSHIPS OF THE SOLDIERS

[*Letters from George Washington to Governor
Caesar Rodney of Delaware*]

Head-Quarters, Morristown,—26 December, 1779.

SIR—The situation of the army with respect to supplies, is beyond description alarming. It has been five or six weeks past on half allowance, and we have not more than three days bread, at a third allowance, on hand, nor any where within reach. When this is exhausted, we must depend on the precarious gleanings of the neighboring country. Our magazines are absolutely empty everywhere, and our commissaries entirely destitute of money or credit to replenish them. We have never experienced a like extremity at any period of the war. We have often felt temporary want from an accidental delay in forwarding supplies, but we always had something in our magazines and the means of procuring more. Neither one nor the other is at present the case.

This representation is the result of a minute examination of our resources. Unless some extraordinary and immediate exertions be made by the states from which we draw our supplies, there is every appearance that the army will infallibly disband in a fortnight. I think it is my duty to lay this candid view of our situation before your excellency, and to entreat the vigorous interposition of the state to rescue us from the danger of an event, which, if it did not prove the total ruin of our affairs, would at least give them a shock they would not easily recover, and plunge us into a train of new and still more perplexing embarrassments than any we have hitherto felt.

I have the honor to be, with great respect, your excellency's most obedient servant.

G. WASHINGTON.

Head-Quarters, near The Liberty Pole,
BERGEN COUNTY, 27 August, 1780

SIR—The honorable the committee of cooperation having returned to congress, I am under the disagreeable necessity of informing your excellency that the army is again reduced to an extremity of distress for want of provision. The greater part of it has been without meat from the 21st to the

26th. To endeavor to obtain some relief, I moved down to this place, with a view of stripping the lower parts of the country of the remainder of its cattle, which, after a most rigorous exaction, is found to afford between two and three days' supply only, and those consisting of milch cows, and calves of one or two years old. When this scanty pittance is consumed, I know not what will be our next resource, as the commissary can give me no certain information of more than 120 head of cattle expected from Pennsylvania, and about 150 from Massachusetts—I mean in time to supply our immediate wants.

Military coercion is no longer of any avail, as nothing further can possibly be collected from the country in which we are obliged to take a position, without depriving the inhabitants of the last morsel. This mode of subsisting, supposing the desired end could be answered by it, besides being in the highest degree distressing to individuals, is attended with ruin to the morals and discipline of the army. During the few days which we have been obliged to send out small parties to procure provisions for themselves, the most enormous excesses have been committed.

It has been no inconsiderable support of our cause, to have had it in our power to contrast the conduct of our army with that of the enemy, and to convince the inhabitants that, while their rights were wantonly violated by the British troops, by ours they were respected. This distinction must, unhappily, now cease, and we must assume the odious character of the plunderers instead of the protectors of the people; the direct consequence of which must be, to alienate their minds from the army and insensibly from the cause.

We have not yet been absolutely without flour, but we have this day, but one day's supply in camp, and I am not certain that there is a single barrel between this place and Trenton. I shall be obliged therefore to draw down one or two hundred barrels from a small magazine, which I had endeavored to establish at West Point, for the security of the garrison, in case of a sudden investiture.

From the above state of facts, it may be foreseen that this army cannot possibly remain much longer together, unless very vigorous and immediate measures are taken by the states to comply with the requisitions made upon them. The commissary general has neither the means nor the power of procuring supplies—he is only to receive them from the several agents. Without a speedy change of circumstances, this dilemma will be involved: either the army must disband, or what is, if possible, worse, subsist upon the plunder of the people. I would fain flatter myself that a knowledge of our situation will produce the desired relief: not a relief of a few days, as has generally hereto-fore been the case, but a supply equal to the establishment of magazines for the winter. If these are not formed before the roads are broken up by the weather, we shall certainly experience the same difficulties and distresses the ensuing winter which we did the last. Although the troops have, upon every occasion hitherto, borne their wants with unparalleled patience, it will be dangerous to trust too often to a repetition of the cause of discontent.

I have the honor to be, with great respect, your excellency's most obe-dient,

G. WASHINGTON

SOME PHILADELPHIANS COMPLAIN OF UNJUST TREATMENT

[To the President and Council of Pennsylvania, 1777]

The remonstrance of the subscribers, freemen, and inhabitants of the city of Philadelphia, now confined in the Free Mason's Lodge.

Sheweth—That the subscribers have been, by virtue of a warrant, signed in council by George Bryan, vice president, arrested in our houses, and on our lawful occasions, and conducted to this place, where we have been kept in close confinement, under a strong military guard, two or more days—that although divers of us demanded of the messengers, who arrested us, and insisted on having copies of the said warrant, yet were not able to pro-cure the same, till this present time, but have remained here unaccused and unheard. We now take the earliest opportunity of laying our grievances before your body, from whom we apprehend they proceed, and of claiming to our-selves the liberties and privileges to which we are entitled by the fundamental rules of justice by our birthright and inheritance, the laws of the land; and by the express provision of the present constitution, under which your board derive their power.

We apprehend, that no man can lawfully be deprived of his liberty, without a warrant from some persons having competent authority, specify-ing an offence against the laws of the land, supported by oath of affirmation of the accuser, and limiting the time of his imprisonment, until he is heard, or legally discharged, unless the party be found in the actual perpetration of a crime. Natural justice, equally with law, declares that the party accused should know what he is to answer to, and have an opportunity of shewing his innocence—These principles are strongly enforced in the ninth and tenth sections of the declaration of rights, which form a fundamental and inviolable part of the constitution, from which you derive your power. . . .

How far these principles have been adhered to, in the course of this business, we shall go on to shew.

Upon the examination of the said warrant, we find it is, in all respects, inadequate to these descriptions, altogether unprecedented in this or any free country, both in its substance and the latitude given to the messengers who were to execute it, and wholly subversive of the very constitution you profess to support. The only charge on which it is founded, is a recommendation of congress to apprehend and secure all persons who, in their general conduct and conversation, have evidenced a disposition inimical to the cause of America, and particularly naming some of us—but not suggesting the least offence to have been committed by us.

It authorizes the messengers to search all papers belonging to us, upon a bare possibility, that something political may be found, but without the least ground for a suspicion of the kind. . . .

It limits no time for the duration of our imprisonment, nor points at any hearing, which is an absolute requisite to make a legal warrant; but confounds in one warrant, the power to apprehend, and the authority to commit, without interposing a judicial officer between the parties and the messenger.

Upon the whole, we conceive this warrant, and the proceedings thereupon, to be far more dangerous in its tendency, and a more flagrant violation of every right which is dear to freemen, than any that can be found in the records of the English constitution. . . .

What adds further to this alarming strength of power is, that we are informed the vice president of the council, has declared to one of the magistrates of the city, who called on him to enquire into the cause of our confinement, that we were to be sent to Virginia *unheard*.

Scarcely could we believe such a declaration could have been made by a person who fills the second place in the government, till we were this day confirmed in the melancholy truth by three of the subscribers, whom you absolutely refused to hear in person, or by counsel.—We would remind you of the complaints urged by numbers of yourselves against the parliament of Great Britain, for condemning the town of Boston *unheard,* and we call upon you to reconcile your *present* conduct with your *then* professions, or your repeated declarations in favor of general liberty.

In the name, therefore, of the whole body of the freemen of Pennsylvania, whose liberties are radically struck at in this arbitrary imprisonment of us; their unoffending fellow-citizens—we demand an audience, that so our innocence may appear, and persecution give place to justice. . . .

4. VOICES OF DISSENT

LOYALISTS PETITION THE KING AND PARLIAMENT

[Address by American Loyalists published in the
London Chronicle, *March 9, 1782]*

The humble and dutiful declaration and address of his majesty's American
loyalists, to the king's most excellent majesty, to both houses of parliament and the people of Great Britain.

We, his majesty's most dutiful and faithful subjects, the loyal inhabitants of America, who have happily got within the protection of the British
forces, as well as those who, though too wise not to have foreseen the fatal
tendency of the present wanton and causeless rebellion, yet, from numberless obstacles, and unexampled severities, have hitherto been compelled to
remain under the tyranny of the rebels, and submit to the measures of congressional usurpation. . . .

The penalty under which any American subject enlists into his majesty's
service, is no less than the immediate forfeiture of all his goods and chattels,
lands and tenements; and if apprehended, and convicted by the rebels, of
having enlisted, or prevailed on any other person to enlist into his majesty's
service, it is considered as treason, and punished with death: Whereas, no
forfeiture is incurred, or penalty annexed, to his entering into the service of
congress; but, on the contrary, his property is secured, and himself rewarded.

In the former case, he withdraws himself from his family and relations,
without any possibility of receiving any assistance from or affording any
relief to either. In the latter, he is subject to no such peculiar self-denials,
and real distresses.—The embodying provincial corps in New York, and
sending them on services to Savannah—or in Philadelphia, and ordering
them to Pensacola, when they might be more usefully employed in the province where they were raised; the drafting troops from the corps, and from
under the command of officers with whom they enlisted, to form new corps,
and to give a command to other officers, are all measures which have had
their discouraging effects on the recruiting service.

The desultory manner also in which the war has been carried on, by first taking possession of Boston, Rhode Island, Philadelphia, Portsmouth, Norfolk, in Virginia, Wilmington, in North Carolina, etc., etc., and then evacuating them, whereby many thousand inhabitants have been involved in the greatest wretchedness is another substantial reason why more loyalists have not enlisted into his majesty's service, or openly espoused and attached themselves to the royal cause; yet, notwithstanding all these discouraging circumstances, there are many more men in his majesty's provincial regiments than there are in the continental service. Hence it cannot be doubted but that there are more loyalists in America than there are rebels; and also, that their zeal must be greater, or so many would not have enlisted into the provincial service, under such very unequal circumstances. Other reasons might be enumerated, why many more have not enlisted into his majesty's provincial service, if we were not prevented from it by motives of delicacy and tenderness to the character of the person to whose management the business of that department was principally committed. . . .

Relying with the fullest confidence upon national justice and compassion to our fidelity and distresses, we can entertain no doubts but that Great Britain will prevent the ruin of her American friends, at every risk short of certain destruction to herself. But if compelled, by adversity of misfortune, from the wicked and perfidious combinations and designs of numerous and powerful enemies abroad, and more criminal and dangerous enemies at home, an idea should be formed by Great Britain of relinquishing her American colonies to the usurpation of congress, we thus solemnly call God to witness that we think the colonies can never be so happy or so free as in a constitutional connection with, and dependence on Great Britain; convinced, as we are, that to be a British subject, with all its consequences, is to be the happiest and freest member of any civil society in the known world—we, therefore in justice to our members, in duty to ourselves, and in fidelity to our posterity, must not, cannot refrain from making this public declaration and appeal to the faithful subjects of every government, and the compassionate sovereign of every people, in every nation and kingdom of the world, that our principles are the principles of the virtuous and free; that our sufferings are the sufferings of unprotected loyalty, and persecuted fidelity; that our cause is the cause of legal and constitutional government, throughout the world; that, opposed by principals of republicanism, and convinced, from recent observation, that brutal violence, merciless severity, relentless cruelty, and discretionary outrages are the distinguished traits and ruling principles of the present system of congressional republicanism, our aversion is unconquerable, irreconcilable.—That we are attached to monarchical government, from past and happy experience—by duty, and by choice. That, to oppose insurrections, and to listen to the requests of people so circumstanced as we are, is the common interest of all mankind in civil society. That to support our rights, is to support the rights of every subject of legal government; and that to afford us relief, is at once the duty and security of every prince and sovereign on earth. . . .

We most humbly and ardently supplicate and entreat, that, by deputies or ambassadors, nominated and appointed by your majesty's suffering American loyalists, they may be permitted to solicit and obtain from other nations that interference, aid and alliance, which, by the blessing of Almighty God, may, in the last fatal and ultimate extreme, save and deliver us, his majesty's American loyalists, who, we maintain, in every one of the colonies, compose a great majority of the inhabitants, and those too the first in point of opulence and consequence, from the ruinous system of congressional independence and republican tyranny, detesting rebellion as we do, and preferring a subjection to any power in Europe, to the mortifying debasement of a state of slavery, and a life of insult, under the tyranny of congressional usurpation.

ANN SEWARD DISPARAGES THE CHARACTER OF WASHINGTON

[A poem written shortly after the execution of the British
spy Major John André, September 30, 1781]

A MONODY ON THE DEATH OF ANDRÉ

BY ANN SEWARD

Oh Washington! I thought thee great and good,
Nor knew thy Nero thirst for guiltless blood:
Severe to use the power that fortune gave,
Thou cool determined murderer of the grave.
Remorseless Washington! the day shall come
Of deep repentance for this barbarous doom;
When injured André's mem'ry shall inspire
A kindling army with resistless fire,
Each falchion sharpen that the Britons wield,
And lead their fiercest lion to the field;
Then, when each hope of thine shall end in night,
When dubious dread and unavailing flight
Impel your haste, thy guilt-upbraided soul
Shall wish, untouched, the precious life you stole;
And when thy heart, appalled and vanquished pride,

Shall vainly ask the mercy you denied,
With horror shalt thou meet the fate thou gave,
Nor pity gild the darkness of thy grave.

5. THE LIGHTER SIDE

THE HISTORY OF JOHN BULL'S CHILDREN

[From the Maryland Gazette, *August 1778, into which it was
copied from the* London Chronicle]

I, sir Humphry Polesworth, who formerly gave the world a true and
faithful account of John Bull, and of his mother, and sister, and wives, and
his servants, now write the history of his children and how they were got,
and how they were educated, and what befel them. Courteous reader, if thou
hast any curiosity to know these things, read the following chapters and
learn.

Chap. I. Of seven natural children, which John Bull had in his younger
days by Doll Secretary, his mother's maid; namely, three boys, John, jun. or
Master Jacky, Yorky, and Jerry; four girls, Penelope, Mary, Virgey, and
Caroline. How the old lady would suffer no bastards in her family; and how
the poor infants were turned adrift on the fish ponds as soon as born; how
they landed on the western shore, and were there nursed by a wild bear, all
under the green wood tree.

Chap. II. How John disowned them, and left them to get over the children's disorders the best way they could, without paying a farthing for nurses,
or apothecary bills; and how, as soon as they had cut their eye teeth, and
were able to walk alone, John claimed them for his own.

Chap. III. How Master Jacky turned fisherman and ship-carpenter;
Yorky and Jerry drove a great trade; Miss Penny dealt in flour, called the
Maid of the Mill, and never courtseyed to any body: How Mary and Virgey
set up a snuff-shop, and Caroline turned dry-salter, and sold indigo; how
they all flourished exceedingly, and laid out every penny they earned in their
father's warehouse.

Chap. IV. Of two children more, which John had afterwards in lawful
wedlock, viz., a boy which he called Georgey, after his great patron, and a
girl, which he called Peg, after his sister Margaret; how he crammed them
with sugar-plums, and how they remained sickly, ricketty brats at this day.

Chap. V. How young Master Baboon, old Louis' only son, fell in love with Miss Virgey; and how he came behind with intent to ravish her; how she squealed and alarmed her dad.

Chap. VI. How John called for his stick and his barge, and crossed the pond to save his daughter's virtue; how young Louis gave him a confounded rap on his fingers, and drove him back, and then at his daughter again.

Chap. VII. How her brother Jack came to her assistance, and threw young Louis on his back; how old Louis Baboon flew to help his son, and carried lord Strutt along with him; how John Bull returned and mustered all his children at his back, and to it they went.

Chap. VIII. How they had a long tustle; how John's children saved their old dad from a broken head, and helped to seize young Louis and tie him; how the old folks agreed to leave young Louis in custody, and drink friends themselves; and how John made his children pay a share of the reckoning without giving them any of the drink.

Chap. IX. How John in his cups bragged of his exploits, and said he had done all himself, and his children nothing; how he made choice of fair George, the gentle shepherd, for his house steward, because he could tell, without the book, that two and three made five, and had the multiplication table by heart.

Chap. X. The whole stewardship of fair George; how he neglected to protest Louis Baboon's note of hand on the day of payment, released lord Strutt from a mortgage on his manor of Eastland; how he took an aversion to cider, and would allow none to be drank in his family; how he rummaged every man's chest for pen, ink, and paper, and obliged those he catched writing to stand a-top of the table, with a wooden neckcloth under their chin, while he counted sixty times sixty: and how this is called the gentle shepherd's benefit of clergy unto this day.

Chap. XI. How fair George took an antipathy to John's children, because he said they put nothing into the box at Christmas; and when they came to pay their shop accounts, they brought in their money at the back door; how he advised John to brand them on the far buttock, as they do stray cattle, that he might know them to be his own.

Chap. XII. How John's children rode restiff, and swore they would not have the broad R. stampt on their b—ck s—des: how John, in heating the irons, burnt his own fingers most d—ly; how all his neighbors laughed, and fair George could not find him a plaster.

Chap. XIII. How John, in a passion, kicked fair George down stairs, and rung up other servants; how they advised him to consult his wife; and how Mrs. Bull bid him let his children alone; that, tho' born in sin, they were his own flesh and blood, and needed no stamp to shew it; how John took her advice, and let the irons cool again; and how some suspected if John's fingers had not smarted, he would not have complied so soon.

Chap. XIV. A dialogue on education, between fair George and lame Will; how Will proved it to be both cruel and impolitic to pinch children till they cry, and then pinch them for crying; and how George answered and said nothing.

Chap. XV. How John, by means of his new servants, became beloved of his children, and respected by his neighbors; how he obliged Louis Baboon to beat down the wall of Ecclesdown castle, because it overlooked his pond, and harbored sea-gulls to gobble up his fish; how he made him also pay up his note of hand and how lord Strutt—

But, Mr. Printer, I have given you enough to judge of the general plan of this history. Pray let me have your opinion as to the publication. My notion at present is, to send it abroad in six-penny numbers, and engage the country carriers to take it down; it may pass for political an hundred miles from town.

A RIDICULE OF GENERAL BURGOYNE'S PROCLAMATION

[*An anonymous reply to General Burgoyne's proclamation to the people of Saratoga, New York, dated July 2, 1777, which called for their submission to the British Army*]

TO JOHN BURGOYNE, ESQ. lieutenant general of his majesty's armies in America, colonel of the queen's regiment of light dragoons, governor of Fort William in North Britain, one of the representatives of Great Britain, and commanding an army and fleet employed on an expedition from Canada, etc. etc.

MOST HIGH, MOST MIGHTY, MOST PUISSANT AND SUBLIME GENERAL!

When the forces under your command arrived at Quebec in order to act in concert and upon a common principle with the numerous fleets and armies which already display in every quarter of America, the justice and mercy of your king, we, the reptiles of America, were struck with unusual trepidation and astonishment. But what words can express the plenitude of our horror, when the colonel of the queen's regiment of light dragoons advanced toward Ticonderoga. The mountains shook before thee, and the trees of the forest bowed their lofty heads—the vast lakes of the north were chilled at thy presence, and the mighty cataracts stopped their tremendous career, and were suspended in awe at thy approach. Judge, then, Oh! ineffable governor of Fort William in North Britain, what must have been the terror, dismay, and despair that overspread this paltry continent of America, and us, its wretched inhabitants. Dark and dreary indeed, was the prospect before us, till, like the sun in the horizon, your most gracious, sublime, and irresistible proclamation, opened the doors of mercy, and snatched us, as it were from the jaws of annihilation.

We foolishly thought, blind as we were, that your gracious master's fleets and armies were come to destroy us and our liberties; but we are happy in hearing from you (and who can doubt what you assert?) that they were called forth for the sole purpose of restoring the rights of the constitution, to a forward and stubborn generation.

And is it for this, Oh! sublime lieutenant general, that you have given yourself the trouble to cross the wide Atlantic, and with incredible fatigue traverse uncultivated wilds? And we ungratefully refuse the proffered blessing? —To restore the rights of the constitution you have called together an amiable host of savages, and turned them loose to scalp our women and children, and lay our country waste—this they have performed with their usual skill and clemency; and yet we remain insensible of the benefit, and unthankful for so much goodness.

Our congress have declared independence, and our assemblies, as your highness justly observes, have most wickedly imprisoned the avowed friends of that power with which they are at war, and most profanely compelled those, whose consciences will not permit them to fight, to pay some small part toward the expenses their country is at, in supporting what is called a necessary defensive war. If we go on thus in our obstinacy and ingratitude, what can we expect, but that you should, in your anger, give a stretch to the Indian forces under your direction amounting to thousands, to overtake and destroy us! or, which is ten times worse, that you should withdraw your fleets and armies, and leave us to our own misery, without completing the benevolent task you have begun, of restoring to us the rights of the constitution.

We submit—we submit—most puissant colonel of the queen's regiment of light dragoons, and governor of Fort William in North Britain! We offer our heads to the scalping knife, and our bellies to the bayonet. Who can resist the force of your eloquence? Who can withstand the terror of your arms? The invitation you have made, in the consciousness of Christianity, your royal master's clemency, and the honor of soldiership, we thankfully accept. The blood of the slain, the cries of injured virgins and innocent children, and the never ceasing sighs and groans of starving wretches, now languishing in the jails and prison ships of New York, call on us in vain; while your sublime proclamation is sounded in our ears. Forgive us, O our country! Forgive us, dear posterity! Forgive us, all ye foreign powers, who are anxiously watching our conduct in this important struggle, if we yield implicitly to the persuasive tongue of the most elegant colonel of her majesty's regiment of light dragoons.

Forbear, then, thou magnanimous lieutenant general! Forbear to denounce the vengeance against us—Forbear to give a stretch to those restorers of constitutional rights, the Indian forces under your direction.—Let not the messengers of justice and wraith await us in the field, and devastation, and every concomitant horror, bar our return to the allegiance of a prince, who, by his royal will, would deprive us of every blassing of life, with all possible clemency.

We are domestic, we are industrious, we are infirm and timid: we shall remain quietly at home, and not remove our cattle, our corn, or forage, in hopes that you will come, at the head of troops, in the full powers of health, discipline, and valor, and take charge of them for yourselves. Behold our wives and daughters, our flocks and herds, our goods and chattels, are they not at the mercy of our lord the king, and of his lieutenant general, member of the house of commons, and governor of Fort William in North Britain?

A.B.
C.D.
E.F. etc. etc.

Saratoga, 10th July, 1777.

PROPOSALS FOR AN EXCHANGE OF GENERAL BURGOYNE

*[A satirical comment ascribed to Governor William Livingston
of New Jersey on the capture of General Burgoyne]*

Should the report of General Burgoyne's having infringed the capitulation, between Major General Gates and himself, prove to be true, our superiors will doubtless take proper care to prevent his reaping any benefit from it; and should he be detained as a prisoner for his infraction of any of the articles, I would humbly propose to exchange him in such manner, as will at the same time flatter his vanity and redound to the greatest emolument of America. To evince the reasonableness of my proposal, I would observe, that by the same parity of reason, that a general is exchanged for a general, a colonel for a colonel, and so on, with respect to other officers, mutually of equal rank, we ought to have for one and the same gentleman, who shall happen to hold both those offices, both a general and a colonel. This will appear evident from the consideration that those exchanges are never regulated by viewing the persons exchanged in the light of men, but as officers; since otherwise, a colonel might as well be exchanged for a sergeant as for an officer of his own rank, a sergeant being, undoubtedly, equally a man, and, as the case sometimes happens, more of a man too. One prisoner, therefore, having twenty different offices, ought to redeem from captivity twenty prisoners aggregately holding the same offices; or such greater or less number as shall, with respect to rank, be equal to his twenty offices. This being admitted, I think General Burgoyne is the most profitable prisoner we could have taken, having more offices, or (what amounts to the same thing in Old England) more titles, than any gentleman on this side of the Ganges. And as his impetuous excellency certainly meant to avail himself of his titles, by their pompous display in his proclamation, had he proved conqueror, it is but reasonable that we should avail ourselves of them now he is conquered; and, till I meet with a better project for that purpose, I persuade myself that the following proposal will appropriate them to a much better use, than they were ever applied to before.

The exchange I propose is as follows:

I. For John Burgoyne, esquire.

Some worthy justice of the peace, magnanimously stolen out of his bed, or taken from his farm by a band of ruffians in the uniform of British soldiers, and now probably perishing with hunger and cold in a loathsome jail in New York.

II. For John Burgoyne, lieutenant general of his majesty's armies in America.

Two major generals.

III. For John Burgoyne, colonel of the queen's regiment of light dragoons.

As the British troops naturally prize every thing in proportion as it partakes of royalty, and under value whatever originates from a republican government, I suppose a colonel of her majesty's own regiment will procure at least three continental colonels of the horse.

IV. For Burgoyne, governor of fort William in North Britain.

Here I would demand one governor of one of the United States, as his multitulary excellency is governor of a fort; and two more, as that fort is in North Britain, which his Britannic majesty may be presumed to value in that proportion; but considering that the said fort is called William, which may excite in his majesty's mind the rebellious idea of liberty, I deduct one upon that account, and rather than puzzle the cartel with any perplexity, I am content with two governors.

V.   For John Burgoyne, one of the representatives of Great Britain.
The first member of congress who may fall into the enemy's hands.
VI.   For John Burgoyne, commander of a fleet employed in an expedition from Canada.
The admiral of our navy.
VII.   For John Burgoyne, commander of an army employed in an expedition from Canada.
One commander-in-chief in any of our departments.
VIII.   For John Burgoyne, etc., etc., etc.

Some connoisseurs in hieroglyphics imagine that these three et ceteras are emblematical of three certain occult qualities in the general, which he never intends to exhibit in more legible characters, viz., prudence, modesty, and humanity. Others suppose that they stand for king of America; and that, had he proved successful, he would have fallen upon general Howe, and afterward have set upon for himself. Be this as it may, (which it however behoves a certain gentleman on the other side of the water seriously to consider) I insist upon it, that as all dark and cabalistical characters are suspicious, these incognoscible enigmas may portend much more than is generally apprehended. At all events, general Burgoyne has availed himself of their importance, and I doubt not they excited as much terror in his proclamation, as any of his more luminous titles. As his person, therefore, is by the capture, become the property of the congress, all his titles, (which some suppose to constitute his very essence) whether more splendid or opaque, latent or invisible, are become, ipso facto the lawful goods and chattels of the continent, and ought not to be restored without a consideration equivalent. If we should happen to over-rate them, it is his own fault, it being in his power to ascertain their intrinsic value; and it is a rule in law, that when a man is possessed of evidence to disprove what is alleged against him, and refuses to produce it, the presumption raised against him, is to be taken for granted. Certain it is, that these three et ceteras must stand for three somethings, and as these three somethings must, at least, be equal to three somethings without rank or title, I had some thoughts of setting them down for three privates; but then as they are three somethings in general Burgoyne, which must be of twice the value of three any things, in any three privates, I shall only double them, and demand in exchange for these three problematical, enigmatical, hieroglyphical, mystic, necromantic, cabalistical and portentous et ceteras, six privates.

So that, according to my plan, we ought to detain this ideal conqueror of the North, now a real prisoner in the East, till we have got in exchange for him, one esquire, two major generals, three colonels of light horse, two governors, one member of congress, the admiral of our navy, one commander in chief in a separate department, and six privates; which is probably more than this extraordinary hero would fetch in any part of Great Britain, were he exposed at public auction for a day and a year. All which is nevertheless, humbly submitted to the consideration of the honorable the congress, and his excellency general Washington.

BENEDICT ARNOLD IS BURNED IN EFFIGY

[The burning of an effigy of Benedict Arnold in Philadelphia,
September 1780, as reported in a local newspaper]

A stage raised on the body of a cart, on which was an effigy of general Arnold sitting; this was dressed in regimentals, had two faces, emblematical of his traitorous conduct, a mask in his left hand, and a letter in his right from Beelzebub, telling him that he had done all the mischief he could do, and now he must hang himself.

At the back of the general, was a figure of the devil, dressed in black robes, shaking a purse of money at the general's left ear, and in his right hand a pitch-fork, ready to drive him into hell, as the reward due for the many crimes which his thirst of gold had made him commit.

In the front of the stage, and before general Arnold, was placed a large lantern of transparent paper, with the consequences of his crimes thus delineated, i.e., on one part general Arnold on his knees before the devil, who is pulling him into the flames—a label from the general's mouth with these words, "My dear sir, I have served you faithfully," to which the devil replies, "And I'll reward you." On another side, two figures hanging, inscribed, "The Traitor's Reward," and wrote underneath, "The adjutant general of the British army, and Joe Smith, the first hanged as a spy, and the other as a traitor to his country." And on the front of the lantern was wrote the following:—

"Major general Benedict Arnold, late commander of the fort West Point. The crime of this man is high treason.

"He has deserted the important post, West Point, on Hudson's river, committed to his charge by his excellency the commander in chief, and is gone off to the enemy at New York.

"His design to have given up this fortress to our enemies has been discovered by the goodness of the Omniscient Creator, who has not only prevented him from carrying it into execution, but has thrown into our hands André, the adjutant general of their army, who was detected in the infamous character of a spy.

"The treachery of the ungrateful general is held up to public view, for the exposition of infamy; and to proclaim, with joyful acclamation, another instance of the interposition of bounteous Providence.

"The effigy of this ingrate is therefore hanged (for want of his body) as a traitor to his native country, and a betrayer of the laws of honor."

The procession began about four o'clock, in the following order:

Several gentlemen mounted on horseback.
    A line of continental officers.
    Sundry gentlemen in a line.
    A guard of the city infantry.
Just before the cart, drums and fifes playing the Rogue's march.
    Guards on each side.

The procession was attended with a numerous concourse of people, who, after expressing their abhorrence of the treason and the traitor, committed him to the flames, and left both the effigy and the original to sink into ashes and oblivion.

VIII

WINNING THE WAR,

1776-1783

THE MILITARY SIDE of the American War for Independence has received exhaustive treatment by historians and laymen alike. Much of it is deeply woven into the fabric of American nationalism: the discouraging defeats of the first year, Washington's brilliant counterattack at Trenton on Christmas Day, 1776, the surrender of Burgoyne at Saratoga in 1777, the bitter winter at Valley Forge in 1777–1778, the victory at Yorktown when the band played "The World Turned Upside Down."

Hezekiah Niles had no intention of documenting the course of battle; his aim was to "represent the feelings that prevailed." Thus the selections in this chapter touch on many phases of the war that ordinarily receive short shrift, though the war itself is not entirely neglected. In fact the first selections give a glimpse of some of the military episodes that heartened Americans—episodes that had much to do with keeping alive the spirit of '76. The achievements of George Washington at Trenton (p. 277), of John Paul Jones off the coast of the British Isles (p. 279), and of "Mad-Anthony" Wayne at Stony Point, New York, are cases in point.

But the war years involved much more. There were the brutalities of Indian allies of the British (p. 283) and the machinations of the tories (p. 285). There was the surprisingly professional work of American diplomats in dealing with both friend and foe (pp. 286, 288, and 289), and there was, after 1778, the pleasant problem of how Americans would respond to an ally who played so large a role in ensuring their independence (pp. 291, 292, 293).

The most notable example of French aid came at Yorktown, and on this crucial battle Hezekiah Niles did collect a number of pertinent documents.

They range from a letter by George Mason shortly before the siege (p. 294), through accounts of the war itself (pp. 296, 300, and 301), to reports on the reaction on both sides of the Atlantic to the news of Cornwallis's surrender (pp. 303, 307).

The victory at Yorktown, Virginia, in October 1781 marked the end of the struggle, although scattered fighting lasted some months longer. For the most part the next two years were occupied by waiting—waiting for peace negotiations to be concluded and for the armies to withdraw from American cities. Finally in November 1783 the last redcoats embarked from New York City. General Washington was present on that occasion to help the citizens of New York celebrate the end of the war (pp. 308, and 309). American independence had come at last.

1. AMERICAN FORCES KEEP THE BRITISH OFF BALANCE

THOMAS RODNEY DESCRIBES THE TRENTON CAMPAIGN

[*Letter from Thomas Rodney to his brother Caesar, from Allen's Town, New Jersey, December 30, 1776*]

Allen's Town, in Jersey, 12 miles from Princeton, 20 do. from Brunswick,
    Dec. 30, 1776.

SIR—I wrote you a long letter on the 24th, which I had no opportunity of sending, and left it in my trunk at Mr. Coxe's, two miles from Bristol; it contains the news to that time, which I cannot repeat here. On the 25th inst. in the evening, we received orders to be at Shamony ferry as soon as possible. We were there according to orders in two hours, and met the riflemen, who were the first from Bristol; we were ordered from thence to Dunk's ferry, on the Delaware, and the whole army of about 2000 men followed, as soon as the artillery got up. The three companies of Philadelphia infantry and mine were formed into a body, under the command of captain Henry, (myself second in command) which were embarked immediately to cover the landing of the troops. We landed with great difficulty through the ice, and formed on the ferry shore, about 200 yards from the river. It was as severe a night as ever I saw, and after two battalions were landed, the storm increased so much, and the river was so full of ice, that it was impossible to get the artillery over; for we had to walk 100 yards on the ice to get on shore. Gen. Cadwallader therefore ordered the whole to retreat again, and we had to stand at least six hours under arms—first to cover the landing and till all the rest had retreated again—and, by this time, the storm of wind, hail, rain and snow, with the ice, was so bad, that some of the infantry could not get back till next day. This design was to have surprised the enemy at Black Horse and Mount Holley, at the same time that Washington surprised them at Trenton; and had we succeeded in getting over, we should have finished all our troubles. Washington took 910 prisoners, with 6 pieces of fine artillery, and all their baggage in Trenton. The next night I received orders to be in Bristol before day; we were there accordingly, and about 9 o'clock began to embark one mile above Bristol, and about 3 o'clock in the afternoon got all our troops and artillery over, consisting of about 3000 men, and began our march to Burlington—the infantry, flanked by the riflemen, making the advanced guard. We got there about 9 o'clock and took possession of the town, but found the enemy had made precipitate retreat the day before, bad as the weather was, in a great panic. The whole infantry and riflemen were then ordered to set out that night and make a forced march to Bordentown, (which was about 11 miles), which they did, and took possession of the town about 9 o'clock, with a large quantity of the enemy's stores, which they had not time to carry off. We stayed there till the army came up; and the general finding the enemy were but a few miles ahead, ordered the infantry to proceed to a town called Croswick's four miles from Bordentown, and they were followed by one of the Philadelphia and one of the New England battalions. We got there about 8 o'clock, and at about 10, (after we were all in quarters), were informed that the enemy's baggage was about 16 miles from us, under a guard of 300 men. Some of the militia colonels applied to the infantry to make a forced march that night and overhaul them. We had then been on duty four nights and days, making forced marches, without six hours sleep in the whole time; whereupon the infantry officers of all the companies unanimously declared it was madness to attempt, for that it would knock up all our brave men, not one of whom had yet gave out, but every one will suppose were much fatigued. They then sent off a party who were fresh, but they knocked up before they got up with them, and came back and met us at this town next morning. They surrounded a house where there was six tories—took three of them—one got off—and one who ran and would not stop, was shot dead. They gave him warning first by calling, and at last shot two bullets over his head, but he still persisted, and the next two shot; one bullet went through his arm and one through his heart. The enemy have fled before us in the greatest panic that ever was known; we heard this moment that they have fled from Princeton, and that they were hard pressed by Washington. Never were men in higher spirits than our whole army is; none are sick, and all are determined to extirpate them from the Jersey, but I believe the enemy's fears will do it before we get up with them. The Hessians, from the general to the common soldier, curse and imprecate the war, and swear they were sent here to be slaughtered; that they never will leave New York again, till they sail for Europe. Jersey will be the most whiggish colony on the continent; the very Quakers declare for taking up arms. You cannot imagine the distress of this country. They have stripped every body almost without distinction—even of all their clothes, and have beat and abused men, women and children, in the most cruel manner ever heard of. We have taken a number of prisoners, in our route, Hessians and British, to the amount of about twenty. It seems likely through the blessing of Providence, that we shall retake Jersey again without the loss of a man, except one gen. Washington lost at Trenton. The enemy seem to be bending their way to Amboy with all speed, but I hope we shall come up with the Princeton baggage yet, and also get a share of their large stores at Brunswick. I hope if I live, to see the conquest of Jersey, and set off home again in two weeks. Some of my men have complained a little, but not to say sick; they are all now well here.

THOMAS RODNEY.

JOHN PAUL JONES GIVES THE BRITISH ISLES A TASTE OF WAR

[Letter from Commodore Jones to the Countess of Selkirk]

RANGER, BREST, 8th May, 1778

MADAM—It cannot be too much lamented, that, in the profession of arms, the officer of finer feeling, and of real sensibility, should be under the necessity of winking at any action of persons under his command which his heart cannot approve; but the reflection is doubly severe, when he finds himself obliged, in appearance, to countenance such action by authority.

This hard case was mine, when, on the 23d of April last I landed on St. Mary's Isle. Knowing lord Selkirk's interest with the king, I wished to make him the happy instrument of alleviating the horrors of hopeless captivity, when the brave are overpowered and made prisoners of war. It was perhaps fortunate for you, madam, that he was from home, for it was my intention to have taken him on board the Ranger, and to have detained him, until through his means, a general and fair exchange of prisoners, as well in Europe as in America had been effected.

When I was informed by some men whom I met at landing, that his lordship was absent, I walked back to my boat, determined to leave the island. By the way, however, some officers who were with me, could not forbear expressing their discontent, observing, that in America no delicacy was shown by the English, who took away all sorts of movable property, setting fire not only to towns, and to the houses of the rich without distinction, but not even sparing the wretched hamlets and milch-cows of the poor and helpless, at the approach of an inclement winter. That party had been with me as volunteers the same morning at Whitehaven; some complaisance, therefore, was their due. I had but a moment to think how I might gratify them, and, at the same time, do your ladyship the least injury. I charged the two officers to permit none of the seamen to enter the house, or to hurt anything about it; to treat you, madam, with the utmost respect, to accept of the plate which was offered; and to come away without making a search, or demanding anything else. I am induced to believe that I was punctually obeyed, since I am informed that the plate which they brought away is far short of the quantity which is expressed in the inventory which accompanied it. I have gratified my men, and when the plate is sold I shall become the purchaser, and will gratify my own feelings, by restoring it to you by such conveyance as you shall please to direct.

Had the earl been on board the following evening, he would have seen the awful pomp and dreadful carnage of a sea engagement; both affording ample subject for the pencil, as well as melancholy reflection for the contemplative mind. Humanity starts back at such scenes of horror, and cannot but execrate the vile promoters of this detested war:

> *For they, twas they, unsheathed the ruthless blade,*
> *And Heaven shall ask the havoc it has made.*

The British ship of war Drake, mounting twenty guns, with more than her full complement of officers and men, besides a number of volunteers, came out from Carrickfergus, in order to attack and take the continental ship of war Ranger, of eighteen guns, and short of her complement of officers and men; the ships met, and the advantage was disputed with great fortitude on each side for an hour and five minutes, when the gallant commander of the Drake fell, and victory declared in favor of the Ranger. His amiable lieutenant lay mortally wounded, besides near forty of the inferior officers and crew killed and wounded. A melancholy demonstration of the uncertainty of human prospects. I buried them in a spacious grave, with the honors due to the memory of the brave. . . . Let me entreat you, madam, to use your soft persuasive arts with your husband, to endeavor to stop this cruel and destructive war, in which Britain never can succeed. Heaven can never countenance the barbarous and unmanly practices of the Britons in America, which savages would blush at, and which, if not discontinued, will soon be retaliated in Britain by a justly enraged people. Should you fail in this, (for I am persuaded you will attempt it—and who can resist the power of such an advocate?) your endeavors to effect a general exchange of prisoners will be an act of humanity, which will afford you golden feelings on a death bed. . . .

General Wayne Prepares to Take Stony Point

[Orders of General Anthony Wayne of the Continental Army to his men on the night before their attack on Stony Point, New York]

Headquarters, Fort Montgomery,
Light Infantry—July 15, 1779

The troops will parade on beating the assemble. Taking it from the right, they will march on beating the troops, and move by the right. Proper halting places will be fixed and every officer and non-commissioned officer will remain with and be accountable for every man of their platoons. No soldier to be permitted to quit the ranks on any pretence whatever until a general halt is made, and then to be attended by one of the officers of the platoons. As soon as the troops assemble, this order to be read at the head of each:

The troops will march from Clement's to Stony Point, at 11 o'clock, and move by the right. Every officer and non-commissioned officer will remain with and be accountable for every man in his platoon. No soldier to be permitted to quit the ranks on any pretence whatever, until a general halt is made, and then to be attended by one of the officers of the platoon.

When the van of the troops arrive in the rear of the hill, col. Fabager will form his regiment in a solid column of half platoons, in front, as fast as they come up; col. Meigs will form next in Fabager's rear and major Hull in the rear of Meigs, which will be the right column; col. Butler will form a column on the left of Fabager, and major Murphy in his rear—every officer and soldier will then fix a piece of white paper in his hat or cap, to distinguish him from the enemy.

At the word march, col. Flury will take charge of 100 determined and picked men, properly officered, with their guns unloaded, their whole dependence to be on their bayonets, will move 20 paces in front of the column by the rout No. 1, enter the sally port C., he is to detach an officer and 20 men a little in front of him, whose business it will be to secure the sentries, and remove the abattes, and other obstructions, for the column to pass through. The column will follow close in the rear, with shouldered arms, under the command of col. Fabager, with gen. Wayne in person; when the works are forced, (and not before) the victorious troops will as they enter give the watchword, the Ford's our own, with repeated and loud voice, driving the enemy from their works and guns, which will favor the pass of the whole; should the enemy refuse to surrender, or attempt to make their escape by water or otherwise, vigorous means must be used to compel them to the former, and prevent their accomplishing the latter. Col. Butler will move by the rout No. 2, preceded by 100 men with fixed bayonets and unloaded muskets, under the command of major Stewart, who will observe a distance of 20 paces in front of the column, which will immediately follow under the command of col. Butler, with shouldered muskets, and will enter the sally-port C. or D.

The officer commanding the above 100 men will also detach a proper officer, with 20 men, a little in front, to remove the obstructions—as soon as they gain the work, they will also give and continue the watch-word, which will prevent confusion and mistakes.

Major Murphy will follow colonel Butler to the first figure, No. 3, where he will divide a little to the right and left and wait the attack on the right, which will be a signal to begin and keep up a perpetual and galling fire, and endeavor to enter between, and pass the work A. A. If any soldier presumes to take his musket from his shoulder, attempts to fire or begin the battle till ordered by his proper officers, he shall be immediately put to death by the officer next to him; for the cowardice and misconduct of one man is not to put the whole in danger and disorder with impunity. After the troops begin to advance to the works, the strictest silence must be observed and the greatest attention paid to the command of the officers; as soon as the lines are secured, the officers of the artillery, with their commands, will take possession of the cannon, to the end that the shipping may be secured and the Fort at Verplank's Point annoyed, so as to facilitate the attack upon that quarter. The general has the fullest confidence in the bravery and fortitude of the corps he has the happiness to command. The distinguished honor conferred on every officer and soldier who has been drafted into this corps, by his excellency general Washington, the credit of the states they respectively belong to and their own reputation will be such powerful motives for each man to distinguish himself, that the general cannot have the least doubt of a glorious victory: And further, he solemnly engages to reward the first man who enters the works with $500 and immediate preference, to the second 400, to the third

300, to the fourth 200, to the fifth 100, and will report the conduct of every officer and soldier who distinguishes himself on this occasion, in the most favorable point of view, to his excellency, who always takes the greatest pleasure in rewarding merit. But should there be any soldier so lost to every feeling, every sense of honor, as to attempt to retreat one single foot, or shrink from the places of danger, the officer next to him is to put him immediately to death, that he may no longer disgrace the name of a soldier, the corps or the state to which he belongs.

As the general is determined to share the dangers of the night, so he wishes to participate [in] the glory of the day, in common with his brother soldiers.

(Signed)   A. Wayne.

2. AMERICANS LEARN THE HORRORS OF WAR

Chatham Decries the Use of Indian Allies

*[Speech by William Pitt, Earl of Chatham, to the House
of Lords in opposition to a proposal that Indians be
employed against the American colonists, 1777]*

My Lords—I am astonished to hear such principles confessed! I am shocked to hear them avowed in this house, or in this country! Principles, equally unconstitutional, inhuman, and unchristian!

My lords, I did not intend to have encroached again on your attention; but I cannot repress my indignation. I feel myself impelled by every duty. My lords, we are called upon as members of this house, as men, as Christian men, to protest against such notions standing near the throne, polluting the ear of majesty. "That God and nature put into our hands!" I know not what ideas that lord may entertain of God and nature; but I know, that such abominable principles are equally abhorrent to religion and humanity.

What! to attribute the sacred sanction of God and nature to the massacres of the Indian scalping knife? to the cannibal savage, torturing, murdering, roasting, and eating; literally, my lords, eating the mangled victims of his barbarous battles! Such horrible notions shock every precept of religion, divine or natural, and every generous feeling of humanity. And, my lords, they shock every sentiment of honor; they shock me as a lover of honorable war, and a detester of murderous barbarity.

These abominable principles, and this, more abominable avowal of them; demand the most decisive indignation. I call upon that right reverend bench, those holy ministers of the gospel, and pious pastors of our church: I conjure them to join in the holy work, and vindicate the religion of their God. I appeal to wisdom and the law of this learned bench, to defend and support the justice of their country. I call upon the bishops to interpose the unsullied sanctity of their lawn; upon the learned judges, to interpose the purity of their ermine, to save us from this pollution. I call upon the honor of your lordships to reverence the dignity of your ancestors, and to maintain your own. I call upon the spirit and humanity of my country, to vindicate the national character. I invoke the genius of the constitution.

From the tapestry that adorn these walls, the immortal ancestor of this noble lord frowns with indignation at the disgrace of his country. In vain he led your victorious fleet against the boasted armada of Spain, in vain he defended and established the honor, the liberties, the religion, the protestant religion of this country, against the arbitrary cruelties of popery and the inquisition, if these more than popish cruelties and inquisitorial practices are let loose among us; to turn forth into our settlements, among our ancient connections, friends, and relations, the merciless cannibal, thirsting for the blood of man, woman and child! to send forth the infidel savage—against whom? against your protestant brethren; to lay waste their country; to desolate their dwellings, and extirpate their race and name, with these horrible hell-hounds of savage warfare!

Spain armed herself with blood-hounds, to extirpate the wretched natives of America; and we improve on the human example even of Spanish cruelty. We turn loose these savage hell-hounds against our brethren and countrymen in America, of the same language, laws, liberty, and religion, endeared to us by every tie that should sanctify humanity.

My lords, this awful subject, so important to our honor, our constitution, and our religion, demands the most solemn and effectual inquiry. And I again call upon your lordships and the united power of the state, to examine it thoroughly, and decisively, and to stamp upon it an indelible stigma of the public abhorrence. And I again implore those holy prelates of our religion, to do away these iniquities from among us. Let them perform a lustration; let them purify this house, and this country from this sin.

My lords, I am old and weak and at present unable to say more; but my feelings and indignation were too strong to have said less. I could not have slept this night in my bed, nor reposed my head upon my pillow, without giving this vent to my eternal abhorrence of such preposterous and enormous principles.

CONGRESS ADVISES RETALIATION AGAINST THE TORIES

*[Resolutions passed by the Continental Congress,
October 21, 1778]*

Whereas, there is every reason to expect that our unnatural enemies, despairing of being ever able to subdue and enslave us by open force, or persuade us to break through the solemn treaties, as having entered into with our great and good ally, his most Christian majesty, and return to the dependence of Great Britain, will, as the last effort, ravage, burn, and destroy every city and town on this continent they can come at:

Resolved, That it be recommended to such inhabitants of these states, as live in places exposed to the ravages of the enemy, immediately to build huts, at least thirty miles distant from their present habitations, there to convey their women, children, and others not capable of bearing arms, and themselves in case of necessity, together with their furniture, wares, and merchandise of every sort; also, that they send off all their cattle; being measures they cannot think hardships in such times of public calamity, when so many of their gallant countrymen are daily exposed in the hardships of the field, fighting in defence of their rights and liberties.

Resolved, That, immediately, when the enemy begin to burn or destroy any town, it be recommended to the good people of these states to set fire to, ravage, burn, and destroy, the houses and properties of all tories, and enemies to the freedom and independence of America, and secure the persons of such, so as to prevent them from assisting the enemy, always taking care not to treat them or their families with any wanton cruelties, as we do not wish, in this particular, to copy after our enemies or their German, negro, and copper-colored allies.

Extract from the minutes,

CHARLES THOMSON, Sec.

3. AMERICAN DIPLOMACY HELPS BRING SUCCESS

THE HOWE BROTHERS ARE REBUFFED

[Address by an unidentified Charlestonian to Admiral Richard Howe and General William Howe, October 22, 1776]

CHARLESTON, S.C., October 22, 1776

MY LORD AND SIR—Your declaration at New York has reached this place. It has occasioned surprise and concern. The known honor and abilities of your excellencies, and your declaration, appear perfect contrasts. The latter is an unnatural production. Hurt, as I am to see your names so prostituted, I cannot restrain myself from making a few remarks to your excellencies upon a subject which, by endangering your reputation, distresses every generous mind. I shall first state your declaration.

"BY RICHARD VISCOUNT HOWE, of the kingdom of Ireland, and WILLIAM HOWE, Esq. general of his majesty's forces in America, the king's COMMISSIONERS for restoring peace to his majesty's colonies and plantations in North America, etc. etc.

DECLARATION

"Although the congress, whom the misguided Americans suffer to direct the opposition to a re-establishment of the constitutional government of these provinces have disavowed every purpose of reconciliation not consonant with their extravagant and inadmissible claim of independence, the king's commissioners think fit to declare that they are equally desirous to confer with his majesty's well affected subjects upon the means of restoring the public tranquility, and establishing a permanent union with every colony as a part of the British empire. The king being most graciously pleased to direct a revision of such of his royal instructions to his governors as may be construed to lay an improper restraint on the freedom of legislation in any of his colonies, and to concur in the revisal of all acts by which his majesty's subjects there may think themselves aggrieved, it is recommended to the inhabitants at large, to reflect seriously upon their present condition and expectations, and judge for themselves, whether it be more consistent with their honor and happiness to offer up their lives as a sacrifice to the unjust and precarious cause in which they are engaged, or return to their allegiance, accept the blessings of peace, and to be secured in a free enjoyment of their liberties and properties upon true principles of the constitution.

"Given at New York, 19th September, 1776.

HOWE,

W. HOWE."

. . . And so your excellencies, besides your military commands as admiral and general, are also "commissioners for restoring the peace." Is there not some error in this title? Ought we not instead of "peace" to read tyranny? You seem armed at all points for this purpose; and your very language detects the latent design. But you are commissioners, and for the important purpose of "restoring peace," you are honored with a power—"to confer." And you have condescended to be mere machines through which, as through speaking trumpets, words are to be sounded from America to Britain! How much lower is it possible for your excellencies to degrade yourselves in the eyes of the world! By this it is most evident, the British king has not one generous thought respecting America. Nor does he mean to grant terms upon the true principles of the constitution. For, if to grant such terms was bona fide the intention of your master, without doubt you would have been vested with competent powers. But he plainly means to grant nothing he can possibly avoid; and therefore he would have the matter of negotiation drawn into length under his own eye. Can we place any confidence in such a prince? His aim is to divide, not to redress and your excellencies' declaration is but a continuation of lord North's conciliatory plan.

Thus, while we remember that lord North declared, on the 20th of February, 1775, that his famous conciliatory plan was rather calculated to break a link in the American chain of union, than to give satisfaction to the people: and that the exercise of the right of taxing every part of the British dominions must by no means be given up; that lord Mansfield, on the third reading of the bill declaring war against the united colonies, affirmed that he did not consider who was originally in the wrong, they were now to consider only where they were, and the justice of the cause must now give way to their present situation: when we consider the king of Great Britain's speech to the parliament on the last of November, and the commons' address and his answer on the 7th of December, 1774—the commons' address of the 9th of February, 1775, and the royal answer: and the speech from the throne at the last opening of the parliament, October the 26th, 1775—all declaring an unalterable purpose to maintain the supreme authority of that legislature over all the dominions of the crown—in other words, their unalterable purpose, to bind us in all cases whatsoever: when we see your hostile array and operations, in consequence of those declarations: I say, when we consider these things, we can be at no loss to form a just idea of the intentions of your king: or to conceive what your excellencies mean, by "the true principles of the constitution." Nor are we to be caught by any allurements your excellencies may throw out—you confess, and we know that you as commissioners, have not any power to negotiate and determine anything. . . .

That your excellencies may "reflect seriously" upon "the unjust cause in which you are engaged:" and that the name of Howe may be enrolled with the names of Marlborough and Effingham, are the wishes of,

A CAROLINIAN.

LOUIS XVI EXHORTS THE FRENCH CANADIANS TO AID AMERICA

[Declaration by the Count d'Estaing on behalf of the King of France to all Frenchmen in North America, from Boston, October 28, 1778]

The undersigned, authorized by his majesty, and thence clothed with the noblest of titles, with that which effaces all others; charged, in the name of the father of his country, and the beneficent protector of his subjects, to offer a support to those who were born to enjoy the blessings of his government—

TO ALL HIS COUNTRYMEN IN NORTH AMERICA.

You were born French: you never could cease to be French. The late war, which was not declared but by the captivity of nearly all our seamen, and the principal advantages of which our common enemies entirely owed to the courage, the talents, and the numbers of the brave Americans, who are now fighting against them, has wrested from you that which is most dear to all men, even the name of your country. . . .

Can the Canadians, who saw the brave Montcalm fall in their defence, can they become the enemies of his nephews? Can they fight against their former leaders, and arm themselves against their kinsmen? At the bare mention of their names, the weapons would fall out of their hands.

I shall not observe to the ministers of the altars, that their evangelic efforts will require the special protection of Providence, to prevent faith being diminished by example, by worldly interest, and by sovereigns whom force has imposed upon them, and whose political indulgence will be lessened proportionably as those sovereigns shall have less to fear. I shall not observe, that it is necessary for religion that those who preach it should form a body in the state; and that in Canada no other body would be more considered, or have more power to do good than that of the priests, taking a part in the government; since their respectable conduct has merited the confidence of the people.

I shall not represent to that people, nor to all my countrymen in general, that a vast monarchy, having the same religion, the same manners, the same language, where they find kinsmen, old friends and brethren, must be an inexhaustible source of commerce and wealth, more easily acquired, and better secured, by their union, with powerful neighbors, than with strangers of another hemisphere, among whom every thing is different, and who, jealous and despotic sovereigns, would sooner or later treat them as a conquered people, and doubtless much worse than their late countrymen, the Americans, who made them victorious. I shall not urge to a whole people that to join with the United States, is to secure their own happiness; since a whole people, when they acquire the right of thinking and acting for themselves, must know their own interest. But I will declare, and I now formally declare in the name of his majesty, who has authorized and commanded me to do it, that all his former subjects in North America, who shall no more acknowledge the supremacy of Great Britain, may depend upon his protection and support.

Done on board his majesty's ship the Languedoc, in the harbor of Boston, the 28th day of October, in the year 1778.

ESTAING.

THOMAS RODNEY DESCRIBES THE FIRST STEPS TOWARD PEACE

[Letter from Thomas Rodney to his brother Caesar]

PHILADELPHIA, June 14, 1781

SIR—You will find by the contents of this, that it is a confidential letter, conveying you very important and pleasing intelligence.

Congress has received a letter from the king of France, and also otherwise officially informed by his minister here, that the empress of Russia threw out an invitation for the belligerent powers to apply for her mediation, at which the court of London eagerly caught, and mentioned the emperor of Germany as another mediator—and a congress was proposed to be opened at Vienna, for the purpose of settling a general peace. The answer of the court of France was, that they could send no plenipotentiaries to said congress, till they had consulted their allies; but, in [that] the mediators are such respectable powers, and may be so fully relied on for justice, the king presses the United States to submit to the mediation—and that the first preliminary he will insist on, previous to any other negotiation, shall be, the independence of the United States, in full—and upon obtaining this, request that the states may be as moderate in all other demands as possible, that the mediating powers, may thereby receive favorably impressions of our equity and justice. The same mediating application was made to the court of Spain, and their answer was, that they could not do any thing but in conjunction with their ally, the king of France—so that the congress of mediation is likely to be delayed till our despatches reach France. However, the king says that, if he is so pressed that he cannot decently delay sending a plenipotentiary till that time, he shall insist on the preliminary before mentioned, and then only proceed in the negotiation so as to have it in such forwardness as will not injure America against their plenipotentiaries and instructions arrived. The king of France thinks that very equitable terms of peace may be obtained through this mediation, but urges us strongly to exert ourselves this campaign—as the wresting the southern states out of the hands of the British, will contribute greatly to lessen their demands and make them more readily incline to equitable terms of peace; and that our exertions ought to be quick and vigorous, lest a truce should take place: and to ensure the success of this mediation we ought to make the most ample and vigorous preparations for carrying on the war. Britain made an attempt, through a Mr. Cumberland, to negotiate a separate treaty with Spain; but this has failed, though Mr. Cumberland is still at Madrid. Spain would not treat but in conjunction with France, and France cannot treat but in conjunction with America. Thus are we linked together, so that the independence of America now stands on prosperous ground, and no further doubt need to remain about it: for this much is certain—all the powers of Europe, (Britain excepted), wish us to be independent. Thus far in confidence, with this addition, that congress have appointed Dr. Franklin, J. Adams, J. Jay, H. Laurens and governor Jefferson, plenipotentiaries for settling the peace. They first agreed to appoint but one, and Adams was appointed before I came up; they then agreed to add two more, then Jay was appointed—then Jefferson had five votes, Franklin four, and Laurens one. The states voted the same way three times. Then I proposed to the members of Virginia and Pennsylvania that we should appoint them both, which being generally agreed to, this day was appointed for the purpose, and then Laurens was included—so the appointment now consists of five, New Hampshire, Pennsylvania, Delaware and Maryland, were for Franklin, South Carolina for Laurens, and Massachusetts, Connecticut, Jersey, Virginia and North Carolina for Jefferson, Rhode Island and New York unrepresented; Georgia absent. Mr. M'Kean wanted to alter in favor of Jefferson and leave Franklin out, which, upon Georgia's coming in, would have carried him; but I would not give up Franklin, and by the manner of proposing to appoint them both, got him appointed—though this was exceedingly against the grain of several members. He will not be put at the head of the commission. His abilities, character and influence are what will be of most use to us in Europe.

I am, your most obedient,
THOMAS RODNEY.

4. FRENCH AID HELPS TURN THE TIDE

AN AMERICAN COMMENTS ON FRENCH SOLDIERS

[Letter from James Tilton to Thomas Rodney]

WILLIAMSBURG, Dec. 16, 1781

DEAR SIR—After the departure of gen. Washington, the French quartered themselves upon the people, of this and some other towns, a la mode militaire, and gave no small offence; but they are now dancing them into good humor again by a ball every week. I had myself a petit guerre with a French officer, by which I was turned out of my quarters, and, consequently, came off but second best. Being summoned before count Rochambeau to answer for my rebellious conduct, I received a long lecture on the subject of politeness to friends and allies, with intimations of his power to punish obstinacy. Although I was put into quarters equally good with those I was compelled to leave, I must confess, I did not perfectly understand the French politeness, in the mode of exchange. The old count, I believe, has either forgotten or forgiven me, as a day or two ago he gave me an invitation to dine with him.

It must be mortifying to our poor devils to observe the comfortable and happy life of French soldiers. They appear on parade every day like fine gentlemen, as neat as their officers, and hardly to be distinguished from them. They are paid once a week, and, by their happy countenance, appear to want nothing. A sentinel is not allowed to stand upon duty without a warm watch-coat in addition to his other clothing. The officers treat the soldiers with attention, humanity and respect, and appear to employ all the means necessary to inspire them with sentiments of honor. Except some horse-jockeying and plundering, at the reduction of York, I have heard of no stealing among them.—Theft is said to be a crime held in universal abhorrence among them. I have not seen or heard of any instance, yet, of a French soldier being whipped. Their desertions, I believe, have been rare, and their sickness but little. When will our army bear the comparison?

JAMES TILTON.

BALTIMORE HONORS GENERAL LAFAYETTE

*[Address by the Citizens of Baltimore to the
Marquis de Lafayette.]*

BALTIMORE, November 15, 1781

It is with peculiar satisfaction that the citizens of Baltimore embrace the present moment, to express a gratitude which they will always owe to major general the marquis de la Fayette; and to congratulate him, personally, on the late important events in Virginia and South Carolina, so glorious and consequential to America.

Among the first in our cause, you early found a way to our affections, with him, who has struggled with our various difficulties since their beginning. At a time when we had no ally, you were our friend; and when we gained an ally, your presence and good offices could not but increase a cordiality which must render our union with France permanent.

In particular, we cannot sufficiently acknowledge, our sense of your late campaign in Virginia, where, with a few regulars and militia, you opposed the British commander, from whose large army, and military talents this state had such serious cause of apprehension.

These things, sir, have rendered you dear to us, and we feel the highest gratification in seeing, once more, in our town, the man who will always hold a first place in our hearts.

*[Reply by General Lafayette to the Address
of the Citizens of Baltimore]*

BALTIMORE, November 15, 1781

In the affectionate attentions of the citizens of a free town, I would find a reward for the services of a whole life. The honor to have been among the first American soldiers is for me a source of the greatest happiness.

I participate with you in the glorious events that have taken place under his excellency, general Washington's immediate command, and under general Greene. I enjoy the effects these will have on the success of our noble cause and particularly the advantages which they will afford to this state.

The time when I had the honor to command the army in Virginia, which you are pleased so politely to mention, has only shewn that the courage and fortitude of American troops are superior to every kind of difficulty.

My campaign began with a personal obligation to the inhabitants of Baltimore; at the end of it I find myself bound to them by a new tie of everlasting gratitude.

LA FAYETTE.

THE MERCHANTS OF BALTIMORE PRAISE GENERAL ROCHAMBEAU

[Address to the Count de Rochambeau by a deputation of Baltimore merchants, July 29, 1782]

TO HIS EXCELLENCY THE COUNT DE ROCHAMBEAU, commander in chief of the auxiliary troops of his most Christian majesty, in the United States.

We, the merchants of the town of Baltimore, impressed with a grateful sense of the important services rendered by your excellency, and the gallant forces under your command, to the United States, and more particularly to the state of Maryland, beg leave to wait upon your excellency, and return you our most sincere thanks, in this public manner, for the distinguished aid and protection, which you have, from time to time, so willingly afforded to the commercial interests of this state, and to inform your excellency, that we are happy in the opportunity of paying you this tribute, so justly due to distinguished merit.

And, permit us, sir, on this occasion, to observe, that when the distresses of this country rendered an application to the French nation for assistance necessary, the wisdom of your sovereign pointed out your excellency as the grand instrument to assist in our salvation; and, with gratitude, we remark, that the objects of your appointment have been fully answered, and the events that have taken place, since your happy arrival in America, and in which you acted so distinguished a part, fully evince the propriety of your sovereign's choice, and the magnanimity of his intentions toward us—for we have seen a British army, numerous and well appointed, become prisoners of war to the united exertions of the combined armies of France and America

—an event that was considerably accelerated by the great experience and military talents of your excellency, and the valor of the officers and soldiers under your command, and which, we trust, will tend eventually to the establishment of the rights and liberties of this country, the purposes for which you have so generously drawn your sword.

And we beg leave also, amid the general joy diffused by the birth of a Dauphin of France to congratulate your excellency on that auspicious event; and it is our fervent wish and prayers, that he may long live to tread the footsteps of his illustrious father, in being the friend of the distressed, and the advocate for the liberties of mankind.

In hopes that your excellency will enjoy health and happiness, while you reside among us, and on return to your native country, may you be rewarded by your sovereign, in proportion to your merits and services—we remain, with sentiments of gratitude and esteem, on behalf of the merchants of Baltimore, your excellency's most obedient servants. . . .

5. VICTORY COMES AT YORKTOWN

GEORGE MASON REPORTS ON THE EVE OF THE CONFLICT

*[Extract from a letter by Colonel George Mason of
Virginia to his son George, then in France, 1781]*

Our affairs have been, for some time, growing from bad to worse. The enemy's fleet commands our rivers, and puts it in their power to remove their troops, from place to place, when and where they please without opposition; so that we no sooner collect a force sufficient to counteract them in one part of the country, but they shift to another, ravaging, plundering, and destroying every thing before them. Our militia turn out with great spirit, and have, in several late actions, behaved bravely; but they are badly armed and appointed. General Greene with about 1200 regular troops and some militia, is in South Carolina: where he has taken all the enemy's posts, except Charleston. The enemy's capital object, at this time, seems to be Virginia. General Phillips died lately in Petersburg; upon which the command of the British troops then devolved upon Arnold. But lord Cornwallis, quitting North Carolina, has since joined Arnold, with about 1200 infantry and 300 cavalry, and taken the chief command of their army in Virginia, now consisting of about 5000 men. They have crossed James river, and by the latest accounts were at Westover; their light horse having advanced as far as Hanover court house. They have burnt Page's warehouses, where the greatest part of the York River tobacco was collected; they had before burned most of the tobacco upon James river, and have plundered great part of the adjacent country. The Marquis de la Fayette is about twenty miles below Fredericksburg with about 1200 regulars and 3000 militia, waiting the arrival of general Wayne, with about 1500 regular troops of the Pennsylvania line.

We have had various accounts of the sailing of a French fleet, with a body of land forces, for America; should they really arrive it would quickly change the face of our affairs, and infuse fresh spirits and confidence; but it has been so long expected in vain, that little credit is now given to reports concerning it.

You know, from your own acquaintance in this part of Virginia, that the bulk of the people here are staunch whigs; strongly attached to the American cause, and well affected to the French alliance; yet they grow uneasy and restless, and begin to think that our allies are spinning out the war, in order to weaken America, as well as Great Britain, and thereby leave us at the end of it, as dependent as possible upon themselves.

However unjust this opinion may be, it is natural enough for planters and farmers, burthened with heavy taxes, and frequently dragged from their families upon military duty on the continual alarms occasioned by the superiority of the British fleet. They see their property daily exposed to destruction, they see with what facility the British troops are removed from one part of the continent to another, and with what infinite charge and fatigue ours are, too late, obliged to follow: and they see too, very plainly, that a strong French fleet would have prevented all this.

If our allies had a superior fleet here, I should have no doubt of a favorable issue to the war: but, without it, I fear we are deceiving both them and ourselves, in expecting we shall be able to keep our people much longer firm, in so unequal an opposition to Great Britain.

France surely intends the separation of these states, forever, from Great Britain. It is highly her interest to accomplish this; but by drawing out the thread too fine and long, it may unexpectedly break in her hands.

God bless you, my dear child; and grant that we may again meet, in your native country, as freemen,—otherwise that we may never see each other more, is the prayer of

Your affectionate father,
G. MASON.

EXTRACTS FROM THE JOURNAL OF AN AMERICAN OFFICER

[*Observations on the siege of Yorktown by a captain in the Continental Army*]

Oct. 12.—A tremendous fire from both sides.

Head-quarters, Oct. 12, 1781.

For to-morrow.

M. G. M. La Fayette,

B. G. Muhlenburg.

The Marquis' division will mount in the trenches to-morrow. The superintendent of the deposite of the trenches, is required to have the quality of saucisson, fascines and gabions brought to the deposite, accurately inspected; to reject such as are not fit for use, and report the corps that offer them.

13—Two Hessian deserters came in; every thing favorable.

Head-quarters, Oct. 13, 1781.

For to-morrow.

B. G. Wayne and

Gist's brigade.

14—This morning a deserter says the infantry refuse doing duty. That Cornwallis promised them they would be relieved from New York, and give each reg. a pipe of wine.

The Marquis, at dark, stormed their river battery, and baron viscount Viomnel stormed another on their extreme, to the left, with little loss. We run our second parallel complete.

Head-quarters, Oct. 14, 1781.

For to-morrow.

M. G. Lincoln,

B. G. Clinton.

Maj. general Lincoln's division will mount the trenches to-morrow.

The effects of the late col. Scammel will be disposed of at public sale, to-morrow at 3 o'clock. P.M. at maj. Rice's tent, in gen. Hayne's Brigade.

15—This night the enemy made a sally and imposed themselves on the French for Americans; forced their works and made themselves masters of an American battery which they spiked. Imposition being found out, they retired, with eight men killed on the spot.

Head-quarters, Oct. 15, 1781.
For to-morrow.
M. G. M. La Fayette,
B. G. Muhlenburg and
Hayne's brigade.
Maj. gen. La Fayette's division will mount the trenches to-morrow.

The commander in chief congratulates the army on the success of the enterprise against the two important works on the left of the enemy's lines. He requests the baron Viomnel, who commanded the French grenadiers and chasseurs, and marquis La Fayette, who commanded the American light infantry, to accept his warmest acknowledgments for the excellency of their dispositions and their own gallant conduct on the occasion; and he begs them to present his thanks to every individual officer, and to the men of their respective commands, for the spirit and rapidity with which they advanced to the attacks assigned them, and for the admirable firmness with which they supported them, under the fire of the enemy, without returning a shot.

The general reflects with the highest degree of pleasure on the confidence which the troops of the two nations must hereafter have in each other. —Assured of mutual support, he is convinced there is no danger which they will not cheerfully encounter—no difficulty which they will not bravely overcome.

The troops will be supplied with fresh beef to Thursday next, inclusive; they will receive 3 pints of salt to every 100 rations, for their allowance of Wednesday and Thursday.

16—Our batteries completing very fast.

Head-quarters, Oct. 16, 1781.
For to-morrow.
M. G. B. Steuben,
B. G. Wayne and
Gist's brigade.
Maj. gen. baron Steuben's division will mount the trenches to-morrow.

The commander in chief having observed that the trenches are constantly crowded with spectators, who, by passing and repassing prevent the men from working, and thereby greatly impede the operations of the siege. He therefore orders that no officer, who is not on duty, shall hereafter enter the trenches, except gen. officers and their aids, and that no inhabitant, or person not belonging to the army, be suffered to enter the trenches, at any time, without permission from the maj. general of the trenches.

In future the relief for the trenches are not to beat their drums after they pass the mill dam; they are from that place to march silently, with trailed arms and colors furled, until they arrive at their posts in the trenches.

Lieut. col. Dehart being relieved from his arrest, the court martial, of which col. Cortland is president, will proceed to the trial of the prisoners confined in the provost.

17—At 11 o'clock, his lordship closes the scene by propositions for deputies from each army, to meet at Moore's house, to agree on terms for the surrender of York and Gloster. An answer was sent by 3 o'clock, when a cessation of arms took place.

> Head-quarters, Oct. 17, 1781
> For the trenches to-morrow.

Maj. gen. Lincoln's division.

18—Flags alternately passing this day.

> Head-quarters, Oct. 18, 1781.
> For the trenches to-morrow.

Maj. gen. marquis La Fayette's division.

19—At 1 o'clock this day, our troops marched in and took possession of their horn-works, and the British marched out. The American and French armies form a lane through which the British pass and ground their arms.

> Head-quarters, Oct. 19, 1781.
> For to-morrow.

M. G. Lincoln,
Col. Butler,
Maj. Woodson,
B. M. Blake.

Gen. Muhlenburg's brigade will hold itself in readiness for duty to-morrow.

20—Lay quiet this day cleaning our arms.

> Head-quarters, Oct. 20, 1781.
> For to-morrow.

M. G. M. La Fayette,
Col. Stewart,
Maj. Bird,
M. M. Cox

Brig. general Hayne's brigade for duty tomorrow, to parade at 10 o'clock on their own parade.

The general congratulates the army upon the glorious event of yesterday: the generous proofs which his most Christian majesty has given of his attachment to the cause of America, must force conviction in the minds of the most deceived among the enemy, relative to the decisive good consequences of the alliance; and inspire every citizen of these states with sentiments of the most unalterable gratitude. His fleet the most numerous and powerful that ever appeared in those seas, commanded by an admiral whose fortune and talents insure success; an army of the most admirable composition, both in officers and men, are pledges of his friendship to the United States, and their co-operation has secured us the present signal success.

The general, upon this occasion, entreats his excellency count Rochambeau, to accept his most grateful acknowledgments for his counsel and assistance at all times. He presents his warmest thanks to the generals baron de Viomnel, chevalier Chastelleux, marquis de St. Simon, count de Viomnel, and to brig. de Choisey (who had a separate command), for the illustrious manner in which they have advanced the interest of the common cause. He requests the count de Rochambeau will be pleased to communicate to the army under his immediate command, the high sense he entertains of the distinguished merits of the officers and soldiers of every corps, and that he will present, in his name, to the regiment of Argenois and Deaponts, the pieces of brass ordnance captured by them, as a testimony of their gallantry in storming the enemy's redoubts, on the night of the 14th inst. when officers and men so universally vied with each other in the exercise of every soldierly virtue.

The general's thanks to each individual of merit, would comprehend the whole army: but he thinks himself bound however by affection, duty and gratitude, to express his obligation to maj-gens. Lincoln, La Fayette and Steuben, for their dispositions in the trenches—to gen. Duportail and col. Carney for the vigor and knowledge which were conspicuous in their conduct of the attacks; and to gen. Knox and col. de Abberville for their great attention and fatigue in bringing forward the artillery and stores; and for their judicious and spirited management of them in the parallels. He requests the gentlemen above mentioned, to communicate his thanks to the officers and soldiers of their commands. Ingratitude, which the general hopes never to be guilty of, would be conspicuous in him, was he to omit thanking in the warmest terms his excellency governor Nelson, for the aid he has derived from him, and from the militia under his command: to whose activity, emulation and courage such applause is due; the greatness of the acquisition would be ample compensation for the hardships and hazards which they encountered with so much patriotism and firmness.

In order to diffuse the general joy in every breast, the general orders those men belonging to the army, who may now be in confinement, shall be pardoned, and join their respective corps.

21—British marched out for their cantonments under militia guards.

22—York affords very good Port-wine.

23—Orders for the troops to hold themselves in readiness to march at the shortest notice.

24—Marquis de St. Simon's troops embark their cannon.

25—Demolish our works by brigades.

26—Expectations of a supply of necessaries from the merchants of York and Gloster.

27—Report says sir H. Clinton has embarked from New York for Virginia.

28—The American cannon put on board vessels for the head of Elk.

29—Nothing material.

30—I was on duty at Gloster.

31—Col. Tarlton dismounted from his horse by an inhabitant, who claimed him in the midst of the street.

Nov. 1—A supply of clothing purchased by agents, appointed for that purpose.

2—Distribution of the supplies.

3—Orders for Pennsylvania and Maryland troops to march tomorrow for South Carolina.

4—General beat at 8 o'clock. Tents struck and loaded. Troops march at 9.

DESCRIPTION OF THE SURRENDER AT YORKTOWN

[An anonymous eyewitness account of the surrender]

At two o'clock in the evening Oct. 19th, 1781, the British army, led by general O'Hara, marched out of its lines, with colors cased and drums beating a British march.

It will be seen in the sequel, that O'Hara, and not Cornwallis, surrendered the British army to the allied forces of France and America. In this affair, lord Cornwallis seemed to have lost all his former magnanimity and firmness of character,—he sunk beneath the pressure of his misfortunes, and for a moment gave his soul up to chagrin and sorrow. The road through which they marched was lined with spectators, French and American. On one side the commander in chief, surrounded by his suite and the American staffs, took his station; on the other side opposite to him, was the count de Rochambeau, in like manner attended. The captive army approached, moving slowly in column, with grace and precision.

Universal silence was observed amidst the vast concourse, and the utmost decency prevailed, exhibiting in demeanor an awful sense of the vicissitudes of human life, mingled with commiseration for the unhappy. The head of the column approached the commander in chief—O'Hara, mistaking the circle, turned to that on his left for the purpose of paying his respects to the commander in chief, and requesting further orders; when quickly discovering his error, with embarrassment in his countenance, he flew across the road, and advancing up to Washington, asked pardon for his mistake, apologized for the absence of lord Cornwallis and begged to know his further pleasure.

The general feeling his embarrassment, relieved it by referring him, with much politeness, to general Lincoln for his government. Returning to the head of the column, it again moved, under the guidance of Lincoln, to the field selected for the conclusion of the ceremony.

Every eye was turned, searching for the British commander in chief, anxious to look at that man heretofore so much their dread. All were disappointed.

Cornwallis held himself back from the humiliating scene; obeying sensations which his great character ought to have stifled. He had been unfortunate, not from any false step or deficiency of exertion on his part, but from the infatuated policy of his superior, and the united power of his enemy brought to bear upon him alone. There was nothing with which he could reproach himself; there was nothing with which he could reproach his brave and faithful army; why not then appear at its head in the day of misfortune, as he had always done in the day of triumph?

The British general in this instance deviated from his usual line of conduct, dimming the splendor of his long and brilliant career.

Thus ended the important co-operation of the allied forces. Great was the joy diffused throughout our infant empire. . . .

WASHINGTON RECALLS THE FINAL CAMPAIGN

[Letter by George Washington from Mount Vernon, approximately seven years after the capture of Yorktown]

MOUNT VERNON, July 13, 1788

SIR—I duly received your letter of the 14th inst. and can only answer you briefly and generally from memory: that a combined operation of the land and naval forces of France in America, for the year 1781, was preconcerted the year before; that the point of attack was not absolutely agreed upon, because it could not be foreknown where the enemy would be most susceptible of impression; and because we (having the command of the water with sufficient means of conveyance) could transport ourselves to any spot with the greatest celerity; that it was determined by me, nearly twelve months before hand, at all hazards, to give out, and cause it to be believed by the highest military as well as civil officers, that New York was the destined place of attack, for the important purpose of inducing the eastern and middle states to make greater exertions in furnishing specific supplies, than they otherwise would have done, as well as for the interesting purpose of rendering the enemy less prepared elsewhere; that, by these means, and these alone, artillery, boats, stores, and provisions, were in seasonable preparation to move with the utmost rapidity to any part of the continent; for the difficulty consisted more in providing, than knowing how to apply the military apparatus; that, before the arrival of the count de Grasse, it was the fixed determination to strike the enemy in the most vulnerable quarter, so as to insure success with moral certainty, as our affairs were then in the most ruinous train imaginable; that New York was thought to be beyond our effort, and consequently, that the only hesitation that remained, was between an attack upon the British army in Virginia, and that in Charleston: and finally, that, by the intervention of several communications, and some incidents which cannot be detailed in a letter, the hostile post in Virginia, from being a provisional and strongly expected, became the definitive and certain, object of the campaign.

I only add, that it never was in contemplation to attack New York, unless the garrison should first have been so far degarnished, to carry on the southern operations, as to render our success in the siege of that place, as infallible as any future military event can ever be made. For I repeat it, and dwell upon it again, some splendid advantage (whether upon a larger or smaller scale was almost immaterial) was so essentially necessary, to revive the expiring hopes and languid exertions of the country, at the crisis in question, that I never would have consented to embark in any enterprise wherein, from the most rational plan and accurate calculation, the favorable issue should not have appeared to my view as a ray of light. The failure of an attempt against the posts of the enemy, could, in no other possible situation during the war, have been so fatal to our cause.

That much trouble was taken, and finesse used, to misguide and bewilder sir Henry Clinton, in regard to the real object, by fictitious communications, as well as by making a deceptive provision of ovens, forage, and boats in his neighborhood, is certain; nor were less pains taken to deceive our own army; for I had always conceived, where the imposition does not completely take place at home, it would never sufficiently succeed abroad.

Your desire of obtaining truth, is very laudable; I wish I had more leisure to gratify it, as I am equally solicitous the undisguised verity should be known. Many circumstances will unavoidably be misconceived, and misrepresented. Notwithstanding most of the papers, which may properly be deemed official, are preserved; yet the knowledge of innumerable things of a more delicate and secret nature, is confined to the perishable remembrance of some few of the present generation.

With esteem, I am, sir, your most obedient humble servant,

GEORGE WASHINGTON.

THE BRITISH GOVERNMENT REACTS TO THE DEFEAT

[Extracts from the Memoirs of N. W. Wraxall]

NOVEMBER, 1781.—During the whole month of November, the concurring accounts transmitted to government, enumerating lord Cornwallis's embarrassments, and the positions taken by the enemy, augmented the anxiety of the cabinet. Lord George Germain, in particular, conscious that on the prosperous or adverse termination of that expedition, must hinge the fate of the American contest, his own stay in office, as well as probably the duration of the ministry itself, felt, and even expressed to his friends, the strongest uneasiness on the subject. The meeting of parliament meanwhile stood fixed for the 27th of November. On Sunday the 25th, about noon, official intelligence of the surrender of the British forces at Yorktown, arrived from Falmouth, at lord Germain's house in Pall-mall. Lord Walsingham, who, previous to his father sir William de Grey's elevation to the peerage, had been under secretary of state in that department, and who was selected to second the address in the house of peers, on the subsequent Tuesday, happened to be there when the messenger brought the news. Without communicating it to any other person, lord George, for the purpose of despatch, immediately got with him into a hackney-coach and drove to lord Stormount's residence in Portland-place. Having imparted to him the disastrous information, and taken him into the carriage, they instantly proceeded to the Chancellor's house in Great Russell-street, Bloomsbury, whom they found at home; when, after a short consultation, they determined to lay it themselves, in person before lord North. He had not received any intimation of the event when they arrived at his door, in Downing-street, between 1 and 2 o'clock.

The first minister's firmness, and even his presence of mind gave way for a short time, under this awful disaster. I asked lord George afterwards, how he took the communication, when made to him? "As he would have taken a ball in his breast," replied lord George. For he opened his arms, exclaiming wildly, as he paced up and down the apartment during a few minutes, "Oh God! it is all over!" Words which he repeated many times, under emotions of the deepest agitation and distress.

When the first agitation of their minds had subsided the four ministers discussed the question, whether or not it might be expedient to prorogue parliament for a few days; but, as scarcely an interval of forty-eight hours remained before the appointed time of assembling, and as many members of both houses were already either arrived in London, or on the road, that proposition was abandoned. It became, however, indispensable to alter, and almost model anew the king's speech, which had been already drawn up, and completely prepared for delivery from the throne. This alteration was therefore made without delay; and at the same time, lord George Germain, as secretary for the American department, sent off a despatch to his majesty, who was then at Kew, acquainted him with the melancholy termination of lord Cornwallis's expedition. Some hours having elapsed, before these different, but necessary acts of business could take place, the ministers separated, and lord George Germain repaired to his office in Whitehall. There he found a confirmation of the intelligence, which arrived about two hours after the first communication; having been transmitted from Dover, to which place it was forwarded from Calais with the French account of the same event.

I dined on that day at lord George's; and though the information, which had reached London in the course of the morning, from two different quarters, was of a nature not to admit of long concealment; yet it had not been communicated either to me, or to any individual of the company, as it might naturally have been through the channel of common report, when I got to Pall-mall, between five and six o'clock.—Lord Walsingham, who likewise dined there, was the only person present, except lord George, who was acquainted with the fact.—The party, nine in number, sat down to table. I thought the master of the house appeared serious, though he manifested no discomposure. Before the dinner was finished, one of his servants delivered him a letter, brought back by the messenger who had been despatched to the king. Lord George opened and perused it: then looking at lord Walsingham, to whom he exclusively directed his observation, "The king writes" said he, "just as he always does, except that I observed he has omitted to mark the hour and the minute of his writing with his usual precision." This remark, though calculated to awaken some interest, excited no comment; and while the ladies, lord George's three daughters, remained in the room, we repressed our curiosity. But they had no sooner withdrawn, than lord George having acquainted us, that from Paris information has just arrived of the old Count de Maurepas, first minister, lying at the point of death: "It would grieve me," said I, "to finish my career, however far advanced in years, were I first minister of France, before I had witnessed the termination of this great contest between England and America." "He has survived to see that event," replied lord George, with some agitation. Utterly unsuspicious of the fact which had happened beyond the Atlantic, I conceived him to allude to the indecisive naval action fought at the mouth of the Chesapeake, early in the preceding month of September, between admiral Graves and count de Grasse; which, in its results, might prove most injurious to lord Cornwallis. Under this impression, "my meaning," said I, "is that if I were the Count de Maurepas, I should wish to live long enough, to behold the final issue of the war in Virginia." "He has survived to witness it completely," answered lord George. —"The army has surrendered, and you may peruse the particulars of the capitulation in that paper," taking at the same time one from his pocket, which he delivered into my hand, not without visible emotion. By his permission I read it aloud, while the company listened in profound silence. We then discussed its contents, as it affected the ministry, the country and the war. It must be confessed that they were calculated to diffuse a gloom over the most convivial society, and that they opened a wide field for political speculation.

After perusing the account of lord Cornwallis's surrender at Yorktown, it was impossible for all present not to feel a lively curiosity to know how the king had received the intelligence, as well as how he had expressed himself in his note to lord Germain, on the first communication of so painful an event. He gratified our wish by reading it to us, observing at the same time, that it did the highest honor to his majesty's fortitude, firmness and consistency of character. The words made an impression on my memory which the lapse of more than thirty years has not erased; and I shall here commemorate its tenor, as serving to show how that prince felt and wrote, under one of the most afflicting, as well as humiliating occurrences of his reign. The billet ran nearly to this effect: "I have received, with sentiments of the deepest concern, the communication which lord George Germain had made me, of the unfortunate result of the operations in Virginia. I particularly lament it, on account of the consequences connected with it, and the difficulties which it may produce in carrying on the public business, or in repairing such a misfortune,—But I trust that neither lord George Germain, nor any member of the cabinet, will suppose that it makes the smallest alteration in those principles of my conduct which have directed me in past times, and which will always continue to animate me under every event, in the prosecution of the present contest." Not a sentiment of despondency or of despair was to be found in the letter; the very hand-writing of which indicated composure of mind.—Whatever opinion we may entertain relative to the practicability of reducing America to obedience by force of arms, at the end of 1781, we must admit that no sovereign could manifest more calmness, dignity or self-command than George III displayed in this reply.

Severely as the general effect of the blow received in Virginia was felt throughout the nation, yet no immediate symptoms of ministerial dissolution, or even of parliamentary defection became visible in either house. All the animated invectives of Fox, aided by the contumelious irony of Burke, and sustained by dignified denunciations of Pitt, enlisted on the same side, made little apparent impression on their hearers, who seemed stupefied by the disastrous intelligence. Yet never probably at any period of our history, was more indignant language used by the opposition, or supported by administration. In the ardor of his feelings at the recent calamity beyond the Atlantic, Fox not only accused ministers of being virtually in the pay of France, but menaced them with the vengeance of an undone people, who would speedily compel them to expiate their crimes on the public scaffold. Burke, with inconceivable warmth of coloring, depicted the folly and impracticability of taxing America by force, or, as he describes it, "shearing the wolf." The metaphor was wonderfully appropriate, and scarcely admitted of denial. Pitt leveled his observations principally against the cabinet, whom he represented as destitute of principle, wisdom or union of design. All three were sustained, and I had almost said, outdone by Mr. Thomas Pitt, who, in terms of gloomy despondency, seemed to regard the situation of the country as scarcely admitting of a remedy, under such a parliament, such ministers and such a sovereign. Lord North, in this moment of general depression, found resources within himself.—He scornfully repelled the insinuations of Fox, as deserving only contempt, justified the principle of the war, which did not originate in a despotic wish to tyrannize over America, but from the desire of maintaining the constitutional authority of parliament over the colonies; deplored in common with the opposition, the misfortunes which had marked the progress of the contest; defied the threat of punishment; and finally adjured the house not to aggravate the present calamity by dejection or despair, but, by united exertions, to secure our national extrication.

CONGRESS PROCLAIMS A DAY OF THANKSGIVING

[Proclamation by the Congress of the United States,
October 26, 1781]

PROCLAMATION

Whereas, it hath pleased Almighty God, the father of mercies, remarkably to assist and support the United States of America, in their important struggle for liberty, against the long continued efforts of a powerful nation, it is the duty of all ranks to observe and thankfully acknowledge the interpositions of his Providence in their behalf. Through the whole of the contest, from its first rise to this time, the influence of Divine Providence may be clearly perceived in many signal instances, of which we mention but few.

In revealing the councils of our enemies, when the discoveries were seasonable and important, and the means were seemingly inadequate or fortuitous;—in preserving and even improving the union of the several states, on the breach of which our enemies placed their greatest dependence;—in increasing the number, and adding to the zeal and attachment of the friends of liberty;—in granting remarkable deliverances, and blessing us with the most signal success, when affairs seemed to have the most discouraging appearance;—in raising up for us a most powerful and generous ally, in one of the first of the European powers;—in confounding the councils of our enemies, and suffering them to pursue such measures, as have most directly contributed to frustrate their own desires and expectations,—above all, in making their extreme cruelty to the inhabitants of these states, when in their power, and their savage devastation of property, the very means of cementing our union, and adding vigor to every effort in opposition to them.

And as we cannot help leading the good people of these states to a retrospect on the events, which have taken place since the beginning of the war, so we recommend, in a particular manner, to their observation, the goodness of God in the year now drawing to a conclusion. In which the confederation of the United States has been completed—in which there have been so many instances of prowess, and success in our armies, particularly in the southern states, where, notwithstanding the difficulties with which they had to struggle, they have recovered the whole country which the enemy had overrun, leaving them only a post or two, on or near the sea;—in which we have been so powerfully and effectually assisted by our allies, while in all the conjunct operations the most perfect harmony has subsisted in the allied army;—in which there has been so plentiful a harvest, and so great abundance of the fruits of the earth of every kind, as not only enables us easily to supply the wants of our army but gives comfort and happiness to the whole people—and, in which, after the success of our allies by sea, a general of the first rank, with his whole army has been captured by the allied forces, under the direction of our commander in chief.

It is therefore recommended to the several states to set apart the thirteenth day of December next, to be religiously observed as a day of thanksgiving and prayer; that all the people may assemble on that day, with grateful hearts, to celebrate the praises of our gracious Benefactor; to confess our manifold sins; to offer up our most fervent supplications to the God of all Grace, that it may please him to pardon our offences, and incline our hearts for the future to keep all his laws; to comfort and relieve all our brethren who are in distress or captivity; to prosper our husbandmen, and give success to all engaged in lawful commerce; to impart wisdom and integrity to our counsellors, judgment and fortitude to our officers and soldiers, to protect and prosper our illustrious ally, and favor our united exertions for the speedy establishment of a safe, honorable, and lasting peace; to bless all seminaries of learning; and cause the knowledge of God to cover the earth, as the waters cover the seas.

Done in congress this twenty-sixth day of October, in the year of our Lord one thousand seven hundred and eighty one, and in the sixth year of the independence of the United States of America.

THOMAS M'KEAN, President.

Attest, CHARLES THOMPSON, Secretary.

6. THE PATRIOTS REGAIN NEW YORK CITY

THE CITIZENS OF NEW YORK THANK GENERAL WASHINGTON

[Response of the people of New York City to the evacuation of British forces, 1783]

A committee had been appointed by the citizens to wait upon General Washington and Governor Clinton and other American officers, and to express their joyful congratulation to them upon this occasion. A procession for this purpose formed in the Bowery, marched through a part of the city, and halted at a tavern, then known by the name of Cape's tavern, in Broadway, where the following addresses were delivered. Mr. Thomas Tucker, late of this town, and, at that time, a reputable merchant in New York, a member of the committee, was selected to perform the office on the part of the committee.

To His Excellency George Washington, Esq.
General and Commander in Chief of the Armies of the United States of
America.
The address of the citizens of New York, who have returned from exile, in
behalf of themselves and their suffering brethren:

Sir—At a moment when the army of tyranny is yielding up its fondest usurpations, we hope the salutations of long suffering exiles, but now happy freemen, will not be deemed an unhappy tribute. In this place, and at this moment of exultation and triumph, while the ensigns of slavery still linger in our sight, we look up to you, our deliverer, with unusual transports of gratitude and joy. Permit us to welcome you to this city, long torn from us by the hard hand of oppression, but now, by your wisdom and energy, under the guidance of Providence, once more the seat of peace and freedom. We forbear to speak our gratitude or your praise. We should but echo the voice of applauding millions. But the citizens of New York are eminently indebted to your virtues; and we, who have now the honor to address your excellency, have often been companions of your sufferings and witnesses of your exertions. Permit us, therefore, to approach your excellency with the dignity and sincerity of freemen, and to assure you that we shall preserve, with our latest breath, our gratitude for your services, and veneration for your character; and accept of our sincere and earnest wishes that you may long enjoy that calm domestic felicity, which you have so generously sacrificed—that the cries of injured liberty may never more interrupt your repose—and that your happiness may be equal to your virtues. . . .

GENERAL WASHINGTON'S REPLY TO THE
CITIZENS OF NEW YORK,

[*November 25, 1783*]

GENTLEMEN—I thank you sincerely for your affectionate address, and entreat you to be persuaded that nothing could be more agreeable to me than your polite congratulations. Permit me, in return, to felicitate you on the happy repossession of your city. . . .

May the tranquility of your city be perpetual—may the ruins soon be repaired, commerce flourish, science be fostered, and all the civil and social virtues be cherished in the same illustrious manner which formerly reflected so much credit on the inhabitants of New York. In fine, may every species of felicity attend you, gentlemen, and your worthy fellow-citizens.

GEORGE WASHINGTON

IX

CREATING A NEW FORM OF GOVERNMENT,

1776-1789

ONE OF THE side-effects of the debate that had raged from 1763 to 1776 over the rights of Englishmen was a sharpening of American thinking on the principles of civil government. It may be true that Americans have produced only a small body of writings on political theory, but the practical documents of the Revolutionary era reflect the Founding Fathers' impressive grasp of the fundamentals of a free society. In instructions to their Congressional delegates (pp. 312, and 313), in Virginia's landmark Declaration of Rights (p. 315), and in innumerable tracts and orations (pp. 317, 318, and 321), Americans of the 1770's enunciated a profound understanding of and attachment to the principles of government they believed worth fighting for.

Americans had two kinds of constitutions to draft during and after the War for Independence. Most pressing was the need for state constitutions, for the removal of British authority left the former colonies without any legitimate civil structures. Much of the political energy of the Founding Fathers went into the drafting, revising, and administration of state constitutions. But even more challenging was the need for an intercolonial union, one that would avoid the perils of the imperial system from which the colonies had rebelled and at the same time would guarantee the fruits of independence.

Not surprisingly America's first effort at a national constitution left much to be desired. The Articles of Confederation had been drafted in the turmoil of war; its defects were neither gross nor illogical. Arguments against central authority had been prominent in the debate with the mother country and they were reflected in the feeble provisions in regard to the executive branch and the coercive powers of the new government. But the Articles of Confederation were at least a promising beginning, one not lightly made (p. 323) nor to be casually discarded. When the postwar period proved trying (p. 331), an increasing number of Americans suspected that the Articles were at least partly to blame (p. 334), and they called for a new and more perfect union.

The Constitution of 1787 was in many respects the institutional fulfillment of the Revolution. Through that hot summer in Philadelphia, the Founding Fathers proposed, argued, and compromised, while the rest of the nation watched and waited (p. 338). Sessions were secret; only scraps of information filtered out to the people (p. 341). But when at last their work was done and offered to the people for a decision, America's political architects could be proud of their work. Even the men who did not vote for the final document took pride, in the end, in the heritage of the American Revolution (p. 342).

The men and women of the Revolutionary generation had brought a new era to America, one which, in the words of Hezekiah Niles, "happily terminated in the establishment of their liberties." If at times they spoke more idealistically than they acted they merely demonstrated that they were men, not angels. If at times they did their work of constitution-making so hastily that it had to be done again a few years later—as in the case of the Articles of Confederation and some of the state constitutions—they only showed that they could learn from experience. The perspective of the twentieth century adds luster to their ideals and their efforts.

1. AMERICANS EXPOUND THEIR POLITICAL PHILOSOPHY

BOSTON INSTRUCTS ITS DELEGATES TO CONGRESS

[Instructions from the town of Boston to its delegates in the Continental Congress, 1776]

GENTLEMEN. . . . The right to legislate is originally due to every member of the community; which right is always exercised in the infancy of a state, but, when the inhabitants are become numerous, it is not only inconvenient, but impracticable, for all to meet in one assembly; and hence arose the necessity and practice of legislating by a few, freely chosen by the many. When this choice is free and the representation equal, it is the people's fault if they are not happy: we therefore instruct you to devise some means to obtain an equal representation of the people of this colony in the legislature:—but care should be taken that the assembly be not unwieldy; for this would be an approach to the evil meant to be cured by representation. The largest bodies of men do not always despatch business with the greatest expedition, nor conduct it in the wisest manner.

It is essential to liberty, that the legislative, judicial, and executive powers of government be, as nearly as possible, independent of, and separate from each other; for where they are united in the same persons, or number of persons, there would be wanting that mutual check which is the principal security against the making of arbitrary laws, and a wanton exercise of power in the execution of them. It is also of the highest importance, that every person in a judiciary department employ the greatest part of his time and attention in the duties of his office; we therefore further instruct you, to procure the enacting such law or laws, as shall make it incompatible for the same persons to hold a seat in the legislative and executive departments of government, at one and the same time: that shall render the judges, in every judicatory through the colony, dependent, not on the uncertain tenure of caprice or pleasure, but on an unimpeachable deportment in the important duties of their station, for their continuance in office: and to prevent the multiplicity of offices in the same person, that such salaries be settled upon them as will place them above the necessity of stooping to any indirect or collateral means for subsistence. We wish to avoid a profusion of the public moneys on the one hand, and the danger of sacrificing our liberties to a spirit of parsimony on the other. . . .

MECHANICS OF NEW YORK CITY ADDRESS THEIR DELEGATES

*[Address by a meeting of New York City mechanics to delegates
of the state of New York in the Continental Congress,
June 14, 1776]*

TO THE HONORABLE THE DELEGATES ELECTED BY THE SEVERAL COUNTIES AND DISTRICTS WITHIN THE GOVERNMENT OF NEW YORK, IN COLONIAL CONGRESS CONVENED.

The respectful address of the mechanics in union, for the city and county of New York, represented by their general committee.

ELECTED DELEGATES. . . . —We, the mechanics in union, though a very inconsiderable part of your constituents, beg leave to represent, that one of the clauses in your resolve, respecting the establishment of a new form of government, is erroneously construed, and for that reason may serve the most dangerous purposes. . . . We could not, we never can believe you intended that the future delegates, or yourselves, should be vested with the power of framing a new constitution for this colony; and that its inhabitants at large should not exercise the right which God has given them, in common with all men, to judge whether it be consistent with their interest to accept or reject a constitution framed for that state of which they are members. This is the birthright of every man to whatever state he may belong. There he is, or ought to be by inadmissible right, a co-legislator with all the other members of that community.

Conscious of our own want of abilities, we are, alas! but too sensible that every individual is not qualified for assisting in the framing of a consti- tution: but, that share of common sense which the Almighty has bountifully distributed among mankind in general, is sufficient to quicken every one's feeling, and enable him to judge rightly what degree of safety, and what ad- vantages he is likely to enjoy, or be deprived of, under any constitution pro- posed to him. For this reason, should a preposterous confidence in the abili- ties and integrity of our future delegates, delude us into measures which might imply a renunciation of our inalienable right to ratify our laws, we believe that your wisdom, your patriotism, your own interest, nay, your ambition it- self, would urge you to exert all the powers of persuasion you possess, and try every method which, in your opinion, could deter us from perpetrating that impious and frantic act of self-destruction; for, as it would precipitate us into a state of absolute slavery, the lawful power which, till now, you have received from your constituents, to be exercised over a free people, would be annihilated by that unnatural act. It might probably accelerate our political death; but it must immediately cause your own. . . .

We never did as a body, nor never will, assume any authority whatso- ever in the public transactions of the present times. Common sense teaches us, that the absurdity of the claim would not only destroy our usefulness as a body of voluntary associators, who are warmly attached to the cause of liberty: but that it would likewise expose every one of us to deserved derision. At the same time, we assure your honorable house, that on all occasions we will continue to testify our zeal in supporting the measures adopted by congresses and com- mittees, in the prosecution of their grand object, the restoration of human rights in the United Colonies. And if at any future time, the silence of the bodies in power give us reason to conceive that our representations may be useful, we then will endeavor to discharge our duty with propriety, and rely

on public indulgence for any imperfection which cannot effect our uprightness.

Signed by order of the committee,

MALCOLM M'EUEN, Chairman.

VIRGINIA ISSUES A DECLARATION OF RIGHTS

[George Mason's draft of the Virginia Declaration of Rights, 1776]

A declaration of rights made by the representatives of the good people of Virginia, assembled in full and free convention; which rights do pertain to
them and their posterity, as the basis and foundation of government, unanimously adopted by the convention of Virginia, June 12th, 1776.

1. That all men are created equally free and independent, and have certain inherent natural rights of which, they cannot, by any compact, deprive,
or divest their posterity; among which are the enjoyment of life and liberty,
with the means of acquiring and possessing property, and pursuing and obtaining happiness and safety.

2. That all power is by God and nature vested in and consequently derived from the people; that magistrates are their trustees and servants, and at
all times amenable to them.

3. That government is, or ought to be, instituted for the common benefit, protection and security of the people, nation or community. Of all the
various modes and forms of government, that is best, which is capable of producing the greatest degree of happiness and safety, and is most effectually secured against the danger of administration; and that whenever any government shall be found inadequate or contrary to these purposes, a majority of
the community hath an indubitable, unalienable, indefeasible right, to reform,
alter, or abolish it, in such manner as shall be judged most conducive to the
public weal.

4. That no man, or set of men, are entitled to exclusive or separate emoluments or privileges from the community, but in consideration of public services; which not being descendible, neither ought the offices of magistrate,
legislator, or judge, to be hereditary.

5. That the legislative and executive powers of the state should be separate and distinct from the judicial; and that the members of the two first may
be restrained from oppression, by feeling and participating the burthens of
the people, they should, at fixed periods, be reduced to a private station, and

return unto that body from which they were originally taken, and vacancies be supplied by frequent, certain and regular election.

6. That elections of members, to serve as representatives of the people in the legislature, ought to be free, and that all men having sufficient evidence of permanent common interest with, and attachment to the community, have the right of suffrage; and cannot be taxed, or deprived of their property for public uses without their own consent, or that of their representatives so elected, nor bound by any law to which they have not, in like manner, assented for the common good.

7. That all power of suspending laws, or the execution of laws, by any authority, without consent of the representatives of the people, is injurious to their rights, and ought not to be exercised.

8. That in all capital or criminal prosecutions, a man hath a right to demand the cause and nature of his accusation, to be confronted with the accusers and witnesses, to call for evidence in his favor, and to a speedy trial by an impartial jury of his vicinage; without unanimous consent he cannot be found guilty, nor can he be compelled to give evidence against himself; and that no man be deprived of his liberty, except by the law of the land, or the judgment of his peers.

9. That excessive bail ought not to be required, nor excessive fines imposed, nor cruel and unusual punishments inflicted. . . .

11. That in controversies respecting property, and in suits between man and man, the ancient trial by jury is preferable to any other, and ought to be held sacred.

12. That the freedom of the press is one of the great bulwarks of liberty, and can never be restrained but by despotic governments.

13. That a well regulated militia, composed of the body of the people trained to arms, is the proper, natural, and safe defence of a free state; that standing armies in time of peace, should be avoided, as dangerous to liberty; and that, in all cases, the military should be under strict subordination to, and governed by the civil power. . . .

15. That no free government, or the blessing of liberty, can be preserved to any people, but by a firm adherence to justice, moderation, temperance, frugality and virtue, and by frequent recurrence to fundamental principles.

16. That religion, or the duty which we owe to our Creator, and the manner of discharging it, can be directed only by reason and conviction, not by force or violence, and, therefore that all men should enjoy the fullest toleration in the exercise of religion, according to the dictates of conscience, un-

punished and unrestrained by the magistrate; unless under color of religion, any man disturb the peace, the happiness, or the safety of society. And that it is the mutual duty of all to practice Christian forbearance, love, and charity toward each other.

JOHN JAY HAILS AMERICAN PRINCIPLES OF GOVERNMENT

[Charge to Grand Jury of the Supreme Court of New York by John Jay, Chief Justice of the state, September 9, 1777]

GENTLEMEN—It affords me very sensible pleasure to congratulate you on the dawn of that free, mild and equal government, which now begins to rise and break from amidst those clouds of anarchy, confusion and licentiousness, which the arbitrary and violent domination of the king of Great Britain has spread, in greater or less degree, throughout this and the other American states. . . .

The Americans are the first people whom heaven has favored with an opportunity of deliberating upon, and choosing the forms of government under which they should live;—all other constitutions have derived their existence from violence or accidental circumstances, and are therefore probably more distant from their perfection, which, though beyond our reach, may nevertheless be approached under the guidance of reason and experience.

How far the people of this state have improved this opportunity, we are at no loss to determine.—Their constitution has given general satisfaction at home, and been not only approved, but applauded abroad. It would be a pleasing task to take a minute view of it, to investigate its principles, and remark the connection and use of its several parts—but that would be a work of too great length to be proper on this occasion. I must therefore confine myself to general observations; and among those which naturally arise from a consideration of this subject, none are more obvious, than that the highest respect has been paid to those great and equal rights of human nature, which should forever remain inviolate in every society—and that such care has been taken in the disposition of the legislative, executive and judicial powers of government, as to promise permanence to the constitution, and give energy and impartiality to the distribution of justice. So that, while you possess wisdom to discern and virtue to appoint men of worth and abilities to fill the offices of the state, you will be happy at home and respectable abroad.—Your life, your liberties, your property, will be at the disposal only of your Creator and yourselves. You will know no power but such as you will create; no authority unless derived from your grant; no laws, but such as acquire all their obligations from your consent.

Adequate security is also given to the rights of conscience and private judgment. They are, by nature, subject to no control but that of the Deity, and in that free situation they are now left. Every man is permitted to consider, to adore and to worship his Creator in the manner most agreeable to his conscience. No opinions are dictated; no rules of faith prescribed; no preference given to one sect to the prejudice of others.—The constitution, however, has wisely declared, that the "liberty of conscience, thereby granted, shall not be so construed as to excuse acts of licentiousness, or justify practices inconsistent with the peace or safety of this state." In a word, the convention, by whom that constitution was formed, were of opinion, that the gospel of Christ, like the ark of God, would not fall, though unsupported by the arm of flesh; and happy would it be for mankind, if that opinion prevailed more generally.

But let it be remembered, that whatever marks of wisdom, experience and patriotism there may be in your constitution, yet like the beautiful symmetry, the just proportions, and elegant forms of our first parents, before their maker breathed into them the breath of life, it is yet to be animated, and till then, may indeed excite admiration, but will be of no use—from the people it must receive its spirit, and by them be quickened. Let virtue, honor, the love of liberty and of science be, and remain, the soul of this constitution, and it will become the source of great extensive happiness to this and future generations. Vice, ignorance, and want of vigilance, will be the only enemies able to destroy it. Against these provide, and, of these, be forever jealous. Every member of the state, ought diligently to read and study the constitution of his country, and teach the rising generation to be free. By knowing their rights, they will sooner perceive when they are violated, and be the better prepared to defend and assert them. . . .

A PLEA FOR LIBERTY OF CONSCIENCE

[Remarks ascribed to Governor William Livingston
of New Jersey, 1778]

If, in our own estimate of things, we ought to be regulated by the importance, doubtless every encroachment upon religion, of all things the most important, ought to be considered as the greatest imposition; and the unmolested exercise of it, a proportionable blessing.

By religion, I mean an inward habitual reverence for, and devotedness to the Deity, with such external homage, either public or private, as the worshipper believes most acceptable to him. According to this definition, it is impossible for human laws to regulate religion without destroying it; for they cannot compel inward religious reverence, that being altogether mental and of a spiritual nature; nor can they enforce outward religious homage, because all such homage is either a man's own choice, and then it is not compelled, or it is repugnant to it, and then it cannot be religious.

The laws of England, indeed, do not peremptorily inhibit a man from worshipping God, according to the dictates of his own conscience, nor positively constrain him to violate it, by conforming to the religion of the state: But they punish him for doing the former, or what amounts to the same thing, for omitting the latter, and consequently punish him for his religion. For what are the civil disqualifications and the privation of certain privileges he thereby incurs, but so many punishments? And what else is the punishment for not embracing the religion of others, but the punishment of practising one's own? With how little propriety a nation can boast of its freedom under such restraints on religious liberty, requires no great sagacity to determine. They affect, 'tis true, to abhor the imputation of [intolerance] and applaud themselves for their pretended toleration and lenity. As contra-distinguished, indeed, from actual prohibition, a permission may doubtless be called a toleration; for as a man is permitted to enjoy his religion under whatever penalties or forfeitures, he is certainly tolerated to enjoy it. But as far as he pays for such enjoyment, by suffering those penalties and forfeitures, he as certainly does not enjoy it freely. On the contrary, he is persecuted in the proportion that his privilege is so regulated and qualified. I call it persecution, because it is harassing mankind for their principles; and I deny that such punishments derive any sanction from law, because the consciences of men are not the objects of human legislation. And to trace this stupendous insult on the dignity of reason to any other source than the one from which I induced it in the preceding essay, I mean the abominable combination of king-craft and priest-craft, (in everlasting indissoluble league to extirpate liberty, and erect on its ruins boundless and universal despotism), would I believe puzzle the most assiduous enquirer. For what business, in the name of common sense, has the magistrate (distinctly and singly appointed for our political and temporal happiness) with our religion, which is to secure our happiness spiritual and eternal? And indeed among all the absurdities chargeable upon human nature, it never yet entered into the thoughts of any one to confer such authority upon another. The institution of civil society I have pointed out as originating from the unbridled rapaciousness of individuals, and as a necessary curb to prevent that violence and other inconveniences to which men in a state of nature were exposed. But whoever fancied it a violence offered to himself, that another should enjoy his own opinion? Or who, in a state of nature, ever deemed it an inconvenience that every man should choose his own religion? Did the free denizens of the world, before the monstrous birth of priest-craft, aiding and aided by the secular arm, ever worry one another for not practising ridiculous rites, or for disbelieving things incredible? Did men in their aboriginal condition ever suffer persecution for conscience sake? The most frantic enthusiast will not pretend it. Why then should the members of society be supposed, on their entering into it, to have had in contemplation the reforming an abuse which never existed? Or why are they pretended to have invested the magistrate with authority to sway and direct their religious sentiment? In reality, such delegation of power, had it ever been made, would be a mere nullity, and the compact by which it was ceded, altogether nugatory, the rights of conscience being immutably personal and absolutely inalienable, nor can the state or community as such have any concern in the matter. For in what manner doth it affect society, which is evidently and solely instituted to prevent personal assault, the violation of property and the defamation of character; and hath not (these remaining inviolate) any interest in the actions of men—how doth it, I say, affect society what principles we entertain in our own minds, or in what outward form we think it best to pay our adoration to God? But to set the absurdity of the magistrate's authority to interfere in matters of religion, in the strongest light, I would fain know what religion it is that he has authority to establish? Has he a right to establish only the true religion, or is any religion true because he does not establish it? If the former, his trouble is as vain as it is arrogant, because the true religion being not of this world, wants not the princes of this world to support it; but has in fact either languished or been adulterated wherever they meddled with it. If the supreme magistrate, as such, has authority to establish any religion he thinks to be true, and the religion so established is therefore right and ought to be embraced, it follows, since all supreme magistrates have the same authority, that all established religions are equally right, and ought to be embraced. The emperor of China, therefore, having, as supreme magistrate in his empire, the same right to establish the precepts of Confucius, and the Sultan in his, the imposture of Mahomet, as hath the king of Great Britain the doctrine of Christ in his dominion, it results from these principles, that the religions of Confucius and Mahomet are equally true with the doctrine of our blessed

Saviour and his Apostles, and equally obligatory upon the respective subjects of China and Turkey, as Christianity is on those within the British realm; a position which, I presume, the most zealous advocate for ecclesiastical domination would think it blasphemy to avow.

The English ecclesiastical government, therefore, is, and all the religious establishments in the world are manifest violations of the right of private judgment in matters of religion. They are impudent outrages on common sense, in arrogating a power of controling the devotional operations of the mind and external acts of divine homage not cognizable by any human tribunal, and for which we are accountable only to the Great Searcher of hearts, whose prerogative it is to judge them.

In contrast with this spiritual tyranny, how beautiful appears our catholic constitution in disclaiming all jurisdiction over the souls of men, and securing, by a law never to be repealed, the voluntary, unchecked moral suasion of every individual, and his own self-directed intercourse with the father of spirits, either by devout retirement or public worship of his own election! How amiable the plan of entrenching, with the sanction of an ordinance, immutable and irrevocable, the sacred rights of conscience, and renouncing all discrimination between men on account of their sentiments about the various modes of church government, or the different articles of their faith!

DAVID RAMSAY PRAISES THE AMERICAN EXPERIMENT

[*Speech by Dr. David Ramsay—the South Carolina physician,
legislator, historian—on the advantages of American
independence, delivered to a public gathering in
Charleston, South Carolina, July 4, 1778*]

. . . It has never yet been fairly tried how far the equal principles of republican government would secure the happiness of the governed. The ancients, unacquainted with the present mode of taking the sense of the people by representatives, were too apt, in their public meetings to run into disorder and confusion. The distinction of patricians and plebeians, laid the foundation of perpetual discord in the Roman commonwealth. If the free states of Greece had been under the control of a common superintending power, similar to our continental congress, they could have peaceably decided their disputes, and probably would have preserved their freedom and importance to the present day. Happily for us, warned by experience, we have guarded against all these evils. No artificial distinction of ranks has been suffered to take place among us. We can peaceably convene a state in one small assembly of deputies, representing the whole in an equal proportion. All disputes between the different states, and all continental concerns, are to be managed by a congress of representatives from each. What a security for liberty, for union, for every species of political happiness! Small states are weak, and incapable of defence, large ones are unwieldy, greatly abridge natural liberty, and their general laws, from a variety of clashing interests, must frequently bear hard on many individuals. But our confederation will give us the strength and protection of a power equal to that of the greatest; at the same time that, in all our internal concerns, we have the freedom of small independent commonwealths. We are in possession of constitutions that contain in them the excellencies of all forms of government, free from the inconveniences of each; and in one word, we bid fair to be the happiest and freest people in the world for ages yet to come. . . .

When I anticipate in imagination the future glory of my country, and the illustrious figure it will soon make on the theatre of the world, my heart distends with generous pride for being an American. What a substratum for empire! compared with which, the foundation of the Macedonian, the Roman, and the British, sink into insignificance. Some of our large states have territory superior to the island of Great Britain; while the whole together, are little inferior to Europe itself. Our independence will people this extent of country with freemen, and will stimulate the innumerable inhabitants thereof, by every motive, to perfect the acts of government, and to extend human happiness.

I congratulate you on your glorious prospects. Having for three long years weathered the storms of adversity, we are at length arrived in view of the calm haven of peace and security. We have laid the foundations of a new empire, which promises to enlarge itself to vast dimensions, and to give happiness to a great continent. It is now our turn to figure on the face of the earth, and in the annals of the world. The arts and sciences are planted among us, and, fostered by the auspicious influence of equal governments, are growing up to maturity; while truth and freedom flourish by their sides. Liberty, both civil and religious, in her noon-tide blaze, shines forth with unclouded lustre on all ranks and denominations of men.

Ever since the flood, true religion, literature, arts, empire and riches, have taken a slow and gradual course from east to west and are now about fixing their long and favorite abode in this new western world. Our sun of political happiness is already risen, and hath lifted its head over the mountains, illuminating our hemisphere with liberty, light, and polished life. Our independence will redeem one quarter of the globe from tyranny and oppression, and consecrate it the chosen seat of truth, justice, freedom, learning and religion. We are laying the foundation of happiness for countless millions. Generations yet unborn will bless us for the blood-bought inheritance, we are about to bequeath them. Oh happy times! Oh glorious days! Oh kind, and indulgent, bountiful Providence, that we live in this highly favored period, and have the honor of helping forward these great events, and of suffering in a cause of such infinite importance!

2. THE FIRST CONSTITUTION

JUDGE DRAYTON ANALYZES THE ARTICLES OF CONFEDERATION

[Speech by William Henry Drayton, Chief Justice of South Carolina, to the General Assembly of the state, January 20, 1778]

MR. CHAIRMAN—A plan of a confederation of the United States of America, is at length by congress, given to the continent: A subject of as high importance as can be presented to their attention. Upon the wise formation of this, their independence, glory and happiness ultimately depend. The plan is delivered abroad for private and public information: It is sent to us for consideration. Sir, my mind labors under the load that is thus thrown upon it.—Millions are to experience the effects of the judgment of those few, whom the laws permit to think and to act for them in this grand business. Millions—posterity innumerable, will bless or curse our conduct!—Their happiness or misery depend upon us—their fate is now in our hands! I almost tremble, while I assist in holding the important balance!—But sir, the great Disposer of all things, has placed us in this important period, pregnant with vast events. He has called us forth to legislate for the new world; and to endeavor to bind the various people of it in durable bands of friendship and union. We must obey: and I trust we shall obey, with courage and integrity. Actuated by these principles, I am incapable of receding from my duty. And conscious that I am bound to consider the subject of a confederation of the United States, upon the broad basis of equality, I shall endeavor to discharge this obligation, first, by viewing the plan before us, with liberality, and with that decency and respect, due to the high authority from which it is derived; and then, by taking the liberty of throwing out my ideas of such terms, as in my opinion are desirable, attainable, and likely to form a beneficial confederation.

The best writers upon government, agree in this as a political truth; that where the liberties of the people are to be preserved, the legislative and executive should ever be separate and distinct; and that the first should consist of parts mutually forming a check upon each other. The consuls, senate and people, constituted such a government in Rome. The kings, lords and commons, erected such a government in Britain. The first, one of the best of antiquity—the last, the most perfect system, the wit of man ever devised; But both, as it is the case with all things temporal, lost their capability of action, and changed their very nature.

We are about to establish a confederated government which I religiously hope will last for ages. And, I must be pardoned when I say that this government does not appear likely to be formed upon those principles, which the wisest men have deemed, and which long and invariable experience prove, to be the most secure defences to liberty. The congress seem to have lost sight of this wise mode of government. At least it is certain, that they have rejected it. I lament their decision: I have apprehension for the consequences, into their own hands, they appear inclined to assume almost all the important powers of government. The second article speaks of the sovereignty of the respective states, but by the time we arrive at the last, scarce the shadow of sovereignty remains to any. "No two or more states shall enter into any treaty," but by consent of congress—"nor shall any body of forces be kept up by any state, in time of peace, except such number only," as congress shall deem requisite—"no vessels of war, shall be kept up in time of peace by any state, except such number only," as congress shall deem necessary—"nor shall any state grant commissions to any ships or vessels of war, except it be after a declaration of war by," Congress—and, these are great and humiliating restrictions upon their sovereignty. It is of necessity, that the sovereignty of the states should be restricted—but I would do this with a gentle hand. Cannot a good confederation be had, without these humiliating restrictions? I think it may. However, independent of the settlement of this point; the two last restrictions require another observation. From the first of them it ought to be presumed, that upon a vacancy in any of the vessels of war, kept up by any state in the time of peace by the permission of congress, the state to which they belong shall in time of peace, be at liberty to issue a new commission. But if this is to be presumed, the sentiment ought to have been precisely expressed; for it is obvious a doubt upon this matter, may arise from the restriction, that no state shall grant commissions to any ships or vessels of war, except it be after a declaration of war. These clauses, if we give due efficacy to the signification of words, really clash—at least displaying an ambiguity, they require a rule of construction, that must destroy the peremptoriness of words. A rule which ought not to be admitted into an instrument of this kind; for it should be maturely considered; and it may be precisely worded, without the formality of a statute law.

There seems to be a dangerous inaccuracy in that part of the sixth article, prohibiting the states respectively from entering into any conference with any king, prince or state. I presume this ought to be understood, to respect a foreign state only: But it may be insisted upon, that the prohibition includes even the United States. And why should not two or more of these have any conference? I would have the doubt absolutely destroyed.

The third section of the article now under my observation, declares, that "no state shall lay any imposts or duties, which may interfere with any stipulations in treaties, entered into by congress with any king, prince or state, in pursuance of any treaties already proposed by congress to the courts of France and Spain:" And I must contrast this with the provision in the ninth article, "that no treaty of commerce shall be made whereby the legislative power of the respective states shall be restrained from imposing such imposts and duties on foreigners, as their own people are subject to, or from prohibiting the exportation or importation of any species of goods or commodities whatsoever."—I am of opinion, we are to understand from the first of these clauses, that no state shall lay any imposts or duties, which may interfere with the present foreign stipulations of congress, in treaties already proposed; and that such stipulations, free of such interference, may be concluded by treaty: But this latter meaning is not expressed. . . .

In the fourth section of the ninth article, congress is vested with the power of "regulating the trade and managing all affairs with the Indians, not members of any of the states, provided that the legislative right of any state within its own limits, be not infringed or violated." I much approve the grant, but I confess I do not understand the grant and proviso combined. For I cannot conceive, in what manner the legislative right of a state within its own limits, can be infringed by an act of congress relative to Indians not members of any state: and therefore not within the limits of any so as to be subject to the operation of its legislative right.

It is of no moment with me, whether the doubts I have raised, are deemed obvious and important, or rather refined and of little consequence.

Grant, and it must be admitted, that they have the appearance of doubts—I ask no more. The honor and interest of America require, that their grand act of confederation, should be a noble monument, free, as far as human wisdom can enable it to be from defect and flaw; Every thing unnecessary should be critically removed—every appearance of doubt should be carefully eradicated out of it. It is not to be thought, but that the present congress clearly understand the confederation. But other congresses will look for the spirit of the law. This "will then be the result of their good or bad logic; and this will depend on their good or bad digestion; on the violence of their passions; on the rank and condition of the parties, or on their connections with congress; and on all those little circumstances, which change the appearance of objects in the fluctuating mind of man." Thus thought the illustrious marquis Beccaria, of Milan, a sublime philosopher, reasoning on the interpretation of laws.—I must be permitted to continue his ideas, yet a little further upon this subject—they are so exactly in point. He says, "there is nothing more dangerous than the common axiom: The spirit of the laws is to be considered. To adopt it, is to give way to the torrent of opinions." "When the code of laws is once fixed, it should be observed in the literal sense." "When the rule of right which ought to direct the actions of the philosopher, as well as the ignorant, is a matter of controversy, not of fact, the people are slaves to the magistrates."—Is it not the intention of the confederation, that the people shall be free?—Let it then be adapted to the meanest capacity—let the rule of right be not matter of controversy, but of fact—let the confederation be understood according to that strict rule by which we understand penal laws. The confederation is of at least as much importance to America, as penal laws are in a small society—safety to the people is the object of both. In a word, the spirit of laws, lays down this maxim, that "in republics, the very nature of the constitution requires the judges to follow the letter of the law."

The fourth article declares, "that the free inhabitants of each of these states, paupers, vagabonds and fugitives from justice excepted, shall be entitled to all privileges and immunities of free citizens in the several states:" A position, in my opinion, absolutely inadmissible. Would the people of Massachusetts have the free negroes of Carolina eligible to their general court? Can it be intended, that the free inhabitants of one state shall have power to go into another, there to vote for representatives in the legislature?—And yet these things are clearly included in that clause. I think there ought to be no doubt, but that the free inhabitants should be white, and that such of one state, should be entitled to the privileges and immunities in another, only by the same means through which the free white inhabitants of that state are by law entitled—This article also provides for the "removal of property imported into any state;" but the removal of property acquired in it, into that "of which the owner is an inhabitant," is neglected. Has not the owner an equal right to enjoy at home, the last kind of property as the first? The provision in behalf of the congress, or a state, is manifestly in contradistinction to that in favor of a private owner. . . .

I have already said, the sovereignty of the states should be restricted with a gentle hand: I now add it ought to be restricted, only in cases of absolute necessity.—What absolute necessity is there, that congress should have the power of causing the value of all granted land, to be "estimated according to such mode, as they shall from time to time direct?" Congress should have no power, but what is clearly defined in the nature of its operation.— But I am absolutely against the position, that the public aids shall be raised by the several states, in proportion to the value of their granted lands, buildings and improvements. At the first blush of this proposition, nothing seems more equitable. But viewing the subject with more attention, I think I see, that it is unequal, injurious and impolitic. . . .

The mode of trial of disputes between any two or more states seems full of delay, and therefore it ought to be amended. The fifth article provides, that the representation of each state, shall not be less than two delegates; But the mode of trial specifies, that in a certain case, "congress shall name three persons out of each of the United States," from whom the judges shall be selected. Now a state may be represented by only two delegates, and then, the trial cannot be had, and considering the expense of paying delegates— the inconvenience of their attendance upon congress at a distance from their private affairs, and from constant experience, a bare representation is oftener to be expected, than a supernumerary one. If it is meant the three shall be taken from the people at large, which I will not imagine to be the case, a court may be picked; and therefore, that plan ought not to be heard of— In this case, I would prefer judges during good behavior, eminent for their knowledge in the law of nations; and who should be obliged to assign at large the reasons upon which they ground their decrees.

The congress would be vested with the sole and exclusive right and power of regulating the alloy and value of coin struck by the authority of the respective states; and of fixing the standards of weights and measures throughout the United States: But I see no necessity for such delegation. To regulate the alloy and value of coin is one of the most distinguished prerogatives of sovereignty, nor can any of the United States part with it without exposing itself to be drained of specie. . . .

Congress desire to be invested with the "appointing all officers in the land forces, excepting regimental officers." And far from seeing any absolute necessity for their having such a power, I can see no degree of common propriety to warrant the claim. The several states are to raise the regiments composing the land forces. Deputy staff officers in particular are absolutely necessary to each of the quotas; and they rank with regimental officers. I cannot see the shadow of a good reason, why the states should not have the appointment of all officers necessary to complete their respective quotas. Their honor, interest and safety are immediately and primarily affected, by the proper formation and regulation of their quotas. Their respective spheres of action, being within a very small circle, in comparison of that, in which the congress preside; they must of consequence be enabled to view objects at a nearer distance—to penetrate into the characters and abilities of candidates, and to make a proper choice with more accuracy and precision, than congress can be supposed to do. They will have enough upon their hands, in actuating the great machine of government. Their attention necessarily engaged in general and important affairs, ought not to be permitted to be drawn off, by those inferior objects which can more minutely and therefore better be examined by the respective states. This ought to be a fundamental maxim in the confederated policy. There is justice in it; and I will be bold to say, it arises from principles of true wisdom. It will display a confidence on the part of congress in the several states; and this must be the grand basis of their independency and freedom. We do not mean, unnecessarily to delegate any part of our sovereignty: We are willing to sacrifice only such parts of it, as are necessary to be sacrificed for the general safety. In short, we enter into this confederacy, on the same principle only, that men enter into society.

But independent of this position, as a matter of right, I will consider the claim upon the footing of common prudence and experience. Whenever congress sit, there will be a number of persons especially from the nearer states, soliciting offices; They will form acquaintances with the members; and we know the common effect of such connection. In consequence, congress may appoint even an unexceptional person, as to his character and capacity, to a post in a state in which he has no connections, and of which he is not a member: This may occasion an envy against the officer, even to the detriment of the public service; and a displeasure against congress, for having made, as it may be deemed, an appointment injurious to those individuals of that state, who were in every respect capable of the office, and whom the public would wish to see in it. Or congress may be induced to appoint a member of the state, but such a one as the people never would have chosen, because they know him to be unequal to the trust. To say such things ought not to be supposed, is to say but little: Every page in history—the known disposition of the human heart inform us, that nothing is more likely to happen. I am therefore clearly against the clause—all officers excepting regimental officers. And indeed I am of opinion, that of as many brigades as the quota of any state may consist so many brigadiers general should that state nominate; the eldest of whom should command the whole, while in the state, and not therein actually assisted by the major part of another quota, commanded by a superior officer. Let congress appoint a generalissimo and major generals—these are proper to command two or more quotas when in conjunction: And the states being divided into departments, a proper number of major-generals may command in them.

In a confederacy of states, for the purpose of general security of arms, I cannot but conceive that there ought of prudence and necessity, to be a clause, at least obliging the parties to furnish their respective quotas, beyond the possibility of a neglect or evasion with impunity. But, I see no such clause in the confederation before us—the main pillar of security therefore is not in it. It is true, there is a long clause respecting quotas. But, it is only directory, And how many such laws are there, which are regarded as nugatory, merely for the want of a penal clause? Have we not had sufficient experience, of the inefficacy of that clause relating to quotas? Before it was inserted in the plan of confederation, did not congress act upon the very principles contained in it? The present quotas of the respective states were arranged upon a computation of their respective abilities. The numbers were sufficient, with the favor of Heaven, nay abundantly sufficient almost without effusion of blood, to captivate all the British forces in America. But when they ought to have crushed the ungenerous foe, they were not even raised in the most populous states. These principles, even in the hour of the most pressing necessity, have been neglected with impunity, at our hands, to the imminent hazard of the liberties of America. Are we not to be instructed, even by a bloody experience? Shall we not receive light, even from the conflagrations spread over our land? Oh! why has our beneficent Creator endowed us with recollection!—Mr. Chairman, pardon me; I am hurt—pierced to the quick, at an omission of the most fatal nature. It is a symptom filling me with torturing apprehensions. . . . .

Sir, when I consider the extent of territory possessed by the thirteen states—the value of that territory; and that the three most southern, must daily and rapidly increase in population, riches and importance. When I reflect, that from the nature of the climate, soil and produce of the several states, a northern and southern interest in many particulars naturally and unavoidably arise; I cannot but be displeased with the prospect, that the most important transactions in congress, may be done contrary to the united opposition of Virginia, the two Carolinas and Georgia: States possessing more than one half of the whole territory of the confederacy; and forming, as I may say, the body of the southern interest. If things of such transcendent weight, may be done notwithstanding such an opposition; the honor, interest and sovereignty of the south, are in effect delivered up to the care of the north. Do we intend to make such a surrender? I hope not, there is no occasion for it. Nor would I have it understood, that I fear the north would abuse the confidence of the south: But common prudence, sir, admonishes me, that confidence should not wantonly be placed any where—it is but the other day, that we thought our liberties secure in the care of Britain. I am assisting to form the confederation of the United States: It is my duty to speak, and to speak plainly: I engage in this great work with a determined purpose, to endeavor, as far as my slender abilities enable me, to render it equal, just and binding. I presume, that all my coadjutors in the several states, in and out of congress, act upon this sentiment; nor can I admit a contrary idea. When all mean fair, equitable terms are not difficult to be adjusted. I therefore hope, I shall not be thought unreasonable, because I object to the nine voices in congress; and wish that eleven may be substituted, to enable that body to transact their most important business. The states general of Holland must be unanimous: Their government is accounted a wise one; and although it causes their proceedings to be slow, yet, it secures the freedom and interest of its respective states. Is not this our great aim?

For the present, I here, sir, limit my particular objection to the plan under consideration: I have made these with the highest reluctance. In a word, I cannot admit of any confederation that gives congress any power, that can with propriety be exercised by several states—or any power, but what is clearly defined beyond a doubt. Nor can I think of entering into any engagements, which are not as equal as may be, between the states—engagements of a compelling nature, and the whole to be understood according to the letter only. Without these five leading principles, a confederation is not a desirable object in my opinion. . . .

JUDGE PENDLETON SPEAKS OF HARD TIMES
IN SOUTH CAROLINA

[Charge to a South Carolina grand jury by Judge Pendleton, 1787]

GENTLEMEN OF THE GRAND JURY . . . No society ever long endured the miseries of anarchy, disorder, and licentiousness. The most vile despotism will be embraced in preference to it. The nations, from which we derive our origin, afford innumerable examples of this. I will, however, mention but one. When the parliament of England had dethroned and beheaded that faithless tyrant, Charles the first—subdued all their enemies at home and abroad—and changed their monarchy into a republic—one would have supposed, that an assemblage of as great talents as ever adorned human nature, which so highly distinguished the patriots of that time, could not fail of forming a wise and just government, and of transmitting it to their posterity. But the event shewed that the disorderly temper of the people, occasioned by the civil war, would not bear the strong curb of legal authority. Expedient after expedient was tried: and government assumed many different shapes to humor their passions and prejudices, and lead them to a willing obedience; but all to no purpose. The public disorders daily increased. Every little club of politicians were for making laws for the whole nation. The fair form of equal and legal liberty became defaced by a thousand fanciful and impracticable whimsies, until the general distress became insupportable. What followed? The very people, who, a few years before had dazzled the world with the splendor of their actions, invited back, and enthroned the son of that king, whom they had formerly put to death; gave him carte blanche to do as he pleased; and seemed to have forgotten, that they had ever lost a drop of blood, or spent a shilling, in defence of their liberty.

Gentlemen, let us not lose sight of this awful precedent. To acquire freedom is nothing, in comparison to a wise and profitable use of it. Nothing can be more certain, than that Great Britain would eagerly seize any opportunity to compass our destruction. She would, to-morrow, pour her fleets and armies into this country, particularly the southern states, if the great powers of Europe could be so allied and connected, as to secure her from a hostile confederacy. The history of those nations every where shews us, what trivial causes occasion the most important changes in their political systems. Surely, then, it is wise to be on our guard, and in the first place to secure a free and just, but, at the same time, a strong government at home. Without this, the citizens are insecure in their persons and estates; that insecurity produces murmuring and discontent: and that discontent will ever produce a disposition favorable for trying new changes. In such a state, to be attacked by a formidable enemy, without soldiers or military stores, and without authority to compel even our own citizens to obey the laws, we must fall a prey to any foreign power, who may think it worth the cost to subjugate us.

I have heard, gentlemen of the grand jury, great complaints against the illiberal and monopolizing spirit of the British government, on the subject of commerce with America—her numerous duties on American produce—and her refusal to enter into treaties for mutual benefits in trade. It must surely be highly ridiculous to abuse one nation for profiting by the follies of another. Do we expect that Great Britain, as a trading nation, will not exert every nerve to hold fast the commercial advantages, which our avidity for her negroes and manufactures hath given her? Is it not the steady policy of every nation in Europe, to promote and extend their own commerce by every possible means, let it be at the expense of whomsoever it will? Yes, gentlemen: and let us act with such caution and punctuality, as to make it her interest to solicit, and we shall soon find her courting, with douceurs, those commercial compacts, which she now so contemptuously declines. At the close of the war, indeed, she stood trembling with apprehension, lest our two allies, France and Holland, should monopolize our trade. A treaty, pressed at that moment, and properly urged—the *sine qua non* of all future amity and intercourse, would in all probability, have produced an inlet of American built vessels into her islands, and an exemption from many other injurious restraints. But the favorable moment slipt through our hands unimproved, and (I fear) never to return. The only possible way left us to recover it, is, to live within our income; to secure a balance of trade in our favor; and to urge the federal government to such general regulations, as shall secure us from the infamous vassalage into which we are hurrying. If three or four thousand pounds sterling worth of merchandise, (annually) which sum will include a great many luxuries, be sufficient for all our rational wants, when our exports greatly exceed that sum, and are annually increasing—is it not obvious to the meanest capacity, that a large balance must yearly return to us in gold and silver? which, in spite of all the paper-money casuists in the world, is the only wholesome political blood that can give union, health, and vigor to the body politic.

If we do not curtail our expenses, and export more than we import, a general bankruptcy must be the inevitable consequence.

Many people call for large emissions of paper-money. For what?—To shift the burdens, which they have incurred by their avarice and folly, from themselves to their better, and more deserving, creditors, whose property they choose to hold fast. Can anything be more fraudulent or astonishing? No, gentlemen: paper medium and sheriffs' sale bills, are only temporary expedients, a repetition of which, in a very short time, would be insupportable. They were intended, at a singular crisis, to open a retreat even to the foolish and extravagant, as well as the unfortunate debtor, by affording an opportunity to retrieve, but not to give impunity to the one, or a release to the other. The honest and industrious man will seize the opportunity to lay up against the day of account and payment, while nothing will correct or reclaim the indolent and fraudulent knave. But, as I said, the period is at hand, when the punctual payment of taxes and debts must take place voluntarily: or the uninterrupted recovery of them, in the courts of justice, be enforced. Palliatives are exhausted. We must either relinquish government, resign our independence, and embrace a military master—or execute our laws by force of arms, if no alternative is left us. But, before we are compelled to resort to this disgraceful and painful ultimatum, let us all exert ourselves, and support each other, as free citizens, acknowledging no master but the laws, which we ourselves have made for our common good—obeying those laws, and enforcing them, when and where we can. Let no man say, this or that is not my business. Whatever materially affects the honor and interest of the state, is every man's business; because he must, in common with all others, share the good or evil brought upon his country. The man who refuses or evades the payment of taxes imposed by his immediate representative, or excites or co-operates in the resistance of lawful authority, is the parricide of his country, as well as the voluntary assassin of his own interest; since it is impossible he can be tranquil or happy, or enjoy his property in peace and security, while his country is convulsed and distracted. . . .

This is not a time to lessen or extenuate the terror, which the present dangerous crisis must inspire. To know our danger, to face it like men, and to triumph over it by constancy and courage, is a character this country once justly acquired. Is it to be sacrificed in the hour of peace, with every incentive to preserve it? I repeat again, that, without a change of conduct, and an union of all the good men in the state, we are an undone people; the government will soon tumble about our heads, and become a prey to the first bold ruffian, who shall associate a few desperate adventurers, and seize upon it.

I confess the subject very deeply affects me. I shall, therefore pursue it no farther. I do not, however, despair of the republic. There are honest and independent men among us, to retrieve every thing, whatever may be opposed by the vicious and unprincipled, if they will but step forth, and act with union and vigor. If they will not, the miseries resulting to their country from the utter destruction of all public and private credit, a bankrupt treasury, and the triumph of all manner of fraud, rapine, and licentiousness, together with the scorn and derision of our enemies, if we should have any left, be on their heads!

BENJAMIN RUSH ADVOCATES MAJOR CHANGES

*[Address by Dr. Benjamin Rush, the Philadelphia physician,
statesman, and author, to the people of the United States,
Philadelphia, 1787]*

There is nothing more common, than to confound the terms of American revolution with those of the late American war. The American war is over: but this is far from being the case with American revolution. On the contrary, nothing but the first act of the great drama is closed. It remains yet to establish and perfect our new forms of government; and to prepare the principles, morals, and manners of our citizens, for these forms of government, after they are established and brought to perfection.

The confederation, together with most of our state constitutions, were formed under very unfavorable circumstances. We had just emerged from a corrupted monarchy. Although we understood perfectly the principles of liberty, yet most of us were ignorant of the forms and combinations of power in republics. Add to this, the British army was in the heart of our country, spreading desolation wherever it went; our resentments, of course, were awakened. We detested the British name, and unfortunately refused to copy some things in the administration of justice and power, in the British government, which have made it the admiration and envy of the world. In our opposition to monarchy, we forgot that the temple of tyranny has two doors. We bolted one of them by proper restraints; but we left the other open, by neglecting to guard against the effects of our own ignorance and licentiousness.

Most of the present difficulties of this country arise from the weakness and other defects of our governments.

My business at present shall be only to suggest the defects of the confederation. These consist—1st. In the deficiency of coercive power. 2d. In a defect of exclusive power to issue paper money, and regulate commerce. 3d. In vesting the sovereign power of the United States in a single legislature: and, 4th. In the too frequent rotation of its members.

A convention is to sit soon for the purpose of devising means of obviating part of the two first defects that have been mentioned. But I wish they may add to their recommendations to each state, to surrender up to congress their power of emitting money. In this way a uniform currency will be produced, that will facilitate trade, and help to bind the states together. Nor will the states be deprived of large sums of money by this mean, when sudden emergencies require it; for they may always borrow them, as they did during the war, out of the treasury of congress. Even a loan office may be better instituted in this way, in each state, than in any other.

The two last defects that have been mentioned, are not of less magnitude than the first. Indeed, the single legislature of congress will become more dangerous, from an increase of power, than ever. To remedy this, let the supreme federal power be divided, like the legislatures of most of our states, into two distinct, independent branches. Let one of them be styled the council of the states and the other the assembly of the states. Let the first consist of a single delegate—and the second, of two, three, or four delegates, chosen annually by the joint ballot of both houses; and let him possess certain powers, in conjunction with a privy council, especially the power of appointing most of the officers of the United States. The officers will not only be better, when appointed this way, but one of the principal causes of faction will be thereby removed from congress. I apprehend this division of the power of congress will become more necessary, as soon as they are invested with more ample powers of levying and expending public money.

The custom of turning men out of power or office, as soon as they are qualified for it, has been found to be absurd in practice. Is it virtuous to dismiss a general—a physician—or even a domestic, as soon as they have acquired knowledge sufficient to be useful to us, for the sake of increasing the number of able generals, skilful physicians—and faithful servants? We do not. Government is a science, and can never be perfect in America, until we encourage men to devote not only three years, but their whole lives to it. I believe the principal reason why so many men of abilities object to serving in congress, is owing to their not thinking it worth while to spend three years in acquiring a profession, which their country immediately afterwards forbids them to follow.

There are two errors or prejudices on the subject of government in America, which lead to the most dangerous consequences.

It is often said, "that the sovereign and all other power is seated in the people." This idea is unhappily expressed. It should be—"all power is derived from the people," they possess it only on the days of their elections. After this, it is the property of their rulers; nor can they exercise or resume it, unless it be abused. It is of importance to circulate this idea, as it leads to order and good government.

The people of America have mistaken the meaning of the word sovereignty: hence each state pretends to be sovereign. In Europe, it is applied only to those states which possess the power of making war and peace—of forming treaties, and the like. As this power belongs only to congress, they are the only sovereign power in the United States.

We commit a similar mistake in our ideas of the word independent. No individual state, as such, has any claim to independence. She is independent only in a union with her sister states in congress.

To conform the principles, morals and manners of our citizens, to our republican forms of government, it is absolutely necessary, that knowledge of every kind should be disseminated through every part of the United States.

For this purpose, let congress, instead of laying out a half a million of dollars, in building a federal town, appropriate only a fourth of that sum, in founding a federal university. In this university let every thing connected with government, such as history—the law of nature and nations—the civil law—the municipal laws of our country—and the principles of commerce—be taught by competent professors. Let masters be employed, likewise, to teach gunnery—fortification—and every thing connected with defensive and offensive war. Above all, let a professor of, what is called in the European universities, economy, be established in this federal seminary. His business should be to unfold the principles and practice of agriculture and manufactures of all kind, and to enable him to make his lectures more extensively useful, congress should support a travelling correspondent for him, who should visit all the nations of Europe, and transmit to him, from time to time, all the discoveries and improvements that are made in agriculture and manufactures. To this seminary, young men should be encouraged to repair, after completing their academical studies in the colleges of their respective states. The honors and offices of the United States should, after a while, be confined to persons who had imbibed federal and republican ideas in this university.

For the purpose of diffusing knowledge, as well as extending the living principle of government to every part of the United States—every state—city—county—village—and township in the union should be tied together by means of the post-office. This is the true non-electric wire of government. It is the only means of conveying heat and light to every individual in the federal commonwealth. "Sweden lost her liberties," says the abbe Raynal, "because her citizens were so scattered, that they had no means of acting in concert with each other." It should be a constant injunction to the post-masters, to convey newspapers free of all charge for postage. They are not only the vehicles of knowledge and intelligence, but the sentinels of the liberties of our country.

The conduct of some of those strangers, who have visited our country, since the peace, and who fill the British papers with accounts of our distresses, shows as great a want of good sense, as it does of good nature. They see nothing but the foundations and walls of the temple of liberty; and yet they undertake to judge of the whole fabric.

Our own citizens act a still more absurd part, when they cry out, after the experience of three or four years, that we are not proper materials for republican government. Remember, we assumed these forms of government in a hurry, before we were prepared for them. Let every man exert himself in promoting virtue and knowledge in our country, and we shall soon become good republicans. Look at the steps by which governments have been changed, or rendered stable in Europe. Read the history of Great Britain. Her boasted government has risen out of wars, and rebellions, that lasted above six hundred years. The United States are travelling peaceably into order and good government. They know no strife—but what arises from the collision of opinions; and in three years, they have advanced further in the road to stability and happiness, than most of the nations in Europe have done, in as many centuries.

There is but one path that can lead the United States to destruction; and that is their extent of territory. It was probably to effect this, that Great Britain ceded to us so much wasteland. But even this path may be avoided. Let but one new state be exposed to sale at a time; and let the land office be shut up, till every part of this new state be settled.

I am extremely sorry to find a passion for retirement so universal among the patriots and heroes of the war. They resemble skillful mariners who, after exerting themselves to preserve a ship from sinking in a storm, in the middle of the ocean, drop asleep, as soon as the waves subside, and leave the care of their lives and property, during the remainder of the voyage, to sailors, without knowledge or experience. Every man in a republic is public property. His time and talents—his youth—his manhood—his old age—nay more, his life, his all, belong to his country.

Patriots of 1774, 1775, 1776—heroes of 1778, 1779, 1780! come forward! your country demands your services!—Philosophers and friends to mankind, come forward! your country demands your studies and speculations! Lovers of peace and order, who declined taking part in the late war, come forward! your country forgives your timidity and demands your influence and advice! Hear her proclaiming, in sighs and groans, in her governments, in her finances, in her trade, in her manufactures, in her morals, and in her manners, "The Revolution Is Not Over!"

3. THE CONSTITUTION OF 1787

JOEL BARLOW COMMENTS ON THE CONSTITUTIONAL CONVENTION

[Speech by the poet Joel Barlow to the Society of the Cincinnati at Hartford, Connecticut, July 4, 1787]

MR. PRESIDENT, GENTLEMEN OF THE SOCIETY, AND FELLOW-CITIZENS,

On the anniversary of so great an event as the birth of the empire in which we live, none will question the propriety of passing a few moments in contemplating the various objects suggested to the mind by the important occasion. But, at the present period, while the blessings, claimed by the sword of victory, and promised in the voice of peace, remain to be confirmed by our future exertions—while the nourishment, the growth, and even the existence of our empire depend upon the united efforts of an extensive and divided people—the duties of this day ascend from amusement and congratulation to a serious patriotic employment.

We are assembled, my friends, not to boast, but to realize—not to inflate our national vanity by a pompous relation of past achievements in the, council, or in the field; but, from a modest retrospect of the truly dignified part already acted by our countrymen—from an accurate view of our present situation—and from an anticipation of the scenes that remain to be unfolded—to discern and familiarize the duties that still await us, as citizens, as soldiers, and as men. . . .

Whatever praise is due for the task already performed, it is certain that much remains to be done. The revolution is but half completed. Independence and government were the two objects contended for: and but one is yet obtained. To the glory of the present age, and the admiration of the future, our severance from the British empire was conducted upon principles as noble, as they were new and unprecedented in the history of human actions. Could the same generous principles, the same wisdom and unanimity be exerted in effecting the establishment of a permanent federal system, what an additional lustre would it pour upon the present age! a lustre hitherto unequalled; a display of magnanimity for which mankind may never behold another opportunity.

Without an efficient government, our independence will cease to be a blessing. Shall that glow of patriotism and unshaken perseverance, which has been so long conspicuous in the American character, desert us at our utmost need? Shall we lose sight of our own happiness, because it has grown familiar by a near approach? Shall thy labors, O Washington, have been bestowed in vain? Hast thou conducted us to independence and peace, and shall we not receive the blessings at thy hands?

The present is justly considered an alarming crisis: perhaps the most alarming that America ever saw. We have contended with the most powerful nation, and subdued the bravest and best appointed armies: but now we have to contend with ourselves, and encounter passions and prejudices, more powerful than armies, and more dangerous to our peace. It is not for glory, it is for existence that we contend.

Much is expected from the federal convention now sitting at Philadelphia: and it is a happy circumstance that so general a confidence from all parts of the country is centred in that respectable body. Their former services, as individuals, command it, and our situation requires it. But although much is expected from them, yet more is demanded from ourselves.

The first great object is to convince the people of the importance of their present situation: for the majority of a great people, on a subject which they understand will never act wrong. If ever there was a time, in any age or nation, when the fate of millions depended on the voice of one, it is the present period in these states. Every free citizen of the American empire ought now to consider himself as the legislator of half mankind. When he views the amazing extent of territory, settled and to be settled under the operation of his laws —when, like a wise politician, he contemplates the population of future ages —the changes to be wrought by the possible progress of arts, in agriculture, commerce, and manufactures—the increasing connection and intercourse of nations, and the effect of one rational political system upon the general happiness of mankind—his mind, dilated with the great idea, will realize a liberality of feeling which leads to a rectitude of conduct. He will see that the system to be established by his suffrage, is calculated for the great benevolent purposes of extending peace, happiness, and progressive improvement to a large proportion of his fellow creatures. As there is a probability that the system to be proposed by the convention may answer this description, there is some reason to hope it will be viewed by the people with that candor and dispassionate respect which is due to the importance of the subject. . . .

The present is an age of philosophy, and America the empire of reason. Here, neither the pageantry of courts, nor the glooms of superstition, have dazzled or beclouded the mind. Our duty calls us to act worthy of the age and the country that gave us birth. Though inexperience may have betrayed us into errors— yet they have not been fatal: and our own discernment will point us to their proper remedy.

However defective the present confederated system may appear—yet a due consideration of the circumstances, under which it was framed, will teach us rather to admire its wisdom, than to murmur at its faults. The same political abilities, which were displayed in that institution, united with the experience we have had of its operation, will doubtless produce a system, which will stand the test of ages, in forming a powerful and happy people.

Elevated with the extensive prospect, we may consider present inconveniences as unworthy of regret. At the close of the war, an uncommon plenty of circulating specie, and a universal passion for trade, tempted many individuals to involve themselves in ruin, and injure the credit of their country. But these are evils which work their own remedy. The paroxysm is already over. Industry is increasing faster than ever it declined; and, with some exceptions, where legislative authority has sanctioned fraud, the people are honestly discharging their private debts, and increasing the resources of their wealth.

Every possible encouragement for great and generous exertions, is now presented before us. Under the idea of a permanent and happy government, every point of view, in which the future situation of America can be placed, fills the mind with peculiar dignity, and opens an unbounded field of thought. The natural resources of the country are inconceivably various and great. The enterprising genius of the people promises a most rapid improvement in all the arts that embellish human nature. The blessings of a rational government will invite emigrations from the rest of the world, and fill the empire with the worthiest and happiest of mankind; while the example of political wisdom and felicity, here to be displayed, will excite emulation through the kingdoms of the earth, and meliorate the condition of the human race. . . .

GEORGE MASON WRITES FROM THE CONVENTION

*[Letter to a friend from George Mason of Virginia, a
delegate at the Constitutional Convention]*

PHILADELPHIA, June 1st, 1787

The idea I formerly mentioned to you, before the convention met, of a
great national council, consisting of two branches of the legislature, a judiciary and an executive, upon the principle of fair representation in the legislature, with powers adapted to the great objects of the union, and consequently
a control in these instances, on the state legislatures, is still the prevalent one.
Virginia has had the honor of presenting the outlines of the plan, upon which
the convention is proceeding; but so slowly, that it is impossible to judge
when the business will be finished, most probably not before August—*festina
lente* may very well be called our motto. When I first came here, judging from
casual conversations with gentlemen from the different states, I was very apprehensive that, soured and disgusted with the unexpected evils we had experienced from the democratic principles of our governments, we should be
apt to run into the opposite extreme, and in endeavoring to steer too far from
Scylla, we might be drawn into the vortex of Charybdis, of which I still think,
there is some danger; though I have the pleasure to find in the convention,
many men of fine republican principles. America has certainly, upon this occasion, drawn forth her first characters; there are upon this convention many
gentlemen of the most respectable abilities; and, so far as I can yet discover,
of the purest intentions; the eyes of the United States are turned upon this assembly, and their expectations raised to a very anxious degree.

May God grant, we may be able to gratify them by establishing a wise
and just government. For my own part, I never before felt myself in such a
situation; and declare, I would not, upon pecuniary motives, serve in this
convention for a thousand pounds per day. The revolt from Great Britain,
and the formations of our new governments at that time, were nothing compared with the great business now before us; there was then a certain degree
of enthusiasm, which inspired and supported the mind; but to view, through
the calm sedate medium of reason, the influence which the establishments
now proposed may have upon the happiness or misery of millions yet unborn,
is an object of such magnitude, as absorbs, and in a manner suspends the operations of the human understanding.

P.S. All communications of the proceedings are forbidden during the sitting of the convention; this I think was a necessary precaution to prevent mis-representations or mistakes; there being a material difference between the appearance of a subject in its first crude and indigested shape, and after it shall have been properly matured and arranged.

4. A FOUNDING FATHER LEAVES A LEGACY TO HIS SONS

GEORGE MASON'S TESTAMENT TO FREEDOM

[An extract from the last will and testament of Colonel George Mason of Virginia]

I recommend it to my sons, from my own experience in life, to prefer the happiness of independence and a private station to the troubles and vexa-tion of public business: but if either their own inclinations or the necessity of the times should engage them in public affairs, I charge them on a father's blessing, never to let the motives of private interest or ambition induce them to betray, nor the terrors of poverty and disgrace, or the fear of danger or of death, deter them from asserting the liberty of their country, and endeavoring to transmit to their posterity those sacred rights to which themselves were born.